Sex

Other Books of Related Interest

Sex

Tamara L. Roleff, *Book Editor*

David Bender, *Publisher*
Bruno Leone, *Executive Editor*
Bonnie Szumski, *Editorial Director*
Stuart B. Miller, *Managing Editor*
James D. Torr, *Series Editor*

Teen Decisions

Greenhaven Press Inc., San Diego, California

Library of Congress Cataloging-in-Publication Data

Sex / Tamara L. Roleff, book editor.
    p. cm. — (Teen decisions)
    Includes bibliographical references and index.
    ISBN 0-7377-0493-4 (pbk. : alk. paper) —
    ISBN 0-7377-0494-2 (lib. bdg. : alk. paper)
    1. Teenagers—Sexual behavior. 2. Sexual ethics. I. Roleff,
Tamara L., 1959–   . II. Series.

HQ27 .S458 2001
306.7'0835—dc21   00-034128
                                                                   CIP

©2001 by Greenhaven Press, Inc.
PO Box 289009, San Diego, CA 92198-9009

Printed in the U.S.A.

Contents

Foreword

The teen years are a time of transition from childhood to adulthood. By age 13, most teenagers have started the process of physical growth and sexual maturation that enables them to produce children of their own. In the United States and other industrialized nations, teens who have entered or completed puberty are still children in the eyes of the law. They remain the responsibility of their parents or guardians and are not expected to make major decisions themselves. In most of the United States, eighteen is the age of legal adulthood. However, in some states, the age of majority is nineteen, and some legal restrictions on adult activities, such as drinking alcohol, extend until age twenty-one.

This prolonged period between the onset of puberty and the achieving of legal adulthood is not just a matter of hormonal and physical change, but a learning process as well. Teens must learn to cope with influences outside the immediate family. For many teens, friends or peer groups become the basis for many of their opinions and actions. In addition, teens are influenced by TV shows, advertising, and music.

The *Teen Decisions* series aims at helping teens make responsible choices. Each book provides readers with thought-provoking advice and information from a variety of perspectives. Most of the articles in these anthologies were originally written for, and in many cases by, teens. Some of the essays focus on ethical and moral dilemmas, while others present pertinent legal and scientific information. Many of the articles tell personal stories about decisions teens have made and how their lives were affected.

One special feature of this series is the "Points of Contention," in which specially paired articles present directly opposing views on controversial topics. Additional features in each book include a listing of organizations to contact for more information, as well as a bibliography to aid readers interested in more information. The *Teen Decisions* series strives to include both trustworthy information and multiple opinions on topics important to teens, while respecting the role teens play in making their own choices.

Introduction

The teen years are a difficult time. With the onset of adolescence and puberty, teen bodies, attitudes, and feelings begin to change. Many teens—and their parents—are confused and uncertain about their developing bodies. Emerging hormones tempt many teens to explore their sexuality. Most parents want their teenagers to abstain from sexual activity until marriage or adulthood, and many are uneasy with the thought of their children becoming sexually active. At the close of the twentieth century, parents' concerns range from whether teens are emotionally mature enough to handle sex to fears of pregnancy and sexually transmitted diseases, especially HIV/AIDS. On the other hand, teens are as curious about sex as they have ever been. While some of the specific concerns about teen sex have changed over the years, a historical view of teen sex can provide valuable insight into why modern society views teen sex with alarm.

Teen Sex Versus Premarital Sex

The ages at which teens first have sex haven't changed much over the course of American history. During the 1990s, about 80 to 90 percent of teens had sexual intercourse by the time they were 20 years old; most teens were between the ages of 15 and 18 when they lost their virginity. In the 1950s the average age was 17½, according to Robert T. Michael, John H. Gagnon, Edward O. Laumann, and Gina Kolata, authors of *Sex in America: A Definitive Survey*. In the 1930s, they cite the average age as 18. And the pregnancy rate for teenage girls under 15 has barely changed during the twentieth century—approximately 12,000 girls under 15 become pregnant every year.

Some aspects of teen sex have changed, of course. For example, during the colonial era, poor diet delayed the arrival of puberty until 15 or 16, whereas today it's no longer uncommon for pre-teens—age 11 or 12—to undergo puberty.

More importantly, what has changed during the past two hundred years is the average age at which people marry. After the American Revolution, the states established their own legal age limits for marriage based on British common law. Although the marriage age varied from state to state, most states required girls to be 12 and boys to be 14 in order to marry (even though records show that very few children of this age were married). At the same time, the age of consent was 7. (Fears by male legislators that raising the age of consent would encourage girls to blackmail men kept the age of consent low. It wasn't until the early 1900s that most states raised the age of consent to 14.) While these ages are now considered quite young, that wasn't the view during Revolutionary times. Children were often apprenticed to learn a trade at age 6 or 7 and by the time they were in their mid- to late teens, they were earning their living.

In colonial times, then, "teen" sex was accepted as long as the teens were married. However, society closely monitored *premarital* sex. Prevailing religious beliefs considered premarital sex to be a sin, and society was also more concerned about illegitimate births. According to Kristin Luker, author of *Dubious Conceptions: The Politics of Teenage Pregnancy*, colonial communities were obligated to provide food and shelter for children who had lost a parent; providing economic aid to children of mothers who were voluntarily single was a burden that many small, rural towns couldn't support. Unmarried parents were punished for having a child out of wedlock (public whippings and fines were the common punishments). However, since unwed mothers were more visible and less able to pay fines than the fathers, women bore the brunt of the whippings. Much like Hesther Prynne in *The Scarlet Letter* was exhorted to name the father of her illegitimate child, pregnant and unwed mothers in the colonial era were commanded to name their lovers, who would then be forced to support their family.

Changing Views of Adolescence

With the advent of the Industrial Revolution, societal views of childhood and adolescence began to change. Many states passed child labor laws in the mid-1800s, which (depending on the state) prevented children under the age of 10, 12, or 14 from working. Since the children couldn't work, more children were able to attend school and communities began building more public schools. It was during this period, when children didn't have to take on the responsibilities of adulthood and they had the opportunity to play, that childhood and adolescence came to be seen as a time of innocence. Teenagers, especially girls, were viewed as vulnerable and in need of protection from the stresses of adult life. According to Luker, social reformers believed that adolescents now needed their teen years to be free of cares and worries in order to develop properly; "'burdening' them with adult concerns such as work, marriage, and sex—especially the latter two" would hinder their development into adulthood, she writes. Consequently, to protect their development, the legal age of marriage was raised to 16 for women and 18 for men.

At the same time, American psychologist G. Stanley Hall became one of the first to propose that the teenage years were a distinct stage of development between childhood and adulthood. He named this period "adolescence" in his 1904 book, *Adolescence: Its Psychology and Its Relations to Physiology, Anthropology, Sociology, Sex, Crime, Religion, and Education.* Hall writes, "The dawn of puberty is soon followed by a stormy period . . . where there is a peculiar proneness to be either very good or very bad." Hall, and many others in the early 1900s, argued that teenagers—who just one hundred years earlier were considered mature enough to work, marry, have sex, and raise children—weren't legally or emotionally developed enough to take on any adult responsibilities.

This way of thinking continued into the mid- to late twentieth century. As the legal age for marriage rose, so, too, did the average age of marriage. However, the age at which teenagers began having sex remained unchanged. Whereas the eighteen- and nineteen-year-olds who were having sex in the 1700s, 1800s, and the first half of the 1900s were usually married, many teenagers in the second half of the 1900s were having illicit sex. Robert T. Michael and his associates note in *Sex in America* that in the 1990s, the average age for marriage was in the mid-twenties. Thus, teenagers and young adults are now expected to ignore their hormones and remain chaste for a longer period than their ancestors ever did. However, many teens follow the example set by their ancestors when they were teenagers hundreds of years earlier: They give in to their urges.

The Sexual Revolution

Up until about the 1960s, society, parents, and political and religious leaders were fairly consistent about the message they gave teens about sex: Wait until marriage. Before this time, sex generally wasn't discussed or portrayed as openly as it is now. Sex education was provided by the parents, who were often too embarrassed to offer any information beyond a brief explanation of the basics. However, the message from society was very firm: "Nice" girls didn't have sex. A double standard was solidly in place: Boys were expected to have sex with as many girls as they could, while girls who were sexually active received a bad reputation. Girls (and adult women) who became pregnant often felt they must leave town so that no one would know their scandalous secret. The media also contributed to this image of innocence. Married couples on television and in the movies slept in twin beds, and girls and women who had illicit sex were usually punished somehow at the end of the script. As a result of the taboo nature of the subject, many teens married without a firm understanding of the mechanics and pleasures of sexual intercourse, and birth control—in the form of condoms—wasn't easily available to unmarried teens.

In the 1960s and early 1970s, Americans' views of sexuality and premarital sex underwent a dramatic change in a phenomenon known as the sexual revolution. Perhaps the most important event of the sexual revolution was the introduction of the birth control pill; now, for the first time, women could control their fertility. The U.S. Supreme Court also played a pivotal role in the development of the sexual revolution. In 1970 it ruled that states couldn't prohibit married couples from obtaining contraceptives, and in 1972, it legalized abortion. The women's rights movement also became a prominent social force in the 1960s, changing the way both men and women thought about gender roles. Together, these changes contributed to a powerful revolution. The easy availability of the pill and abortion allowed girls and women to have sex with little fear of pregnancy. The sexual revolution also destigmatized unwed motherhood for those girls and women who decided to keep and raise their babies. The change in how Americans viewed premarital sex is staggering, according to a Roper poll in 1969, nearly 80 percent of Americans believed that premarital sex was wrong. Four years later, that percentage dropped to 50 percent.

The Media and Sex

The media began to reflect this new, open attitude toward sex by portraying more sexual situations and language. Today, sex is the featured topic of talk shows, soap operas, and dramatic and sitcom television shows. Talk show hosts such as Jerry Springer feature sexual topics that become more and more outrageous in a bid to attract viewers. Studios use explicit heterosexual and homosexual love scenes, as well as rape, bondage, and sado-masochistic sex to draw attention to their movies and shows. Big name stars are more willing to be nude in their films. Movie and TV characters, whether friends or strangers, fall into bed and have sex with little or no discussion of contraception, pregnancy, STDs or AIDS. But Hollywood isn't the only party guilty of using sex to draw attention to its products. Music lyrics are just as explicit in words as film is in pictures. Madison Avenue produces slick ads using sex appeal to promote its products. Commercials for Victoria's Secret feature close-ups of female breasts to sell its bras; breweries use scantily-clad women to entice viewers to buy their brands of beer.

Whether parents like it or not, these continual messages and images influence teens' ideas about sex. Michael J. Basso, author of *The Underground Guide to Teenage Sexuality*, argues that teens are absorbing media messages such as:

> Sex is good. The more sexually experienced you are, the more accepted you will be. The cool guys are studs. Promiscuity is in. Fun and popular girls have sex. Girls want to have sex, even when they say no. Sex is an all-night fantasy filled with simultaneous, earth-shattering, multiple orgasms. Only the physically beautiful people really enjoy life. You don't need birth control or condoms because only other people get pregnant, STDs, or AIDS. Sex makes you a respected adult.

Peer Pressure

Teens aren't only pressured by media images to have sex, they also face pressures from their friends and peers. Teens may feel left out when they hear others talking about "doing it," "going all the way," "scoring," and "getting lucky." Boyfriends or girlfriends may pressure their partner into having sex by saying "If you loved me, you would" or other lines designed to instill feelings of guilt for not giving in. Some teens may be embarrassed to admit that they still are a virgin, and so they have sex at the first opportunity. Other teens are simply curious about the experience. Julia Anderson, a teenager in Detroit, talks about the conflicting messages teens receive about sex:

In our culture we're taught that sex is evil but you're supposed to have as much of it as possible. We're living in this huge double standard and it's really frustrating because you hear different things: Your parents tell you "Don't do it," the church tells you, "Don't do it," but your friends say, "Do it, do it, do it." TV says do it and it's in every conversation you have even if it comes up in a little inside joke or a little metaphor or something, it's in everything. I can totally understand how people just give in and say, "Fine, I want to be let in on the big, huge secret."

Parental Messages About Sex

Teens do receive a lot of conflicting messages about sex. Parents try their best to raise their children to become healthy sexual beings, but many times their advice runs contrary to teens' own hormones and the messages broadcast by the rest of society. With the benefit of age and experience, many parents know that teen sex isn't always a wise, healthy, or positive experience. Parental involvement in their children's sex education is critical to the health and well-being of their teenagers. Teens need to know what their parents' values and morals are and the possible consequences of sexual activity before they find themselves in a position where they are confronted with having to make a decision about sex.

However, parental attempts to dissuade their children from teen sex aren't always successful, and often send mixed messages. For example, parents may follow their religion's teaching that sex should be reserved for the sanctity of marriage, but if the parents weren't virgins at their wedding, it may be difficult for them to explain why they could have sex outside of marriage and why their children shouldn't. Parents may also tell a teen, "Wait until you're old enough" without making it clear when they believe their child is "old enough" to have sex. According to Basso in *The Underground Guide to Teenage Sexuality*, telling a teen that "you'll know when the right time is" or "when you meet someone special and fall in love" doesn't answer the question. Since even adults have trouble deciding when the time is right, teens are bound to feel that an answer of "You'll know" is unsatisfactory. Furthermore, Basso notes that it's also difficult trying to explain what love is:

> Teens fall in and out of love frequently. Does this mean that when young people are in love, sex is a way of expressing true love? A parent might come back with "That's just puppy love or infatuation." So what is the difference between love and infatuation? Guess what—you lose! Sure you can find all kinds of people who might be able to come up with a few goodies yourself, but when you are in love or infatuated, you experience the same emotions. Both bring very strong and very real feelings of passion.

Parents know that sex is a wonderful expression of love, but sometimes it's not easy for them to explain its complexities and prepare teenagers for its intensity and consequences.

Consequences

Nevertheless, parental guidance is crucial in the areas of teen sex. Many teens who rely on the media and their friends for their information about sex are often ignorant about the possible consequences of sexual activity. In the case of sex, ignorance can be deadly and can change a teen's life forever.

The most obvious consequences of having sex are the possibilities of becoming pregnant or contracting a sexually transmitted disease. While pregnancy and most STDs can be prevented through contraception, many teens who do have sex don't use contraception. This may be because teens receive conflicting messages about sex and contraception from the media, their peers, their parents, and their sex education classes. Teens are often told that "everyone" is having sex, and therefore, they must have sex to be a part of the "in" crowd. However, media images of sexual intercourse rarely portray the couple stopping to put on a condom. Finally, parents and religious leaders urge teens to abstain from sex. So, to appease their conscience and their parents, teens often try to prevent giving the appearance that they are ready for sex. For many teens, especially girls, this means they avoid using contraception. Luker explains the paradox in *Dubious Conceptions*:

> One simple way of showing that one is a "nice girl" is to be unprepared for sex—to have given no prior thought to contraception. . . . A woman who obtains contraception in anticipation of sexual activity is thought to be "looking for sex" (as teens say) and is culturally devalued. More to the point, she risks being devalued within the relationship. When it comes to contraception, she is caught in a net of double binds. She is the one who is supposed to "take care of it," the one at whom most contraceptive programs are aimed, and the one for whose body the most effective methods have been developed. Yet she is expected to be diffident about sex, and interested in it only because love and erotic arousal have spontaneously led her to be "carried away."

This reluctance to be prepared for sex explains why many girls say they didn't intend to become pregnant, "it just happened." And it also is partly responsible for the soaring rate of STDs—estimated at 25 percent—among sexually active teenagers.

Other, less obvious consequences of teen sex are more emotional than physical. Teens—again, mostly girls—face being labeled with a bad reputation if they appear too eager or too ready to have sex. Others may regret the circumstances surrounding the time when they lost their virginity or had sex with someone for the first time. Yet others who think they are ready for sex may be surprised at and unprepared for the feelings of loss, regret, or guilt they may experience after sex.

These consequences—pregnancy, STDs, and emotional unpreparedness—are often at the heart of debates over what types of sex education teenagers should be taught. Some parents believe that teens are going to be sexually active no matter what they are told; therefore, they argue, teens should be taught how to protect themselves from pregnancy and STDs by using contraception and other methods of "safe sex." Other adults claim, however, that telling teens about "safe sex" gives them the implied—and wrong—message that teen sex is acceptable behavior. Thus they believe that teens should receive "abstinence-only" sex education, a program that teaches teens how to say no to sex and therefore avoid the emotional and physical consequences of having sex at too young an age.

A Difficult Decision

All of these factors—the later age at which teens marry, the pervasiveness of sex in the media, and the conflicting views about sex that teens receive from their parents, peers, and society—make choices about sex some of the most difficult decisions that teens must make. And because the decision to have sex can have serious and potentially life-altering consequences for teens, it's not one that should be taken lightly. The essays in *Teen Decisions: Sex* are meant to help you identify and understand the aspects involved in making this important decision. In Chapter One, **Common Concerns About Sex**, teen advisers answer some of the questions teens might ask about their own sexuality, such as when is a teen ready to have sex? Is masturbation normal? What is sex like? In Chapter Two, **Thinking About Virginity**, teens discuss why they decided to remain a virgin and their feelings about their first sexual experience. Chapter Three, **The Pressures Teens Face to Have Sex**, examines not only peer pressure on boys and girls, but also the pressure women face from society to have sex. Sexually transmitted diseases and pregnancy are some of the topics discussed in the fourth chapter, **Sex and Consequences**. The authors in the following chapters provide advice about these subjects and try to help you understand the issues involved and to make wise and responsible choices concerning sexual activity.

Chapter 1

Common Concerns About Sex

Only Thirteen

Teen Advice Online

Today, even thirteen-year-old girls are making decisions about having sex. However, when you decide to lose your virginity, you should think about aspects besides the physical act. Below, teen counselors advise a teenage girl that she needs to consider the emotional aspects of sex as well as the risks she faces by deciding to have sex at such an early age. The authors are peer counselors with Teen Advice Online, a teen counseling website (www.teenadviceonline.org).

I am always so horny. I have done some pretty stupid things. Like I agreed to let a 19—almost 20-year-old—go down on me. Anywayz . . . I have met this guy who's 14 and he's really sweet and funny, and adorable and HOT and like. . . . we might go out. But . . . he's not a virgin. And I am. And I'm afraid if I start fooling around with him and he wants to have sex I won't be able to say no. I mean, just hearing him talk I wanna have sex with him. But I'm also afraid I would do it wrong or that like it would hurt to much and. . . .

I think I'm ready for sex . . . but it makes me feel bad that I'm only 13. Yet I feel ready. What should I do?

Female 13 yrs.
USA

Reprinted with permission from "Being Horny Means 'Ready for Sex?'" *Teen Advice Online,* 1998. Article available at www.teenadviceonline.org/archive/19984.html.

Answers

Being physically ready and emotionally ready are two very different things. Most people can say they are physically ready for sex. I would even venture to say that. However, I know that, not only is it meant to be more of an emotional thing, there are SO many consequences to consider. Especially for you, since the guy you like is not a virgin. Having sex with someone who has had sex with other people is, essentially, like having sex with all of their other partners, and their partner's partners!! Do you see what I mean? If you know it would be hard for you to control, then I suggest making this known to this guy, or refraining from seeing him. There are too many consequences that can happen from 5 seconds of pleasure :-). Good Luck. ~Peace~

> "I think I'm ready for sex . . . but it makes me feel bad that I'm only 13."

Amanda

Consider the Consequences

Well you can have sex if you want to, but do consider the consequences—you could get pregnant, acquire an STD, have complications—did you know the sooner you have sex the greater the chances of getting cancer of the cervix, etc? There are many risks to consider when having sex, especially making sure it's the right guy and the right time.

You should wait to make sure the relationship will last, just because you're horny doesn't mean you're ready—it just means your hormones are in overdrive—it's okay to fool around but don't sacrifice your virginity to "the fool"—you may take it for granted now, but when you meet THE GUY, the one you plan to spend your life with, it will be worth the wait. If you plunge into the lusty behavior you may regret it so much later. Bad reputations are about as hard to unspread as butter.

Tina

Plenty of Time

Raging hormones are pretty much the bane of every teenager's existence. You hit puberty, and all of a sudden those hormones are going crazy. Unfortunately, a lot of teens mistake these sexual feelings to be an indication that they're ready to have sex. In reality, there's a whole lot more to being ready to become sexually active than just feeling "horny."

Mike Smith. Reprinted by permission of United Feature Syndicate, Inc.

First off, you have to know the risks and consequences, and be prepared for those. Having sex can lead to unwanted, unplanned pregnancy, contraction of sexually transmitted diseases, and a lot of emotional baggage. Could you handle it if you got pregnant? Do you know how to protect yourself from such a possibility? Do you know that no manner of protection works 100% of the time? What about STDs? Do you know how to protect yourself from those? Again, do you know that no manner of protection works 100% of the time? Do you know that some STDs are deadly and/or incurable? Sex is a big responsibility, and you have to be sure that you can handle that responsibility before you even think about taking it on.

You're young, only thirteen years old. You have plenty of time to become sexually active. It's a big decision, so just take your time and don't rush into anything. Before you have sex for the first time, you should know beyond a shadow of a doubt that this is what you want, that you're 100% ready to handle it and be responsible about it. If you can, talk to people you trust about this decision you're trying to make—your friends and family. They might have some valuable advice for you. I hope this helps. Best of luck to you.

Love, Jen

Barely a Teenager

I'm not going to lecture you that you're too young for sex. If you really want to do it you're going to whether I tell you to or not, but I would like you [to] step out for a second and look at yourself.

You're 13—barely a teenager. Do a lot of the 13-year-olds you know have sex lives? I doubt it. Sex is something mature people do and at that age you're still developing. Throwing sex into your life (as good as it may feel) isn't always the best choice.

You're at an age where your hormones are going to tell you to do a lot of things, but this is a time when you really should be listening to your mind. I can tell you're a smart person because you admit that you have second doubts about it. You're not sleeping around with a bunch of guys simply because it "feels good." You've gotta be smart about this. Do you want to get pregnant or AIDS before you're 14? Do you think a 14-year-old guy is old enough to be a responsible sexual partner? Or are you so hypnotized by his voice and body that you'd be willing to throw caution in the wind in exchange for an hour or two of hot sex?

I can't tell you what to do, but it would be a shame for you to write back in a year or so asking me about a pregnancy or a sexually-transmitted disease.

You're a smart girl and I trust you'll make the right decision. Take care,

Laura

Masturbation Is Healthy

Liberated Christians, Inc.

Although a lot of myths still surround masturbation, over the years societal and medical views of masturbation have changed from considering it a sin to viewing it as a means of sexual and emotional release. According to this author, masturbation is a natural, healthy, and risk-free way to experience sexual pleasure. In fact, sex researchers believe that regular masturbation keeps you healthy mentally and physically. Finally, it can help you learn what sexual activities you enjoy the most; this knowledge, when passed along to your partner, can enhance your sexual pleasure. Liberated Christians, Inc., is a couples fellowship group that promotes sexual intimacy in alternative, nonmonogamous relationships.

You are not insane. You are not blind. You have not grown hair on your palms. You are a completely competent member of society—despite all the times you've done it. Kinsey and the latest *Sex in America* report show there's a whole lot of shaking going on. Today's sex researchers have come to grips with the fact that masturbation has important physical and emotional benefits for both men and women.

Getting a Grip

"Masturbation is a normal, natural activity throughout life," says Robert Pollack, a psychology professor at the University of Georgia. It may even contribute to mental health and not doing it may lead to psychosexual problems.

For men, masturbation or regular sex is good for the prostate and can prevent painful prostate blockage. For women it can help reduce cramping and for both men and women has been shown to have a healthy effect on the immune systems as well as reducing overall tension and helping emotions.

Besides being healthy for the body, a private grope can help both a man and a woman better understand their own sexuality. If you can learn to lie back and enjoy it and really pay attention to the pleasure it gives your body—no one knows better than you what gives you maximum pleasure—you can share that knowledge with a partner and have more mutually fulfilling sexual pleasure sharing. The self-awareness gained from masturbation makes it a central feature of many sex therapy programs.

An Evolutionary Design

Evolution may have even designed us to be masturbators. Notice when you are standing where your hand falls if you hang it in front of you. Apes do it, dogs and cats do it, elephants do it and even porcupines have been observed doing it, probably very carefully. One reason we may be so programmed, paradoxically, is to increase our odds of producing offspring. Older sperm can lose their ability to swim well. A good masturbatory flush guarantees fresh, robust sperm for mating.

> [Masturbation] may even contribute to mental health and not doing it may lead to psychosexual problems.

Storing seminal fluids for long periods can also cause prostate congestion, which in turn can lead to urinary and ejaculatory pain. Regular ejaculations, either through masturbation or intercourse, can help ward off this condition, also called non-specific prostatitis and, for obvious reasons, "sailor's disease" and "priest's disease."

Masturbation is also an ever-renewable health resource. In fact, the people who start the earliest and do it the most often are the ones who do it longest into old age. So, as with all sexual activity, it's "use it or lose it."

Normal and Common

Some things you need to know about masturbation:

• It's normal. Two-thirds of men and women questioned for the 1993 Janus Report on Sexual Behavior agreed with the statement that "Masturbation is a natural part of life and continues on in marriage"; 48 percent of the single men and 68 percent of the divorced men reported doing it daily to weekly. And in a 1995 international survey, *Playboy* found that at least 15 percent of its American readers masturbated daily.

• It's a mark of intelligence. Maybe. *Sex in America*, the 1994 University of Chicago study, linked the practice to education: Eighty percent of men with graduate degrees reported masturbating in the current year, as opposed to less than 50 percent of the high-school dropouts.

• Even married guys do it. It isn't limited to the romantically challenged. According to the Janus report, 44 percent of married men masturbate once a week or more.

Stephen Rae, *Men's Health,* September 1995.

Another reason why nature designed us to masturbate is to strengthen PC muscles, much like "Kegel" exercises. This is especially true in females where strong PC muscles are practically the sole factor in whether labor is easy and fast or long and difficult. Females masturbating regularly with multiple orgasms would develop strong PC muscles and should have easier labor.

Another potential concern is reliance on masturbation for sexual pleasure to the exclusion of intimacy with another person. But in such cases, masturbation is probably a symptom, not a cause, of larger psychological barriers to intimacy. Most people want relationships. But if you're scared of them, you might stick with masturbation exclusively.

How Masturbation Got Its Bad Rap

First came the misunderstanding of the biblical passage related to Onan whose sin was not masturbation but not impregnating his dead brother's wife. Then came the twisted Christian tradition that sex was only proper for procreation, not just enjoyment. The stigma was later compounded by the 18th century Swiss physician Samuel August Tissot who believed that while blood-flow changes during any kind of sex would cause nerve damage and insanity, masturbation was especially hazardous.

> Besides being healthy for the body, a private grope can help both a man and a woman better understand their own sexuality.

Tissot's teachings were picked up by American physician Benjamin Rush. Besides signing the Declaration of Independence, Rush wrote several influential articles on masturbation that helped make it one of the most feared activities in the new United States. Antimasturbatory devices became available, including a tube lined with metal spikes that fit over the penis. Until this century, young men were sometimes put to bed in straitjackets or with their hands tied to bedposts to make sure they didn't do it.

John Harvey Kellogg, of cornflakes fame, was a virulent crusader against masturbation and invented the cereal as one element of a diet he thought would quench the sex drive. (Mr. Sylvester Graham came up with the Graham cracker for the same purpose.) For those masturbators whom snacks could not cure, Kellogg suggested circumcision without anesthesia.

Finally, around the turn of the century, physicians started to realize that masturbation was not the evil earlier generations thought it was. Still, it was not until 1940 that a respected textbook, *Diseases of Infancy and Childhood,* removed its discussion of masturbation from the chapter titled "Functional and Nervous Disorders."

An internet message in reply to above post:

Quite true. The sad preoccupation with masturbation came from Jansenism, a heresy which said the Human Body is inherently evil. . . . As a Catholic Priest, I have sorrowed greatly at the unnecessary neurosis our Catholic Church has fostered regarding masturbation. . . . Glad you have this out there.

A women said on the internet:

Sexual release is just as important as any kind of emotional release. Saying that you shouldn't masturbate is like saying that you shouldn't cry when you're upset or hurt, or that you should hold in anger and other emotions. I see no difference between sexual release and emotional release. Not releasing will only result in stress and health problems. And I know that I need no more stress in my life. I figure, if something helps a person relieve stress, clear their mind, and make them feel better (that doesn't hurt others, mind you), then more power to them.

Ready for Sex

Joshua

In this personal narrative of his first sexual experience, Joshua writes about the hopes and expectations he had for his first time. He writes about how he turned down an opportunity to have sex with his girlfriend because of the pressure and awkwardness of the moment. However, when he and his girlfriend eventually did have sex, it happened during a moment of spontaneous passion that he doesn't regret. Joshua is a teenager who writes for *Teenwire,* a Planned Parenthood online magazine.

Mom and Dad's idea of sex education: If you're gonna have sex with someone, you'd better make sure you love them. Cause if you don't, you're gonna roll over the next morning and hate them. This idea did wonders for keeping me a virgin.

Julie was my best friend's girlfriend. I was their counselor, their go-between. She'd call me to complain, I'd call him to explain, they'd get together and make up while I sat around and wondered what it would be like to be in their shoes.

They broke up for good a couple of months later. Junior year. She wore red velvet sunglasses. I fell in love with her. Sweet Julie . . .

When you fall in love with a friend it's easy to create an ideal present and fantasy future. We were together for a couple of years. I'd have Christmas brunch at her grandmother's. She'd play board games and dance with my folks on Christmas night.

Once we stayed up late making a list of baby names. When she got her first car, we'd drive around and choose houses. She gave me a bowl of cherries on the Fourth of July.

> "I don't know if other couples talk about it . . . , but I wanted it to be natural and spontaneous."

Her parents were pretty cool about us hanging out in her room. Yeah, we fooled around a bit. Fingers flying and bodies rubbing, but never going all the way. I don't know if other couples talk about it ("When do you wanna do it? Tonight? Next Saturday? After six months?"), but I wanted it to be natural and spontaneous.

If Not Tonight, When?

Senior Prom came. Her dad rented us a limo and we had dinner at the Ritz-Carlton. The night was romantic but contrived. After dinner, the limo took us to the beach for a long walk and a little illegal champagne. We dropped by the prom for a couple of dances and some pictures, then she surprised me—her friend's parents had a condo on the beach.

The mood changed as soon as we walked into the condo—all this pressure swooped down on us. There we were alone in this condo, and not to watch TV or kick back to music. We were there for sex. It wasn't right. It was like a movie set, and we were the actors, ready to start "hittin' it" on cue. I knew there were probably a lot of couples hittin' it on prom night, but I'm not about playing the part. I dare to be different. We didn't do it. She wasn't happy.

The rest of the night was awkward. A bunch of our friends had rented hotel suites. We joined them for an all-night party chasing each other with fire extinguishers, smoking cigars, and yes, some were having sex.

But though the night was awkward, it was also cool. Watching our friends head off to have sex kind of disgusted Julie—all of a sudden it's like we were the adults, and our friends were these kids stupidly humping away their virginity on a drunken prom night. I was off the hook.

When the Time Is Right

A couple of weeks later I was hanging out at my buddy's house while his parents were out of town. It was about two in the afternoon, hot and humid. It was the kind of day you don't expect much from, just the chance to chill with your friends. Julie came over. When she arrived, the air was electric. The heat gave her a thin film of sweat, she was slightly out of breath, and she smelled like summer. We kissed like it was the first time, and quickly fell into bed. "This is it," I'm thinking.

Every conversation I'd ever had about sex, every image of sex I'd ever seen came flooding through my mind. I was completely obsessed with how I was doing, and whether this would be memorable. I'm not going to admit I was nervous. It's weird how we were naked, getting all private, but we never asked each other out loud what we wanted each other to do next. She did ask me if I had a condom. I did (the old wallet standby, which thankfully didn't break).

> "I was completely obsessed with how I was doing, and whether this would be memorable."

I opened it up and she put it on, and . . . it was a beautiful day.

Looking back I'm pretty cool with having waited until the end of high school to have sex. Right after we all graduated I went to a party and a bunch of guys were talking about virginity. It's like we all thought each other got laid for the first time at 15 or 16. But just about all of us were virgins until senior year or after. Figures.

Not Ready for Sex

DeDe Lahman

Many teens consider losing their virginity as a rite of passage, an act that turns them into men or women. Some teens are so anxious for this transformation that they'll have sex with someone at the first opportunity, a decision that they often later regret. DeDe Lahman describes how she felt as her close girlfriends lost their virginity, and discusses her own feelings about her virginity. She decides that she really doesn't like or trust any boy well enough to have sex with him, a sign that she takes to mean that she's not ready for sex. She's proud of her decision to wait, and realizes that sex isn't something that you lose or give away. Lahman writes for *Seventeen* magazine.

I never actually planned on being a virgin all through high school. I mean, it's not like I wasn't interested in sex. In fact, I thought about it all the time, envisioning my first experience to be very romantic—a fun evening, a warm, safe place, a guy I really loved and trusted and cared about a lot. I think that's what most people hope for. But when I hit high school, everyone else seemed to, like, forget that vision and replace it with a different attitude: Just do it.

There were only 205 kids in my class at a New England prep

Reprinted from "Sex Appeal," by DeDe Lahman, *Seventeen,* March 1997. Reprinted with permission from Primedia Publications.

school (if someone even tripped in the lunchroom, everyone else knew about it by next period). Freshman year, my four closest girlfriends and I all started out in the same place sexually: Most of us had made out with a few guys, and some of us had even gotten to second base (at least over the shirt, if not under the bra).

But then we were invited to the first upperclass party of the year, and everything changed.

The Party

It was thrown by Veronica Leeds,* the coolest senior in school. Veronica had brown hair with chunky blond streaks and wore black lipstick. Every guy worshiped her. When we arrived at the party, my friends and I tried to play it cool, babbling to each other nervously but not actually saying anything coherent except "Oh, my God, [*fill in the name of someone hot*] is here." I felt way out of my league and spent most of the night maneuvering through the sweaty, crowded rooms, stepping over clusters of bodies, trying not to stare while people danced and hooked up and seriously partied.

Though my friends and I stayed in our group, a couple of senior guys flirted with us—a minitriumph, considering the majority of girls who scoffed at us condescendingly (that was just how you treated frosh girls at my school). Then, around the time of my curfew, I watched my friend Samantha slip through the back screen door with A.J.—one of the guys we had been talking to (who was also rumored to be one of the biggest players in school). She grinned back at the rest of us and mouthed, "Leave without me."

> I never actually planned on being a virgin all through high school.

At our lockers Monday morning, we all crowded expectantly around Samantha, who acted way too nonchalant about the

*All names have been changed.

whole thing and dodged our probing questions like a skilled politician. But by the very end of first period, she had turned into somewhat of a celebrity, which made it hard for her to blow it off. All the freshman girls had heard the rumors, and as we ushered Samantha toward the bathroom, they scanned her up and down, clutching their books tightly against their chests. It dawned on us that the whole school knew, and as we walked through the halls to our classes, guys who had never even glanced our way before were saying hi.

Empty and Cold

At noon, when Samantha and I finally reached the cafeteria alone, I pumped her for info. I was so excited to get the scoop. I mean, wow. Sex. It was such a major, adult thing. I wanted to know everything: What happened? What did he say? Did it hurt?

I held my breath, waiting for the tales of romance—the really cool story about the way he had first kissed her, what it had felt like, the deep connection they now shared. But Samantha just looked blankly at me, her eyes red-rimmed and watery.

It was no big deal, she said. Basically, they had gone outside to talk, she got very drunk on cranberry juice and vodka, and the next thing she knew, they were on the ground having sex—kind of in the bushes on the perimeter of the backyard. She didn't really remember many details and had no clue about whether he'd used a condom, but she was pretty sure he hadn't.

While she was talking, I got this weird feeling. It was as if she hadn't really been there in her body—as if what she was describing had happened to somebody else. I'd always thought that sex, especially sex for the first time, was supposed to be this huge expression of love (or at least very serious *like),* something that two people did when they really trusted and cared about each other—so getting "done" in the bushes on top of wet, smelly leaves didn't seem very loving or warm to me. Suddenly, it didn't seem like what had happened was very exciting at all. In fact, it seemed kind of empty and cold.

Later that day, we walked by A.J. in the library, and he looked right through Samantha, like she was Casper or something. Luckily, Samantha didn't end up getting pregnant or contracting an STD or anything, and a few weeks later, she started going out with a new guy. And then, one by one, almost every one of my friends lost her virginity—as if being a virgin were some trend that wasn't "in" anymore, like baby barrettes or strappy sandals.

I Wasn't Ready

As each girl went through her big post-losing-it phase (talking about it incessantly, reveling in her new "womanhood," worrying about late periods), I couldn't help but feel further and further out of the loop. It was like all of my closest friends were part of this secret club to which I didn't belong, and it started to get me down. Fortunately, my friends were cool enough not to make a big deal out of my "hymenally challenged" status: Since I wasn't questioning my decision, they weren't either. And as much as they thought they'd been ready, deep down inside I had plenty of reasons that let me know I wasn't.

> I'd always thought that sex, especially sex for the first time, was supposed to be this huge expression of love.

Like, first of all, what guy would I do it with? There wasn't anyone I was truly in love with—or even very much in like with. And even if there were, he'd have to be the type who would still talk to me and respect me and hang out with me the next day. And what if we broke up afterward—would I be able to deal? Second, I had a hard enough time being completely stark naked with *myself,* let alone parading around in front of some guy. (I couldn't even think about going to the gyno without breaking into a cold sweat.) Third, I could never imagine buying a condom, not to mention just whipping out a trusty tube of spermicidal gel in the middle of the whole event and, like, casually talking it over with my crush. Fourth, I didn't know one guy who would have sex with me and not announce it over the PA system. And fifth? I was scared of the pain—too scared to get past it and think about the rest, like how I'd be sharing myself with someone in a really major way.

Weeding Out the Jerks

All this was a clear signal that I was not ready, but what wasn't clear was how to handle the sex thing when I was with someone I liked. So what I decided to do was to be up front with the guy: After a few weeks of getting closer, I'd let him know the deal. Which you'd think might make a lot of guys walk away, but I could tell that most of them respected my honesty and appreciated that there were some boundaries (I found that not every guy automatically wanted to leap into bed, either). This became an easy way for me to weed out the jerks: If they couldn't deal with my decision, then they couldn't deal with me.

A few years ago, I read a cool passage about virginity in a psychology book. It said that the word "virgin" did not originally refer to a women who had not yet had intercourse but to a woman who was not tied to—or possessed by—any man. In other words, it meant a woman who was her own person, both sexually and socially. Reading that made me feel really good about myself and proud of my decision not to have treated virginity as this part of me I had to "lose" or "give away." I'd always known that sex is meant to be an experience that makes you—and your relationship—strong and whole and complete. And until I was sure that was how it would make me feel, why should I have settled for anything less?

The First Time

Tanya Maloney

For some teens, the decision to have sex isn't something that they plan, "it just happens." Most people hope that their first time will be like a romantic love scene in a Hollywood movie, but the reality usually does not live up to expectations. A man's first sexual experience is usually quite different than a woman's, who may not even reach orgasm. Tanya Maloney, an advice columnist for Sex Etc., a website written by and for teens, describes what sex is like for both men and women.

"Are you still coming to get me after school tomorrow?" Jessica asked her boyfriend, James.

"Yeah, I'll meet you out front," he said.

"All right, see you tomorrow."

The First Time

And that was the only thing the couple planned. The rest just happened. James picked Jessica up from school and they went to his house. They went straight to his room, watched some music videos and started to kiss. The kiss led to so much more.

The two had been dating on and off for almost two years and often considered having sex. James suggested it first, but Jessi-

Reprinted from "Losing It: What's the First Time Really Like?" by Tanya Maloney, *Sex Etc.*, Winter 1997. Reprinted with permission from *Sex Etc.*, a national newsletter written by teens for teens of high school age, published by the Network for Family Life Education, Rutgers University School of Social Work.

ca wasn't sure it was the right thing to do. They never really came to an agreement. But that day after school, without saying it out loud, James and Jessica agreed to have sex.

"We didn't say what we were going to do. It was just something we assumed was going to happen," explains Jessica, 16, who lost her virginity that day just a couple of months ago.

Jessica agreed to talk to SEX, Etc. about her first time to dispel some of the mystery surrounding sex. Of course, everybody's first time is different. But since it's tough to make smart decisions when all those emotions and hormones are kicking around, we thought a look at what happened to two teens would help us all become better informed—and more sexually responsible.

> For most people, the first time is filled with high expectations and worries over whether you'll "perform" OK.

For most people, the first time is filled with high expectations and worries over whether you'll "perform" OK. Little communication or planning, no birth control and disappointment are also usually part of the picture, psychologist and American University professor Dr. Barry McCarthy explains in *Losing It: The Virginity Myth,* a book about first sexual experiences, edited by Louis M. Crosier. But with solid information, teens can make the right decisions about their own sexuality. That means waiting until you and your honey can rap seriously about sex, take precautions (read: use birth control and condoms) and understand how your bodies work sexually. Doing this before losing your virginity can make sex a source of pleasure, rather than guilt, confusion or shame, writes Dennis M. Dailey, a professor at the University of Kansas School of Social Welfare, in *Losing It: The Virginity Myth.*

Getting Physical

Most teens wonder what sex feels like the first time. The answer is usually different for guys and girls. Most guys have an orgasm the first time. A lot (one in four) have problems, though. Some can't get an erection, some ejaculate (come) before the penis penetrates the vagina, some just can't reach orgasm. "Young men are so anxious about doing well that the anxiety overpowers their ability to gain control," explains Dailey.

What's more, less than 5 percent of women have an orgasm the first time they have sex. Why? "Young men do not under-

---

Is Sex Really Like It Is in the Movies?

We live in a media (TV, movies, music, news) controlled society. The media repeatedly show us sex in ways that are inaccurate, unbelievable, idealistic, and often harmful to us. Media myths say that in order for the male to be a "stud," he should have a ten-inch monster penis, keep an erection for at least half an hour, and know where to touch and how to excite his partner. And of course the male must be aggressive. Media myths say that for the female to excite and stimulate her partner, she should be aggressive or the exact opposite: let herself be dominated. Also for the female to be successful, she should know where and how to touch her partner, have big breasts, moan and scream, and of course have an orgasm.

Constantly watching these media myths will soon start you thinking that this is how intercourse is supposed to be. This is not good.

Many people have problems with intercourse because of what could be called "performance anxiety." These people believe that if they do not do it "right" (as seen on TV), they will be inadequate, degraded (put down), and embarrassed.

To repeat, intercourse is not a performance or an Olympic event. Ideally it should be an extension or enhancement of love. The things that you see on TV and in the movies are faked performances for an audience.

Michael J. Basso, *The Underground Guide to Teenage Sexuality,* 1997.

stand very much about female sexuality (or their own for that matter) and neither do a lot of women," writes Dailey. "Thus, women cannot tell men what they want and most men do not have a clue."

Jessica confirms this. She says that sex hurt a little, almost like a pinch, but that "after awhile the pain eases up." So when the pain fades, does it feel pleasurable? Yes, says Jessica, but she never hit the point where you scream and yell for God, like in the movies. And she didn't have an orgasm.

Tim, who lost his virginity in seventh grade, had a different experience. Now 19, he says that, physically, sex was "the best feeling in the world. Only love feels better." And he did have an orgasm.

The emotional side of sex was trickier. Looking back now, Tim feels he was way young for sex. He remembers having the jitters, big time. "Don't let anyone try to tell you they weren't nervous the first time because they'll be lying," says Tim. Seeing a naked girl for the first time can overwhelm a teenage boy.

> Most teens wonder what sex feels like the first time. . . . Most guys have an orgasm the first time.

Plus, the girl expects the boy to know what he's doing, Tim says, admitting he didn't have a clue.

"All you can go by is what you see on TV and jump in bed and do it," he adds. (It's a bummer, but surveys show that many teens think that "Hollywood" sex is the way it really happens. Guess again).

"If I knew then what I know now, I wouldn't have done it so early," he says, referring to issues like pregnancy and disease. But, he adds that he and his girlfriend discussed sex before they did it, and they agreed to use a condom. Jessica didn't take those precautions and so she started worrying about pregnancy afterward. She wished that she had used a condom. She was lucky—she didn't become pregnant.

Now, Jessica says she feels closer to her boyfriend and can even positively say that she loves him. But she is reluctant to have sex with him too often. "I don't want him to think the relationship revolves around having sex," Jessica explains.

Healthy Sexuality

It's pretty safe to say that at one point or another, most people will lose their virginity. It's only natural.

"The healthy question is how and when to express sexuality," writes McCarthy. It's also important to consider the many reasons to wait to express your sexuality by having sexual intercourse with someone.

Adolescence is a time to learn about yourself. That means exploring your own values and beliefs and resisting pressure to have sex before you feel ready, says McCarthy. You might turn to books (check out your local library) or a trusted adult to learn how sex feels physically and emotionally for both guys and girls and how it affects relationships. Masturbation is also a good way to explore your own body.

"A healthy guideline is to view sexuality as a positive part of yourself and express it in a way that enhances your life and relationships," writes McCarthy. "At a minimum, this means trying to avoid behavior that is harmful to you or your partner—unwanted pregnancy, STDs, HIV/AIDS, sexual victimization and force or coercion. Hopefully, it means being a sexual friend who is aware and responsible."

Point of Contention: Are Homosexual Feelings Normal for Teens?

Attitudes toward homosexuality—in which an individual has sexual feelings for another person of the same sex— have generally not been very accepting, and many homosexuals have responded by keeping their sexual orientation a secret. Since the gay liberation movement of the 1970s, more and more gays and lesbians have "come out" about their sexual orientation. This openness doesn't necessarily mean that all of society has become more tolerant of homosexuality, however, and teens who experience homosexual feelings may receive conflicting messages. Many people believe the Bible condemns homosexuality as sinful and immoral behavior. They claim that individuals who become gay or lesbian have made a choice to do so, and that intensive counseling can convert them from homosexuality to heterosexuality. Others maintain that homosexuality is a normal part of the human condition that can't be changed. Since no one would willingly choose to be a gay or lesbian and become an outcast from society, these supporters argue, homosexuality must be genetically based. Understanding the argument over whether homosexuality is a result of environmental or genetic factors can help you decide for yourself whether homosexuality is a normal part of human sexuality. Kevin Cranston and Cooper Thompson wrote this brochure for gay youth and young men questioning their sexuality with the help of the Boston Area Gay and Lesbian Youth organization. Tim Stafford is the author of *Love, Sex, and the Whole Person: (Everything You Want to Know)*.

Yes: Homosexual Feelings Are Normal for Teens

Kevin Cranston and Cooper Thompson

What Does It Mean to Be Gay?

Men who call themselves gay are sexually attracted to and fall in love with other men. Their sexual feelings toward men are normal and natural for them. These feelings emerge when they are boys and the feelings continue into adulthood. Although some gay men may also be attracted to women, they usually say that their feelings for men are stronger and more important to them.

We know that about one out of ten people in the world is gay or lesbian (lesbians are women who are attracted to other women). This means that in any large group of people, there are usually several gay people present. However, you cannot tell if someone is gay or not unless he or she wants you to know. Gay people blend right in with other people. But they often feel different from other people.

Gay teenagers may not be able to specify just why they feel different. All of the guys they know seem to be attracted to girls, so they don't know where they fit in. And, they may not feel comfortable talking with an adult about their feelings.

How Do I Know if I'm Gay?

I don't remember exactly when I first knew I was gay, but I do remember that the thought of sex with men always excited me.—Alan, age 19.

I never had any real attraction towards women, but I really knew that I was gay when puberty began. I felt an attraction toward the other boys and I was curious to find out what they were like.—James, age 17.

One day I was flipping through a magazine, there was a cute guy, and bam! I knew.—Antonio, age 16.

You may not know what to call your sexual feelings. You don't have to rush and decide how to label yourself right now. Our sexual identities develop over time. Most adolescent boys are intensely sexual during the years around puberty (usually between 11 and 15 years old), when their bodies start changing and their hormones are flowing in new ways. Your sexual feelings may be so strong that they are not directed toward particular persons or situations, but seem to emerge without cause. As you get older you will figure out who you are really attracted to.

> We all choose to have sex in different ways, whether we are gay or straight.

Boys with truly gay feelings find that, over time, their attractions to boys and men get more and more clearly focused. You may find yourself falling in love with your classmates or maybe developing a crush on a particular adult man. You may find these experiences pleasurable, troubling, or a mix of the two. By age 16 or 17 many gay kids start thinking about what to call themselves, while others prefer to wait.

If you think you might be gay, ask yourself:
- When I dream or fantasize sexually, is it about boys or girls?
- Have I ever had a crush or been in love with a boy or a man?
- Do I feel different than other guys?

• Are my feelings for boys and men true and clear?

If you cannot answer these questions now, don't worry. You will be more sure in time. You and only you know how to label yourself correctly.

Making Contact

So, you may be ready to find out more. Start by reading. If you feel comfortable, ask the librarian in the "Young Adult" section of your public library. Librarians are usually glad to help. If your library does not have much on sexuality you may want to check out the "GAY" section of a large bookstore, or possibly order books and other material through the mail. Please note that not all books about gay people are supportive.

Try calling a gay hotline. Most major cities have one. You may want to call from a phone booth for privacy. They will let you talk about your feelings and will direct you to organizations that help gay people. There may even be a gay youth group in your area. . . .

Remember, gay people are out there, wherever you are. Trust your instincts. Sooner or later you will meet someone who feels some of the same things you do.

> When I first met another gay person, I felt excited, anxious, nervous and happy. There was an indescribable relief to know that I was not alone, that there was someone else like me. It was also intimidating, not knowing what to expect, but I quickly loosened up and felt relaxed.—Nathan, age 18.

> When I first made contact with another gay man, I felt a tremendous relief. I couldn't believe I had made a connection. I felt happy but also scared. I felt that I could do or say anything and not worry about it.—Alan, age 19.

> When I first met another gay person, it was incredible, refreshing, reassuring, touching, awesome, and wonderful.—James, age 17.

Will I Ever Have Sex?

Naturally, you think about finding an outlet for your sexual feelings. Becoming a healthy sexual person is part of the coming out process. You may be scared at the prospect of having sex. This is normal for everyone. No one should start having sex until they are ready. Until then, you may choose to masturbate or fantasize.

Sex should only happen between mature individuals who care about each other. You will know when the time is right.

We all choose to have sex in different ways, whether we are gay or straight. Gay men choose from a wide range of sexual practices, including masturbation (either alone or with another person), oral sex, anal intercourse, kissing, hugging, massage, wrestling, holding hands, cuddling or anything else that appeals to both partners. You are in complete control over what you do sexually and with whom.

What About AIDS?

All sexually active people need to be aware of AIDS as well as other sexually transmitted diseases. Being gay does not give you AIDS, but certain sexual practices and certain drug use behaviors can put you at risk for catching the virus that causes AIDS. AIDS is incurable, but is preventable.

Here's how to reduce your risk of getting AIDS:

- Do not shoot up drugs. Sharing needles is the most dangerous behavior in terms of getting AIDS.
- Avoid anal intercourse or other direct anal contact. Anal intercourse transmits the virus very efficiently. If you do engage in anal sex, use a condom every time.
- Use condoms whenever you engage in anal or oral sex (or vaginal sex if you have sex with women). You

should choose latex condoms that are fresh and un-damaged. Store them away from heat (your wallet is not a good place to keep them). Use a condom only once. Try to choose condoms with "reservoir tips," and be sure to squeeze out the air from the tip as you put it on. Hold on to the condom as you remove your penis; sometimes they slip off after sex.

- Choose sexual activities that do not involve intercourse: hugging, kissing, talking, massaging, wrestling or mas-turbating (on unbroken skin).

Learning to Like Yourself

I had to reject a lot of negative heterosexual and reli-gious programming that made me feel lousy about my-self as a gay person. I began to like myself by meeting other gay people and going to a gay support group. Af-ter that I was content with myself.—Bill, age 18.

My aunt is a lesbian, and she made it clear to me, before I even knew I was gay, that being gay was OK.—Anto-nio, age 16.

I accepted the facts, which means that I don't deny be-ing gay and I don't pretend to be someone I'm not.—Alan, age 19.

It's not easy to discover that you are gay. Our society makes it very clear what it thinks of gay people. We all hear the terrible jokes, the hurtful stereotypes and the wrong ideas that circulate about gay people. People tend to hate or fear what they don't understand. Some people hate lesbians and gay men. Many people are uncomfortable be-ing around lesbians and gay men.

It's no wonder that you might choose to hide your gay feelings from others. You might even be tempted to hide them from yourself.

You may wonder if you are normal. Perhaps you worry

about people finding out about you. Maybe you avoid other kids who might be gay because of what people will think. Working this hard to conceal your thoughts and feelings is called being in the closet. It is a painful and lonely place to be, even if you stay there in order to survive.

It takes a lot of energy to deny your feelings, and it can be costly. You may have tried using alcohol or other drugs to numb yourself against these thoughts. You may have considered suicide. If so, please consult the phone book for the Samaritans or other hotline. There are alternatives to denying your very valuable feelings. Check out the resources listed on the back of this brochure.

Who Should I Tell?

> I only tell other people that I'm gay if I've known them for a long time and if they are accepting and tolerant. I think it's important that they know about this special part of me.—Bill, age 18.

> Since I'm normal, I don't have to hide how I feel. But you should make sure that you are comfortable with your preference before you blurt it out to just anyone.—Nathan, age 19.

> I tell people that I'm gay if I know that they won't reject me, will accept me for what I am, and won't try to 'straighten' me out. I test them, I suppose, then I judge if I want to risk telling them.—James, age 17.

More and more gay kids are learning to feel better about themselves. As you start to listen to your deepest feelings and learn more about what it means to be gay you will begin to be comfortable with your sexuality. This is the process called coming out.

The first step in coming out is to tell yourself that you are gay and say, "That's OK." Later you may want to tell someone else—someone you trust to be understanding and sympathetic. You might choose a friend or an adult. You will probably want to meet other gay kids for friendship or a more intimate relationship. Some gay kids are able to come out to their families. You need to decide whether or not to tell your family, and to choose the right time. Lots of people, including parents, simply don't understand gay people and are difficult to come out to. In the beginning, be cautious about whom you tell.

But it is crucial to be honest with yourself. Just as self-denial costs you, coming out pays off. Most kids who accept their sexuality say they feel calmer, happier and more confident.

> No matter what people say, you are normal. God created you, and you were made in this [sic] image. If you are non-religious, you were born and you have a purpose, and being gay is only part of it.—Nathan, age 19.

> Stand up for what you believe in, and don't listen to what hatemongers have to say. Stay proud and confident.—James, age 17.

Reprinted from "I Think I Might Be Gay . . . Now What Do I Do?" by Kevin Cranston and Cooper Thompson. Reprinted with permission from The Campaign to End Homophobia.

No: Homosexual Feelings Are Not Normal

Tim Stafford

Q: I am gay. Or at least bisexual. I am also a Christian. I have been a Christian for four years. Most people's response to these facts is, "Well, if you made a true commitment, you wouldn't struggle with this." Or, "You can't be a Christian and be gay too." So I am a poor excuse for a Christian. I know what I do is wrong, but I still go on and do it. That is why I am writing to you. What's wrong with me? Do I need psychological help? Are you going to give me the "Jesus is the true answer" bit? (Though I know he is.) I just can't do it alone. I don't even know if I want to change. What should I do?

A: Let me start with your comment that you are a poor excuse for a Christian. There, at least, we are on common ground. I am a poor excuse for a Christian. We all are, if I read my Bible correctly. Nobody deserves to be treated lovingly by God; we all act in ways that would justify his turning away from us. Recognizing our total lack of credibility before him is a necessary starting point for grasping his attitude toward us. Because instead of turning from us, God welcomes us into his family and calls us his children.

God does not stop there, however. Any loving father trains his children, wanting them to grow up healthy. For your own good, God has expressed his expectations regarding your choices. He is not ambiguous. God does not want you living a gay lifestyle.

The Bible's Views

The Bible considers homosexual actions wrong. There isn't a great deal of material dealing with it; in the Old Testament it simply is declared off-limits, and that is carried over in the New Testament. The only passage that gives a hint of why it is wrong is Romans 1:26–27. There Paul discusses homosexuality in the context of people that have turned their back on God and have succeeded in twisting far away from what is "natural." Paul probably was thinking of the story of creation in Genesis, where it is said that God made man in his own image "male and female." We're sexual people—that's what's "natural"—and sex was made to be between male and female. We learn something about ourselves and about God through the wonderful erotic attraction and interaction of male and female. We learn even if we never marry, for we take part in those interactions at other levels.

That is the basic threat—that you would lose out on part of your identity. Your true identity in Christ isn't homosexual. Some experts say nearly everyone has homosexual desires to some extent. But the sexual focus of our lives is meant to be the opposite sex, for that is how we discover more about ourselves.

The Big Lie

It is important to distinguish between your personality structure and the way you live it out. In other words, there is a difference between homosexual tendencies and a homosexual lifestyle. Everyone has certain dispositions that lead to particular strengths and weaknesses. The Big Lie of the sexual-freedom revolution is that you have to follow you sexual preference (whatever it is), that you have no choice. If I fall in love with someone, it's inevitable we'll end up in bed—unless I am a repressed and unhappy individual determined to stay in an unhappy marriage. If you feel attracted to other men, you will either "stay in the closet," repressed and unhappy, or you will enter the free-flowering splendor of the gay community.

> "The sexual focus of our lives is meant to be the opposite sex."

But this is sheer nonsense. It's really just a variation on the old line a guy gives who wants to take a girl to bed: "Fate meant us to be together. It's bigger than both of us. It's chemistry." One difference between human beings and animals is that we can control our sexuality; it doesn't have to control us. If we all did everything we felt like doing, the world would be sheer chaos. Instead, as rational, thinking creatures, we take our many desires into consideration—desires for sexual release, for personal intimacy, for long-lasting friendships, for marriage and children, for many things—and we decide on a course. We choose a lifestyle that really suits us. We may need to say no to certain desires, but the overall result will be positive, fitting our personal needs.

Temptations

Scripture does not indicate that it is wrong to be tempted. In fact, temptations are normal. The fact that you are tempted to have sexual relations with other men may reflect badly on our sex-crazed society, which inflames our tendencies, or it may reflect badly on your family background, as some psychologists say. I don't see that it reflects badly on you. How you came by the desires that trouble you I do not know. I suspect that most people feel a certain amount of sexual ambiguity, some people more than others.

I get many letters from young people who are afraid they are homosexuals. They've never lived a gay lifestyle, but they feel some variance in their sexual longings—maybe the opposite sex does not attract them in the way they expect is normal, or maybe they have tender feelings for a friend of the same sex. The gay movement claims that one out of ten people is a homosexual and that if you are one you can't do a thing about it. So the question arises: "Am I one?" Once the idea is planted, it tends to grow. And if a person tries it out, he will probably find that, indeed, he can be sexually aroused by his own sex. Therefore, he thinks, he must be gay. In reality, he may merely be ambivalent. In another society, in another time, he would have channeled his sexual desires in a different direction. Sexuality is more fluid than the gay movement leads people to believe. Sexual attraction is as much mental as physical.

Choose Your Lifestyle

You cannot choose your desires, but you can choose your lifestyle. As you say, your feelings and desires for sex will still be there. But what does that prove? Mine are still there too, but I have chosen to focus them within the marriage relationship. That means saying yes to some desires and no to a great many others. Some Christians are single, and they live with continuing heterosexual or homosexual desires. Need they be unhappy? The Bible answers a resounding no! The single, celibate life is honored in the New Testament without reservation. Everyone is called to it for some portion of his or her life. Some are called to it permanently. Jesus was, Paul possibly was, and countless other great and inspiring Christians through the ages have been celibate. Jesus' words in Matthew 19:12 suggest that the call to singleness is not always based on great religious feeling. Practical factors enter: "For some are eunuchs because they were born that way, others were made that way by men; and others have renounced marriage because of the kingdom of heaven." All three causes are honorable.

I believe singleness is the healthy and blessed lifestyle for you at this point. It won't be sheer bliss—I don't know of any lifestyle that is, realistically. And because your struggles are less acceptable in our society than mine, you will suffer a special loneliness in them. Given the judgmental disgust that many people feel regarding homosexuality, you can't expect the sympathies of vast numbers of people. However, you can hope to find the help and support of some.

Don't exaggerate the difficulty of sharing your situation privately with concerned, caring Christians. Many will not be able to accept and understand your situation, but many others will. I know some Christians who would be delighted to commit themselves to regular prayer and encouragement for someone in your shoes.

You cannot change your lifestyle alone. That is why I strongly encourage you to begin today asking God to put before you one or more people whom you can confide in with complete confidence. You need them not just to listen to you and accept you, but to play an active, caring part in your life, meeting regularly with you for prayer and Bible study. You need to take the risk of revealing your inner thoughts so that you can quit living in lonely secretiveness and begin to develop satisfying, deep relationships. Jesus is the answer to all our problems, but he doesn't work in a purely spiritual way. He has a physical and relational reality, what the Bible calls the "body of Christ"—that is, the church.

I look for the day when Christians will get over their homophobia and realize that those with homosexual temptations differ very little from the rest of us. We all struggle with temptations, and the Bible never treats one sin as worse than another. In the fellowship of the Holy Spirit, which is the togetherness binding Christians, we come closest to grasping Christ's full and final victory over sin.

You Can Change
There is no mysterious, awesome power in homosexual temptations. Temptation is temptation—we all know how impossible it can be when we are in the wrong situation and how easy to resist when we leave that situation. You

say you are not sure that you want to change. I think you do want to change, but you are not sure you can. The gay movement says that you cannot, that you can only repress your natural feelings. That is not so. It is most natural to follow Jesus. You were made to do that.

Excerpted from *Love, Sex, and the Whole Person,* by Tim Stafford. Copyright ©1991 by Campus Life Books. Used by permission of Zondervan Publishing House.

Chapter 2

Thinking About Virginity

The Importance of Virginity

Tara Bonaparte

Virgins used to receive a lot more respect for their decision to save themselves for marriage, writes Tara Bonaparte. She believes virgins still deserve that respect. In her opinion, virginity is the most precious gift you can give to someone. There are too many consequences associated with being sexually active to risk having sex before you're ready, she notes. She concludes that you'll appreciate sex more if you wait until you're with someone you truly love. Bonaparte is a teen who writes for *Foster Care Youth United*, a magazine for youth in the New York City foster care system.

Wuz up, people!!!! Well, this is the high yellow, big mouth, funny writer who comes correct with all the facts, coming at ya with an article that is strictly for the ladies. (But guys, feel free to read too.)

This article may help you understand some of the stresses that we ladies have to go through in being virgins. And ladies, this article may help you to understand things about yourselves.

This article can also speak to male virgins. The same way that some females have to worry about males, males also need to

Reprinted from "Virgin Power," by Tara Bonaparte, *Foster Care Youth United*, January/February 1999. Reprinted with permission from Youth Communications.

worry about some females. Because there are a lot of girls (and you girls know who you are) who want to take away the virginity from the last batch of virgin males that exists.

When my mother and father were growing up, it was a good thing for a girl to be a virgin. My grandparents made sure that all of their five daughters (including my mom) ran around claiming what was between their legs was 14 carat gold. My grandparents always let their daughters know the importance of being a virgin. And that is why I know the importance of being a virgin.

No Respect

Today it seems as if nobody has any respect for themselves. Girls (not all of them) are running around having sex with any and every boy who says they love them.

And the boys. I just have no words. They are running around reproducing more children than rabbits. Having sex with any girl who has a big butt and a nice smile.

Where did the respect for being a virgin go?

Being a teenager, I know that one of the biggest things that teens worry about is self-image. We teenagers are always worried about what our friends think. We're always trying to be down with the latest craze.

And when I look around, the newest craze is for people to talk about all the sex they have. And if you happen to be that one teenager who hasn't experienced the "wonder" of having sex, it can be very difficult.

Name Calling

"Man, you ain't had sex yet?"

"You scared or something?"

"What, are you gay?"

If you are a virgin, these statements are probably very familiar to you. Most of the time they come from your friends, but sometimes they even come from your partner. These statements can make the strongest person feel like an idiot.

Well, let me shine some light on these problems.

If you've heard these comments from a friend, then there are some things that you really need to know. Ninety-nine percent of the time your friend is lying about her own sex experience. And liars always try to make themselves look good by putting others down.

> Being a virgin is the most precious thing in the universe.

Does your friend usually bring up the topic of sex when he/she is around a large group of people? If your friend does, then I'm sorry to say that he/she is probably still a virgin too. Because if a person is having sex, there is no need to brag about it.

If you've heard those statements from your partner, there is only one reason he/she is telling you that. He/she is obviously trying to make you feel bad that you're a virgin. Bad enough to give it up to him/her.

Don't be fooled, because if your partner really loved you, then he/she wouldn't be trying to make you rush into a serious, life or death decision. And believe me, it is.

Be Sure

To all the virgins out there—if your mama or daddy didn't tell you this, then I think that it is time that we have "The Talk." So to everyone who is reading this article, take these words as seriously as the air that you are breathing.

To me, being a virgin is the most precious thing in the universe. And when I finally do decide to lose my virginity, it will be when I'm ready. And when I'm in love.

Don't let anyone pressure you into doing anything that you don't want to do. And please don't be fooled by those silly lines like "I have needs" or "It will make our relationship grow stronger."

Give me a break. Everyone makes sex seem like a holiday in the Bahamas, but nobody bothers to explain the consequences. And there are plenty.

Party's Over

Sex (if done right) can be a beautiful thing. But everything is not beautiful about sex. So, to that young virgin who is about to take that first step to sex—listen up. I don't care where you are either. You could be at your boyfriend's/girlfriend's buck naked and just happen to pick up this article. You better get your clothes and run.

Just like they say that weed is a gateway drug, sex can lead to a baby or a serious disease. And virgins can get pregnant the very first time they have sex.

Teens Are Remaining Virgins Longer

- In 1995, 50% of girls and women aged 15 to 19 had had sex, down from 55% in 1990.
- 55% of single males aged 15 to 19 have had sex, down from 60% in 1988.
- 70% of 18- and 19-year-old women have had sex, down from 74% in 1990.
- 38% of girls aged 15 to 17 have had sex, down from 41% in 1990.
- The average age at which teens have their first sexual experience has risen from 15.8 in 1997 to 16.3 in 1998.

National Center for Health Statistics, Urban Institute, Durex Global Survey.

There was this one girl I knew when I was younger. Her name was Taisha. She was pretty, smart and funny. Everyone wanted to be just like her. Every time my family and I played house, I would be her. She was 18 and still a virgin. I was seven and still believed in the stork. But still, I always told everyone that Taisha was my best friend.

When I reached 12, I knew all I needed to know about sex. I knew that I could get pregnant. I also knew about AIDS. I guess Taisha didn't know. The last I heard she was 25, had AIDS and was pregnant for her third time. And I heard that her children have the AIDS virus. Not everyone can pass on the AIDS virus to their children, and I was hoping that she didn't pass it on to hers. But she did. Sad, isn't it?

Her First Time

Taisha's cousin told me that the first person she had sex with gave her the AIDS virus. So don't sit there and say, "It can't happen to me." Because as long as there are teenagers and sex out there, it can happen to you.

You could be having sex for 50 years (even though the thought is very scary) and never catch a disease. Or you can have sex just once and end up with the AIDS virus. So be careful.

> There are a lot of good things about making love. But don't be in such a rush to find out what's so good.

Along with babies and diseases, sex also gives you a reputation. And once you gain a reputation, it is going to stick with you for a long time. You could have the reputation of a "goodie two shoes," but all it takes is for you to have sex with one not-so-special person to be labeled a h-c. And I know that isn't right, but unfortunately that is the world that we are living in today.

To be honest, a boy is not really going to be called anything but "The man" for having sex. So ladies, you and your boyfriend can have sex, but only you will get the bad reputation. Hmmm, something to think about.

Making Love

Now, at this point, I know you are probably saying, "Damn, this girl is trying to keep our legs closed forever."

Well, that is not completely true. I'm just trying to make sure that before anyone goes out and does something as serious as sex, they should know about the good and the bad.

There are a lot of good things about making love. But don't be in such a rush to find out what's so good. Because the longer you wait, the more you will appreciate sex when you finally have it. And you will appreciate it more if it's with somebody you really love. So people, let me end this article with a little advice.

Make your decision right, because it could change the rest of your life.

Deciding to Wait

Lilybird

One reason why many teens decide to have sex is because they're simply curious about the experience. Lilybird is a teenager who was anxious to lose her virginity before she became "too old"; however, she wants her first time to be with someone special. In her quest to lose her virginity, Lilybird began to change her ideas about being a virgin until she realized that sex will have a lot more meaning for her if she waits until she's in love and is emotionally ready. Lilybird is a teen writer for *Foster Care Youth United*, a magazine written by and for teens in the New York City foster care system.

The way I felt about my virginity was I wanted to lose it before I got too old, but I didn't wanna lose it to just anybody. When I spoke to my friends about it they would say, "Girl, you're stupid, I wish I was a virgin," or "I wish I waited." But I felt like they didn't understand because it wasn't their problem. I wanted to know what it was like before I got too old.

I'm 16 and for a while I thought I was waiting too long. I didn't know what the right time was, so I wanted to lose it quick before it was too late. In some ways I thought that by having sex I would mature and not be the same little girl.

Reprinted from "My Virginity: I Wanted to Lose It Quick," by Lilybird, *Foster Care Youth United*, March/April 1996. Reprinted with permission from Youth Communications.

I had been in situations where I was about to have sex, but I was so scared my whole body was shaking. I was scared of exposing my body to a guy and finding out later that I didn't know him well enough.

Not Wanting to Rush

People would always say to me "It's alright to be nervous," or "It's normal to be a 16-year-old virgin." But teenagers now are expected to grow up a lot faster than teenagers in the past.

Getting a man was not the problem, it was finding the right one. I didn't wanna rush into anything and later say to myself, "I should never have lost it to him."

I also was worried that the word would get out that I was "sexin' this brotha" and I'd get treated like a chicken around my way. I've seen it happen to mad girls and I refuse to let it happen to me. In my neighborhood, when guys find out you're having sex, they hound you like you're raw meat.

When someone asks me if I'm a virgin, I'm not ashamed to admit I am. But when they want more detail, I get embarrassed because they probably think I'm hot in the pants.

> I wanted to lose [my virginity] quick before it was too late.

I began to think of my virginity as a big problem around the time one of my good friends lost it last year. After that, it was on my mind nonstop. I felt like if I didn't lose it, my friend and I would have nothing to talk about and she would eventually outgrow me.

Too Scared

I had boyfriends who I could have lost it to, but they weren't the right guys and I would have regretted it.

For example, there was this guy Jaquan. He and I weren't really serious from the get, so I wasn't gonna do anything with him. Besides, he knows mad people around my way. If I had done something with him, news would have gotten out.

I remember one time I was going out with this guy Richard. We were in his room making out and it started to go further. I wanted to, but I was too scared to expose my body. He asked me if I was alright.

> I felt like if I didn't lose [my virginity], my friend and I would have nothing to talk about and she would eventually outgrow me.

I jumped off his bed with the quickness and made up some excuse about how I was hungry and wanted to go to the store. I think he knew I was scared because he didn't push the issue. We went to the store, he walked me to the bus stop, then I went home.

I was kicking myself when I got on the bus. I had wanted it for so long but when I had the opportunity I got scared. I felt like I was gonna make a fool of myself. I know now that having sex with him would have been a mistake, because he and I didn't last that long. I would have felt used.

As months passed I started to change my ideas about being a virgin. I looked around and saw what happened to some girls who rushed into having sex, or girls who caught STD's from their man messin' around on them.

I know one girl who got played by her man. He told her to stop calling him, saying "You're too immature," and even called her a hoe. She still kept stressing him. Her close friend had sex and she wanted to try it out so bad, she did it with a guy who she knew was not faithful to her.

A New Attitude

I think God made an example of her to help me see the light, because I don't want to get played like that. I feel there are other things I can think about, like my clothes and hair, rather than sex. After a while it got to the point where I had to say to myself, "Why are you stressin' it so much?"

My friends talk about sex like it's regular and boring because they've been doing it for so long and so much. I don't want it to become regular for me at such a young age, for it to become "just sex." That's why I say to myself now, "When I get older and finally do it, I'm gonna have a lot more thrills in my life than the ones who already went through it."

I don't know if time has changed my whole perspective on this issue, or seeing other teenage sexual relationships gone bad. For some reason "having sex" doesn't seem as big and over-powering as before. Its kind of like money in the bank—the longer you wait, the more loot you'll have because of interest.

It's Better to Wait

I want to wait to find the right guy. Not just some guy who looks mad good, is nice only when he's not drunk, and mad funny. I need to know he is mature emotionally, not just physically. Some guys think just because they've had a lot of partners, they're mature enough to handle sex. Anybody can have sex, but not everyone can handle sex. Waiting until you're married to me is kind of long, but having sex just because it might be going out of style is crazy.

So, it's still on my mind but not like before. As time passed I realized that life is not gonna end just because I'm not having sex yet. There's other things I can do with my boyfriends. Virginity should be given to someone you care about or love, and he should feel the same for you.

Alternatives to Intercourse

Tara McCarthy

There are lots of ways that you can express your sexuality without having sexual intercourse. Below, Tara McCarthy explains how she is able to remain a virgin yet still have an active sex life. During a re-examination of her sexual past, McCarthy discovered that sexual play has more meaning for her if she's with someone she cares about. She's proud that she has stayed true to her ideals so she can give her future husband the gift of her virginity. McCarthy is a freelance writer who writes about teen and women's issues.

I've always hated that Madonna song "Like a Virgin"—the "touched for the very first time" bit, in particular— because at 26, *I'm* still a virgin, and I've been touched, kissed, prodded, rubbed, caressed, licked, nibbled—you name it. More times than I'd like to admit. I don't fit the image of a virgin except for one salient fact: I've never had sexual intercourse.

A Life Without Sex

I am not a religious fanatic or a prude. I'm not a wallflower, nor have I ever had any trouble finding guys who wanted to sleep

Excerpted from *Been There, Haven't Done That,* by Tara McCarthy. Copyright ©1996 by Tara McCarthy. Reprinted with permission from Warner Books, Inc.

with me. I go to movies and concerts. I have good days and bad days at pool. I buy a lot of CDs. I have a life.

The decision to have a life without having premarital sex isn't an easy one, but I made it a long time ago and have had few regrets. It would be convenient to say that I decided to wait because of AIDS; not having sex because you fear for your health is somehow easier for people to understand. But my decision was made before I'd even heard of AIDS, so disease was not the deterrent. Maybe my decision was made *for* me, to an extent, when my mother stood at our kitchen sink peeling a cucumber, of all things, and told 10-year-old me that sex is something that two people do when they really love each other.

For years I waited with great anticipation for my attitude to change. I knew that Catholic girls were supposed to go nuts when they got to college. Alas, four years at Harvard passed without any change in my sexual status. After graduation I moved to Dublin, landed a job at a music magazine and felt I was truly living my own life for the first time. It was such a rock-and-roll life—I frequented pubs and clubs and spent nights with spiky-haired synthesizer players—it only made sense that having sex would follow.

What stopped me? The same reasoning that kept me from sleeping with a long-term serious boyfriend when I returned to the States: Since intercourse is the only thing that can get you pregnant and the only act that physically joins two people together, I've imbued it with symbolic meaning and reserved a special place for it in my life.

> At 26, I'm still a virgin, and I've been touched, kissed, prodded, rubbed, caressed, licked, nibbled—you name it.

I've allowed myself other physical pleasures for reasons that are equally clear—I'm human, I have sexual impulses and I don't see anything wrong with acting on them.

Truth is, I've had very satisfying, very intimate physical and emotional relationships with men in my life. Sure, I've left some of them hanging, but not as a general rule. A lot of people think that I've come so close I might as well have done it, that my cut off point is completely arbitrary, and that therefore I'm not *really* a virgin. Well, if the words *chaste* and *pure* enter into your definition of *virgin,* I would never claim to be one. I'm probably more in tune with what I like and don't like in bed than a woman who has slept with one or two guys and hasn't really fooled around with anyone else.

> There's so much emphasis on intercourse that people aren't given the chance to figure out what else there is and how to be a sexual being without having actual sex.

But if you get caught up in semantics you miss my point, which is that the traditional definition of virginity is pretty outdated. You can venture far beyond innocent goodnight kisses on the front porch and explore your sexuality without risking pregnancy, disease and your sense of self.

Too Much Emphasis on Intercourse

A boyfriend once told me that if his parents knew what we did in bed together, they'd probably wish we were just having sex. What's that all about? I don't own handcuffs. I'm not a contortionist. But society shies away from anything that isn't standard missionary-position screwing. There's so much emphasis on intercourse that people aren't given the chance to figure out what else there is and how to be a sexual being without having actual sex. We forget that two people can enjoy each other's bodies—and their own—with less risk.

Of course, sex will never be risk-free. People make mistakes, and I'm no exception, but the best ones are those you can learn from and promptly forget, not the ones that you have to put through college.

Some of my own worst missteps involved not being honest about who I am and what I want out of life and romance. When

The Benefits of Outercourse

You're not saying no to sex when you practice Outercourse. You're saying *oh, God, yes* to all the things that get overlooked when you fall into an intercourse rut (as it were). Below, five Outercourse aficionados speak out. Their true tales might make true believers of you.

• "My fiancé and I decided to follow the advice from a sex book and not have intercourse, or even oral sex, for a while. We just touched, talked, groped. I went from not having orgasms to having them all the time. Now, when I look at other couples and wonder if they're having the great sex we're having, I feel smug!"—Jennifer, 27, graduate student, Seattle

• "To have good sex, you have to let your guard down. It's hard not to be embarrassed about doing things like dry humping. Once you do, it's like being a teenager again and having all this sexual energy and not knowing what to do with it."—Cara, 25, account executive, Minneapolis

• "We waited four months to have intercourse. I said I wasn't ready for a commitment, but really, I just knew that the holding back was more exciting for me. It was like, 'The suspense is killing me; I hope it lasts.'"—Heather, 24, caterer, Middlebury VT

• "We don't want sex to be routine. My boyfriend and I waited until we couldn't take it any longer before we finally had sex. Now we'll sometimes go without intercourse for a week. I'm a romantic. I don't want it to be ordinary."—Elizabeth, 24, researcher, New York City

• "I was raised Catholic. So I held off on intercourse for as long as I could. My friends who were having sex didn't have orgasms, but I did, all the time. Even now that I'm not a virgin, there's something special about holding off—once you have intercourse, the mystery is gone. Restraint is exciting."—Andrea, 27, model booker, New York City

Suzanna Markstein, *Mademoiselle*, October 1996.

I somehow got on the subject of sex with Bill,* a musician I'd met in Belfast—OK, it came up because we were in bed together—I told him that I had had very few relationships involving sex in the past (wild understatement). Later, he asked me playfully to tell him the strangest place I had ever done it, and I considered making something up but blanked.

> A part of me has always felt that my virginity set me apart.

"I can't answer that question," I began, "because I've never had sex . . ."

I thought about adding "in any strange places," which would have been perfectly true. But I couldn't do it, so there it was, just hanging out there: "I've never had sex . . ."

"But you were just talking about relationships where sex had been involved."

Caught.

Ah yes, I attempted, but only in the sense that it had been brought up, discussed and decided against.

"What are you, saving yourself for marriage or something?" he asked. All of a sudden I felt ridiculous.

An Exception to the Norm

Not because *waiting* was ridiculous, but because attempting to dodge the subject of my virginity was a ridiculous thing for me to be doing. I knew how much of an exception to the norm I was, and that my virginity made me less attractive in some men's eyes. The fact that I went to an Ivy League college had had the same effect in certain situations; a temp agent once told me to take Harvard off my resume because it would hurt my chances of getting a summer job as a secretary. I could have lied—sparing potential employers the "Harvard" and potential boyfriends the "virgin"—but what was the point if all it got me was a job I didn't want and a guy who didn't want the real me?

* All names have been changed.

These days, the embarrassment factor—such a huge part of the virgin experience—is gone. I know that for me, the right time, place, guy and circumstances have yet to coincide. I'm hardly going to isolate myself from the world or lie to it in the meantime.

When will it happen? Maybe not for some time, given the fact that my selection of single men is somewhat limited. I believe so strongly that sexual intercourse is not to be taken lightly that it's impossible for me to have a relationship with someone who doesn't feel the same. I sometimes wish there were more

> The physical pleasure isn't nearly so important to me as the emotional release of giving myself to someone— the right one—body and soul.

potential partners for me to choose from, but I'm not bitter—unlike Dan,* a fellow virgin I used to know. When I last saw him, he went on and on about how the world would be a better place if there were more people "like us," and I suddenly realized why virgins so often get a bad rap. Not only was Dan unbearably self-righteous—as many vocal virgins in the media tend to be—but he appeared to be carrying an enormous chip on his shoulder.

Like a Tattoo

For all my frustrations with not having found the right person, a part of me has always felt that my virginity set me apart, and not necessarily in a negative way—more like a cool tattoo on an obscure body part. In fact, virginity and tattoos have a lot in common. Getting rid of them often proves difficult and painful. And just as a skull and crossbones, an I Love Mom or a simple rose tattoo can mean different things to different people, the way we view our virginity—and losing it—is unique to each of us (so much so that Hallmark could put out a line of cards for the occasion, ranging from "Happy Hump Day" to "We're sorry for your loss"). I imagine Dan saw his virginity as an actual cross to bear, something the whole world could see and pass judgment on. Mine I've often seen as an anchor tattoo, perhaps hidden away on an ankle or butt cheek. Something that grounded me when other aspects of my life were out of control. Something that would one day give way and let me set sail.

I considered raising anchor with my most recent boyfriend, Mark.* We'd met in passing several years before, but our relationship really started while he was living in Sweden, finishing research for his master's degree. In the course of a 10-month correspondence, Mark and I went from being friends to lovers, and when he moved to New York City we became an established couple. That isn't to say we were perfectly compatible. Take our romantic histories: Mark could count on his fingers the dates he'd had, while I'd need an abacus. He was in love with all of the women he'd had sex with, and he simply couldn't fathom how I could have been intimate with so many guys I didn't care for deeply.

A Re-Examination

Mark's questions forced me to reexamine my sexual history, and I found that I wasn't so thrilled with it either. I'd always felt, on some level, that resisting intercourse made up for all my flings. But looking back, it seemed that in my search for the right man, I'd gone places and done things I would no longer feel comfortable doing. It took loving and being loved by Mark, someone who understood my ideals but challenged whether I'd really lived up to them, to help me realize that, intercourse aside, I don't want to be doing *anything* sexual with just anybody.

> When I do decide to have sex, it will be the biggest gift I've ever given anyone in my life.

I no longer feel that need to find "the one" with such urgency, in no small part due to the way in which Mark and I eventually ended our year-plus romantic involvement. Agreeing that we would be better off as friends felt like the most mature decision I'd ever made in my

love life. Now that I've reached that level of maturity, I don't
think there's any going back. I know what I want and I still believe it's out there, but until I find it, I simply can't see myself
hooking up with random men or fooling around with a guy I've
only had a few dates with. It's not who I want to be.

It's possible that when all is said and done and my first real
lover has fallen asleep beside me, I'll lie there and say to myself,
"You idiot, you could have been doing that for years!" But I
don't have any romanticized notions of the mechanics of intercourse. In spite of an ever-increasing desire for what I imagine
it feels like, I'm not expecting a mind-blowing orgasm or the
best sexual experience of my life. The physical pleasure isn't
nearly so important to me as the emotional release of giving myself to someone—the right one—body and soul.

The Biggest Gift

For a long time I was looking for someone worthy, someone
who understood and deserved a gift of this magnitude. But that
feeling of superiority has been replaced over the years with a
quieter sense of power and pride at having stuck to my guns.

I know, simply, that it will happen with someone who loves
me and whom I love back—unreservedly. I also know that when
I do decide to have sex, it will be the biggest gift I've ever giv-
en anyone in my life. It just took me a long time to understand
that I'd be giving it to myself.

A Born-Again Virgin

David Erikson

For many years, David Erikson, a freelance writer, believed that if the sexual chemistry was right between him and his sexual partner, then love and intimacy would follow. He discovered, however, that the lack of emotional bonds between him and his partners just led to meaningless sex and feelings of loneliness. The way to make sex meaningful, he has decided, is to build the emotional bonds first. He has resolved to abstain from sex until he's willing to give his body and soul to his one true love on his wedding night.

We started kissing just outside her door, our hands feeling through coats and shirts and sweaters. "Why don't you come in?" my date whispered, making it clear that sex was there for the asking. But I didn't ask; I walked away.

"What? No sex?" my buddies said, stunned. "Man, you'd better think that over." I have. But casual sex—while exciting for about, oh, 15 minutes—has never given me what I really want. I want something that lasts past bagels and cream cheese in the morning. I want a relationship that's laced with intimacy, trust— and no sex until we're married.

I've tried it both ways. (Who would listen to me if I hadn't?) In college, my weekends revolved around the hook-up scene, and the first step in most relationships was testing our chemistry in bed. I figured that if the sex was good, the rest—communication, humor, maybe even *love*—would follow. But instead of being the start of something fulfilling and intertwining, sex always left me feeling lonelier than before.

The Facts About Secondary Virginity

Right now you are probably thinking, "Why do I want to be a virgin? When I was a virgin I was dying to lose it, why should I find it now?" There are some benefits from being a virgin that you probably haven't considered.

• Orgasms experienced by recovered virgins are 200% stronger than those by non-virgins.

• After regaining their virginity, 34.8% of the users claimed that food tasted better. . . .

• The death rate among virgins is 300% lower than that among non-virgins. . . .

• Virgins are 86.1% less likely to get into hazardous automobile accidents. . . .

• Hair loss is 45.6% less prevalent among male virgins than non-virgins.

• 67% of all American Olympians are virgins.

• Mother Theresa *and* the Pope are virgins.

• Extensive testing has shown weight loss is substantially easier while you are a virgin.

• Donald Trump first started off as a virgin.

Society for the Recapture of Virginity, Inc., www.thebluedot.com/srv/facts.html

---

Flashback to the instant this truth hit home for me: It was our third date, and we lay naked in bed, laughing, tickling . . . you get the picture. In the immediate moment after the immediate sex, I realized that I barely knew the woman next to me. What was her middle name? Her favorite color? Did she have a good singing voice?

Not long after that night, filled with maybe 900 seconds of thrill, we broke up. I suppose we could have continued to just do it for several months until we finally admitted it wasn't going to work. But things somehow felt wrong between us. No doubt other flaws plagued our romance, too—but the fact that our physical relationship had jumped way ahead of anything we were ready for emotionally seemed to amplify our rifts and harm our chances to mend them. Ultimately, I just couldn't find a way to bridge the chasm between the intimacy of our sex life and the hollowness of our conversations.

> Casual sex—while exciting for about, oh, 15 minutes—has never given me what I really want.

That was when I stopped laughing off abstinence—a concept that had always conjured up images of God as the Great Cosmic Killjoy. Perhaps, I began to think, the no-sex-before-marriage rule was more than a centuries-old joke. Maybe it wasn't so much a barrier designed to keep me from something good as a boundary set in place to guide me to something *better.* Maybe there was something contradictory about the fact that I'd given my body to someone, but kept parts of my heart and soul to myself. The more I thought about it, the more I saw the logic and beauty of total union—no holds barred—and, for me, that meant waiting for sex until marriage.

Dating Sans Sex

Sometimes I wonder if I've lost my mind. Believe me, plenty of women would agree with that theory. "You're on a power trip," one date told me, insisting (in the middle of a crowded restaurant, I might add) that my whole celibacy deal was nothing more than a way to show off my superior will.

"You won't have sex? That's bullshit! You're just scared," another said. (So much for the stereotype that men want to screw and women crave endless foreplay.) But let me assure anyone still with me here, I'm not trying to be a male tease. It's just that I dream of saving my sexual energies for one woman.

Worth the Wait

I often fantasize about my wedding night. The entire ordeal of the ceremony, reception, dancing and thank-you's is over, and at last I'm alone with my wife. I dream that this night will be amazing, and that dream helps me wait. But what if the sex isn't mind-blowingly wonderful? Won't I be sorry I didn't find out before it was too late? Sometimes that worries me. I've decided, though, that the most important thing about our relationship will be our spiritual and emotional connection—after all, that's what will keep us in love with each other long after the passion fades. If we build our commitment on a deeper level, then sex will be a wonderful bonus. Then we can truly say we're making love.

Point of Contention: Will Abstinence-Only Sex Education Programs Reduce Teen Sex?

In 1996, concern over the high teen pregnancy rate led Congress to allocate $50 million over five years to states that agreed to teach abstinence-only education programs in the nation's public schools. Schools that accepted the funds must teach students that premarital sex and sex outside of marriage are frowned upon by society, and that the only guaranteed way to prevent pregnancy and sexually transmitted diseases is through abstinence. Supporters of the abstinence-only programs contend that comprehensive sex education programs—which teach teens about contraception and how to protect themselves from STDs—essentially give teens permission to have sex. They claim that teens are less likely to have sex if they're told that premarital sex is unacceptable. Opponents argue that these abstinence-only programs don't work. They say that teens are going to have sex no matter what they're told, therefore, it's better to teach them how to avoid the consequences, such as pregnancy and STDs.

The two viewpoints presented here offer both sides of this debate. Ellen Goodman is a syndicated columnist. Joseph Perkins is an editorial writer for the *San Diego Union-Tribune*.

Yes: Abstinence-Only Sex Education Will Reduce Teen Sex

Joseph Perkins

Alexandra Stevenson, a recent graduate of La Jolla Country Day School, raised a lot of eyebrows when she made it all the way to the Wimbledon semifinals. And the 18-year-old almost certainly raised as many eyebrows when she recently revealed in a nationally televised interview that she has never been kissed.

Indeed, it's one thing for a teen-ager to make an overnight transition from a promising high school tennis player to a serious contender for a Grand Slam tennis title. But to think that she made it all the way through high school without having sex, without having so much as a kiss. Forget about it.

Well, as it happens, young Alexandra is not such an aberration. In fact, an increasing number of her fellow teens are also practicing chastity. And much of the credit for this must go to the growing number of abstinence-only programs that are reaching youngsters throughout the country.

The teen-abstinence movement got a major boost by the 1996 welfare reform law, which included a provision setting aside $250 million over five years for a federal program to discourage teen sex.

The ground rules of the program are to teach younger Americans "the social, psychological and health gains to be realized by abstaining from sexual activity" and to caution teens that "sexual activity outside of . . . marriage is likely to have harmful psychological and physical effects."

States can get a share of the federal money by putting up

$3 for every $4 they request from Washington. The maximum yearly grant a state may receive is $5.7 million, which the state must match with $4.2 million of its own.

> If teens get the message that underage, premarital sex is not normative, . . . then youngsters will be less inclined to have sex.

Over the past two years, the states have created nearly 700 new abstinence-only programs, bringing the nationwide total to roughly 1,000. And even the lone state government that has chosen not to participate in the federal program, California, is funding abstinence-only programs out of state coffers.

This represents a radical shift in public policy with respect to teens and sex. For the past quarter-century, at least, the prevailing wisdom has been that the government ought not waste time and tax dollars trying to discourage the underaged from having sex.

The more "realistic" and "sensible" approach, the thinking went, was for the government to bend its efforts to preventing unwanted pregnancies and sexually transmitted diseases by supporting programs that make condoms and birth control pills more readily available to youngsters.

Well, this "teens-will-be-teens" orthodoxy has not withered away by any stretch of the imagination, but it does face a serious challenge today from the abstinence-only movement. And this challenge has the "sex education" crowd (which teaches chastity as one of several sexual "options" for kids) plenty worried.

And with good cause. The abstinence-only movement is producing desired results. Indeed, since federal funds started flowing to abstinence-only programs in 1997, the number of teen-age pregnancies, abortions and births have fallen. Moreover, the average age at which youngsters have their first sexual experience has risen from 15.8 in 1997 to 16.3 in 1998, according to the Durex Global Survey.

These developments show that the prevailing wisdom about teen sex—that kids simply cannot control their raging hormones, that they are bound to have sex—is a fallacy. Kids live up or down to expectations.

Indeed, if adults impart the message to teens that they are expected to be sexually active, that it's OK as long as they use a condom or take the pill, then those teens are that much more likely to engage in sexual activity.

On the other hand, if teens get the message that underage, premarital sex is not normative, that adults will not tacitly condone teen promiscuity by providing contraceptives-on-demand, no questions asked, then youngsters will be less inclined to have sex.

There are millions of responsible teens out there, like Alexandra Stevenson, who are living proof that younger Americans are quite capable of waiting at least until they are adults before becoming sexually active.

They recognize that the best way to avoid unwanted pregnancies and sexually transmitted diseases is not by practicing so-called "safe sex"—by using condoms and birth control pills—but by refraining from sex altogether.

Reprinted from "The Best Choice for Teens Concerning Sex," by Joseph Perkins, *The San Diego Union-Tribune,* August 13, 1999. Reprinted with permission from the author.

No: Abstinence-Only Sex Education Programs Will Not Reduce Teen Sex

Ellen Goodman

I have always had a soft spot for the folks who preach abstinence. For one thing, I like their rap lines. You know, "Pet Your Dog, Not Your Date." "Do the Right Thing, Wait for the Ring."

Reprinted by permission of Kirk Anderson.

Then, too, they were also the ones who came up with the idea of "Secondary Virginity," which is a kind of biological annulment. This prompted a young lawyer in my family to ask, "Can you have a third or a fourth virginity? Or is it two strikes and you're out?"

In any case, I can happily agree with the rightest wing of this movement in lamenting the number of kids who start having sex far too young and far too unhappily with far too many consequences. Do teens need help saying no when all the messages around them, from media to partners, are saying yes, yes, yes? Do they need adults to talk with them about waiting? Sure.

Abstinence Only
Why then do I find myself queasy when the government offers to pass out some $50 million a year for educational pro-

grams that will teach abstinence only? Try the word "only."

In one of those after-hours maneuvers for which Washington is famous, a provision offering money for abstinence-only programs was snuck into the 1996 welfare reform bill.

The logic that welded abstinence to welfare was that unwed teen moms often end up on AFDC. No sex, no teen moms. Ergo no welfare. Teach kids abstinence and nothing but abstinence.

Under the guidelines, any approved government program must have "as its exclusive purpose, teaching the social, psychological and health gains to be realized by abstaining from sexual activity." Exactly which sexual "activity" to be avoided—masturbation? French-kissing?—remains undefined.

But the guidelines do clearly say that kids must be taught that sex is only for marriage. Despite the fact that 90 percent of Americans—including parents and members of Congress—had their first sex outside of marriage, abstinence-only teaches that married intercourse is "the expected standard of human sexual activity."

There's no reliable evidence that current abstinence-only programs reduce sexual activity.

To get government money, a program must even teach that unmarried sex is "likely to have harmful psychological and physical effects."

If that sounds like legislated fear-mongering, a recent California study of abstinence programs bears it out.

In one "educational" video, a student asks what happens if he wants to have sex before marriage. The instructor answers, "Well, I guess you'll just have to be prepared to die."

If the idea of federally funded disinformation is troubling enough, the lack of information is worse. Under these guidelines, abstinence-only programs can't teach about contraception. Nor talk openly and frankly about those banned "sexual activities." This "education" is monosyllabic.

I agree that abstinence should have a strong role in a comprehensive program. But this is all-or-nothing money, meant to replace any other programs, not enrich them with, say, an abstinence unit. The states have to find $3 for every $4 they get from Washington.

And there's no reliable evidence the current abstinence-only programs reduce sexual activity.

Today we know a fair amount about kids who have early, too early, intercourse. They're likely to be physically mature, to come from poor single-parent families. The kids who delay sex tend to have mentors, to read and write better, to have fewer stereotypes about sex roles, to be busy and connected. I still think the best abstinence program is an after-school program.

But now the states have to decide whether to ask for this hush money.

Just Say No

Debra Haffner of SIECUS, the Sex Information and Education Council of the United States, says, "We are giving states the same advice we are giving teens. Abstain, and if you are not going to abstain, act responsibly."

So far all but half a dozen states have caved to peer group pressure. Some states like Maine want to use the money for a media campaign. Others say they'll use it to teach just the youngest kids. Still others are trying to find a creative end run around the restrictions. But even those states will have to take money from another pot.

Money, especially federal money, can be awfully seductive. It's hard to just say no to government dollars. But this is one time when states should practice abstinence—and not preach it.

Chapter 3

The Pressures Teens Face to Have Sex

Peer Pressure on Teenage Boys

Robin Chan

Boys often boast about their sexual conquests to their friends and ridicule their classmates who admit they are still virgins. In the following essay, Robin Chan writes that many boys are still virgins and proud of the fact. He notes that virgins don't have to worry about sexually transmitted diseases or their girlfriends getting pregnant and he urges teens not to give in to the peer pressure to have sex. Chan writes for *New Youth Connection*, a New York City magazine written by and for teens.

The names in this story have been changed.

One time in the boys locker room in the local YMCA, three guys who were changing clothes across from me and my friends started talking about who they had "done" the night before. Then they asked us who we had done. We told them we didn't do anyone because we were virgins. One of the guys rolled on the floor laughing while another one said, "They're virgins! HA-HA, they're little boys that get dressed up by mommy!"

A virgin is not an easy thing for a teenage guy to be. It seems like everywhere we turn, whether we're at the mall or watching

Reprinted from "Handling the Pressure," by Robin Chan, *New Youth Connection*, November 1996. Reprinted with permission from Youth Communications.

TV, something sex-related is going on. Sure we feel the pressure, sure we are curious to try it out, and sure we feel awkward talking about it when everyone around us says they're doing it.

Odd Men Out

We also know that we don't want to have sex yet. But people like those guys at the Y make it seem like being a virgin is a major crime or sin, that virgins are "losers" and not real men. Why can't they accept and respect the way we choose to be? If you're "doing it," good for you. You don't have to bring us into this when we're not ready.

I'm not the only teenage guy who's a virgin. I've interviewed some other guys who haven't had sex yet. Some feel ashamed that in this sex-crazed world, they're virgins. Others, like me, take pride, in the fact that we are who we are.

What's the Rush?

Most guys I interviewed had several reasons for abstaining from sex. Keith, 18, said, "My family wouldn't allow it." But he also said that he's just not ready for sex at his age. "When I'm 21, I'll know that I'm old enough for something like that," he told me. "My brother influenced my belief because he's a virgin and he's 24."

George, 16, of Bronx Science HS, feels the same way. "I'm too young to have sex," he said, adding that he believes in "sex after marriage."

> A virgin is not an easy thing for a guy to be.

Like George, Jim, 15, of Stuyvesant HS, believes in waiting until after marriage to have sex. "Besides," he said, "I feel safer not doing it." Jim feels that the risks and dangers of having sex, like AIDS, STD's, or getting a girl pregnant, are things he isn't ready to handle. "I choose to be a virgin because if anything bad happens, that's not good. I'm responsible."

Pressures and Temptations

But guys who want to wait often find that they don't get a lot of support. "We are pressured by friends and the stereotype that guys who have sex are macho and cool," said Nick, 15, of Bronx Science HS. Nick says he doesn't let this get to him but Keith admitted that it can be tough to stand up to all the pressures and temptations lurking out there.

> Don't give in to the pressure, don't have sex to impress someone and don't do it just to satisfy your curiosity.

"Sometimes I'm tormented by the fact that I'm a virgin," Keith said, "because when I see people around, and they say what they did, and I didn't do anything, I feel like the odd man out." Other guys will also "say stupid things like, 'Your d-ck will fall off [if you don't have sex],' but I don't listen to those stupid things," Keith said.

It's not only other guys who can pressure you; women do it too. Keith told me about a woman he worked with who used to come on to him. "She would say, 'Step into my office' and she would start complimenting me. One time she tried to touch me, but I said to her, 'I don't play like that.'" The woman apologized but Keith still thinks the experience "was a little like sexual harassment."

It was easy for Keith to say no in this case, but what if it was a girlfriend that was pressuring him? Keith says that "from the beginning" he would tell any girl he was really interested in that "I don't want to have sex, I just want to have a nice relationship."

All these guys agree that, as Nick put it, "sex isn't mandatory in a relationship." Jim said, "[Sex] is not that important because a relationship is about love and caring about each other and other stuff." Keith feels that a relationship is about "being with a companion, a person to say words of compassion to," not about sex.

I hope this article will enlighten the people who think virgins are losers. I also hope it will make anyone who is considering having sex because they're sick of being pressured think twice about doing something they might regret or that will change their whole life forever.

Worth Waiting For

I thought that only other virgins would agree with me but I was wrong. One guy I talked to who is 17 and sexually active said, "Virgins are not losers. They are probably better people because they know what they want and when they want it." As Jim said, "We choose not to have [sex] yet because we are worth waiting for, like the commercial said."

So, to the other virgins out there, I say: Don't give in to the pressure, don't have sex to impress someone and don't do it just to satisfy your curiosity. Do it when you're good and ready.

As for me, right now I am more concerned about family, friends, school, the SAT, and my future. There'll be a time for me to have sex but it won't be any time soon.

Societal Pressures on Women and Girls

Noelle Howey

Pressure to have sex comes in many forms and from many sources. Many women have sex even when they're not emotionally ready for the experience. Noelle Howey, a freelance writer who writes about teen problems and women's issues, discusses some of the pressures women face to have sex. Many women have sex, she writes, because they want to feel desirable, because they want to seem sexually uninhibited, or because they do not want to come across as a tease.

You would never describe Melissa,* 25, known for belting out raunchy drinking songs at office parties, as sexually timid. But she knew she didn't want to have sex on her first date with Ryan. "I wasn't up for it," she says. "I thought, 'Maybe we'll do it on the third or fourth date.'" So, at midnight, as she stood up to leave his apartment after chatting with him for a few hours, she was surprised when he blocked the door. "Don't go," he coaxed. "I don't want you to leave." Half an hour later, when

*Names have been changed to protect privacy.

she tried once more to go home, he grabbed her hand and asked her to stay. They had sex. Though she didn't object, Melissa was furious with him for being so insistent—and with herself for giving in.

Pressured and Manipulated

Chances are, Melissa's experience isn't that foreign to you. Almost all sexually active women have similar stories to tell—about times when they felt pressured, manipulated, intimidated or trapped into having intercourse, when they didn't say no but never said yes—but many of them maintain a self-defeating policy of silence about these episodes. Says Melissa, "I know it would have helped to confide in my friends, but I was so ashamed of myself for not doing anything more to stop him."

Anna, 28, shudders whenever she remembers her date with Doug five years ago. After they went out to dinner, they came back to his place and kissed for a while. She wasn't that attracted to him, but she enjoyed making out. He removed her shirt and bra. They kissed some more, then he excused himself. When he reentered the room, he was wearing nothing but an open terry-cloth bathrobe and was carrying a condom. "I was stunned," Anna says. "But since Doug acted like it was a given we'd have sex, I felt like I couldn't turn him down." Afterward, he smoked a cigarette. She spent a sleepless night lying next to him.

> Almost all sexually active women have . . . felt pressured, manipulated, intimidated or trapped into having intercourse, when they didn't say no but never said yes.

A few weeks later, she ran into him on the street. He asked in a flirtatious way, "Why haven't you called me?" She stammered something about being busy, and fled. She was livid, but she felt unjustified in being so angry, because, as she puts it, "It was my fault. If I hadn't fooled around with him, this wouldn't have happened. And it's not like he raped me or anything."

That's true. According to Carol Sanger, J.D., a professor at Columbia University Law School, rape is generally defined in most states as forcible sexual intercourse. But high-pressure sex—or sex obtained without regard for the woman's desire, through pressure, intimidation or intentional manipulation—seems to be much more common. According to the landmark 1995 Sex in America study conducted by researchers at the University of Chicago—astonishingly, the only recent major study to address this topic—more than one out of five women say they have been coerced into having sex. Feminist Naomi Wolf, author of *Promiscuities* (Fawcett Columbine, 1998), thinks the real numbers are higher: "It's absolutely universal. Every woman I've talked to about this has gone through it." Liz Grauerholz, Ph.D., associate professor of sociology at Purdue University and coeditor of the book *Sexual Coercion* (Lexington, 1991), agrees. "When I get together with groups of women, just about everybody has had this experience to different degrees," she says. "But women are hesitant to label it. Also, they don't want to seem like they're saying they've gone through something that's in any way the same as being a rape victim."

> [High-pressure sex] relies more heavily on manipulation and subtler forms of psychological warfare—pleading, presuming or wearing the other person down.

High-pressure sex shouldn't be confused with date rape, though the line between them is blurry. The difference lies in the use of force. Date rape often involves a degree of physical force, but it may also be marked by intense intimidation or some other overt form of psychological coercion, like social or emotional blackmail. Another crucial point: The woman expresses her lack of consent in an obvious way—either by trying to fend the man off, by saying, "No," "I don't want to" or "Please don't," or by expressing emotional distress or anger—and the date rapist overrides, ignores or pretends to misread her.

But, unlike date rape, which isn't consensual at all, high-pressure sex is ambiguous because it does involve some form of consent. It relies more heavily on manipulation and subtler forms of psychological warfare—pleading, presuming or wearing the other person down. While the date rapist actively inspires and exploits a woman's terror, the man in high-pressure sex plays on emotions like pity, guilt, insecurity, embarrassment or, in some cases, fear.

Why "No" Can Be Such a Difficult Word

Just saying "No" has never been as easy as it sounds. Many smart, independent women who can forcefully assert their opinion in a meeting or argue a point in a courtroom have found themselves relinquishing power in the bedroom. Why do we persist in going along?

• *We don't want to be a bad date.* Melissa, for instance, was interested in pursuing a relationship with Ryan: "I wasn't that attracted to him, but he seemed nice. I liked him." If a guy is insistent, we may think, "Oh, this is important to him, so I might as well." In a context of trust and equality, that might be okay. But without that trust—which can only be established over time—the woman who has sex before she's ready is likely to end up feeling used.

> The woman who has sex before she's ready is likely to end up feeling used.

"Women are taught to put men's needs above their own," points out Dr. Grauerholz. "By the time girls hit puberty, they can clearly see that men are more privileged, which reinforces the idea that men have a right to make these demands and to pressure them into having sex." Those lessons may come from home, where Mom has a job but still does all the housework, while Dad relaxes with the newspaper. Or they may come from school: Studies repeatedly show that teachers call on girls less frequently than on boys, and take their opinions less seriously.

Such everyday situations convey to girls that males possess more authority, so that by the time we're in the crucible of junior high and our self-esteem frequently plummets—we've already learned to muffle ourselves, to question our own judgment and to realize that to get along, it might be better to give in.

Female Bullies

Women aren't the only ones feeling pressured. Sixteen percent of men in a recent survey said they'd been blackmailed, guilt-tripped or otherwise psychologically coerced into intercourse, says Cindy Struckman-Johnson, Ph.D., professor of applied psychology at the University of South Dakota in Vermillion and coauthor of *Sexually Aggressive Women: Current Perspectives.* While male and female "bullies" have some similarities— they're highly aroused and driven by the prospect of dominating and controlling another person—there's a distinct difference in how victims from each gender cope. "Women who've been sexually intimidated tend to avoid sex and men in general," says Dr. Struckman-Johnson, while men who described themselves as "strongly affected" by a traumatic incident try to steer clear of particularly aggressive women but still retain the same openness toward women and relationships.

Noelle Howey, *Mademoiselle*, August 1998.

• *We don't want to come across as a "tease."* It's a common assumption that women only have a small window of time in which to speak up. "I'm already in his apartment," we might think. "Can I still say no? What about if I've kissed him? Let him touch my breasts? Or taken off my clothes?" Rationally, most women realize that they have the right to say no at any point up to—and even during—intercourse. But that doesn't always silence the nagging feeling that we can't say no after a certain point, because then, we fear, we'll be accused of leading him on.

When she was a teenager, Audrey would get to a point, somewhere between heavy petting and getting completely naked, when she felt she had to "follow through" whether she wanted to or not. "I took it for granted that you had to get guys off once it got to a certain point," Audrey, now 25, says, "So I ended up going down on a lot of guys or having sex with them because I thought I had to, that it was part of the bargain. My friends and I all assumed we had to."

> Rationally, most women realize that they have the right to say no at any point . . . but that doesn't always silence the nagging feeling that . . . we'll be accused of leading him on.

• *We want to seem sexually uninhibited and savvy.* Women are not only afraid of letting down their male partners; they're also afraid of disappointing themselves. Thanks to the sexual revolution, women feel they have the total and complete power to say . . . yes. But what if we don't want to, because we're not ready, we're not feeling well or simply aren't in the mood? Anna remembers wanting to say no, but she "didn't want to seem like this little girl."

"Some women think, 'Oh, I'm a hip, liberated chick. I can't say no,'" points out Wolf. "The ideal is this Ally McBeal-by-day, Debbie Does-Dallas-by-night figure who always manages to deliver a high-quality sexual experience. Most young women don't want to be seen as backward." Ironically enough, the price we pay for living up to that sexy modern image may be our voice.

• *On the other hand, we're afraid of coming across as too sexually savvy.* Much of this confusion would be alleviated if women simply asked for what they *did* want in bed. Kate, who reluctantly ended up having sex with a blind date, would have been "perfectly happy doing a little petting, you know? He could have touched my breasts, but I didn't want to have sex." But as Wolf says, "Women aren't allowed to be clear about what they want. You're not supposed to say something like 'You can go down on me, but let's not have intercourse,' because our culture says not to talk about these things. Our culture says if you use those words, you're a slut."

Kate agrees. "There's no way I could have told him what I was okay with. I would have felt like I was trying to talk dirty. I would rather have had sex I didn't want than say anything to him." According to Wolf, this phenomenon is incredibly common. "You're not supposed to talk about anything," she says. "Instead, you're supposed to get swept away, like when people get drunk and hook up. That's supposed to be sexy."

• *We need to feel that men find us desirable.* Anna says, "I have a friend, Kim, who's successful and beautiful and intelligent, but she doesn't see any of these good points." Some women focus on male attention as the main measure of their self-worth and see a man's sexual interest—even if he's slick or pushy—as validation. "Kim met a cute guy at a party the other night, and she ended up having sex with him," recounts Anna. "She hadn't wanted to sleep with him, but she gave in because, she told me, 'I felt lucky that he noticed me.'"

Men Aren't Always the Villains

What makes high-pressure sex even harder to deal with is that in some cases, no one is to blame. The guy—far from being an assailant—is baffled about what his female partner wants, and honestly believes she's interested in having sex.

This isn't unusual, even among experienced men. "Some guys don't know how to recognize female desire," says Wolf. "Many can't tell whether a woman is sending out signals she doesn't want to go further." And some women assume that men can interpret their body language, and are irritated when they don't.

But there are also men who don't try to understand what's going on. They're the ones who've bought into an idea that still permeates popular culture: Women secretly long to be sexually dominated. These men might not actually assault their dates, but they rely on the implied passive threat of physical violence to get their way.

From *Sex Respect*® by Colleen Kelly Mast, ©1997. Used with permission from Respect, Inc.

Suzanna, 24, had sex with Daniel on the third date—only because she wasn't sure he'd take no for an answer. After she had a drink with him at her apartment, he held her against the wall and kissed her. "Let's slow down," Suzanna whispered. "All he said was, 'Why? Don't you like me?' He had this smile on his face, a weird smile, like he didn't want to stop. All I could think was 'It's better if I just go along with him. I won't get hurt this way.'" Although she submitted to Daniel out of fear, Suzanna insists that he didn't rape her. "I could have told him to leave," she says. "I could have spoken up, at least. I definitely wasn't his victim. But he knew what he was doing; he knew he was freaking me out, and I think that excited him."

Dealing with the Aftermath

Coping with the consequences of high-pressure sex can be difficult. As Suzanna explains, "I felt pissed and angry and helpless. There was no way to get revenge."

Certainly not through the court system: These situations are *not* prosecutable. But, as Dr. Grauerholz asserts, "That doesn't mean it's moral and excusable." Unlike a rape victim, a woman who suffers after being manipulated into sex bears some responsibility for its occurrence. And that feeling of culpability keeps many women silent about what actually went on.

According to Andrea Parrot, Ph.D., associate professor of policy analysis at Cornell University and an acquaintance-rape expert, turning blame inward—common among victims of assault or rape—is endemic in high-pressure sex cases. "In so-called 'gray zone cases,'" says Dr. Parrot, "fewer people believe you have genuinely suffered as a result of the incident. You're less likely to tell others how you feel, including your friends. You're more likely to deal with it yourself, thinking it's all your fault because it's not a straightforward assault." This self-blame is harmful, says Dr. Grauerholz, because "pressured sex has negative emotional effects: lowered self-esteem, and the feeling that you're not in control of your sexuality. The idea that women are painting themselves as victims and need to quit whining can end up silencing them."

The social critic Camille Paglia has even suggested that coercive incidents should be considered a rite of passage, a consequence of being sexually active. Many women believe this, too, and dismiss high-pressure sex as "just bad dates." Audrey says, "It could be thought of as bad sex, as something everyone goes through." But these experiences are about being intimidated or manipulated into intercourse, and, frequently, they involve the implicit threat of assault to obtain consent. Such an abuse of male power should never be considered "normal" sex.

How to Get Your Own Way in Bed

Women need to realize they're entitled to say no, and they should practice saying it out loud. "Come up with five sentences that you can say to a date, like 'I don't want to do this' or 'I have to leave because I have to get up early for work,'" advises Madeline Breckinridge, A.C.S.W., clinical social worker and director of the Sexual Abuse Treatment and Training Institute in New York City. If you've had high-pressure sex in the past, you need to figure out why. "I wanted to impress Doug," notes Anna. "He was older and so much more experienced, and I was nervous about seeming unsophisticated." Revisit your "bad dates." Was it fear of rejection? Or disappointing yourself? Then, consider: Was caving in to that fear worth feeling crummy afterward? Realize that each time you "give in," you're chipping away at your belief in your right and power to speak up. "I kept beating myself up because I did nothing to stop him," says Anna. "It was only one incident, but it made me feel so weak and stupid."

Finally, we need to take these experiences seriously. Because as long as we keep quiet about high-pressure sex and its often painful consequences, it will go unrecognized. After all, before the term "date rape" was coined, few people believed it existed, and women were assigned responsibility for any "unpleasantness." "It would help if there were a word," says Dr. Grauerholz. "It would give us the language to help process our feelings." Call it "high pressure sex," and talk about your experiences with your friends and male partners. Audrey agrees: "The awful times I had shouldn't be accepted as a part of life."

My Boyfriend Wants Sex

Liz

A fourteen-year-old girl writes that her boyfriend says she should have sex with him to prove that she loves him. She's not ready for sex yet, she says, despite the fact that he tells her all their friends are doing it. But, she's afraid he'll break up with her unless she gives in. Liz, an online teen counselor, tells her that if her boyfriend really cared about her, he wouldn't ask her to have sex when she's not ready.

Chris, 14, has a boyfriend, Rick, who wants to have sex with her. She doesn't think she wants to, but she's afraid she'll lose him.

Chris's Story

Rick keeps pushing me. I don't know if he's telling the truth—that they're all doing it . . . I mean, it's not exactly the kind of thing I can ask my friends in school, is it? Not even Dara. We're close, but not that close.

I don't really want to, but he keeps saying if I love him, I should prove it. I'm happy with the way things are now. It feels good just to fool around and touch each other, and I like the kissing. Not so much when he tries to put his tongue in my mouth,

Reprinted with permission from "How Far Should I Go: A Monologue in One Act," by WholeFamily Inc., available at www.wholefamily.com.

that's kind of pushy. But I feel safe just having him hold me. I even let him put his hands under my blouse. Why do we have to do more than that, anyway? And what about all that AIDS stuff, and getting pregnant? I wouldn't want a kid at my age! Rick says, "Don't worry, I'll take care of everything." But he's missing the point.

> He keeps saying if I love him, I should prove it.

I'm afraid if I don't go along with him, he'll drop me and find someone else. I really don't want that, but I don't like feeling pressured either. Anyhow, who says my next boyfriend won't ask for the same thing?

I wonder if April and Andy really did it. Rick says that Andy told him they do it all the time—whenever her parents are out and she baby-sits for her baby sister he comes over. But I can't imagine them. Maybe I can just ask her if it hurt the first time. . . I'm afraid of that too. It's easy for the boy—he's not the one it's gonna hurt.

I'm Not Ready Yet

Every time we're alone somewhere, Rick keeps asking me if I'm ready, or am I still chicken. He even showed me the condom he keeps in his wallet for when I'll say yes. I want to keep checking to see if he still has it or if he gave up on me and tried it with someone else, but I can't ask that! He says he really loves me, but it makes me think that if he loved me, he wouldn't ask me to do it, knowing how I feel about it.

The problem is. . . . I'm not so sure how I really feel.

I saw him looking at Laura. Maybe he'll ask her out if I don't say yes. I wish I could decide if I really want to do this—I don't feel ready yet. Once we start, he'll probably want it all the time.

Why can't we leave things the way they are right now? I just feel it's going too fast for me. Rick says it's not healthy for a guy to get so hot and then stop—but what about me? I get turned on, too, but nothing happens to me when we stop. It just takes a while to cool down and then I'm okay. Could he be right about guys, though? I wouldn't want to hurt him in any way, but I don't want to do it just for that reason.

It's not fair that he says I don't really love him if I won't say yes. I do love him . . . I think so, anyway.

It's too bad Mom's gone. I know I could have talked this over with her. I guess I'll just have to work it out for myself. I wish there was someone I could talk to.

Why can't we just leave things the way they are till we're older?
Chris, 14

Liz Tells It Like It Is

To all the "Chris's" out there saying "I wish there was someone I could talk to," you need to know that sometimes there isn't. In the real world, you may sometimes feel as if you're alone, which is too bad, since this topic may be the most difficult one you'll ever have to deal with in your teen years.

Hopefully, there will be parents or friends or school counselors who can help you out, but part of becoming an adult is acknowledging that the buck stops with you. And this is certainly the case when the issue is your sexual life.

So here's Liz, to tell it like it is. Chris, all Rick wants is to feel good for a while. He could care less about your mind, your emotions and your soul. Maybe some day he'll grow up and he will care about those things, but from your description of him, he's still far, far away from that point.

> I'm afraid if I don't go along with him, he'll drop me and find someone else.

Because if he really cared about you as a person, he wouldn't just be trying to have sex with you. I know that's hard to hear. Everyone wants to feel wanted, for whatever reason. Maybe you haven't yet experienced the wonderful high you can feel when a guy wants to hang out with you because you're bright, or funny, or fun, and not just because he wants to have sex with you.

It would be great if you could find someone to talk to, but this is a topic that is difficult to discuss with anyone, even your closest girlfriends. And maybe the average teenage girl won't feel comfortable discussing this with a parent, relative or teacher.

But sometimes help comes from strange places, like a cool staff member at the school, an adult neighbor who you babysit for and—who knows—maybe you're one of those lucky kids who can talk to her parents. Hey, when I'm not doing this WholeFamily stuff, I'm a parent and teacher, and I'd sure like to believe that my kids or students could come to me.

> If he really cared about you as a person, he wouldn't just be trying to have sex with you.

As for friends—sometimes it's even hard for good friends to keep a secret. And you never know what's going on in the head of a friend. For instance, if you have a girlfriend who's doing it, but she's not so sure she's doing the right thing, it might make her feel better if she knows that you're doing it too.

But me, I'll keep your secret, because I don't know you from Eve anyway and I have no plans to contact your parents, so trust me—you're safe.

Which is maybe a poor choice of words—safe—since if there is one thing that teenage sex is not, it's "safe."

Teenage sex is not safe.

Teenage Sex Is Not Safe

And here are some of the reasons it's not safe:

1. Sex is a heavy responsibility, not just a feel-good sport. And the first responsibility you have is to yourself. For girls, more than for boys, it's something that involves your deepest feelings, your most intimate connection between your body and your soul, and it's not something that you should share lightly. I mean, who is this guy, anyway? Do you really feel like letting him deep into

your soul? Into your body? Just so you'll have someone to hang out with on Saturday nights?

2. You can get AIDS from sex (not to mention a lot of other diseases), and anyone who tells you that condoms are foolproof is a proven fool. Some doctors say condoms are only 80% foolproof (and if they are really 90% foolproof, or 95%—does that make you feel any better?).

3. You can get pregnant from sex. So there's good news and bad news:

4. If you didn't get pregnant, there's nothing to worry about (physically, maybe) and if you did, there's good news and bad news:

5. If your parents don't make you feel like a lowlife for the rest of your life for getting an abortion, then there's good news and bad news:

6. If the abortion goes okay, you'll be back on the market for the next cruising cat, but if it doesn't, then there's good news and bad news:

7. If you only get slightly messed up, you might still have a kid or two, but if not, then there's good news and bad news:

8. If you lose your ability to have children, you might not want children anyway, but if you do, then there's good news and bad news:

9. If there are still girls out there stupid enough to get pregnant, then you might consider adoption, but then there's good news and bad news:

10. If they're all having abortions like you, there'll be no babies left to adopt.

The Real Questions

The real questions that you may (or should) be asking yourself are:

How does this sex thing fit in with my values, my emotions,

my comfort or discomfort with myself sexually, my place (status?) among my friends—both girlfriends and male friends, my feelings about what my parents and other adults whom I respect would think about this, etc.

Each person is different so each person has different questions. Obviously, you have questions, or you wouldn't be reading this.

Chris, take it from me—if you want sex to be a special part of your life, save it to share with someone whom you want to make a special part of your life, too.

And I'm not talking about your high school life (unless you plan on settling down at the age of seventeen). Sure, you'll be missing out on a lot of superficial fun right now—maybe even on some stuff that isn't so superficial—but hang in there. If all we cared about was feeling good for the moment, we'd still be swinging from trees.

I know this doesn't sound cool and some of the guys will laugh at you, but when the right one comes along, he'll think that you're amazing.

But a question still remains: If you're not having sex with him and you feel that you don't really know why, and you feel a void in your life because of it, and you feel you should be filling that void with something, what are you going to fill it with?

That's a question that only you can answer.

Hang in there.

Keep in touch.

Fondly,

Liz

My Girlfriend Wants Sex

Lucie Walters

In this question-and-answer column, a teenage boy asks for help in resisting his girlfriend's pressure to have sex. Lucie Walters, whose syndicated advice column is published in newspapers in Louisiana, Alabama, and Florida, tells him that people who pressure their partners into having sex show no concern for their partners' feelings. Recent columns by Lucie Walters are available at www.lucie.com.

L ucie—I'm 15 and being pressured. I have an older girlfriend who wants to have sex. I want to, but don't know if I should.

I have to ask advice from a total stranger off the Net. Sad, huh? No offense. What should I do?

—Peace Out

Peace out—No offense taken. I am a stranger, but helping teens anonymously is my job. That probably fits for you right now because you seem to be looking for an objective opinion. If you read my bio online, you'll see that I have been doing this for many years.

Reprinted with permission from "Dear Lucie Says to Keep Your Morals and Ask Lots of Questions," *Adolessons* column from March 15, 2000, at www.lucie.com.

Who would you feel safe to ask? Your parents would be up-set, and probably try to end the relationship (which may be a safe way out for you). My guess is that most of your male friends would not be able to relate and may start teasing you. You realize that, so you found me.

A Life-Altering Decision

I don't know your girlfriend's age or where you live. Having sex with you could get her into legal trouble.

Unfortunately, many people consider your situation enviable. In fact, they wouldn't see a problem here. Some readers won't even believe your letter.

You seem like a moral guy struggling with deciding when and

The Effect of Peer Pressure on Teens

Peer pressure, "the most blamed" factor, . . . contributes to in-creased teen sexual activity. B. Herjanic states that young ado-lescents below the age of 15 were probably the most vulnerable to pressures to engage in sex, as well as to the consequences of pregnancy. In a survey of 625 teens . . . , 43 percent of boys aged 15–18, 65 percent of girls aged 15–16, and 48 percent of girls aged 17–18 answered affirmatively to the question, "Have there been times when you have been on a date, when you had sexual contact even though you really did not feel like it?" J. Billy and J. Udry's research showed that best male friends influence females' sexual activity, but they could not determine if the best friend was a sexual partner of the girls questioned. Despite the assumption that females become sexually active because they cannot say no to their boyfriends, research by G. Cvetkovich and B. Grote suggests that neither can some boys say no to their girlfriends.

La Wanda Ravoira and Andrew L. Cherry Jr., *Social Bonds and Teenage Pregnancy,* 1992.

---

with whom you should begin having sex. I don't know if the issue is simply whether or not to have sex with this girl. Could be the reason you're feeling so pressured is because this is a *life-altering decision,* and it encompasses a great deal more than this one situation.

You are right! Your life would never be the same again. Maybe you believe that sex means love and commitment, even marriage, and you don't want this relationship to become that involved. To many females, making love means making a commitment.

Being Pushed Feels Uncomfortable

Also, your girlfriend is pressuring you. Regardless of gender, being pushed feels uncomfortable. Can you trust her?

My suggestion is to decide (as objectively as you can) what is the appropriate time and situation for you to begin having sexual intercourse. Factor in your moral and religious beliefs. Include the dangers involved vs. the pleasures derived.

Decide in the cool of the day, not the heat of the night.

Until then, congratulate yourself on good boundaries and morals.

Chapter 4

Sex and
Consequences

The Emotional Side of Sex

Shauna

Having sex is an act of physical and emotional intimacy. Despite all the hopes and plans you may have for your first time, you may not be prepared for the emotions you'll experience afterwards. In the following essay, Shauna describes how her expectations of a beautiful and romantic experience were shattered by the totally unexpected emotions she felt afterward. With the help of her understanding boyfriend, Shauna was able to work through her feelings, but she warns that some teens may not be prepared for the emotional intensity of sex until they are more mature. Shauna is a teen writer for TeenWire.com, an online teen magazine published by the Planned Parenthood Federation of America.

I didn't lose my virginity—I know exactly where I left it.
It was three days past my 18th birthday with my boyfriend, Curtis, who was also a virgin. We were in love—in crazy, desperate, earthshaking love, and we wanted our first time to be special.

Everything was perfect: He was a wonderful, caring, decent man. I knew I didn't have to worry about him running back to his buddies to brag about his "score." We were in my own bed, we used protection, we were "old enough," and we were relaxed and happy.

I remember the romantic way I had envisioned it happening—it would feel wonderful and I was supposed to feel wonderful afterwards—mature and fulfilled.

"The Big Lie"

I now refer to that idea as "The Big Lie."

I'm not saying it can't be that way, I'm just saying that soap operas and romance novels don't exactly paint an accurate picture of losing your virginity.

> "Soap operas and romance novels don't exactly paint an accurate picture of losing your virginity."

Here's the truth:

It's awkward.

It's confusing.

It can hurt.

And for most women, having an orgasm is very unlikely.

Worse yet, I was completely unprepared for how emotionally lost I would feel afterward.

Unexpected Feelings

Instead of feeling like I'd crossed some sacred threshold into true womanhood, I felt like I'd just slammed the door on ever being a little girl again. I was 18—an adult by legal standards—and yet there was still a little girl inside of me who wasn't quite ready to let go of who she was. I felt as if I'd given away a part of me that I could never get back.

I think I assumed too much. I thought that since my partner loved me a great deal and we'd given the event so much forethought, I would be left with a rosy "afterglow" instead of the emptiness I felt.

Simply because I was 18—older and more emotionally mature than many are when they lose their virginity—I was strong enough and resilient enough to get through it. My partner and I already had a strong relationship, so I talked to him about the feelings I was having. We worked through them together and had a loving relationship for two more years before we finally went our separate ways.

I don't think it would have been any easier for me if I'd waited longer, but I'm grateful that I waited as long as I did—and that I chose the right boy. It helped me to deal with the unexpected feelings that came up.

Although I think we'd all like sex to be spontaneous, I've learned that it requires a great deal of thought and planning—for adults and teens alike. And that involves several things: choosing a partner, making sure you have and use protection against pregnancy and infection, keeping realistic expectations of the experience, and waiting until you know that you can handle the feelings that may come up afterward.

In the end, I have no regrets about how or with whom it happened. But I always feel so sad for the girl or boy who has a first sexual experience too early and may be unable to cope with feelings that might have been much easier to handle later on.

Loss of Self-Respect

Fetima Perkins

It's said that girls and women often use sex to get love, meaning that they'll have sex with someone with the hope that a one-night stand will turn into a long-term relationship. What many don't realize, however, is that those who constantly search for "love" in this manner frequently lose their sense of self-esteem and self-respect. Fetima Perkins describes how her search for love led to her promiscuous behavior with guys who were just using her for sex, and her realization that she doesn't have to have sex with every guy she meets. Fetima Perkins writes for *New Youth Connections*, a New York City magazine by and for teens.

My boyfriend had always known about my past, but one day toward the beginning of our relationship, he asked me how many guys I'd had sex with.

"A lot," I said. But he wanted a specific number.

I was shocked when I counted and realized the answer was 21. That even shocked him.

So then I asked him the same question, and when he answered, I was speechless for the first time in my life.

He said, "One."

I don't think I ever felt so bad in my life. Not even when

Reprinted from "Looking for Love," by Fetima Perkins, *New Youth Connections*, January/February 1998. Reprinted with permission from Youth Communications.

people called me names did I ever feel that bad. When I came out of shock, I burst into tears.

Looking for Mr. Right

He told me I shouldn't be upset—I really am a nice girl who didn't know what she wanted from a man, he said.

Actually, I did know what I wanted from a man—the problem was, I didn't know how to get it.

I wanted someone who would give me all the love and support I didn't feel like I got at home. What I got instead was just sex.

I guess I figured that if I could find a nice guy to treat me right, he would automatically take the place of my father, who left home when I was in the sixth grade.

I was very hurt when my father left because we had such a good relationship. We would go to Florida by ourselves for the weekend and leave my mother home.

> I wanted someone who would give me all the love and support I didn't feel like I got at home. What I got instead was just sex.

We'd go out to dinner and to the movies. And it meant a lot to me that (and this may sound silly) we even had special names for each other.

If we had such a good relationship, why was he leaving me? What had I done wrong?

I Started to Rebel

After my father left, I was upset and depressed, and I began to rebel against my mother.

I felt like I couldn't really depend on her for the love I needed because she's not very open. She says I can talk to her, but I don't think I can.

I didn't know any other way to vent my feelings, so I would keep all my anger inside and wait until she got me upset. Then I'd go off on her.

I always wanted to tell her my problems and tell her what I was doing with my life, but it seems like the older I got, the harder it was for me to tell her anything. I feel like my life is one big secret.

After my dad left, I also shrugged off all my girl friends. They couldn't do anything for me except tell me where all the cute guys were going to be at. They couldn't help me with my real problems.

Feeling Empty Inside

I felt like I had no one to talk to and I didn't feel close to anyone anymore. Eventually I started to feel empty inside.

I only knew one way to fill that empty space, and that was to depend on a guy emotionally the way that I used to depend on my father.

I was 12½ years old when my father left, and by my 13th birthday, I had lost my virginity. I wasn't proud of it, but how could I change it, it was already gone.

The first time I had sex, it was the biggest surprise in my life that it happened.

At the time, I was mad at my boyfriend and wanted to get back at him. My other boyfriend took me to a friend's house and we had sex in his brother's room.

"The Most Naive Virgin in the World"

I had no intention of doing that. I went to our friend's house as the most naive virgin in the world, honestly thinking that nothing would happen if we were alone.

Later I found out we weren't even alone: There was one guy watching from under the bed and another guy watching from the next room.

Once it was all over and the audience was gone, I didn't even know how to feel. But I didn't feel bad until I found out that the guy under the bed wanted to know if he was next.

When I got home, I went into my room and wrote in my diary. That's when it really hit me. I thought to myself, "Fetima, you just had sex with someone who doesn't even love you!"

I sat there and cried.

To make things worse, that boyfriend broke up with me two days later.

I didn't have sex again for a while. I figured I wouldn't want to do it again. But when the urge did arise, I didn't fight it. I made out with all these guys who came my way, and my name was scattered all over my neighborhood.

I Thought They'd Love Me

I never really felt that I had to go all the way with these guys, but that's the way it happened.

I had this l-don't-care attitude, but I did care even though I wouldn't admit I did. I would cry every night thinking about what I was doing and how I felt. Still, I couldn't seem to change.

I always wondered to myself, "What the hell is your problem? Don't you know you could catch something and die?"

I never had an answer for any of the questions that I asked myself. I felt like a lost soul walking through a graveyard, trying to find someone to take care of me, but never picking the right one.

10 Times out of 10, I Was Wrong

I would always go into the bedroom thinking this guy might actually like me. Then when we finished and everyone knew about it the next day, I would realize I was wrong again.

But again and again my feelings would get intertwined way too much. I'd get a big knot in my chest and think it was love.

Then I would get upset with the guys when they didn't return my feelings, even though I knew deep down inside that they hardly even knew me. And the truth is that I really didn't know them either.

Like I met this one guy who didn't act like a typical guy. After we had sex, he didn't say, "Get out of my house." He let me sleep over and he made me lunch.

After that, I wanted to tell him, "I love you."

It's not so much that I thought that sex would lead to love, but I guess that as a girl, I thought everyone felt close after they had sex. Ten times out of 10, I ended up being the only one who felt something at the end of the night.

I guess I just had to learn the hard way that some guys will tell you anything to keep you in their houses a little while longer.

Called a "H-" and a "Sl-t"

Most people who found out what I was doing labeled me a h- and a sl-t. They never tried to find out what was wrong, and just assumed I was doing this for the fun of it.

> I would always go into the bedroom thinking this guy might actually like me. Then when we finished . . . I would realize I was wrong again.

But I never enjoyed myself. I mean, I enjoy having sex whether I like the sex or not but mostly because I enjoy pleasing the person I'm with.

I don't know why I feel I have to satisfy other people all the time. I don't want to hurt anyone's feelings and I'm afraid they might think less of me if I don't do what they want me to do.

I tend not to tell people what I truly feel. Even when I can't or just don't want to do what they ask, I usually just say what the person wants to hear.

For example, I was going out with this guy who didn't bother acting slick like the other guys. He made it clear he just wanted me for sex.

Hard to Say "No"

One day I didn't feel like being bothered, but I also didn't feel like I could tell him I didn't want to have sex. So while he was in the bathroom, I just took my stuff and left.

The next day I saw him driving as I was walking home from work. He stopped the car in the middle of the street and yelled, "That was really f—ked up what you did, you stupid b-tch!"

Being with that guy made me look at my other relationships. I said to myself, "Fetima, you're so stupid!"

If I'd had two other hands, I would have beat myself up.

Trying to Change

I never knew just how bad I felt about myself until a good male friend of mine wrote me a letter telling me it was high time I take a look in the mirror and saw that I was not the person I was being.

When I read his letter, I started to cry. I had never really thought I was a h- or a sl-t, because I always wanted to be something and stay in school. I thought that made me different.

I mean, some girls get caught up in guys so much, they don't even go to school. I didn't go to school at times because being with this one guy seemed more important.

But after a while I stopped letting guys interfere with my education. At least they couldn't call me a *stupid* sl-t.

My friend's letter made me see that I was acting like a sl-t, even though I knew I was worth more than that.

A Serious, Not Sexual, Relationship

The person who really helped me calm down is my boyfriend. He and I have been together for almost three years now, even though we've argued, cheated on each other and even broken up.

He has helped me realize who I am and who I want to be. I didn't have sex with him for a whole year, kind of as a test to see if he'd wait—and he did.

He wanted a serious, not just a sexual, relationship. That made me feel more confident in myself.

Now I can proudly say that while I haven't made a 180 degree turnaround in my life, I have made a 90. I'm really proud of myself for that. Some people can't even make a 9.

I Wish I Never Had Sex

These days, I am still flirty and I still feel like having sex with some guys I meet (and sometimes I do). But I'm working on being monogamous.

When I tell guys, "No," I feel proud of myself. To myself, I'm like, "You go, girl!"

I always tell younger girls that I wish I had never had sex in the first place. I know that if someone had told me that, like most teenagers I probably would have gone and tried it anyway.

> I was acting like a sl-t, even though I knew I was worth more than that.

But I think it's important for girls to know that having sex with every guy, or even a select few, isn't cool.

In my opinion, there is nothing wrong with having responsible sex, but if you don't want to have sex, or you don't enjoy having sex, you shouldn't do it.

Show a Girl You Care

Plus, sex is risky. Of course, you can get pregnant. And it's the '90s—there are millions of people out there with AIDS and other diseases. We teenagers think that it's never going to happen to us. (It does!)

And if you're the type to call a girl names and make her feel bad—well, take it from someone who has been there, it hurts like hell.

In the same time that it takes to call someone a slut or a whore, you could take some time out to talk to her. Ask her why she chooses to do the things that she does.

She may be surprised at first by your asking, but I bet she will be happy that you cared enough to ask.

Being Used for Sex

Rebecca Lanning

Teens who are going through a difficult time, such as a move to a new school, may feel like they don't fit in and sometimes have less confidence in themselves. In an attempt to overcome these feelings of loneliness and become popular, they may sometimes make decisions they'll later regret. In this essay, a lonely teenage girl finds that attention from a cute boy in her new school makes her feel better about herself. Because she's lost her self-confidence, she's easily persuaded to have sex with him when he tells her things she wants to hear about herself. When she discovers he was just using her for sex, she realizes that self-esteem must come from within, not from others. Rebecca Lanning is a writer for 'Teen magazine.

If you didn't know her, you might think 16-year-old Brittany* had it all together. She's really cute, in a Meg Ryan kind of way, with swingy blond hair and a smile that can light up a room. You'd think she'd never had one moment of self-doubt. But she keeps a secret tucked inside of her, a secret of shame, sadness and loss. Here is her story.

*Names and identifying details have been changed.

Excepted from "He Only Wanted Me for Sex," by Rebecca Lanning, 'Teen, August 1995. Reprinted with permission from 'Teen magazine.

Brittany's Story

This is really hard for me to talk about. Whenever I think back on all that's happened, I feel these waves of grief. Like someone died or something. And I want to go back and try to fix it, change the whole story so that it has a different ending. But I can't do that. I used to pray that I'd wake up and be my old self again. But then I'd run into him somewhere. Or someone would mention his name. Or I'd just see a car like his, and I'd fall apart.

> I wish I could just take a giant eraser, and erase the whole thing from my life.

Sometimes, my eyes would tear up and I could squeeze them shut and swallow hard and kind of swallow the pain and be OK. But other times, I couldn't shut it off that easily. Like one day at school. I was sitting there in biology, and I saw him pass by in the hall. I saw him for, what, a millisecond? And I lost it. I had to be excused. I went to the girls' bathroom and closed myself up in a stall and leaned against the door and just cried. Total sobbing. Those giant, heaving sobs, like when you can't even catch your breath. I felt so stupid, but I couldn't get a grip. And then my face was all red and splotchy, and I looked like I'd been beaten up or something. And I guess I had been, in a way, beaten up from the inside. It's hard to make the hurt go away.

It's not like I even want to be with him again. I mean, I did for a while, but now I just want to put it all behind me. I want it all to be like ancient history. Or not even history. I want it to be like it never happened at all. I wish I could just take a giant eraser, and erase the whole thing from my life.

Trying to Connect

I think things started to unravel when my family moved. We built this house that was like a mile from our old house, and we moved at the end of my freshman year. When I was a freshman, I was really popular. I was on student council, and I was a junior varsity cheerleader and I had a great boyfriend named Hayes. He was really good to me. Even though he wanted us to have sex, he never pressured me. And at that time, having sex was the last thing on my mind. I never even considered it.

Then, during that summer, before my sophomore year, the school district changed, and that fall, I had to go to a different high school where I knew only about two people. Even though I tried to make friends and get involved in stuff at my new school, it just didn't come that easily for me. It was like everybody was already in their set groups. I couldn't find a niche, you know, where I felt accepted. I ate lunch by myself a lot. I was really lonely. I went to some club meetings, but nobody would really talk to me that much. I felt like I was invisible. I'd try to get together with some friends from my old school, but it's like I didn't really fit in with them anymore. I guess I didn't want them to know what a hard time I was having at my new school, so I didn't really reach out to them. Then Hayes and I started having problems because we didn't see each other as much. And when we were together, I was always so bummed out that he didn't know how to handle it. We broke up the last week in September. Over the next couple of weeks, I sort of gave up on myself. Then in October, I met Tad.

I had never felt that kind of attraction before in my life! He had wavy, brown hair and brown, sort-of-flirty eyes and these shoulders that went on for miles. He played soccer, so he was really in shape. I could just look at him and melt. He had Spanish right before I did, and I always passed him coming out of the room where the class was. At first, we just smiled at each other. And then one day he said, "hi," and pretty soon we were meeting between classes and talking. Every morning when I woke up, I thought about when I would see Tad and that gave me en-

> He tried to get me to go further, but I wouldn't. He said I wasn't any fun. I wanted him to think I was fun so that he'd want to be with me.

ergy, you know, to get up and get going. All morning, I'd think about stuff I could say to him. And then after we'd talked, I'd feel pumped up and that would help me get through the day.

One day when we were talking, he invited me to eat lunch with him. I thought it was just going to be us, but he showed up with two of his friends, Ward and Peter. They were juniors like him; they were on the soccer team too, and we walked over to this deli. They were pretty wild, kind of loud and acting crazy. I remember, Tad pulled me on his lap. I was kind of nervous, but at the same time I was really happy. It felt so good to be close to him and to be eating lunch with him. I soaked up the attention. I ended up paying for everybody's lunch.

After that, I ate lunch with Tad, Ward and Peter every day. I wouldn't say much. But I'd smile a lot and laugh at their jokes. Sometimes, they'd ask me personal stuff. Looking back, I realize that these guys were jerks. But at the time, I thought I was privileged to hang out with them.

Crossing the Line

One night, I went out with Tad and Peter and Ward. We drove around and went to a couple of parties. Later, after they dropped me off, Tad threw rocks at my bedroom window, and then he climbed up the rain gutter, onto the roof and into my room. My parents weren't there; they were at the symphony, but I didn't tell Tad that. We talked quietly, and then he turned off the light and stood close to me. I let him kiss me and unbutton the top of my nightgown. He tried to get me to go further, but I wouldn't. He said I wasn't any fun. I wanted him to think I was fun so that he'd want to be with me.

> I think I felt that having sex . . . was going to make everything better.

The next weekend, I went out with Tad and his friends again. This time, they got some beer and we went out to this field near the airport.

The next thing I knew, Tad had grabbed a sleeping bag and he was leading me by the hand away from the Jeep and into the woods. He was being sort of funny about it, sort of dancing with me. He had a couple of beers with him, and he was trying to get me to drink one, but I wouldn't. Then he spread the sleeping bag out, and he pulled me down next to him. He started telling me how beautiful I was, how much he liked me. The next thing I knew, he was on top of me. He was saying all these wonderful things to me, like how right it was for us to be together. He was being really gentle, really sweet. It felt so good to be close to him, but at that point I still wasn't going to give in. But then he said I was beautiful. And that made me feel so happy. I started feeling my old confidence coming back, and it's so ironic because that's when I started giving in. I think I felt that having sex with Tad was going to make everything better. I'd just been doubting myself so much, and here was this guy who didn't have any doubts about me. I think I wanted to be accepted so bad, I wanted to feel like I belonged somewhere again, and so we had sex.

> I think maybe he liked the challenge of trying to get me to have sex more than he liked actually having sex.

Holding On

The next few days were kind of weird. Those bad feelings about myself hadn't gone away. If anything, I felt worse. I couldn't make sense of it all. Tad was still nice to me, but it's like something had shifted between us. He didn't look at me the same way. Maybe it was my imagination, but it seemed like he didn't look at me at all.

My interest in him grew. Even though I was beginning to make some friends at school, I started feeling really dependent on Tad. He hadn't promised me anything. I'd just assumed that we'd be together because we'd had sex. But, obviously, he didn't feel the same way. I couldn't believe that Tad could've said all those things to me and then tossed me aside. Was it just a big act so he could get me to have sex with him?

I think maybe he was surprised that I had given in to him, even though that's what he wanted. I think maybe he liked the challenge of trying to get me to have sex more than he liked actually having sex. And I guess I wasn't much of a challenge anyway, so he sort of lost interest.

> Being self-assured, feeling good about who I am, has to come from the inside.

I became really clingy, calling him up all the time and crying if he couldn't meet me somewhere or see me. I constantly tried to figure out where he was.

We ended up having sex again, twice. Both times I was the one who initiated it. One time was at Peter's house after school. The other time was at my house, in my room. I really regret that time especially because whenever I look at my bed that's what I think about. That will never go away.

I thought having sex would make things better, but it didn't. After I lost my virginity, I guess I felt like I didn't have anything else to offer.

Looking Back

My friend finally talked me into seeing a school counselor. That's when I knew things were out of control. The counselor helped me put together the pieces of what had happened. She helped me deal with all the stuff that I was feeling.

It's been over a year now, and things are better. I can actually have a conversation with Tad and not break down. I don't even blame him so much for what happened anymore. I just feel sad. He smooth-talked me into doing something I wasn't ready for. I was at a very vulnerable place, and I was looking to him to make it all better. He took something from me that I'll never be able to get back. But I also learned something. That being self-assured, feeling good about who I am, has to come from the inside. Nobody can make me feel secure but me.

I'm on the gymnastics team now, and I was elected to the homecoming court and the National Honor Society. That meant a lot to me, but I'm still not completely over what happened. I have a hard time dating guys because I think that they know I'm not a virgin and that's why they're interested in me. There's this little voice inside of me that keeps trying to convince me that I'm OK. That I'm still a good person. But when I look in the mirror, it's not always her voice I hear. Sometimes it's a nagging, critical voice.

I wish I could go back in time and change what happened. I'd go back to the first day at my new school. I'd try harder to make friends and not expect to fit in overnight. I'd reach out more. I'd be more honest about how hard all the changes were for me instead of pretending that everything was OK.

I'd like to go back to that night in the woods with the planes going overhead. I wouldn't have gone anywhere near that sleeping bag. What I'd really like to do is to go back to that first night I let Tad come in my room. I wouldn't have let things go so far.

A Ruined Relationship

Mari Kinney

There are many different reasons why teens decide to have sex. Mari Kinney writes about a friend of hers who had sex with her boyfriend in an attempt to save her relationship. She found out sex doesn't always act as glue; her boyfriend soon dropped her anyway for someone else. Kinney was sixteen years old in 1996 when this essay was written.

Everyone who is anyone seems to be having sex. I'm not saying that every single person is having sex, but having sex is just as common as smoking weed. Pretty much everyone has tried it at least once.

It's too scary out there for me. Even safe sex doesn't seem that safe. But I think the thing that scares me most about sex is how much it hurts when your relationship doesn't work out. This happened to my friend and it broke my heart– hers too, I guess.

When Lovers Break Up

When I was 12, I hooked up two friends of mine. I knew they would be a great couple. They were both sweet and thoughtful and had great personalities. At school everyone envied them. They were always holding hands, totally lovey-dovey. He got her rings and bracelets for her birthday. One time at school he

Reprinted from "Teen Sex: Too Scary Out There for Me," by Mari Kinney, *LA Youth,* December 7, 1996. Reprinted with permission from *LA Youth.*

hired some guys to come and sing her favorite song, "Always and Forever," then later took her and her family out to the Red Lobster. She once got him an autographed Cowboys jersey, his favorite team.

He'd carry her books for her, and one Christmas, gave her all his hard-earned Christmas money so she could visit her family in Guatemala for the holidays.

> The more she wouldn't put out, the more aggravated and distant he got.

But two years later, things took a turn for the worse. The spark was fading. They didn't go out much. The couple that everyone had once envied seemed just like any other couple. He wanted to do more than just make out. To be honest, so did she, but her family was Catholic. Her mom always said, "Your virginity is everything. Don't ever give it away. Only to the man that you marry and love."

The more she wouldn't put out, the more aggravated and distant he got. It was, "Sorry, I forgot about the date." "I forgot about your birthday." "I forgot to call you back—I was busy." They were breaking up and getting back together every other day.

Fighting to Save a Relationship

One day she told me she had the solution—to have sex. She said, "This will make everything better." I said, "No, this is what he wants." I tried to convince both of them it was just going to make everything worse. But they were like, tonight's the night. They shut me out. She was fighting to save a relationship that wasn't meant to be.

The next day they were all happy, holding hands again. Then two weeks later, she came to me. "What am I going to do? My period hasn't come."

She called me the next day. She was pregnant. She had to tell her boyfriend and her parents.

She invited me over to be there when she told him. His response was: "Are you sure it's mine?" She gave away her treasure to this guy, and he was basically saying she was a tramp.

The next day, he wanted to know why she didn't get an abortion. She told him she could never do that because it was against the teachings of the Catholic church. Meanwhile, her parents were upset. They wanted to know how she was going to take care of a baby.

She was a smart, college-bound girl with good grades. So they looked into adoption. I think this was the right decision, because she couldn't excel in school and take care of a baby.

The months went by. Everybody at school could tell she was pregnant. But her relationship with her boyfriend got worse. He wouldn't take her calls, he wasn't there. When my friend was six months pregnant, he wanted to see other people. She reminded him that it was his kid, too. He said, I'm too young to be taking care of a kid. So she was on her own.

In her seventh month she stayed home because of complications. She had her baby in her eighth month and gave it away for adoption. I haven't seen her since then because her parents sent her away to Guatemala so she could learn some values.

Sex Messed Everything Up

So in the end, they split up and I lost both their friendships. Sex messed everything up. I think teens should think about the love and friendship they are putting at risk when they have sex, not to mention the risk of pregnancy and AIDS. These days, the only person you can trust is yourself. That's why I have better things to do than go out there and lose my virginity.

> We all feel lonely and want to feel loved, but sex won't fix that.

I think we all feel lonely and want to feel loved, but sex won't fix that. It's just a temporary physical act. I don't know exactly how you find love, but I know you can't fix things instantly by having sex.

Pregnancy

Marshall Brain

The following article by Marshall Brain, author of *The Teenager's Guide to the Real World*, gives sexually active girls the facts about their chances of becoming pregnant. No contraception, except abstinence, is 100 percent effective against pregnancy, so pregnancy can result even if a couple uses protection. The purpose of sex is to create a baby, writes Brain, so a couple should not have sex unless they are prepared to make the commitment—both financial and personal—to raise a child for the rest of their lives.

Should you pursue or have sex as a teenager? This is an option, and you get to make the decision. Like any other decision, however, there are things you should keep in mind. Here are three of the more important:

- Fact #1: If two people have unprotected sex long enough, they will get pregnant.
- Fact #2: This comes from the October 1996 issue of *Scientific American* magazine: "Six out of 10 women having abortions used protection." What that says is two people who have protected sex have a pretty good chance of pregnancy as well.
- Fact #3: If two people have sex and one of them is carrying a sexually transmitted disease, then the other person has

Reprinted from "Teenage Sex Is an Option," by Marshall Brain, *The Teenager's Guide to the Real World*. Reprinted with permission from BYG Publishing.

some probability of getting the disease, even when the couple uses protection.

Think of these three facts as "disadvantages." They tend to be good reasons not to have sex as a teenager. None of them have ever stopped anyone from having sex, however. You can look at the rate of infection for STDs, the number of abortions performed every year and the number of unwed teenage mothers to see that.

> If two people have unprotected sex long enough, they will get pregnant.

To any adult the three disadvantages make it "obvious" that teenagers should not have sex. What adults generally forget is that for many teens the brain and body are sending signals that indicate otherwise. The question for you as a teenager is, "Should logic win this one?" Your body has a desire to reproduce. To your body sex is important. Can you discipline yourself enough to live with the urges and wait until you get married? That is the question.

The Purpose of Sex Is to Make a Baby

Here are two things to keep in mind as you are making that decision:

- By having sex, you are making a hidden commitment to the child that results. The purpose of sex is to create a baby. Therefore, by having sex you are saying, "I am willing to care for the baby."
- Babies carry with them a lot of baggage. They need constant attention, they cost a lot and they require two people. Therefore, once you and your friend create a baby you will need to get married, and then the two of you will need to care for the child for the next 20 years. That means you will give up a tremendous amount of personal and financial freedom. Spend some time with someone who has a baby and see how much work is involved before you underestimate the amount of care a baby requires.

If you decide to have pre-marital sex, do it with the understanding that once a child is conceived, you are responsible for the care and well-being of your mate and the child for the next 20 years. The hospital bill alone for a normal childbirth is $5,000 to $10,000. Do you have that money? If not, then why would you have sex? Never mind the cost of housing, feeding, clothing your spouse and the child.

Facts About Teen Pregnancy

How widespread is teen pregnancy in the U.S.?

More than 4 out of 10 young women become pregnant at least once before they reach the age of 20. Nearly one million teen girls become pregnant every year, (that's 12% of all teen girls who have had sexual intercourse.)

Don't a lot of teens want to get pregnant?

No. The overwhelming majority—78 percent—of pregnancies to 15–19 year old teen girls are not planned. Among younger teens, 15–17 year olds, 83 percent of pregnancies are unplanned. In addition, most . . . sexually active teens today use contraception.

What's the future for teen parents and their babies?

• Only 1/3 of teenage mothers receive a high school diploma.

• Nearly 80 percent of unmarried teen mothers end up on welfare.

• The children of teenage mothers have lower birth weights, are more likely to perform poorly in school, and are at greater risk of abuse and neglect.

• The sons of teen mothers are 13% more likely to end up in prison. The daughters of teen mothers are 22% more likely to become teen mothers themselves.

National Campaign to Prevent Teen Pregnancy, *Facts and Figures*, no date.

The correct path is to find someone you are madly in love with and want to spend the rest of your life with, then decide that the two of you want to have a child, then get married, then save up enough money to provide a stable environment for a baby and then conceive a baby. Have a baby within a strong marriage that is ready to support the child: It is best for the baby and best for the parents.

> Once a child is conceived, you are responsible for the care and well-being of your mate and the child for the next 20 years.

As an unmarried teenager there is one other fact that you should keep in mind. You generally don't hear much about this fact, but it is important. You are doing your thing right now. You are meeting people, going out, having fun. That is all fine. You have this vague notion in your head that one day you will get married. That is also fine. But eventually you will find someone who you want to marry, and it will become much less vague. You are going to be deeply in love with this person. You are going to be with this person for the rest of your life. That is a fact.

On the night of your wedding you are going to be with that person in bed. There are two options on that first night you are together. Either it will be the first time for you, and therefore it is going to be special. Or it will not. If both of you are able to come to bed and learn about sex with each other and share that throughout your lives, it is a good thing. It is an incredible gift to give to someone. Maybe your partner cannot give it to you. That is OK. You can still give it to him or her.

A Long-Term Commitment

In general, teenage sex is like drugs. It seems like it should feel good when you do it, but longer term it often feels bad. It is a "cheap thrill" that has little or no value. It also tries to separate sex from babies, which is impossible. Keep in mind that the purpose of sex is to create a baby, and that a baby is an incredible long-term commitment. You should not be attempting to create a baby unless you are willing to make that commitment. If you want to make that commitment, you should be getting married first for the sake of the baby. That is a fact of life.

Abortion

Liz

For women, discovering that you're pregnant when you don't want to be gives new meaning to the word "panic." Liz, an advice columnist for an online teen advice website, *www.wholefamily.com*, writes about her decision to have an abortion when she was a teenager. Although her abortion went smoothly, her relationship with her boyfriend was never the same, and the experience was one she'll never forget.

Y ou're late. At first you figure it's just nerves. After all, you took precautions. I mean, you were always careful, except maybe that one time.

So you buy one of those home pregnancy tests. You sneak it into the house and spend one crazy, long night reading the instructions over and over again. The next morning, your entire being becomes fixated upon that unmistakable, red POSITIVE circle sitting at the bottom of a plastic tube.

Panic

For the first time in your life, you understand the full meaning of the word "panic." Your heart drops into a deep, dark place you had no idea existed in your body, but you know it's not moving until you get yourself out of this mess.

The crazy thing is that while your world is falling apart, some

Reprinted with permission from "Liz on Teen Pregnancy," by WholeFamily Inc., available at www.wholefamily.com.

neighbor down the street took that same test and also got a positive. Only she's running down the hall to tell her husband the good news. But life's sort of funny that way.

Okay girls, Liz knows how you're feeling—believe me, 'cause I've been there. Now, we're not going to talk about Pro Life vs. Pro Choice—this is not about that. This is about taking control of a difficult situation by surrounding yourself with the people who love and care about you the most and getting some good, solid guidance.

> For the first time in your life, you understand the full meaning of the word "panic."

Your first step may be to contact a school counselor or empathetic teacher. You'll probably need someone to help you approach your parents. Now you're thinking, "Liz, there's no way I can tell my parents." As rough as this may seem, believe me, it can be done. . . .

Liz's Story

But now I'd like to share something with you. Liz has her own story to tell. Several years ago I was staring at my positive result at the bottom of a cup. If only I had known then what I know now, but Liz was just too full of herself to ask for assistance from the right people. I decided to do things my way.

Back then, I figured that "Pro Life" meant no life left for me and whoever coined the phrase "Pro Choice" had a sick sense of humor. I mean wasn't it my need to be free and make my own choices that got me into this mess? Believe me, there was nothing free about being a pregnant teen. And feeling that there was no way out other than abortion wasn't much of a choice.

I couldn't bear the secret alone, so I told my best friend and of course, I also told him, after all, he was the father. But I guess this news was just too hot for them to handle, 'cause by the time I got to school, all eyes were upon me (or maybe it was just my imagination).

My trusted "friend" volunteered to contact the local abortion clinics. Meanwhile the other "responsible" party figured he could raise at least most of the cash. After all, he was the father.

As the days went by, the panic and fear only became worse. I couldn't sleep. I looked like hell and my body sort of floated through space, like I was no longer grounded and I didn't know where I was headed. And I kept saying over and over to myself, "What have I done? What have I done?"

Then my day at the clinic arrived. He came with me and so did my "friend," who had by now told the whole continent.

Facts About Abortion

- Nearly 4 in 10 teen pregnancies (excluding those ending in miscarriages) are terminated by abortion. There were about 274,000 abortions among teens in 1996.

- Since 1980, abortion rates among sexually experienced teens have declined steadily, because fewer teens are becoming pregnant, and in recent years, fewer pregnant teens have chosen to have an abortion.

- The reasons most often given by teens for choosing to have an abortion are being concerned about how having a baby would change their lives, feeling that they are not mature enough to have a child and having financial problems.

- 29 states currently have mandatory parental involvement laws in effect for a minor seeking an abortion: AL, AR, DE, GA, ID, IN, IO, KS, KY, LA, MD, MA, MI, MN, MS, MO, NE, NC, ND, OH, PA, RI, SC, SD, UT, VA, WV, WI and WY.

- 61% of minors who have abortions do so with at least one parent's knowledge; 45% of parents are told by their daughter. The great majority of parents support their daughter's decision to have an abortion.

Alan Guttmacher Institute, *Facts in Brief: Teen Sex and Pregnancy,* 1999.

The counselors were nice enough. They calmly informed me of the procedure and risks. They answered questions and for one selfless minute I thought to ask, "will the baby—er . . . fetus, embryo or whatever—feel pain?" But that fleeting thought was overtaken by fears for myself and instead I asked, "Will this hurt a lot?"

Things Were Never the Same Again

A few hours later, I lay at home no longer pregnant and the relief that I thought I'd feel took the form of reflective depression mixed with anxiety, 'cause I had to keep hiding all bathroom evidence from my mother.

Aside from a phone call, I didn't hear from him much. But that's okay, 'cause I didn't want to repeat this episode again. But believe it or not, two weeks down the road when I was feeling lonely, hurt and vulnerable, he showed up at the door. You see, he had that urge and I was fair game once again. But things were never the same between us.

Hey, don't get me wrong, it's not like I didn't survive all of this. It's just that, well . . . take it from me, Liz—there are some things in life that you never forget.

Sexually Transmitted Diseases

Angie Maximo

Contracting a sexually transmitted disease is a real risk for teens, as they make up nearly 25 percent of all new cases of STDs. Angie Maximo discusses some of the most common sexually transmitted diseases—how they are contracted, what their symptoms are, and how (and if) they can be cured. Abstinence or condoms are the best defense against most STDs. Maximo is a writer for *Seventeen*.

N eed a good reason not to lose your virginity? How about six? Here's the deal on the most common sexually transmitted diseases (STDs).

Gonorrhea (aka the clap)

What is it? A supercontagious disease. Left untreated, it can cause pelvic inflammatory disease, stomach pain, bleeding between periods and infertility (translation: You can't have kids—ever). Women are less likely to notice symptoms than men.

How do you get it? Sexual intercourse or oral sex.

How do you know you have it? You have a greenish-yellow discharge and pelvic pain; you feel like you have to pee all the time, and it burns when you do. It usually takes about 10 days

Reprinted from "Sex Files: The Deal on STDs," by Angie Maximo, *Seventeen,* March 1997. Reprinted with permission from Primedia Publications.

for these symptoms to show up, but 80 percent of women who have it don't even get symptoms (that's why it's *so* important to visit a gynecologist if you're sexually active).

How do you get rid of it? Antibiotics. Many people with gonorrhea also have chlamydia and must be treated for both.

Your best defense? Condoms or abstinence.

Herpes (simplex virus 1 and 2)

What is it? A virus that causes painful blisters and sores on the genitals, mouth or other areas of the body.

How do you get it? Although the cold sores and blisters you get on your mouth are usually caused by herpes simplex 1, both kinds of herpes can be sexually transmitted. That means you can get it through touching, kissing, oral sex or intercourse.

> [Gonorrhea is] a supercontagious disease. Left untreated, it can cause pelvic inflammatory disease, stomach pain, bleeding between periods, and infertility.

How do you know you have it? Most people get blisters and open sores (ouch!) within two to 20 days after infection. But—warning—it can take *years* before you have that first breakout (um, surprise!). Other symptoms include itching and burning, fever and feeling run-down.

How do you get rid of it? Sorry—you can't. A drug called acyclovir can clear up the yucky sores and blisters, but the actual virus stays in your body forever. That means you can get breakouts again, and again, and again. . . .

Your best defense? Condoms or abstinence.

HPV (Human Papilloma Virus)

What is it? There are 60 different HPVs—some of which cause genital warts. HPV is often linked to cervical cancer.

How do you get it? Sexual intercourse or oral sex. Here's the tricky part: You can get HPV *even if* you use condoms. Because they don't cover all areas that might be infected.

How do you know you have it? Warts will usually pop up about two to three weeks after infection. They look like, well, warts. Some even resemble little cauliflowers. But this is another sneaky STD—-you can have it and experience no symptoms. Or you can have the virus and not have a breakout until years later. The virus can also show up on a Pap smear, which you can have done by your gynecologist.

STD Stat

There are 12 million new cases of STDs every year, three million of them among teens.

One in four sexually active teens gets an STD by age 21.

The earlier you start having sex, the greater your chance of getting an STD.

Anyone can get an STD, whether the person has had one or 100 partners and showers twice a day or twice a week. No one has an I HAVE AN STD stamped on the forehead, so don't assume anything.

Teenagers are at greater risk of getting STDs because their immune systems are still developing.

Using condoms (rubbers, raincoats, love gloves—whatever) during sex can help protect you from STDs. But your best defense? Don't have sex—or wait until you've found a partner (someone you love would be ideal) who will get tested and be honest with you about his sexual history.

Angie Maximo, *Seventeen*, March 1997.

How do you get rid of it? The actual warts can be removed with special medicine (and we don't mean Compound W; this medicine must be prescribed by your gynecologist), laser surgery (zapping them with a laser beam) or cryosurgery (freezing them with liquid nitrogen). But, like herpes, this virus stays in your body forever.

Your best defense? Condoms (but again, condoms don't cover all areas that might be infected) or abstinence.

HIV (Human Immunodeficiency Virus)

What is it? This infection weakens the body's ability to fight disease and can cause AIDS (Acquired Immune Deficiency Syndrome). In the U.S., it's *the* leading cause of death for American women and men between the ages of 25 to 44.

How do you get it? The virus is in blood, semen, vaginal fluids and breast milk. That means you can get it through intercourse, oral sex, sharing contaminated needles or blood transfusions. Infected women can pass it to their babies while pregnant and in childbirth. You *can't,* however, get it from kissing, touching or from toilet seats. Keep in mind that HIV can live in the body for years before it causes symptoms, so you *can't* tell whether your partner is infected just by looking at him.

> HIV can live in the body for years before it causes symptoms, so you *can't* tell whether your partner is infected just by looking at him.

How do you know you have it? AIDS can cause rapid weight loss, diarrhea, flulike symptoms, thrush (a thick white coating on the tongue), major yeast infections and purple growths on the skin called lesions. Again, you could be infected with HIV and not show any symptoms for years.

How do you get rid of it? New treatments are giving AIDS patients hope, but so far there's no cure.

Your best defense? Condoms or abstinence.

Pubic Lice (aka crabs)

What is it? Critters that latch on to pubic and underarm hair, eyelashes and eyebrows. These little guys really do look like mini crabs (they're pale gray but get darker when they're swollen with blood).

How do you get it? Mostly through sexual contact (including petting), but you can also pick them up from infected sheets and clothes.

How do you know you have it? You'll know. Symptoms include intense itching (and we're not talking mosquito-bite itchy) of the genitals, a mild fever, irritability and fatigue, not to mention the freak-out factor of *seeing* the tiny critters on your body.

How do you get rid of it? Over-the-counter medicines like A-200 and Rid (the same stuff used to treat head lice).

Your best defense? You can't really protect yourself from crabs, so your best defense is abstinence.

Chlamydia

What is it? A bacterial infection that happens to be the most common STD—about four million cases a year in the U.S.! In women it can cause bladder infections, pelvic inflammatory disease and possibly even infertility.

How do you get it? Sexual intercourse.

How do you know you have it? This one's tricky. Most women have zero symptoms. But if it hurts to have sex (not just the first time but every time), if you have a weird discharge (read: anything that seems different from your usual discharge) or if it burns when you pee, you might have a case. As for your partner? Possible symptoms for him include penile discharge, burning and/or frequent urination and pain or swelling in his testicles.

How do you get rid of it? Take antibiotics prescribed by your doc.

Your best defense? Condoms or abstinence.

HIV and AIDS

Michelle Towner, as told to Stephanie Booth

AIDS is a sexually transmitted disease caused by the human immunodeficiency virus. The virus weakens your immune system to the point that it can no longer fight off infections, cancer, and other diseases. People can be infected with HIV and not even know it since it can take a decade or more before they start to show symptoms of the disease. In the following story, a teenage girl discovers that her longtime boyfriend unknowingly infected her with HIV. She's afraid to let her friends know her secret. Stephanie Booth is a freelance writer who writes about teen issues. Michelle Towner is the pseudonym of a teenage girl who contracted HIV.

I was 15 when I decided to have sex with Ben,* my first serious boyfriend. I worried that I'd get pregnant, not that I'd end up HIV positive. But that's exactly what happened.

I met Ben at the movie theater when I was 14. We ran in different circles because he was three years older than I was, but we liked a lot of the same music and movies and were both big Chicago Bulls fans. Ben was cute and sweet, and things between us got serious fast. When Ben brought up the idea of sex a few

* All names have been changed.

Reprinted from "I'm HIV Positive," by Michelle Towner, as told to Stephanie Booth, *Teen*, October 1999. Reprinted with permission from Stephanie Booth.

months later, it seemed right to me. We were in love.

We used a condom only about half the time we had sex. I knew you could get STDs that way, but Ben told me not to worry, and I trusted him. I knew he was more experienced than I was, so I figured he knew what he was talking about. The thought of HIV never crossed my mind—I would never have suggested we get tested before we had sex.

We dated for a year and a half, until I moved away. My father died when I was younger, and my mom and I never got along that great. So I decided to go live in a different section of Chicago with my aunt, who I was very close to. I knew that would mean Ben and I wouldn't see each other as much, and I worried that we'd drift apart.

Soon after the move, we did break up. I was crushed. I went back to my old neighborhood a couple of times, hoping to bump into him, but no one had seen him. I figured he had a new girlfriend, which made me feel even worse.

A Bad Diagnosis

About six months after I moved, I got really sick. I was running a high fever and throwing up, and I didn't have the energy to crawl out of bed for two days. My aunt made an appointment for me at the doctor, but she had to work, so I went by myself.

> I worried that I'd get pregnant, not that I'd end up HIV positive.

While the doctor examined me, he asked one question after another: "Do you drink?" "Do you do drugs?" "Do you smoke?" The answers were all no, until he asked if I'd had unprotected sex. "Just with my boyfriend," I said. He asked if he could test me for HIV, and I was like, "Why not?" I was sure I didn't have it. They took some blood and said to call in a few days for the results. I blew it off because I still felt so sick and just wasn't in the mood.

The nurse wound up calling me and asked me to come back

in as soon as possible. I just thought, or hoped, they were going to give me different antibiotics. The HIV test was still in the back of my mind, though. Then I knew something was wrong when the nurse made me wait in the doctor's private office. By the time the doctor came in, my hands were all clammy and I was shaking. Then he dropped the bomb: "Michelle, you're HIV positive," he said.

My first thought was, "I'm dying." I felt so angry and confused. Then I asked myself, "How did this happen?" "Who gave this to

---

HIV and AIDS

- As of December 1998, 688,200 Americans had been reported with AIDS, and 410,800 of them had died, since the beginning of the epidemic in 1981. In 1997, an estimated 270,841 persons were living with AIDS. This represented a 12 percent increase in people living with AIDS from 1996 and was due, in large part, to new drug therapies that have improved survival rates and decreased the number of deaths among people with AIDS. Despite this decrease, AIDS remains a leading cause of death in most age groups—in 1997 it was the fifth leading cause of death in the 25–44 age group, the seventh leading cause of death in those aged 15–24, and the ninth leading cause of death in those aged 5–14.

- The greatest proportion of AIDS cases in the U.S. has always been among people in the 25–44 age group. In 1996, nearly 75 percent of Americans diagnosed with AIDS were in this group.

- While there has been a declining trend in the number of AIDS diagnoses, the number of HIV diagnoses has remained relatively stable. Estimates suggest that 650,000 to 900,000 Americans are now living with HIV, and at least 40,000 new HIV infections occur each year.

Planned Parenthood Federation of America, *Fact Sheet: Sexually Transmitted Infections*, October 1999.

---

me?" I didn't want to think it was Ben, but I hadn't had sex with anyone else. The doctor asked if there was anyone he could call for me, but I didn't want to tell my aunt. I was too ashamed.

The next week I faked being sick and hid in my bedroom. I worried that everyone at school would suddenly be able to tell I was HIV positive and wouldn't want to come near me, and I was scared that I would accidentally infect someone. Every time my aunt tried to talk to me, I screamed at her to leave me alone. The doctor gave me brochures about HIV, but I was too depressed to read them. I didn't feel like eating or sleeping. I just felt so alone. Then one night, I finally snuck the phone into my room and called an AIDS hotline that was on one of the brochures.

Return to the Living

I felt weird calling, but it was the best thing I could have done. The woman I spoke to that night was so understanding; she didn't preach to me. She referred me to an AIDS clinic, and I went the next day. Neal, a social worker there, gave me a shoulder to cry on. He told me lots of people with positive status live pretty normal lives for a long time, but I had to face up to being sick.

> I asked myself, . . . "Who gave this to me?" I didn't want to think it was [my boyfriend], but I hadn't had sex with anyone else.

The next time I met with Neal, I brought my aunt. She knew I was seeing someone for depression but didn't know the details. When Neal told her I was HIV positive, my aunt didn't believe it. She demanded I take a second blood test. When that came back positive, she hugged me for what felt like forever. "You have to take care of yourself," she said. My aunt's been so supportive. She helped me break the news to the rest of my family, and she tells them how I'm doing when I don't feel like talking about it.

The doctor gave me medicine, AZT, to take at exact times twice a day. At first it made me tired, and I got monster headaches and stomachaches. The side effects aren't as bad now, but I get sick really easily. I caught my aunt's cold and was in bed for days. Another time, I got dehydrated and was in the hospital for more than a week. A lot of people with HIV lose weight or get bad rashes, and every day I wake up scared to look in the mirror and see those symptoms. I go to the doctor every three months, and each time, I dread bad news—that I have full-blown AIDS. I'm OK so far, but I'll be on AZT for who knows how long.

Everything Has Changed

I'm trying to keep everything normal, but it feels like everything has changed. Eventually I'm going to have to tell my friends. Keeping this secret is so hard. But what do I say, "Hey, great outfit, and by the way, I'm positive"? I still hide my pills if they come over. Or if we're out and I have to take one, I make an excuse and run to the bathroom. Sleepovers are impossible. I think my friends would understand, but I don't want them to feel sorry for me or think I'm contagious and be scared off.

It's the same with any guy I date. I had a boyfriend, but I didn't let it get too intense. I'm not ready to go there. I kinda push guys away right now. Of course, if I found the right guy, I definitely would tell him before things got serious.

Looking back, I think Ben slept with a lot more girls than he told me about. I guess we should have talked more about sexual history and practised safe sex all the time. I'll never know whether or not he knew he was HIV positive. He's moved away, and I've moved on. I'm 17 now and training to be a peer counselor so I can talk to other kids about HIV. At least I have a chance to warn others. Each day I'm alive gives me another opportunity to get the word out.

Bibliography

Books

Eleanor Ayer

It's OK to Say No: Choosing Sexual Abstinence. New York: Rosen, 1997.

Brent A. Barlow

Worth Waiting For: Sexual Abstinence Before Marriage. Salt Lake City, UT: Deseret, 1995.

Nathalie Bartle und Susan Lieberman

Venus in Blue Jeans: Why Mothers and Daughters Need to Talk About Sex. Boston: Houghton Mifflin, 1998.

Michael J. Basso

The Underground Guide to Teenage Sexuality: An Essential Handbook for Today's Teen and Parents. Minneapolis, MN: Fairview Press, 1997.

Ruth Bell

Changing Bodies, Changing Lives: A Book for Teens on Sex and Relationships. New York: Times Books, 1998.

Karen Bouris

The First Time: What Parents and Teenage Girls Should Know About "Losing Your Virginity." Berkeley, CA: Conari Press, 1995.

Marshall Brain

The Teenager's Guide to the Real World. Raleigh, NC: BYG Publishing, 1997.

Jack Canfield, Mark Victor Hansen, and Kimberly Kirberger
Chicken Soup for the Teenage Soul: 101 Stories of Life, Love, and Learning. Deerfield Beach, FL: Health Communications, 1997.

Julie Endersbe
Teen Sex: Risks and Consequences. Mankato, MN: LifeMatters/Capstone Press, 2000.

E. James Lieberman and Karen Lieberman Troccoli
Like It Is: A Teen Sex Guide. Jefferson, NC: McFarland, 1998.

Beth McNeill and Bonnie Benson
Teen Sexuality: Responsible Decisions. Waco, TX: Health Edco, 1995.

Susan Browning Pogány
SexSmart: 501 Reasons to Hold Off on Sex. Minneapolis, MN: Fairview Press, 1998.

Michael A. Sommers and Annie Leah Sommers
Everything You Need to Know About Losing Your Virginity. New York: Rosen, 2000.

Joe White
Pure Excitement: A Radical Righteous Approach to Sex, Love and Dating. Colorado Springs, CO: Focus on the Family Publishing, 1996.

Periodicals

Rebecca Barry
"Are You Ready for Sex?" *Seventeen*, January 1996.

Bob Bartlett
"Intimacy 101 for Teens," *U.S. Catholic*, August 1999.

Elizabeth Benedict   "Please Touch Me," *Esquire*, September
                          1997.

Keith Blanchard   "From Here to Virginity," *Sassy*,
                          September 1996.

Jane E. Brody   "Teenagers and Sex: Younger and More
                          at Risk," *New York Times*, September
                          15, 1998.

Beth Dawes   "I Had an Abortion," *'Teen*, February
                          1997.

Kristina   "From Here to Virginity," *Men's Health*,
DeKoszmovsky   November 1996.

Francesca Delbanco   "The Spin on Teen Sex," *Seventeen*,
                          September 1998.

Kathy Dobie   "The Only Girl in the Car," *Harper's*,
                          August 1996.

Katherine Dowling   "Condoms Won't Keep Our Teens
                          Safe," *U.S. Catholic*, January 1995.

Jill Eisenstadt   "The Virgin Bride," *New York Times
                          Magazine*, June 16, 1996.

Nina Elder   "Teenagers and Herpes," *Better Homes
                          and Gardens*, October 1999.

Thomas R. Eng   "The Hidden Epidemic," *Issues in
                          Science and Technology*, Summer 1997.

Charlotte Faltermayer   "Listening in on Boy Talk," *Time*, June
                          15, 1998.

Sandy Fertman   "I Had a Sexually Transmitted Disease,"
                     'Teen, November 1997.

Gayle Forman   "Sex? No Thanks!" *Seventeen*, August
                     1999.

Valerie Frankel   "Almost Sex," *Mademoiselle*, October
                     1996.

Christine Gorman   "Teen Girls Beware," *Time*, August 24,
                     1998.

Susan Hayes   "AIDS in America," *Scholastic Update*,
                     October 20, 1997.

Sarah E. Hinlicky   "Subversive Virginity," *First Things*,
                     October 1998.

Amy M. Holmes   "Hook-Up U," *National Review*,
                     September 13, 1999.

Thomas Lickona   "Ten Consequences of Premature
                     Sexual Involvement," *U.S. Catholic*,
                     April 1996.

David Lipsky   "Sex on Campus," *Rolling Stone*, March
                     23, 1995.

———   "To Be Young and Gay," *Rolling Stone*,
                     August 6, 1998.

Linda Liu   "If You Have Sex, Read This . . . ,"
                     Mademoiselle, February 1999.

Lance Loud   "Sex, HIV, and You: Three Girls Living
                     with HIV Speak Out," *Sassy*, December
                     1996.

Hara Estroff Marano   "Sexual Issues Fan Parents' Fears," *New York Times*, July 2, 1997.

Angie Maximo   "Sex Files: The Deal on STDs," *Seventeen*, March 1997.

Celia Milne   "Sex and the Single Teen," *Maclean's*, December 28, 1998/ January 4, 1999.

Marianne R. Neifert   "Why Teen Sex Is Riskier than Ever," *McCall's*, August 1995.

Anne Novitt-Moreno   "Our Battle Against AIDS," *Current Health*, February 1996.

Stephen Rae   "Party of One," *Men's Health*, September 1995.

Billy Rayman   "Losin' It! Hey, Guys Are Virgins, Too . . . ," *Sassy*, August 1995.

Katie Roiphe   "The End of Innocence," *Vogue*, January 1998.

Rex Roberts   "AIDS: The New Generation," *Scholastic Update*, October 20, 1997.

Robert Rorke   "Coming Out in America," *Seventeen*, April 1999.

Jeannie I. Rosoff   "Helping Teenagers Avoid Negative Consequences of Sexual Activity," *USA Today*, May 1996.

Nancy Jo Sales   "The Sex Trap," *New York*, September 29, 1997.

Roger Scruton   "Very Safe Sex," *National Review*, July
                         28, 1997.

Michael Segell   "The Sex Men Lie About," *Esquire*,
                         September 1996.

Wendy Shalit   "Daughters of the (Sexual) Revolution,"
                         Commentary, December 1997.

Shaynee Snider   "STDs: Don't Be a Statistic," *'Teen*,
                         December 1999.

Leora Tanenbaum   "I Was a Teenage 'Slut'," *Ms.*
                         November/December 1996.

Sadie Van Gelder   "It's Who I Am," *Seventeen*, November
                         1996.

Peter Vilbig   "Life, Death, Sex," *Scholastic Update*,
                         October 20, 1997.

Paul C. Vitz   "Cupid's Broken Arrow," *Phi Delta
                         Kappan*, March 1999.

Catherine Walsh   "Catholic Singles and Sex," *America*,
                         February 11, 1995.

Julie Weingarden   "The High Price of Popularity," *'Teen*,
                         June 1999.

Naomi Wolf   "The Making of a Slut," *Ms.*, March/
                         April 1997.

Organizations and Websites

The editors have compiled the following list of organizations concerned with the issues debated in this book. The descriptions are derived from materials provided by the organizations. All have publications or information available for interested readers. The list was compiled on the date of publication of the present volume; the information provided here may change. Be aware that many organizations take several weeks or longer to respond to inquiries, so allow as much time as possible.

Advocates for Youth

1025 Vermont Ave. NW, Ste. 200, Washington, DC 20005
(202) 347-5700 • fax: (202) 347-2263
e-mail: info@advocatesforyouth.org
website: www.advocatesforyouth.org

Advocates for Youth is the only national organization focusing solely on pregnancy and HIV prevention among young people. It provides information, education, and advocacy to youth-serving agencies and professionals, policy makers, and the media. Among the organization's numerous publications are the brochures *Advice from Teens on Buying Condoms* and *Spread the Word—Not the Virus* and the pamphlet *How to Prevent Date Rape: Teen Tips.*

Alan Guttmacher Institute

120 Wall St., New York, NY 10005
(212) 248-1111 • fax: (212) 248-1951
e-mail: info@agi-usa.org • website: www.agi-usa.org

The institute works to protect and expand the reproductive choices of all women and men. It strives to ensure that people have access to the information and services they need to exercise their rights and responsibilities concerning sexual activity, reproduction, and family planning. Among the institute's publications are the books *Teenage Pregnancy in Industrialized Countries* and *Today's Adolescents, Tomorrow's Parents: A Portrait of the Americas* and the report "Sex and America's Teenagers."

American Civil Liberties Union (ACLU)

125 Broad St., 18th Fl., New York, NY 10004
(212) 549-2500 • fax: (212) 549-2646
website: www.aclu.org

The ACLU is a national organization that works to defend Americans' civil rights as guaranteed by the U.S. Constitution. It supports confidential reproductive health care for teens and civil rights for homosexuals. ACLU publications include the monthly *Civil Liberties Alert*, the quarterly newsletter *Civil Liberties*, the briefing paper "Reproductive Freedom: The Rights of Minors," as well as handbooks and pamphlets.

Child Trends, Inc. (CT)

4301 Connecticut Ave. NW, Ste. 100, Washington, DC 20008
(202) 362-5580 • fax: (202) 362-5533
e-mail: swilliams@childtrends.org
website: www.childtrends.org

CT works to provide accurate statistical and research information regarding children and their families in the United States and to educate the American public on the ways existing social trends, such as the increasing rate of teenage pregnancy, affect children. In addition to the annual newsletter *Facts at a Glance*, which presents the latest data on teen pregnancy rates for every state, CT also publishes the papers "Next-Steps and Best Bets:

Approaches to Preventing Adolescent Childbearing" and "Welfare and Adolescent Sex: The Effects of Family History, Benefit Levels, and Community Context."

Coalition for Positive Sexuality (CPS)

3712 N. Broadway, PMB #191, Chicago, IL 60613
(773) 604-1654
website: www.positive.org

The Coalition for Positive Sexuality is a grassroots direct-action group formed in the spring of 1992 by high school students and activists. CPS works to counteract the institutionalized misogyny, heterosexism, homophobia, racism, and ageism that students experience every day at school. It is dedicated to offering teens sexuality and safe sex education that is pro-woman, pro-lesbian/gay/ bisexual, pro-safe sex, and pro-choice. CPS publishes the pamphlet *Just Say Yes.*

Family Research Council (FRC)

801 G St. NW, Washington, DC 20001
(202) 393-2100 • fax: (202) 393-2134
e-mail: corrdept@frc.org • website: www.frc.org

The council is a research, resource, and education organization that promotes the traditional family, which the council defines as a group of people bound by marriage, blood, or adoption. It opposes schools' tolerance of homosexuality and condom distribution programs in schools. It also believes that pornography breaks up marriages and contributes to sexual violence. Among the council's numerous publications are the papers "Revolt of the Virgins," "Abstinence: The New Sexual Revolution," and "Abstinence Programs Show Promise in Reducing Sexual Activity and Pregnancy Among Teens."

Family Resource Coalition of America (FRCA)
20 N. Wacker Dr., Ste. 1100, Chicago, IL 60606
(312) 338-0900 • fax: (312) 338-1522
website: www.frca.org

FRCA is a national consulting and advocacy organization that seeks to strengthen and empower families and communities so they can foster the optimal development of children, teenagers, and adult family members. FRCA publishes the bimonthly newsletter *Connection*, the report "Family Involvement in Adolescent Pregnancy and Parenting Programs," and the fact sheet "Family Support Programs and Teen Parents."

Focus on the Family
Colorado Springs, CO 80995
(719) 531-5181 • fax: (719) 531-3424
website: www.fotf.org

Focus on the Family is an organization that promotes Christian values and strong family ties and that campaigns against pornography and homosexual rights laws. It publishes the monthly magazine *Focus on the Family* and the books *Love Won Out: A Remarkable Journey Out of Homosexuality* and *No Apologies . . . The Truth About Life, Love, and Sex.*

The Heritage Foundation
214 Massachusetts Ave. NE, Washington, DC 20002-4999
(202) 546-4400 • fax: (202) 546-8328
e-mail: info@heritage.org • website: www.heritage.org

The Heritage Foundation is a public policy research institute that supports the ideas of limited government and the free-market system. It promotes the view that the welfare system has contributed to the problems of illegitimacy and teenage pregnancy. Among the foundation's numerous publications is its Backgrounder series, which includes "Liberal Welfare Programs: What the Data Show on Programs for Teenage Mothers," the paper "Rising Illegitimacy: America's Social Catastrophe," and the bulletin "How Congress Can Protect the Rights of Parents to Raise Their Children."

National Campaign to Prevent Teen Pregnancy

21 M St. NW, Ste. 300, Washington, DC 20037

(202) 261-5655

website: www.teenpregnancy.org

The mission of the National Campaign is to reduce teenage pregnancy by promoting values and activities that are consistent with a pregnancy-free adolescence. The campaign's goal is to reduce the pregnancy rate among teenage girls by one-third by the year 2005. The campaign publishes pamphlets, brochures, and opinion polls that include *No Easy Answers: Research Finding on Programs to Reduce Teen Pregnancy*, *Not Just for Girls: Involving Boys and Men in Teen Pregnancy Prevention*, and *Public Opinion Polls and Teen Pregnancy.*

National Organization on Adolescent Pregnancy, Parenting, and Prevention (NOAPPP)

2401 Pennsylvania Ave., Ste. 350, Washington, DC 20037

(202) 293-8370

e-mail: noappp@noappp.org • website: www.noappp.org

NOAPPP promotes comprehensive and coordinated services designed for the prevention and resolution of problems associated with adolescent pregnancy and parenthood. It supports families in setting standards that encourage the healthy development of children through loving, stable, relationships. NOAPPP publishes the quarterly *NOAPPP Network Newsletter* and various fact sheets on teen pregnancy.

Planned Parenthood Federation of America (PPFA)

810 Seventh Ave., New York, NY 10019
(212) 541-7800 • (212) 245-1845
e-mail: communications@ppfa.org
website: www.plannedparenthood.org

Planned Parenthood believes individuals have the right to control their own fertility without governmental interference. It promotes comprehensive sex education and provides contraceptive counseling and services through clinics across the United States. Its publications include the brochures *Guide to Birth Control: Seven Accepted Methods of Contraception, Teen Sex? It's Okay to Say No Way*, and the bimonthly newsletter *LinkLine*.

Project Reality

PO Box 97, Golf, IL 60029-0097
(847) 729-3298
e-mail: preality@pair.com
website: www.project-reality.pair.com

Project Reality has developed a sex education curriculum for junior and senior high students called Sex Respect. The program is designed to provide teenagers with information and to encourage sexual abstinence.

Sex Information and Education Council of Canada (SIECCAN)

850 Coxwell Ave., Toronto, ON M4C 5R1 Canada
(416) 466-5304 • fax: (416) 778-0785
e-mail: sieccan@web.net • website: www.sieccan.org

SIECCAN conducts research on sexual health and sexuality education. It publishes the *Canadian Journal of Human Sexuality* and the resource document *Common Questions About Sexual Health Education*, and maintains an information service for health professionals.

Sexuality Information and Education Council of the United States (SIECUS)

130 W. 42nd St., Ste. 350, New York, NY 10036-7802
(212) 819-9770 • fax: (212) 819-9776
e-mail: siecus@siecus.org • website: www.siecus.org

SIECUS is an organization of educators, physicians, social workers, and others who support the individual's right to acquire knowledge of sexuality and who encourage responsible sexual behavior. The council promotes comprehensive sex education for all children that includes AIDS education, teaching about homosexuality, and instruction about contraceptives and sexually transmitted diseases. Its publications include fact sheets, annotated bibliographies by topic, the booklet *Talk About Sex*, and the monthly *SIECUS Report*.

Teen-Aid

723 E. Jackson Ave., Spokane, WA 99207
(509) 482-2868 • fax: (509) 482 7994
e-mail: teenaid@teen-aid.org • website: www.teen-aid.org

Teen-Aid is an international organization that promotes traditional family values and sexual morality. It publishes a public school sex education curriculum, *Sexuality, Commitment and Family*, stressing sexual abstinence before marriage.

Websites

All About Sex

www.allaboutsex.org

This organization encourages teens to feel good about their sexuality. It believes that everyone—regardless of their marital status or sexual orientation—should enjoy and participate in sex. The website offers articles on virginity, sexual intercourse, masturbation, and sexual orientation, among other topics.

Dear Lucie

www.lucie.com

Lucie Walters writes a syndicated newspaper and online advice column for teens called Adolessons. Her columns discuss incest, sex, sexually transmitted diseases, pregnancy, love and relationships, and health. Visitors to the site can read archives of her columns as well as participate in message boards and chat rooms.

Teen Advice Online

www.teenadviceonline.org

TAO's teen counselors from around the world offer advice for teens on relationships and dating, sex and sexuality, gender issues, internet relationships, health, family, school, and substance abuse. Teens can submit questions to the counselors or read about similar problems in the archives.

Teenwire

www.teenwire.org

This website was created by Planned Parenthood to provide teens with information about sexuality and sexual health issues. The site offers an online teen magazine, searchable archives, a question-and-answer forum, and informative articles about teen issues.

Whole Family

www.wholefamily.com

This source is designed for both parents and teens. The site's advice columnist, Liz, answers questions about pregnancy, teen sex, drugs, drinking, and body image, while online articles discuss other issues such as divorce, relationships, and health.

Index

ADVERTISING
MEDIA
A TO Z

ADVERTISING MEDIA A TO Z

THE DEFINITIVE RESOURCE FOR MEDIA PLANNING, BUYING, AND RESEARCH

Jim Surmanek

McGraw-Hill

New York Chicago San Francisco Lisbon London Madrid Mexico City
Milan New Delhi San Juan Seoul Singapore Sydney Toronto

Library of Congress Cataloging-in-Publication Data

Surmanek, Jim.
    Advertising media A to Z : the definitive resource for media buying, planning,
and research / by Jim Surmanek.
        p.   cm.
    ISBN 0-07-142214-5 (pbk. : alk. paper)
    1. Advertising media planning—Dictionaries.   I. Title

    HF5826.5 S848   2003
    659.1′03—dc21   2003003684

ISBN 0-07-142214-5

Interior design by Scott Rattray

This book is dedicated, with love, to my wife Paula.

About This Book

S ome people tell me that my books have helped them understand the dynamics of media planning and buying. My friends tell me that my books are a sure cure for insomnia. Notwithstanding, media, like many technical subjects, cannot be swallowed whole and fully remembered. I have found that many who have read all or parts of my previous books continue to use them as handy references. Those key words *handy references* were the impetus for this work.

This book focuses on advertising media: media planning, media buying, and media research. I have wanted to write a book about brain surgery, but I know nothing about the subject. The same goes for rocket science, anthropology, and a host of other subjects. So I continue to stick with what I've been involved in for most of my career: media.

This book is a combination of a dictionary (for those wishing to have a media term defined), an encyclopedia (for those interested in knowing a bit of the history behind certain terms, research companies, etc.), and a training manual (for the serious media student). Overall, I hope you find it a handy reference.

It should not be a surprise that all the terms are in alphabetical order. It's easier to find things that way. Terms with numbers in them are treated as if they are spelled out, so "30-sheet" is alphabetized as if it were "thirty-sheet." Only letters are considered for alphabetizing;

asterisks, dashes, colons, and slashes are completely disregarded. So "A/B split" is alphabetized as if it were "AB split."

Acronyms, such as "CPM," are listed, but they are defined under their full name, in this case, "cost per thousand." This is done for two reasons: first, it reinforces the name, which is often by itself a definition of the acronym and therefore more memorable; second, some people might look up the acronym while others will look up the term itself. The definition could have been listed under both the acronym and the full name, but listing the definition only once saves a tree.

Mathematical formulas are shown at the end of various definitions, along with an example of the math. The serious professional is urged to work out the math at least once to fully understand the definition. An advanced degree in mathematics is not needed. For quick reference and reminder, media formulas are also reprised in a separate section at the end of this book.

Words with multiple definitions have numbered definitions for reading ease, but the numbers do not indicate any order of priority for the definitions. For example, the two definitions of "average audience" are equally important.

If there are related terms not shown within the definition of a term, it will be suggested that you "also see" these other terms. If a website is associated with the term, the uniform resource locator (URL) will be listed. If you cannot find a word in this book, first make sure you are correctly spelling the word. If you are, you will have to look it up in another dictionary.

Enjoy!

AA   *See* average audience.

AAAA   *See* American Association of Advertising Agencies.

AAF   *See* American Advertising Federation.

Abandonware   Computer software that is no longer manufactured nor distributed by the company that created it.

ABC   *See* Audit Bureau of Circulations.

ABCD counties   *See* Nielsen county size groups.

ABCi   *See* Audit Bureau of Circulations.

Above the fold   1. Advertising or editorial content on a Web page that a user can see without having to scroll down. 2. Ad or edit content that appears in the top half of a standard-size newspaper. *Also see* below the fold.

A/B split   Two versions of an advertisement, or two entirely different ads for the same company, with each version distributed in every other copy of the magazine. Each version is ostensibly delivered to all of the geographic areas covered by the magazine. The two versions combined account for 100 percent of the magazine's circulation. A/B splits often are used to test two versions of an advertisement to determine, for example, which has the higher level of readership or response (as gauged by coupon redemption, reader phone calls).

AC *See* adult contemporary.

Academy of Marketing Science (AMS) An international, scholarly, professional organization dedicated to promoting high standards and excellence in the creation and dissemination of marketing knowledge and the furtherance of marketing practice. AMS has a role of leadership around the world within the discipline of marketing. Website: ams-web.org

ACB *See* Advertising Checking Bureau.

Access *See* TV dayparts.

Access channels Cable TV channels that are leased by a cable system operator (with or without cost) for use by the public, educational institutions, or local governments.

Access charge A fee charged to subscribers or other telephone companies by a local exchange carrier for the use of its local exchange networks.

Access provider *See* Internet service provider.

Accordion insert An advertising circular, leaflet, or pamphlet that has been folded in an accordion fashion for binding into a magazine.

Accrual **1.** The amount of a cooperative (co-op) fund earned on a per-dollar or per-unit basis through purchases over a stated period. **2.** An accounting procedure where revenue and expenses are recorded in the period in which they are earned or incurred, regardless of whether cash is received or disbursed in that period.

ACORN A geodemographic segmentation system. ACORN's neighborhood segments are divided into 43 clusters and 9 summary groups. ACORN was created by CACI and then sold to ESRI. It is an acronym for "A Classification of Residential Neighborhoods." Website: esri.com

A counties   *See* Nielsen county size groups.

ACR   *See* Association for Consumer Research.

Across the board   A type of scheduling in which a radio or TV program airs at the same time for five consecutive days for each week that it airs. Purchasing commercials in each airing is therefore an across-the-board commercial schedule. *Also called* strip programming.

ACRT   *See* all communications receiver transmitter.

ACTA   *See* America's Carriers Telecommunications Association.

Active rock   A radio programming format similar to alternative rock but pushed to the extreme edge.

ADA   A computer programming language developed for the U.S. Defense Department. Although a general-purpose language, ADA is often the language of choice for large systems that require real-time processing, such as banking and air traffic control systems. ADA is named after Ada Byron, who in 1843 predicted that a machine would be created that could compose music and produce graphics.

Ad bank   *See* time banks.

Ad blocker   Software on a user's browser that can block advertisements from being displayed.

Ad Council   *See* Advertising Council, The.

Adcume   Software that allows the user to view gross and net target audience delivery for any specified target on a week-by-week basis. A product of Interactive Market Systems.

Added deficiency units (ADUs)   In network television, the commercial units added to an audience-guaranteed buy (at no additional charge) to make up for impression or target rating point (TRP) underdelivery as reported in a post-analysis. An ADU differs from a makegood, because it has to do with rating point underdelivery versus the TRP delivery agreed to at the time of purchase, as opposed to a commercial being missed or preempted.

Added value   The goods or services received gratis as part of a media buy. This may include merchandise—such as a TV set, paid travel, or concert tickets—that the advertiser can use for a sales contest, or services—such as additional advertising within the purchased medium or advertising within a medium owned by the purchased medium, or participation in a media-driven promotion.

Add-on rate   A different rate, established during the negotiation for the original advertising schedule, that applies to any subsequent additions to the schedule.

Addressable   The ability of media such as direct mail, magazines, and TV to direct advertising to specific individuals.

Addressable converter   Equipment in cable households that allows subscribers to order, and cable operators to deliver, pay-per-view events.

Addressable TV   Technology that allows households with digital cable connections to receive (and conceivably interact with) programming or advertising directed specifically to that household.

Ad:edit ratio   The ratio of advertising to editorial pages. For example, a 60:40 indicates that 60 percent of all pages in a publication is advertising and 40 percent is nonadvertising (i.e., editorial). The term can also apply to radio and TV (by substituting programming for editorial), but is never used because all vehicles within a venue (e.g., TV networks within the network TV category) have approximately the same level of commercial load.

Ad hoc network   A group of radio or TV stations that contract to broadcast a program. The network exists solely for the purpose of broadcasting a particular program and ceases to exist after the stations fulfill their contractual agreement to air the program.

ADI   (Obsolete) *See* area of dominant influence.

Ad-IDs   *See* advertising digital identification.

Adjacency   The placement of a TV commercial in a time slot between two TV programs. It is the opposite of an in-program placement. *Also called* break position.

ADM   *See* Association of Directory Marketing.

Adnorms   A RoperASW study that compiles all Starch magazine ad readership scores of the previous year (or two). Adnorms is used in qualitative analysis of advertising recall of ads.

Ad page exposure (APX)   An estimate of the number of times the average reader of a magazine looks at (is exposed to) an average page of advertising in a magazine issue. The concept, proven with various research studies, exists because of the permanency of printed material; that is, a reader can read a given issue of the same magazine or sections of the magazine more than once. APX actually increases the potential reader impressions generated by a magazine. For example, if a magazine has 1 million readers and an APX of 1.1, the magazine produces 1.1 million reader impressions. APX was a popular concept before videocassette recorders and the Internet came on the scene. Now, TV and the Internet can also lay claim to the same advertising exposure phenomenon.

AdRelevance   A research company providing advertising expenditure measurement data for online advertisers. Nielsen//NetRatings purchased it from Jupiter. Website: adrelevance.com

Ad:sales ratio (A:S)   Advertising dollars as a percentage of a product or service's sales. For example, a 2 percent A:S states that 2 percent of sales are invested in advertising. Advertising includes any form of paid communication (such as brochures, direct mail, magazines, point-of-purchase displays, radio, TV), the costs to produce the advertising, and the fees paid to advertising agents (e.g., advertising agencies and media agencies). A:S is usually pronounced "A to S."

Ad*Sentry   A technology known as "computerized pattern recognition" that permits Nielsen Media Research to monitor commercial activity on broadcast and cable networks as well as on local television stations in most of the major markets.

Ad server   A software program or type of computer server that distributes Internet advertisements, and can keep track of and report website usage statistics, such as ad banner exposure by types of individuals. Ads can then be targeted toward certain types of individuals. An ad server also provides the ability to rotate banners so a user won't see the same ad every time the same Web page is hit.

ADSL   Asymmetric digital subscriber line. *See* digital subscriber line.

Adstock   The amount of carryover or retention of advertising (e.g., awareness, recognition, recall) for a selected target audience through time, during and following media advertising. Adstock assumes that in addition to a "full-life," that is, when commercials are actually airing, commercials have a "half-life," or residual effect. Almost immediately after advertising exposure ceases, memory of the commercial to which a viewer was exposed begins to decay—memory fades. However, even after the advertising ceases, people will still remember the advertising (i.e., retain it) for some period of time, with the time period varying by individual. This retention level is known as adstock. Adstock happens even if advertising continues; that is, the effect of week one's advertising lingers into week two, even if week two has additional advertising. Stated with arithmetic, if a commercial has a decay rate of 50 percent for each week following the cessation of advertising, and the commercial aired for one week at a level of 100 target rating points (TRPs), the adstock for that commercial (that schedule) is 50 TRPs in week two (100 TRPs times 50 percent), 25 TRPs in week three (the carryover of 50 TRPs from week two times 50 percent), and so forth. Adstock is the compensating opposite of the advertising decay rate. For example, if a commercial decays at the rate of 75 percent each week, then adstock maintains at a rate of 25 percent each week. The concept, born in the United Kingdom and sometimes used in the United

States, is used to adjust weekly TRP levels or rationalize an advertising hiatus. With the former use, a media planner recognizes that carryover TRPs have real value—that is, in a sense carryover TRPs provide audience delivery at no cost. With the latter use, the media planner may opt to schedule a hiatus to either use funds for higher priority weeks or avoid the purchase of TRPs during high cost periods.

ADU   *See* added deficiency units.

Adult alternative   A radio programming format known as Triple A (adult alternative airplay) or progressive adult radio that is not as repetitive as Top 40 and does not include heavy metal, rap, or syrupy ballads.

Adult contemporary (AC)   A radio programming format that is a blend of current and recent hits, sometimes with a mixture of music from the 1960s and 1970s.

Advanced Analytic Solutions (A2S)   A research company that serves broadcast, cable, and radio networks, providing consulting services in many areas, such as television audience segmentation studies, custom analysis software, advertising sales research, methods evaluation and research, and consumer panels. A2S was formerly known as Symmetrical Resources, which was founded in 1992. It is now a subsidiary of Symmetrical Holdings, Inc. Website: a2solutions.com

Advanced TV (ATV)   The name given by the Federal Communications Commission to digital TV (DTV), including high definition TV (HDTV).

Advertising agency   A service organization that typically creates advertising messages on behalf of its advertiser clients and places those messages in various media forms. A "full service" advertising agency performs all of the advertising functions, such as conducting consumer or business research; formulating media plans; developing creative messages for media such as magazines, newspapers, radio, and television; producing (or overseeing the production of) the creative messages for insertion into print media, airing on radio or TV, and so on; and placing the creative messages in the media. *Also see* 1. boutique advertising agency, 2. media agency.

Advertising Checking Bureau (ACB) A nationwide service that (among other things) monitors and evaluates print advertising. Website: acbcoop.com

Advertising contract A written agreement made between the advertiser (or the advertiser's media buying agent) and the advertising medium, which states in detail the content, cost, and placement of the advertisement for which both parties are bound.

Advertising Council, The Since 1942, the Ad Council's major activities include the production, distribution, promotion, and evaluation of public service communications programs. Some of their most notable public service announcements were Smokey Bear ("Only You Can Prevent Forest Fires"), the "Friends Don't Let Friends Drive Drunk" campaign, McGruff the Crime Dog ("Take a Bite Out of Crime"), and for the United Negro College Fund ("A Mind Is a Terrible Thing to Waste"). Website: adcouncil.org

Advertising digital identification (Ad-IDs) A 12-digit code digitally encoded on all forms of media that stores a wide variety of information about ads, including which agency created them, who was involved in their creation, and when and where they run. In 2002, the Association of National Advertisers and the American Association of Advertising Agencies created Ad-IDs to replace ISCI (International Standard Commercial Identification) codes.

Advertising Media Internet Center (AMIC) An organization that offers a broad collection of links to media-related resources, message boards, a media bookstore, and research tools. It was created by Telmar to serve the advertising industry. Website: amic.com

Advertising Research Foundation (ARF) Founded in 1936 by the Association of National Advertisers and the American Association of Advertising Agencies, the ARF is a corporate-membership, non-profit association for advertising, marketing, and media research. Its combined membership represents more than 400 advertisers, advertising agencies, research firms, media companies, educational institutions, and international organizations. The principal mission of the ARF is to improve the practice of advertising, marketing, and media research in pursuit of more effective marketing and advertising communications. Website: arfsite.org

Advertorial   A print advertisement styled to look like an editorial format. The format and typeface usually resemble what is used by the publication in its editorial. Most publishers require advertorials to be labeled "advertisement" at the top.

Ad*Views   Software that allows the user to work with Nielsen Monitor-Plus information directly from a desktop or laptop computer.

Advocacy advertising   Advertising that pleads or argues in favor of a cause, idea, or policy, as opposed to advertising that sells a product or service.

Aero (.aero)   *See* domain name.

Affidavit (of performance)   A notarized or sworn statement from a broadcast station that confirms the commercial actually ran at the time shown on the station's invoice. Most affidavits also include the commercial number (ISCI code) and the price of each spot that aired.

Affiliate   **1.** A broadcast station that has a contractual relationship with one or more networks (e.g., ABC, CBS, FOX, NBC) to carry the network's programs and commercial announcements. *See* owned and operated. **2.** A marketing tactic wherein a website contains one or more links to one or more other websites with the purpose of driving users of the first website to the other websites.

Affinity marketing   Targeting and selling (usually directly) to people who have an affinity for purchasing specific kinds of products or services.

Afternoon drive   *See* radio dayparts.

AFTRA   *See* American Federation of Television and Radio Artists.

Agate line   A newspaper space measurement that is one column wide by 1/14 of an inch high (14 agate lines to the inch). Replaced (for the most part) as an advertising measurement by the standard advertising unit (SAU).

Agency of record (AOR)   An advertising agency or media agency to which an advertiser has assigned its account, in whole or in part, for all services (e.g., creative, market research, media) or segments within specific services. An agency might, for example, be assigned all media planning and buying, or one or the other, for national TV.

Agency spot buying pool   *See* spot-buying pool.

AHAA   *See* Association of Hispanic Advertising Agencies.

AI   *See* artificial intelligence.

Aided recall (awareness)   A research method used to determine an audience's recollection of specific advertising, brand names, and so on. The respondent is aided with prompts, such as being given the advertised product or service's name and asked if she or he recalls the name. With unaided recall, no prompts are given.

AID Run   It was an acronym for Arbitron Information on Demand. The name has been changed to Maximi$er Run.

AIM   *See* Association for Interactive Marketing.

Air check   A broadcast recording (audio, video, or both) that serves as a file copy of that broadcast. Sometimes an air check is requested by the advertiser or its buying agent to verify program content, the specific commercial that aired, or placement of the commercial within the program.

Airlog   A report that contains the exact time and identification of program and commercial material telecast during the broadcast day.

Album-oriented rock (AOR)   A radio programming format that features recent or current rock music.

Algorithm   A step-by-step procedure or formula for solving a problem. It is not named after Al Gore, but is after Abu Ja'far Muhammad ibn Musa al-Khwarizmi.

All communications receiver transmitter (ACRT)   Coined by Jim Surmanek in his 1995 book, *Media Planning*, an ACRT is the marriage of a TV set and a computer that allows for broadcaster and consumer interactivity.

All Media Planner, The   Software used to calculate reach/frequency for single and multiple target audiences and schedules. A software product of Telmar.

Allotments   The number of outdoor panels in a showing, usually tallied to meet specific GRP (gross ratings points) objectives.

Alpha test   The first test of an experimental product or service, carried out by the creator. A beta test is the second test of the experimental product or service, but is carried out by an outside organization not the creator.

Alternate weeks   The method of scheduling advertising for a period of one week, then skipping a week, and then running it again for a week, and so forth. Sometimes referred to as lightbulb (on/off) flighting.

Alternative   A radio programming format that includes many different types of music, especially those not found on conventional music stations. Also known as progressive.

AM   *See* 1. amplitude modulation, 2. radio programming formats.

AMA   *See* American Marketing Association.

Amateur radio   Private radio communication operating on various narrow frequency bands from 1.8 megahertz to several hundred gigahertz. Operators must pass an examination to be licensed. Amateur operators communicate with each other directly or through ad hoc relay systems and amateur-satellites. They exchange messages by voice, teleprinting, telegraphy, facsimile, and television. Amateur radio is also known as "ham" radio, and the operators are mostly called "hams." *Ham* is the verbal abbreviation of the first two letters in *amateur*. *Also see* Citizen's Band Radio.

AM drive   *See* radio dayparts.

American Advertising Federation (AAF)   A federation that protects and promotes the well-being of advertising, accomplished through a unique, nationally coordinated grassroots network of advertisers, agencies, media companies, local advertising clubs, and college chapters. Website: aaf.org

American Association of Advertising Agencies (4As)   Founded in 1917, the 4As is the national trade association representing the advertising agency business in the United States. Its membership produces approximately 75 percent of the total advertising volume placed by agencies nationwide. Website: aaaa.org

American (country)   A radio programming format that is out of the mainstream country music, blended with rock, jazz, blues, folk, and Tejano.

American Federation of Television and Radio Artists (AFTRA)   A national labor union affiliated with the AFL-CIO. AFTRA represents its members in four major areas: news and broadcasting, entertainment programming, the recording business, and commercials and nonbroadcast media. Its 80,000 members are seen or heard on television, radio, and sound recordings and include actors, announcers, news broadcasters, singers (including royalty artists and background singers), dancers, sportscasters, disc jockeys, talk show hosts, and others. Website: aftra.com

American Marketing Association (AMA)   The AMA serves marketing professionals in both business and education, and serves all levels of marketing practitioners, educators, and students. It has over 40,000 members in 82 countries. The AMA was created in 1937 from the merger of National Association of Teachers of Marketing (founded in 1915) and the American Marketing Society (founded in 1931). Website: marketingpower.com

American National Standards Institute (ANSI)   A private, nonprofit organization that fosters the development of technology standards in the United States.

American Newspaper Publishers Association   *See* Newspaper Association of America.

American Standard Code for Information Interchange (ASCII) A standard way for computers to use bits and bytes to represent characters. An ASCII file contains simple text without any special formatting codes. It is a standard instituted by the American National Standards Institute (ANSI).

American Teleservices Association (ATA)   An organization that represents the call centers, trainers, consultants, and equipment suppliers that initiate, facilitate, and generate telephone, Internet, and e-mail sales, service, and support. Website: ataconnect.org

America's Carriers Telecommunications Association (ACTA) A lobbying organization of over 165 small long-distance telephone carrier companies that was founded in 1985.

AMIC   *See* Advertising Media Internet Center.

AMIN   Advertising and Marketing International Network. An alliance of over 65 independently owned advertising agencies based in North America, Europe, and the Pacific Rim. Website: amin worldwide.com

AMOL   *See* automated measurement of lineups.

Amplitude modulation (AM)   The transmission of sound in radio broadcasting in which the amplitude (power) of a transmitting wave is modulated (changed) to simulate the original sound. A signal is a technical method used to superimpose sounds onto a radio wave.

AM is conveyed to the radio wave by varying the wave's strength—like varying the brightness of a lightbulb with a dimmer switch. AM operating frequencies are expressed in kilohertz (kHz)—for example, a 960 kHz station has a frequency of 960,000 cycles per second. All AM stations operate on frequencies that are at least 10 kHz apart from each other, such as 960, 970, 980.

AMS   *See* Academy of Marketing Science.

AM stereo   *See* stereo.

ANA   *See* Association of National Advertisers.

Analog (or analogue)   The electronics of a circuit or device having an output that is proportional to the input. Loosely, it means the measuring of data on more physical grounds as opposed to digital, which is a more electronic or "wired state." The word is often used to denote the opposite of digital.

Analog signal   A signaling method that uses continuous changes in the amplitude or frequency of a radio transmission to convey information.

Anchor listing   A reference line in the Yellow Pages that directs the consumer to a display ad.

Animatic   A TV commercial created from semifinished or unfinished artwork, or pickup art, used only for demonstration purposes (such as in an advertising agency's presentation to a client) or for test purposes. An animatic (commercial) is not meant for broadcast.

Announcement   An advertising message in broadcast media, commonly 10, 15, 30, or 60 seconds in length. Synonymous with "commercial" and usually referred to as a "spot."

Announcer voice-over   *See* voice-over.

Annual average daily traffic (annual ADT)   A count of the number of vehicles passing a given outdoor unit. It is based on 24 counts taken over an entire year. *Also see* daily effective circulation.

Annualize A statistical technique whereby figures covering a period of less than one year are extended to cover a 12-month period. For example, if a media effort during a 3-month period costs $1,000, a 12-month effort would cost $4,000 (adjusted up or down according to normal cost fluctuations for the media and months in question).

ANSI *See* American National Standards Institute.

Answer print An almost-finished print of a television commercial that contains all of the optical effects, titles, and so forth but is not ready for airing until it is corrected for such things as color and quality.

Antisiphoning A Federal Communications Commission rule that prohibits cable operators from cablecasting programming for pay cable channels that would otherwise be available on broadcast channels.

AOR *See* 1. agency of record; 2. album-oriented rock.

Applet A computer program or application written in Java that can be executed from within another application. It runs on a Web browser and can perform database queries or display animation.

Approach The distance between the out-of-home advertising structure and the point where it first becomes viewable to a passerby. An approach does not necessarily indicate at what distance a specific advertising message will become viewable.

APX *See* ad page exposure.

AQH *See* average quarter hour.

Arbitron An international media and marketing research firm serving radio broadcasters, cable companies, advertisers, advertising agencies, and outdoor advertising companies in the United States, Mexico, and Europe. Arbitron's core businesses are measuring network and local market radio audiences across the United States; surveying the retail, media, and product patterns of local market consumers; and providing application software used for analyzing media audience and marketing information data. This research, gathered through the Arbitron radio listening diary, forms the basis of the audience estimates published in Arbitron Radio Market Reports (RMR). Diary-keepers account for all radio listening estimates. The diary covers seven days of radio listening, designed to be personally maintained by each member of the household (up to a maximum of nine persons per household) over the age of 12. In the diary they are asked to record listening start and stop times, station identifiers, AM/FM indicators, listening locations (home, work, car), and whether or not they listened at all to radio that particular day. In the back of the diary, respondents are asked to provide their age, sex, employment status, city, county, and ZIP code. In Arbitron's Qualitative Diary markets (markets where Arbitron gathers information that describes consumers' demographic, socioeconomic, and lifestyle characteristics, as well as purchase intentions), 21 qualitative questions are also included at the back of the diary in order to determine the preceding descriptors. Arbitron Webcast Services measures the audiences of audio and video content on the Internet, commonly known as webcasts. The company is developing the Portable People Meter, a new technology for radio, TV, and cable ratings. Through its Scarborough Research joint venture with VNU Media Measurement and Information, Arbitron also provides media and marketing research services to the broadcast television, magazine, newspaper, and online industres. Website: arbitron.com

Area of dominant influence (ADI)   (Obsolete) The term used by Arbitron to describe the geographic boundaries of a TV market. Arbitron ceased reporting TV ratings and TV market definitions in 1993. *See* designated market area.

ARF   *See* Advertising Research Foundation.

ARPA   *See* Internet.

Arrears   As reported by the Audit Bureau of Circulations, these are magazine copies sent to subscribers up to three months after subscription expiration. *Also called* post-expiration copies.

Artificial intelligence (AI)   The use of computer technology to strive toward the goal of machine intelligence.

Arts (.arts)   *See* domain name.

A:S   *See* ad:sales ratio.

ASCII   *See* American Standard Code for Information Interchange.

As it falls   A method of simulating a national test media plan into one or more test markets whereby each market receives the media weight (e.g., target rating points [TRPs]) it would normally receive if the national plan were implemented nationally. This method is used to test the viability of one or more national media plans before it is implemented nationally or rolled out across the United States. The methodology treats the test market(s) as if it was actually receiving the implementation of a national media plan. National media in the national media plan are translated into the test market(s) using their local equivalents; for example, spot TV is used to simulate national TV using the same dayparts, local or regional editions of magazines are used to simulate national editions, and where local or regional editions are not available, either similar magazines or newspaper supplements are used. The test market(s) receives what it normally would receive from the national media forms, which is not necessarily the average of the national forms. For example, network TV might deliver more or less than the national average TRP level in any given market. A complete local market delivery analysis must therefore be done for all national media forms in each of the test markets. Local media in the national plan are directly implemented into the test market(s). For example, if the national plan calls for 100 TRPs of spot TV in market X, and market X is a test market, then market X receives 100 TRPs. Conversely, if the national plan does not have planned local activity in market X, then market X does not receive any local activity. As with any in-market test, it is very important to select test markets that are representative of the United States at large (either individually or collectively). It is also wise to select more than one test market in the event that any one market suffers the consequences of dramatic economic or environmental change during the test. *Also see* **1.** Little America, **2.** rollout, **3.** weighted average.

Associated   The percentage of a magazine's readers who saw the advertiser's name in the ad. *See* Starch readership scores.

Association for Consumer Research (ACR)   A society of individuals who have a professional interest in consumer research. Its mission is to advance consumer research and facilitate the exchange of scholarly information among members of academia, industry, and government worldwide. Website: acrweb.org

Association for Interactive Marketing (AIM)   A nonprofit trade organization devoted to helping marketers use interactive opportunities to reach their respective marketplaces. Founded in 1993, AIM works closely with its corporate members to promote and protect the future of interactive marketing. As an independent subsidiary of the Direct Marketing Association, AIM serves diverse corporate interests, including e-mail marketing, e-tailing, online marketing, content provision, e-commerce, customer relationship management, market research, broadband access, and the rollout of interactive television. Among others, the membership consists of companies who have a vested interest in the use of interactive technologies for marketing across multiple channels. Website: imarketing.org

Association of Directory Marketing (ADM)   An association of Yellow Pages certified marketing representatives, directory publishers, and suppliers whose mission is to grow advertisers' businesses and, in turn, industry revenues by maximizing the value of directory advertising. Website: admworks.org

Association of Hispanic Advertising Agencies (AHAA)   A trade organization founded in 1996 established specifically for advertising agencies working within the U.S. Hispanic advertising industry. Website: ahaa.org

Association of National Advertisers (ANA)   A trade association dedicated exclusively to marketing and brand building. It represents more than 300 companies with 8,000 brands that collectively spend over $100 billion in marketing communications and advertising. Founded in 1910. Website: ana.net

Association of Newspaper Classified Advertising Managers   *See* Newspaper Association of America.

Asymmetric digital subscriber line (ADSL)   *See* digital subscriber line.

ATA   *See* American Teleservices Association.

Attentiveness   A term used to describe how attentively people view TV by time period and by program. The common designators are "paying full attention" and "paying partial attention." The inference is that people who pay full attention to a program stand a better chance than the average viewer of being exposed to the commercials in that program. Although logical, the theory has not been proven and is therefore a leap of faith. Attentiveness levels are self-judged by the respondent in answering a questionnaire.

Attenuation   Any reduction in a signal's strength between any two points in a circuit. If signal strength is lost over a long distance in cable transmission, a repeater can be inserted to boost the signal.

Attosecond   *See* second.

Attribute   A characteristic inherent in or ascribed to something, such as media forms. *Also see* the individual media forms' attributes, for example, listed as "Internet, attributes."

ATV   *See* Advanced TV.

A2S   *See* Advanced Analytic Solutions.

Audience   The gross or net number of homes or people exposed to a media vehicle, such as to TV in total, or to a specific program, or for a specific time within that program. All audience measurements are estimates based on a sampling of specific population groups.

Audience accumulation   The total net number of people (or homes) exposed to a medium during its duration (or life). For example, a half-hour TV program might have an average quarter hour (AQH) audience of 1 million people, but would have accumulated a total audience of more than 1 million people who viewed five minutes or more of the program at any time during its airing. The reason is that some people tune in and some tune out a program while it is being aired. This audience churn typically results in a total audience that is greater than represented by the AQH. Likewise, a magazine with a circulation of 1 million would accumulate much more than 1 million readers by nature of the magazine being passed on from one reader to the next. *Also see* **1.** audience flow, **2.** audience turnover, **3.** inherited audience, **4.** reach, **5.** readers per copy.

Audience composition   The demographic profile of a medium's audience. This is typically expressed as percentages of the total audience and is usually reported for basic demographics, such as age groups, gender, and income groups. Sometimes referred to simply as "comp," these calculations can be compared to the percent of population in each demographic cell via an index. An inspection of the resulting indices can reveal audience skews.

Formula:

Audience of a demographic cell ÷ total audience = composition

Example:

500,000 ÷ 2,000,000 = 25%

Audience duplication   *See* duplication.

Audience flow   Describes the source of the total audience for a network television program—that is, how many viewers carry over from audiences who viewed the previous program on the same channel, and how many are new tune-ins from other channels or from people who were not previously watching TV.

Audience fragmentation   The splintering of mass media's audience into small segments due to the increasing number of media outlets available to the total audience. Generally, the more outlets (TV programs, cable channels), the less the audience delivery of each outlet, on average.

Audience guarantee   A guarantee made by a media seller to an advertiser that a certain amount of audience (e.g., target rating points [TRPs]) will be delivered by the programs or time slots purchased by that advertiser. The guarantee is predicated on both parties agreeing to specific research methodology, such as basing audience delivery on a specific Nielsen rating book.

Audience holding index   A unit used to measure the ability of a program to hold its audience—that is, to keep its audience tuned in as opposed to tuning out. Research companies measure the index on a minute-by-minute or quarter-hour (15 minutes) basis.

Audience potential   A broad statement of the total audience available or deliverable by a specific medium or specific media schedule. A statement of audience potential is typically a boxcar number used to describe or sell a medium but has no basis in true media planning. *Also see* reach.

Audience spillover   *See* spillover.

Audience turnover   The ratio of the total accumulated media audience (i.e., the audience accumulated over the entire duration of a program or time segment) divided by the average audience listening or viewing during the average minute or average quarter hour (AQH). For example, a program that has an AQH rating of 1.0 and an accumulated audience of 2.0 has a turnover ratio of 2:1.

Audimeter   Nielsen Media Research's original name for an electronic device that is attached to a TV set and provides minute-by-

minute records of TV receiver tunings in sample households. *Also
see* **1.** diary, **2.** sweeps.

Audio   The sound portion of a TV/radio commercial or program.

AudioAudit   A company that monitors and verifies TV and radio
airplay of advertising. Website: audioaudit.com

Audiotex   A Yellow Pages service that allows the caller to receive
timely information on the advertiser's product or service.

Audit Bureau of Circulations (ABC)   A nonprofit organization
established in 1914 that audits and reports on the circulation of
consumer magazines, business magazines, daily and weekly newspapers, and farm publications. A Publisher's Statement of circulation (commonly called the Pink Sheets because it is printed on pink
paper) is issued every six months and is subject to an audit. Magazine statements cover the periods ending June 30 and December 31;
newspaper statements cover the periods ending March 31 and September 30. Publisher's Statements are issued online approximately
two months after the statement period, with hard copies distributed soon thereafter. An Interim Publisher's Statement is issued for
all publications and covers the first half—i.e., the first three
months—of the Publisher's Statement's period. The Audit Report
(commonly called the White Audit because it is printed on white
paper) is issued annually for all publications and verifies the circulation claims made on the Publisher's Statements. The Audit Report
also provides additional information, such as circulation by county.
ABCi audits the Internet. Website: accessabc.com

Audit report   Any kind of detailed information about the performance of a medium, media vehicle, or media schedule that is typically provided by an impartial third party. This can also include a
financial accounting of media billing and expenditures.

Audit Report   A report (commonly called the White Audit) published annually by the Audit Bureau of Circulations provides audited

verification of the published circulation figures of newspapers and magazines.

Audit trail   A step-by-step record by which media and media-related data can be traced to its source, such as tracing media buy changes or financial records.

Authorization   Approval from an advertiser given to its buying agent to purchase media on the advertiser's behalf.

Automated measurement of lineups (AMOL)   Nielsen Media Research's primary source of information about which programs are airing for each station or cable channel, which comes from a coded ID number that is part of almost every TV picture. It is a series of lines and dots that is found in the top edge of the picture and labels the program and episode.

AV   Abbreviation for audio/visual.

Availability   The commercial position in a program or between programs on a given station or network that is available for purchase by the advertiser. "Avails" for short.

Avails   *See* availability.

Average audience (AA)   1. The number of homes (or individuals) tuned to the average minute of a radio or TV program. 2. The number of individuals who looked into an average issue of a publication and are considered readers.

Average four weeks   Usually refers to reach/frequency tabulations that report audience delivery during the average four weeks of a media schedule that runs for four weeks or longer. To calculate the average, divide a campaign's total gross rating points (GRPs) or target rating points (TRPs) by the number of on-air weeks, multiply the answer by four, and then calculate reach/frequency.

Average frequency   *See* frequency (average).

Average hours of viewing   The number of hours (and minutes) a household (or demographic group) views TV during a particular time frame, such as daily or weekly.

Average issue audience (readership)   The projected number of people who have read or looked into an average issue of a magazine. Audience reader figures are larger than circulation due to the fact that a single issue of a magazine has multiple readers. *Also see* readers per copy.

Average net paid circulation   The average number of copies of a publication sold per issue, as opposed to copies distributed free to recipients.

Average quarter hour (AQH)   An estimate of the percentage of an audience exposed to the typical 15-minute segment across all such segments within a broader daypart. Depending on the research method used, a person is counted as a listener or viewer if she or he tuned in for at least three to five minutes within a quarter-hour segment.

Average time spent listening (TSL)   The time spent listening to radio by the average listener.

Awareness   A measure of a person's knowledge of an advertisement, commercial, company, product, or service. *Also see* **1.** aided recall, **2.** top-of-mind awareness, **3.** unaided recall.

Baby boomers   People born between 1946–1964. *Also see* Generation X, Y, Z.

Backbone   **1.** The Internet's high-speed data highway that serves as a major access point other networks can connect to. **2.** The outside edge of a book, booklet, brochure, catalog, or magazine where pages are bound and where the title (or other material) may be printed.

Back cover   The outside back cover of a magazine. A magazine has four covers: front, inside front (commonly called second cover), inside back cover (third cover), and back cover (fourth cover).

Back-end/front-end   A front-end computer application or program is one a user interacts with directly; a back-end is one that supports the front end service.

Back issue   An issue of a magazine or newspaper that was published prior to the current issue.

Backlit   An out-of-home display (kiosk, poster, taxi-top) where the advertising message is printed on translucent plastic (or other material) and backlit with lights.

Back of book   Refers to the back section of a magazine—that is, any pages after the first 50 percent of pages. Advertising appearing in the back of the magazine was believed to garner lower readership scores because "main" editorial items appeared in the first half of a magazine. Most publishers have since reformatted editorial material to carry through the magazine whereby feature editorial items also appear in the second 50 percent of the magazine, or those articles beginning in the first 50 percent of pages carry over into the second half. This has had a demonstrable effect on readership. There is virtually no difference in readership scores for ads appearing in the first half versus the second half. It does appear, however, that ads placed in and near related editorial improves ad readership scores—for example, placing an ad for food near food editorial.

Back-to-back commercials   Commercials scheduled consecutively without programming interruptions.

Backup space   Advertising space in a magazine that is placed next to an insert—for example, a coupon, return card, or recipe book that has been bound into the magazine.

Bait and switch   An illegal tactic in which a seller advertises a product with the intention of persuading customers to purchase a more expensive product.

Balance sheet   An itemized statement that lists the total assets and the total liabilities of a given business to portray its net worth at a given moment of time. The amounts shown on a balance sheet are generally the historic cost of items and not their current values.

Band   A specific range of radio frequencies. Very low frequencies range from 3 to 30 kilohertz (kHz) and are used for time signals. Low frequencies range from 30 to 300 kHz and are used for navigational systems and radio broadcasting. Medium frequencies range from 300 to 3,000 kHz and are used for maritime mobile and radio broadcasting. High frequencies range from 3 to 30 megahertz (MHz) and are used for amateur radio and radio broadcasting. Very high frequencies range from 30 to 300 MHz and are used for TV broadcasting. Ultra high frequencies range from 300 to 3,000 MHz and are used for radio and TV broadcasting. Super high frequencies range from 3 to 30 gigahertz (GHz) and are used for satellite communication. Extremely high frequencies range from 30 to 300 GHz and are used for earth and space exploration. Amplitude modulation radio operates within a band of 535 kHz to 1.7 MHz; frequency modulation radio within 88 to 108 MHz; shortwave radio within 5.9 to 26.1 MHz; Citizen's Band Radio within 26.96 to 27.41 MHz; TV channels 2 to 6 within 54 to 88 MHz; TV channels 7 to 13 within 174 to 220 MHz. *Also see* 1. baseband, 2. bandwidth, 3. C-band, 4. Ka-band, 5. Ku-band, 6. narrowband, 7. wideband.

Bandwidth   1. The range of electromagnetic frequencies a transmission line or channel can carry, or the amount of data that can be transmitted in a fixed amount of time—that is, how fast data can flow on a given transmission. For digital devices, the bandwidth is usually expressed in bits per second (bps), such as kilobits per second (kbps), megabits per second (Mbps), and gigabits per second (Gbps). For example, a modem that works at 58 kbps is twice as fast as one that works at 29 kbps. For analog devices, the bandwidth is expressed in cycles per second, or hertz (Hz). For example, the higher fidelity of FM radio takes 10 times as much bandwidth per station as does AM radio. TV channels require 33 times more bandwidth than FM radio. The higher the frequency, the higher the bandwidth and therefore, the greater the capacity of a channel to carry information. 2. A measurement of the amount of time it takes for a Web page to fully load. *Also see* 1. narrowband, 2. wideband.

Banner ad   An advertisement on a Web page that typically links to an advertiser's website or buffer page. Ad banners are the most common unit of advertising on the Web. It is called a "banner" because the original online advertisements were always in the shape of a banner, usually at the top of a page. There are many sizes of online ad banners. *Also see* interactive marketing unit.

BAR   Broadcast Advertisers Reports. *See* TNS Media Intelligence/ CMR.

Bar code   A series of lines and spaces affixed to retail items, postal addresses, and other similar items that identify the product, price, location, and other necessary information for the item, and can be read by a computer. *See* Universal Product Code.

Barter   The exchange of goods and services without the use of cash, such as the acquisition of media time or space in exchange for merchandise. The purchaser of bartered media sometimes sells commercials or ads in the media, usually at a profit.

Barter show   A TV program that an advertiser or its agent offers to a TV station free of charge in lieu of payment for commercial announcements during the program or elsewhere during the broadcast day.

Barter syndication   An arrangement between syndicators, advertisers, and stations in which the syndication company acquires the rights to a program, sells commercial positions within the program to national advertisers, and places the program on a noninterconnected network of TV stations. The term *barter* comes into play because the syndicator typically gives a local station commercial availabilities within the program, which the local station can sell; the syndicator and the local station trade goods for services instead of using cash. Unlike network TV programs, syndicated programs can air at different times or days from market to market. "Jeopardy," "Wheel of Fortune," and "The Oprah Winfrey Show" are examples of syndicated properties.

Base   1. In media research, the number of survey respondents from whom projections are made. For example, Nielsen Media Research has a sample base of approximately 5,000 homes in the United States from which it projects national TV ratings. 2. In media planning, base is the target market universe that serves as a point of reference for evaluating media vehicle performance. For example, the base of 100,000 women population in market X can be used to calculate a medium's reach of that target in that market.

Baseband   Electronic transmission of digital signals carried on a single un-multiplexed channel. *Also see* **1.** broadband, **2.** narrowband, **3.** wideband.

Base rate   *See* open rate.

BASIC   One of the earliest and simplest computer programming languages. It is an acronym for Beginner's All-purpose Symbolic Instruction Code.

Basic cable   The offering to subscribers of broadcast and cable-TV originated programs as part of a basic service agreement in which a subscriber pays a cable TV operator or system a monthly fee. It does not include "pay" services that might be offered by the cable operator, such as HBO.

Basic input-output system (BIOS)   The basic set of instructions that tell a computer how to act. It is built-in software that determines what a computer can do without accessing programs from a disk. It is often called a ROM BIOS.

Baud rate   The speed of a digital code. The baud rate of a modem is how many bits it can send or receive per second. Bits per second (bps) is now the more common term for baud rate.

BB   *See* billboard.

BCC   *See* blind carbon copy.

BCFM   *See* Broadcast Cable Financial Management Association.

B channel   An integrated services digital network (ISDN) channel used to carry voice or data connections at 56 or 64 kilobits per second (kbps).

B counties   *See* Nielsen county size groups.

BDI   *See* brand development index.

BDS   *See* Nielsen Broadcast Data Systems.

Beautiful music   *See* easy listening.

Bell curve Also called normal distribution, it is the curved shape of a graph that is highest in the middle and lowest on the sides, resembling a bell. If U.S. population and income were graphed with population counts on the y-axis (vertical) and income levels on the x-axis (horizontal), the resulting picture would be a bell curve with the majority of the population falling within the middle income groups and small portion of the populations polarized at the low and high income levels. *Also see* S curve.

Below the fold 1. Advertising or editorial content on a Web page that can only be seen if the user scrolls down. 2. Ad or edit content that appears in the bottom half of a standard-size newspaper. *Also see* above the fold.

Benchmark 1. A standard by which something can be measured or judged. 2. The average media costs paid by all advertisers, or by all advertisers within a particular product or service category, against which an advertiser's costs are compared. SQAD (Service Quality Analytics Data) costs, for example, are used for radio and television benchmarks. An advertiser can also conduct its own research to determine media costs paid by other advertisers, although this rarely occurs since the majority of advertisers are reluctant to reveal their media costs. 3. The media costs paid by an advertiser for a previous campaign(s). In this case, the advertiser is comparing current or future media costs to the costs it paid for a past media effort. Relative costs changes are then compared to industry averages using, for example, SQAD indicators or advertising industry trade press estimates of marketplace conditions. 4. An initial research study or media plan that serves as a standard by which all other studies and plans can be measured and compared.

Bespoke A term used in the United Kingdom that signifies a custom-made or proprietary product or service.

Best food day The day on which a newspaper carries the majority of its weekly food and grocery advertising and editorial. The day is determined by the shopping habits of the people in the newspaper's market and can therefore vary from market to market, albeit Wednesday and Thursday seem to be the prominent best food days.

Best practices   The optimal philosophies, processes, strategies, or tactics used by a business to manage its company.

Beta test   The second test of the experimental product or service, carried out by an outside organization and not the creator. The first test of an experimental product or service, which is carried out by the creator, is known as an alpha test.

Bias   A statistical error in research findings caused by the favoring of some outcomes over others as a result of the order or wording of questions, or by an interviewer's statement to the interviewee.

Biased sample   A research study sample of people that is not representative of the population universe being measured.

Billboard   1. Free (usually) airtime, generally five seconds long, given to an advertiser as part of a package of airtime that the advertiser has purchased. It is typically noted on contracts and printed schedules as "BB." Billboards are a popular "add-on" given to advertisers that sponsor a TV or radio program (i.e., advertisers that have purchased multiple commercials within a program). Often, a billboard is considered added value in a media buy. Some media buyers and planners place a rating point value on billboards and count them toward the achievement of goals. Two methods are used: (1) giving a billboard the same rating as the program in which it appears, or (2) reducing the program rating relative to the proportion that the five seconds represents vis-à-vis a 30-second commercial. Some find either method of valuing a billboard a spurious undertaking. 2. A large-format out-of-home advertising display intended for viewing from extended distances, generally from more than 50 feet. Billboard displays include, but are not limited to, 30-sheet posters, 8-sheet posters, vinyl-wrapped posters, bulletins, wall murals, and stadium or arena signage.

Billboard alley   *See* clutter.

Binary numbers   A numbering system known for its "0" and "1" (or on/off) representation. By comparison, decimal numbers have a base of 10, measurements of feet and inches have a base of 12, and time has a base of 60. Binary numbers are preferred for computers because using them is easier and less expensive than building circuits that detect the difference among 10 states, as with decimals.

Bind-in card   An insert card in a magazine that is bound in with the printed pages. *Also called* a tip-in card. *Also see* blow-in card.

Bingo card   *See* reader service card.

BIOS   *See* basic input-output system.

Bit   The basic unit of information in a binary numbering system. Basic high/low, either/or, yes/no units of information are called bits. Eight bits comprise what is called an octet, but is commonly referred to as a byte. A kilobit (kb) is 1,000 bits, a megabit is 1 million bits, and a gigabit is 1 billion bits. Bit is commonly used when referring to data transfer speeds in a telecommunications system, while byte is used to express the amount of computer storage (memory) or disk capacity.

Bitmap   Any picture seen on a Web page is a bitmap. Bitmaps come in many file formats such as BMP, DIB, GIF, JPEG, TIFF, PCX, and PICT.

Bit rate   The speed at which data travels from one place to another on a computer network such as the Internet. It is usually measured in kilobits per second (kbps).

Bits per second (bps)   The rate of data or information that moves in and out of a modem. If a user is operating at 30.0, he or she is moving 30,000 bps.

Bitstream   The flow of data across, over, and through a computer network. *Also see* clickstream.

Biz (.biz)   *See* domain name.

Black and white (page)   An advertisement that is printed with black ink on (usually) white paper, or in reverse type (white on black paper). Abbreviated as PB/W. Smaller black-and-white ads are notated accordingly, such as 1/2 PB/W.

Black box   A computer program, research model, or software that gives answers (outputs) based on the user's input, but does not reveal to the user how the program, model, or software arrived at those answers. The black box creator opts to keep the "how" a secret.

Blackout   A contractual agreement that a sports league imposes to prohibit a local TV station or cable channel from providing live coverage of a sports event. This is to ensure that attendance at the sport's venue will not suffer as a result of the event being broadcast.

Black/rhythm & blues   A radio programming format whose descriptive term has never had a clear, single meaning. In its broadest sense, the format denotes black pop music. However, as black pop music changes, it has become a term that is often defined by whatever black musical style it is attached to at a given point in time, rather than vice versa. *Also see* rhythm and blues.

Blanket contract   A written agreement between an advertiser and a media vehicle covering all products to be advertised. It is also known as a master contract.

Blanket coverage   A statement, even if not technically correct, that a medium or media vehicle totally covers a specific geographic area. For example, if a newspaper claims blanket coverage of its market, it indicates that nearly all, if not all, neighborhoods in the market receive (purchase) the newspaper.

Blanking   On outdoor posters, a white paper border applied between an advertisement's copy area and the panel molding. Although not obsolete, it soon will be, as more and more units are posted with wraparound vinyl or are fully papered within the poster frame.

Blank out   Covering an out-of-home painted bulletin advertising message in preparation for a new advertisement. *Also called* coat out and paint out.

Bleed   1. To extend the illustration or copy to the edge of a page so there is no white border. 2. An out-of-home poster panel that uses the entire available space.

Bleed in the gutter   *See* gutter bleed.

Blind carbon copy (BCC)   A copy of a memorandum or e-mail that is sent to a specific recipient, but whose name and address do not appear on the copies received by the other recipients to whom the memo or e-mail is addressed. *Also see* carbon copy.

Blind test   A research technique that is used to evaluate packaging or a product and does not reveal the brand name to the respondent. The respondent does not have to be blind.

Blitz   *See* saturation.

Block   A time segment of consecutive hours in a broadcast advertising schedule.

Block group   As defined by the Census Bureau, a block group is a combination of census blocks. The total number of block groups delineated for the 1990 decennial census was 229,466. *Also see* 1. block numbering areas, 2. census areas, 3. census tracts.

Block numbering areas   Geographic entities similar to census tracts and delineated in counties (or the statistical equivalent of counties) without census tracts. For the 1990 decennial census, the Census Bureau recognized 11,586 block numbering areas in the United States, Puerto Rico, and the outlying areas under the U.S. jurisdiction (American Samoa, Guam, the Northern Mariana Islands, Palau, and the Virgin Islands of the United States). *Also see* 1. block group, 2. census areas, 3. census blocks.

Block programming   Scheduling TV or radio programs of similar appeal and therefore directed to similar demographic groups (audiences) within a two- to four-hour time period.

Blow-in card   A loose (not bound in or glued to) insert of an advertising message in a magazine, used primarily by the publication to sell subscriptions (or subscription renewals), but which advertisers can also use. *Also see* bind-in card.

Blues   A radio programming format with roots in rural black America where music was used to communicate the trials and tribulations of life.

BMA   *See* Business Marketing Association.

Bmp (or .bmp)   *See* bitmap.

Bold listing   A unit in a Yellow Pages directory in which the company name is printed in bold letters (bold font).

Bonus circulation   The circulation of a publication that is greater than the circulation generally delivered by the publication. Advertisers are not charged for this additional circulation. The circulation generally delivered by the publication is based, for example, on audit reports (such as those conducted by the Audit Bureau of Circulations).

Bonus spot   A commercial given to an advertiser by a media vehicle free of charge to make up for underdelivered audience, or as an inducement to buy additional spots or in appreciation of past buys placed with the media vehicle.

Bookends   Two TV spots of one advertiser (often :15 [15-second spot]) placed within a commercial pod but separated from each other by other commercials. Two :15s scheduled as bookends command a media cost equal to that of a :30—there is no cost premium for separating the commercials. The supposed media advantage is that the advertiser has two chances of reaching the targeted audience instead of one. It can also be argued that the advertiser has a better chance of reaching a consumer who might be channel switching during a commercial break. Reach/frequency calculations favor frequency in the former case and reach in the latter case. Some media planners double the target rating points (TRPs) for bookend schedules when calculating reach and frequency. For example (and hypothetically), if a schedule of 100 TRPs (all :30s) yields a 50/2.0, a schedule of 100 TRPs in all :15 bookends will tally 200 TRPs and will yield either a 50/4.0 (the reach is held constant and the frequency is doubled) or a 60/1.7 (the reach is calculated for 200 TRPs and frequency calculated within a 100 TRP level). Because there is no research to determine the exact reach/frequency of a bookend schedule, some media planners opt to average the two preceding methods, hypothetically recording the delivery at a 55 reach with a 3.6 frequency. Stations and networks cannot always guarantee that bookend commercials will necessarily air as the first and last commercial within a pod, but they can guarantee that the two commercials will be separated by other commercials.

Bookmark   Another term for the "favorites" that appear at the top of a computer screen when accessing the Web. A bookmark is a website or Web page that a user has saved in order to quickly access it again.

Boolean logic   A mathematical system that uses the words AND, OR, NOT, and IF . . . THEN to sort data. It is used on most search engines to find relevant information based on inputting keywords. For example, a search for "information OR retrieval" will produce documents containing the words "information" or "retrieval"; a search for "information AND retrieval" will produce documents containing both words.

Boosters   Low-powered transmitters that pick up the signal of a parent station and instantly retransmit the signal on the same channel. Broadcast stations use boosters when coverage from the main station is not adequate, such as in mountainous terrain. Also referred to as a repeater station.

Boot up   The process of turning on a computer, which includes many functions that happen automatically once the power switch is turned on.

Bottom-up   Analyzing a subject or creating a media plan starting from the lowest level and working toward the top. For example, a national bottom-up media plan is created by first planning local market efforts and then adding national media (if needed and affordable). *Also see* top-down.

Boutique advertising agency   An organization that specializes in the creative portion of the advertising process and does not typically offer other services such as media planning or media buying. *Also see* 1. advertising agency, 2. media agency.

Boxcar numbers   A big number or large quantity of items. The related reference is to the number of items found in a railroad freight car.

BPA International   A global provider of audited data to the marketing, media, and information industries. Founded in 1931 by a group of publishers, advertisers, and agencies. BPA is an independent, nonprofit, self-regulating organization governed by a tripartite board of directors. Audited data presently includes circulation of print publications, website traffic, newspapers, trade shows, industry databases, wireless communication, and other advertising-supported information providers. For business publications and consumer magazines, BPA International verifies all-paid, all-controlled, or any combination of paid and controlled circulation. Website: bpai.com

Bps   *See* bits per second.

Brand awareness   Consumers' knowledge of an existing product's or service's name, its attributes, or both. Brand awareness measures are typically obtained from a sampling of the population by using various research techniques, such as telephone interviews or written questionnaires. Brand awareness research usually contains data for the advertiser conducting the research as well as one or more of the advertiser's competitors. More often than not, the research also probes on product attributes. The research findings guide advertisers in anything from formulating marketing or advertising strategies, to creative strategies, to media planning and buying.

Brand development index (BDI)   A numerical display showing the geographic areas or demographic segments of a brand's relative strength or weakness. The relativity is gauged by the numerical distance from 100, where 100 represents the "average" market or demographic. It is calculated by dividing the percentage of sales in a market by the percentage of population represented by that market. For example, if market A accounts for 20 percent of the population in a brand's geographic universe (i.e., the total geography in which a brand is distributed) and 25 percent of total sales, the BDI is 125 [(25 percent ÷ 20 percent) × 100]. Market A therefore is 25 percent above average. Likewise, if the percentages are reversed wherein market A represents 25 percent of population and 20 percent of sales, the BDI is 80 [(20 percent ÷ 25 percent) × 100]. With BDI, population is the base and sales are the variable being evaluated. Calculating BDI allows for quick visual scanning of markets to see which are average, above average, and below average, and by what magnitude. Note that BDI numbers are void of decimal places and are rounded to the nearest whole number. Using decimals defeats the purpose of easy visual scanning. All BDI calculations require that sales and population must equal 100 percent for all markets combined (i.e., putting both sets of data within the same geographic universe). Often, BDI is used in conjunction with a CDI (category development index) analysis.

Formula:

[(market A brand sales as a percentage of total universe sales) ÷ (market A population as a percentage of total universe population)] × 100 = BDI

Examples:

(10 percent ÷ 20 percent) × 100 = 50 (decimal and percentage sign deleted)

(10 percent ÷ 5 percent) × 100 = 200

BRC   *See* business reply card.

Break   The time within or between radio or television programs when non-programming material appears, such as commercials and tune-in promotions. From a media buyer's perspective, however, a break typically refers to the time between two TV programs or at the half-hour point of a one-hour-or-longer TV program. *Also see* in-program.

Break-even analysis   A method to determine the quantity of items (e.g., products sold, revenue) to reach a break-even point in a business.

Break-even point   The volume point at which revenue and costs are equal, thereby producing no profit or loss.

Break position   A TV commercial aired between programs as opposed to in-program. *Also called* adjacency.

Broadband   A type of data transmission in which a single medium (wire) can carry video, voice, and data simultaneously. Cable TV, for example, uses broadband transmission. In contrast, baseband transmission allows only one signal at a time. Broadband channels are carried on coaxial or fiber-optic cables and have a wider bandwidth than conventional telephone lines. Broadband operates at rates of 1.544 megabits per second (Mbps) or higher, compared to the slower narrowband, which typically operates at 64 kilobits per second (kbps) or less, and wideband, which operates at speeds ranging from 64 kbps to 1.544 Mbps. *Also see* baseband.

Broadcast   Any radio or television program sent out over the airwaves for public or general use. Broadcast TV programs can be received on a TV set whether or not the set is equipped with cable TV.

Broadcast Advertisers Reports   *See* TNS Media Intelligence/CMR.

Broadcast Cable Financial Management Association (BCFM)   A professional society of over 1,200 radio/TV financial, management information systems, and human resource executives, plus associates in auditing, data processing, software development, credit, and collections. Website: bcfm.com

Broadcast calendar   An industry-accepted 52- to 53-week (depending on the year), 12-month calendar used for developing media schedules, for making radio or TV media buys, and for media vendors to bill advertisers. It is composed of four- or five-week months: each week begins on a Monday, and the month ends on the last Sunday of the month.

Broadcast coverage area   The geographic area within which a signal from an originating radio or TV station can be received. The total area covered is a function of a station's signal strength, tower location, booster use, and surrounding terrain.

Broadcast data systems (BDS)   Name changed. *See* broadcast verification system.

Broadcasting   Transmission of over-the-air radio or TV signals for public use, as opposed to transmission via cable TV, which is not over the air.

Broadcast month   *See* broadcast calendar.

Broadcast network   *See* network.

Broadcast verification system (BVS)   A system of tracking any television broadcasted material including commercials, video news releases, promos, public service announcements, and programs. BVS encodes TV commercials using VEIL (video encoded invisible light) technology. Among other uses, this service provides overnight verification, allowing advertisers to detect exactly when their commercials aired, and to track the effectiveness of direct response campaigns (assuming the data is tied into a database of consumer calls). It is a product of TNS Media Intelligence/CMR (Competitive Media Reporting).

Broadcast week   *See* broadcast calendar.

Broadsheet   Synonymous with a "standard" size newspaper (e.g., *Chicago Tribune*), as compared to a "tabloid" size (e.g., *Chicago Sun-Times*).

Browser   Software that allows a user to navigate the World Wide Web. A browser is as integral to the presentation of data on the Web as a TV set is in making sense of NTSC (National Standards Television Committee) signals.

B2B   Business-to-business (marketing or advertising).

B2C   Business-to-consumer (marketing or advertising).

Buffering   Occurs when a streaming media player saves portions of a streaming media file until there is enough information for the stream to begin playing.

Buffer page   A Web page that appears after a user clicks on an ad banner, which either gives more information about the advertisement (or offer) or connects the user to the advertiser's home page.

Bulk circulation   Two or more copies of a magazine or newspaper sent to a single addressee who, in turn, distributes individual copies.

Bulk discount   A cost discount offered to advertisers who place large space or time orders in a medium.

Bulk sales   Quantity sales of a publication to one purchaser.

Bulldog edition   The daily newspaper's morning edition that is usually distributed the night before its issue date. It can also refer to sections of the Sunday edition that are printed and distributed prior to the Sunday issue.

Bulletin   A standard outdoor format commonly measuring 14 feet by 48 feet in overall size. It is sold either as a permanent display or in rotary packages. Bulletin copy can be rendered using hand-painting techniques, computer production, or printing on paper.

Bump rate   The cost that must be paid by an advertiser to secure a radio or TV commercial position previously sold to another advertiser. To bump (replace) the previous advertiser, the new advertiser must pay a higher rate than paid by the original advertiser.

Bundled (media) deals   The purchase of advertising space or time in two or more media forms (e.g., print and TV) from a media conglomerate that owns multiple media forms. It is akin to a multi-platform deal but involves only media forms as opposed to nonmedia elements (e.g., a promotion).

Burke Test   A research tool, designed by Burke Marketing Research, Inc., that measures audience recall of a commercial message—for example, DAR: Day After Recall.

Burner   *See* CD burner.

Burn rate   The rate at which a company uses up its capital to finance overhead before generating positive cash flow from operations.

Bus   A local area network (LAN) in which all the nodes are connected to a single cable.

Bus bench   An advertising message affixed to a freestanding bench, often located at a bus stop.

Business Marketing Association (BMA)   Started in 1922 and known as the National Industrial Advertising Association, BMA is a service organization for business-to-business professionals. Website: marketing.org

Business news   A radio-programming format that is similar to news or news/talk but oriented to business and financial subjects.

Business Publication Audit of Circulation   *See* BPA International.

Business Publication Audit Report   *See* Audit Bureau of Circulations.

Business Publisher's Statement   *See* Audit Bureau of Circulations.

Business reply card (BRC)   A preaddressed and (usually) prepaid, postcard-type response mechanism that is inserted in magazines or newspapers, allowing the consumer to fill out necessary information (name, address, etc.) and conveniently mail it to the advertiser.

Bus shelter   Advertising posters positioned as an integral part of a freestanding covered structure or bench, often located at a bus stop.

Button ad   A small advertising unit found on a Web page. It is usually a graphic (of any shape, including a circle that resembles a button) that a user can click on to do something, such as download a program or be automatically connected to another Web page or website. Also refers to a small ad banner. *Also see* interactive marketing unit.

Buyer's market   A media marketplace environment in which there is relatively less demand for advertising time or space and media buyers are able to negotiate for lower media costs. It is the opposite of a seller's market.

Buying guidelines   The parameters outlined for an impending media purchase. Guidelines are typically devised by the media planner based on what the planner believes are important specifications for the buyer to fulfill in order that the buy be as effective as possible. Guidelines vary from one medium to another, from one advertiser to another, and sometimes from one period of time to another. For example, they might include the amount of target rating points (TRPs) by daypart, programming requirements or restrictions, day of the week requirements, magazine editorial priorities, or positioning requirements.

Buying service   (Almost obsolete) A company that primarily buys and plans media, as opposed to an advertising agency, which generally also offers creative development and other services. *Also see* media agency.

Buying specifications   Also known as buy specs. *See* buying guidelines.

Buying target   The media audience segment(s) against which a media buy is directed—for example, adults ages 18 to 49. A buying target can be different from the planning target (as specified in a media plan), because the research used to execute a buy might not be as rich in detail as the research used to plan a buy. For example, TV program formats can be analyzed based on audience lifestyle characteristics (using, for example, Mediamark Research, Inc.), but lifestyle audience delivery is not available in Nielsen's program ratings data. *Also see* target audience.

Buyout   1. The same thing as a 100 percent sponsorship: buying all commercial positions in a radio or TV program. 2. A onetime payment to talent appearing in commercials or advertisements that grants the advertiser unlimited use of the commercials in which the talent appears without further talent payments. *Also see* residual.

BVS   *See* broadcast verification system.

B/W   *See* black and white (page).

Byte   A unit of computer storage consisting of (usually) eight bits or binary digits. A kilobyte (KB) is 1,024 bytes, a megabyte (MB) is 1,024 KBs, a gigabyte (G or GB) is 1,024 MBs, a terabyte is 1,024 Gs, a petabyte is 1,024 terabytes, and an exabyte is 1,024 petabytes. Byte is used to express the amount of computer storage (memory) or disk capacity, while bit is commonly used when referring to data transfer speeds in a telecommunications system.

C *See* computer programming language.

CAB *See* Cabletelevision Advertising Bureau.

Cable and Telecommunications Association of Marketing (CTAM)
An industry organization dedicated to the discipline and development of consumer marketing excellence in cable TV, new media, and telecommunications services. Website: ctam.com

Cablecasting As distinguished from broadcasting, this is programming originated by cable networks or cable systems that is delivered to cable subscribers.

Cable FM *See* low power radio.

Cable interconnect *See* interconnect.

Cable modem (CM) A device, usually located at the cable TV subscriber's home, that hooks up the subscriber's computer with a local cable TV line to receive data at a very high speed (typically 1.5 megabits per second). *Also see* **1.** digital subscriber line, **2.** data over cable service interface specifications, **3.** integrated services digital network.

Cable modem termination system (CMTS) The component that is part of a head end, which exchanges digital signals with cable modems on a cable network.

Cable network   *See* network.

Cable nonduplication rule   A Federal Communications Commission rule requiring cable operators to blackout the network programming of a distant affiliate (i.e., an affiliate located outside of the cable operator's home market).

Cable operators   The person or company responsible for owning, maintaining, and operating the cable TV system(s) in one or more communities.

Cable penetration   The percentage of TV households that subscribe to cable TV within a given geographic area (e.g., a designated market area or the United States at large).

CableQ   *See* Marketing Evaluations/TvQ.

Cable-ready   A TV set with built-in circuitry that enables it to receive and translate cable signals without the use of a separate converter (box).

Cable television   Reception of TV signals via cable (wires) rather than over the air (via a TV antenna). Cable TV in the United States began in the late 1940s as a means of providing a TV signal, or an improved signal, to households in areas unable to receive over-the-air signals. These households were generally located in mountainous regions where the topography interfered with normal transmission. The cable operator built a high antenna designed to receive signals from the closest TV stations. The name at that time was fitting: community antenna television (CATV). No records were kept on how many CATV operations were in existence until 1952, at which time there were only 70 systems servicing 14,000 subscribers. In 2002, about 11,000 systems were servicing over 75 million subscribing homes.

Cabletelevision Advertising Bureau (CAB)   An industry organization that represents ad-supported cable networks and most cable systems that accept advertising. It was founded in 1981 when only 30 percent of U.S. homes had cable TV. In 2002, cable penetration was at 75 percent of U.S. homes. The CAB provides information and resources to the advertising community to support their marketing and media planning. Website: cabletvadbureau.com

Cable television relay services (CTRS)   A microwave frequency band used to relay cablecasting, FM radio, TV, and other band signals from their original site to the cable head end for distribution over the cable system.

Cable TV system   A nonbroadcast facility that has a legal license and technological equipment designed to distribute signals of one or more TV stations and other nonbroadcast services (e.g., network cable programming) to one or more homes within a defined geographic area.

CAC   *See* Certified Audit of Circulations.

Cache   The area of a computer's memory that stores frequently used data to speed up viewing time on a computer.

Caching   The process of copying material from a Web page (text, graphic, etc.) for later reuse.

CACI Marketing Systems   A research company that provides data for many industries, nonprofits, and government agencies. The industry-specific marketing applications, products, and services include customer profiling and segmentation, custom target analysis, demographic data reports and maps, direct-mail campaign implementation, media planning, merchandise mix analysis, site evaluation and selection, and target marketing. CACI products include the ACORN segmentation study, which is licensed to ESRI. Website: caci.com

Calendar year   The 12 months from January 1 through December 31, as opposed to a fiscal year, which is any 12-month period defined by a company in which accounts are balanced.

Call letters   A radio or television station's identification, such as WGN-TV. The Federal Communications Commission regulates that the first letter of stations located east of the Mississippi River be a *W* and for stations west of the Mississippi a *K* (although there are exceptions for stations that began to broadcast before the FCC assignments). Station call letters beginning with the letter *X* broadcast from Mexico; those beginning with the letter *C* broadcast from Canada.

Camera ready   A complete print advertisement, including artwork, photography, and copy, that is ready for photographic reproduction.

Campaign   An advertising effort for a product or service over a given period of time.

Campbell Soup position   The first right-hand, four-color page advertisement in magazines following the main body of editorial. It was so named because for many years the Campbell Soup Company purchased this position.

Cancellation   To terminate a scheduled media buy.

Carbon copy (cc)   A copy of a memorandum or e-mail sent to a recipient who is not the main (or primary) recipient. It is sometimes abbreviated as "fcc" for first carbon copy. The term originated when mechanical typewriters were used. Paper was inserted into a typewriter with a sheet of "inked" paper (called carbon paper) between each piece of blank paper. Typing on the top page would produce copies (carbon copies) on the succeeding pages. *Also see* blind carbon copy.

Car card   In transit advertising, an advertisement displayed, for example, inside a bus, train, or subway car.

Card pack   A cooperative mailing of postage-paid business reply cards returned to advertisers who share the costs of mailing the card pack to potential buyers.

Carpal tunnel syndrome (CTS)   A physical ailment in the wrist that is caused by the compression of a nerve in the carpal tunnel. It has been suggested that it may be linked to activities that require repetitive use of the hands, such as typing.

Carriage   The procedure used by cable systems to carry TV broadcasting signals on its various channels. The Federal Communications Commission regulates which signals may or must be carried.

Carrier-current   *See* low power radio.

Carryover   *See* adstock.

CARS   *See* community antenna relay service.

Cart   A piece of equipment that holds scheduled TV commercials. Commercial tapes are received by a radio or TV station and transferred onto a cart. Commercials are computer generated from the cart and telecast or broadcast in their appropriate time slots. The cart operates independently from the programming feed.

CartoonQ   *See* Marketing Evaluations/TvQ.

CARU   *See* Children's Advertising Review Unit.

Cascade   A scheduling technique wherein high levels of media weight are scheduled during the initial week(s) of a campaign with succeeding weeks receiving decreasingly less weight. For example, in a four-week TV flight, a cascading schedule might include 200 target rating points (TRPs) in week one, 150 in week two, 100 in week three, and 50 in week four. The rationale driving this technique is that a new campaign must launch with high levels of media delivery to obtain high levels of reach, but can sustain with decreasingly lower levels that provide frequency—that is, "reminder" advertising.

Case allowance   A discount offered by a marketer to a retailer based on the number of purchased cases of a product.

Cash cow   A business or product that generates a steady, dependable flow of cash.

CASRO   *See* Council of American Survey Research Organizations.

Category development index (CDI)   A numerical display showing the geographic areas or demographic segments of a product category's or service category's relative strength or weakness (e.g., the beer category, financial services category). The relativity is gauged by the numerical distance from 100, where 100 represents the "average" market or demographic. It is calculated by dividing the percentage of category sales in a market by the percentage of population represented by that market. For example, if market A accounts for 20 percent of the population in a category's geographic universe (i.e., the total geography in which one or more brands in a category is distributed) and 25 percent of total sales, the CDI is 125 [(25 percent ÷ 20 percent) × 100]. Market A therefore is 25 percent above average. Likewise, if the percentages are reversed wherein market A represents 25 percent of population and 20 percent of sales, the CDI is 80 [(20 percent ÷ 25 percent) times 100]. With CDI, population is the base and sales is the variable that is being evaluated. Calculating CDI allows for quick visual scanning of markets to see which are average, above average, and below average, and to what magnitude. Note that CDI numbers are void of decimal places and are rounded to the nearest whole number. Using decimals defeats the purpose of easy visual scanning. All CDI calculations require that sales and population must equal 100 percent for all markets combined (i.e., putting both sets of data within the same geographic universe). Often, CDI is used in conjunction with a BDI (brand development index) analysis.

Formula:

[(market A category sales as a percentage of total universe sales) ÷ (market A population as a percentage of total universe population)] × 100 = CDI

Examples:

(10 percent ÷ 20 percent) × 100 = 50 (decimal and percentage sign deleted)

(10 percent ÷ 5 percent) × 100 = 200

Cathode ray tube (CRT)   A vacuum tube in which images are produced when an electron beam strikes a phosphorescent surface. It is the picture tube on a conventional TV set and computer monitor. *Also see* **1.** liquid crystal display, **2.** plasma screen.

CATV   Community antenna television. *See* cable television.

Cause related marketing   Linking the selling of a product or service to a specific cause (e.g., a charity).

CB   *See* Citizen's Band Radio.

C-band   A microwave range of frequencies operating between 3.7 and 4.2 gigahertz and used for distribution of programming by satellite and cable networks. *Also see* 1. Ka-band, 2. Ku-band.

CBB   *See* closing billboard.

CC   *See* 1. closed captioning, 2. closed-circuit TV, 3. carbon copy.

C counties   *See* Nielsen county size groups.

CD   *See* compact disc.

CD burner   An electronic device that can record data on a compact disc (CD), or copy the data on a CD onto another CD.

CDI   *See* category development index.

CDMA   *See* Code Division Multiple Access.

CDMA-One   *See* Code Division Multiple Access.

CDMA2000   *See* Code Division Multiple Access.

CD-ROM   *See* compact disc read-only memory.

Cellular   Anything characterized by, divided into, or containing cells or compartments, such as the cellular construction of a beehive. A cellular phone (known as a mobile phone in many parts of the world) uses a network of short-range transmitters located in overlapping cells.

Cellular Telecommunications Industry Association (CTIA)   The international organization that represents all elements of wireless communication—cellular, personal communication services, enhanced specialized mobile radio, and mobile satellite services—serving the interests of service providers, manufacturers, and others. It was founded in 1984.

Census   A complete canvassing of the population being studied, such as the U.S. Census.

Census areas   The Census Bureau defines specific geographic areas within the United States for which it reports various and sundry statistical data, such as for the decennial census. Several research companies use this geography-based data to segment the U.S. population into lifestyle clusters. The most commonly used geographic areas for media planning or media research are census blocks, block groups, census tracts, block numbering areas, metropolitan statistical areas, consolidated metropolitan statistical areas, primary metropolitan statistical areas, counties, states, regions, and the nation at large.

Census blocks   The smallest geographic areas for which the Census Bureau collects and tabulates decennial census data. They are formed by streets, roads, railroads, streams and other bodies of water, other visible physical and cultural features, and the legal boundaries shown on Census Bureau maps. For the 1990 decennial census, the Census Bureau tabulated data by census block for the entire nation, as well as Puerto Rico and the outlying areas (American Samoa, Guam, the Northern Mariana Islands, Palau, and the Virgin Islands of the United States)—a total of 7,020,924 census blocks. The next level above a census block (i.e., a larger geographic area) is a block group. *Also see* 1. block numbering areas, 2. census areas, 3. census tracts.

Census tracts   Census tracts are small, relatively permanent geographic entities within counties (or the statistical equivalent of counties) delineated by a committee of local data users. Generally, census tracts have between 2,500 and 8,000 residents, and boundaries that follow visible features. When first established, census tracts were to be as homogeneous as possible with respect to population characteristics, economic status, and living conditions. In the 1990 decennial census the Census Bureau recognized 50,690 census tracts in the United States, Puerto Rico, and the outlying areas under the U.S. jurisdiction (American Samoa, Guam, the Northern Mariana Islands, Palau, and the Virgin Islands of the United States). *Also see* 1. block group, 2. block numbering areas, 3. census areas, 4. census blocks.

Center for Media Research   An online source of research material, breaking market conditions, projectable data for media planning and buying, synthesized studies on topics of interest to buyers and planners, and links to identified sources and resource material. A product of MediaPost Communications. Website: mediapost.com

Center spread   The facing pages (usually advertising) in the exact center of a magazine. *Also see* double truck.

Central processing unit (CPU)   The CPU is a computer's brain and where most calculations take place. It is also commonly referred to as a microprocessor.

CEO   *See* C titles.

Certified Audit of Circulations (CAC)   Established in 1956 as a nonprofit circulation audit and research organization, the CAC serves publishers, advertisers, and advertising agencies. Website: certifiedaudit.com

Certified marketing representative   A person or company authorized by the Yellow Pages Integrated Media Association to sell Yellow Pages advertising space to national advertisers.

CFML   *See* ColdFusion Markup Language.

CFO   *See* C titles.

CGI   *See* common gateway interface.

Chain break   The time between network programs when a network-affiliated station identifies itself to viewers and during which commercial announcements usually air. Commercials, of course, also air at other times. *Also see* **1.** break, **2.** in-program.

Channel capacity The number of different channels of programming that a cable system technically can transmit to subscribing households.

Channel planning A marketing or media process for determining which "channels" will be used to communicate with consumers. The channels refer to the communications channels (i.e., the course or pathway through which information—advertising—will be transmitted), such as various types of media (direct mail, Internet, magazines, newspapers, on-site media, radio, TV), packaging, public relations, in-store displays, or movie product placement.

Channel surfing Perusing different TV channels, usually with a remote control device and generally stopping at each channel for a very short period of time.

Chat room A computer facility that allows two or more users in separate locations to communicate with each other in real time. It is akin to instantaneous back-and-forth e-mail.

Checkerboard **1.** A varied lineup of TV programs during the same time period on consecutive days. **2.** A print advertisement intermingled with editorial matter in which the appearance of the page is similar to a checkerboard pattern.

Checking copy A copy of a magazine or newspaper that is sent to an advertiser as proof that the ad ran in the publication in the requested position. *Also called* a tear sheet.

Children's Advertising Review Unit (CARU) Part of the Council of Better Business Bureaus, CARU reviews advertising and promotional material directed at children in all media, and online privacy practices as they affect children. When these are found to be misleading, inaccurate, or inconsistent with CARU's Self-Regulatory Guidelines for Children's Advertising, CARU seeks change through the voluntary cooperation of advertisers. Website: caru.org

Children's Online Privacy Protection Act of 1998 (COPPA)   A congressional act to prohibit unfair or deceptive acts or practices in connection with the collection, use, or disclosure of personally identifiable information on the Internet from and about children under 13 years old. The act requires operators of websites directed to children and operators who knowingly collect personal information from children to (1) provide parents notice of their information practices; (2) obtain prior verifiable parental consent for the collection, use, or disclosure of personal information from children (with certain limited exceptions for the collection of "online contact information," such as an e-mail address); (3) provide a parent, upon request, with the means to review the personal information collected from his or her child; (4) provide a parent with the opportunity to prevent the further use of personal information that has already been collected, or the future collection of personal information from that child; (5) limit collection of personal information for a child's online participation in a game, prize offer, or other activity to information that is reasonably necessary for the activity; and (6) establish and maintain reasonable procedures to protect the confidentiality, security, and integrity of the personal information collected.

Children's Online Privacy Protection Rule (COPPR)   Issued by the Federal Trade Commission in October 1999, the Children's Online Privacy Protection Rule went into effect on April 21, 2000. It implements the requirements of the COPPA by requiring operators of websites or online services directed to children, and operators of websites or online services who have actual knowledge that the person from whom they seek information is a child, to (1) post prominent links on their websites to a notice of how they collect, use, or disclose personal information from children; (2) with certain exceptions, notify parents that they wish to collect information from their children and obtain parental consent prior to collecting, using, or disclosing such information; (3) not condition a child's participation in online activities on the provision of more personal information than is reasonably necessary to participate in the activity; (4) allow parents the opportunity to review and have their children's information deleted from the operator's database and to prohibit further collection from the child; and (5) establish procedures to protect the confidentiality, security, and integrity of personal information they collect from children.

CHR *See* contemporary hit radio.

Christian A radio-programming format composed of Christian rock, gospel, choral and instrumental music, and information or teaching.

Cinema advertising Advertising on-screen in movie theaters.

CIO *See* C titles.

Cipher text *See* encryption.

Circular A special advertising supplement inserted in a newspaper or mailed directly to a consumer.

Circulation 1. The number of copies sold or distributed by a publication. 2. The number of homes owning a radio or TV set within a station's coverage area. 3. The number of households that subscribe to the cable service that carries particular networks. 4. The number of people who pass an out-of-home advertisement and who have an opportunity to see it.

Citizen's Band Radio (CB) A two-way voice communication service for use in personal and business activities with a communication range of up to five miles. *Also see* amateur radio.

City zone The geographic area bounded by the corporate limits of a community. It is usually used when analyzing newspaper circulation.

Claritas A marketing information resources company servicing companies engaged in consumer and business-to-business marketing. Claritas provides targeted and measurable marketing programs and enterprise-wide technology solutions. Founded in 1971, it is owned by VNU. Website: claritas.com

Class A, B, C   *See* radio, types of stations.

Classical   A radio programming format featuring symphonic, chamber, operatic, and show music.

Classic country   A radio programming format of traditional country music, often featuring bluegrass and older works by established performers.

Classic hits   A radio programming format that is essentially Top 40 music from the 1970s and 1980s, without disco or dance music.

Classic rock (CR)   A radio programming format that primarily includes popular rock hits of the 1970s, 1980s, and 1990s.

Classified advertising   Advertising that usually appears in newspapers, but can appear in magazines, online, and other media, and is arranged according to specific categories of ads within its own section, such as help-wanted ads.

Class I–IV   *See* radio, types of stations

Clearance   The broadcast stations carrying a network or syndicated program. This list is usually accompanied by a coverage percentage indicating the collective percent of U.S. homes (TV or total) accounted for by the markets in which the program airs.

Clear channel   An AM radio frequency transmitted with 50,000 watts on which only one station in the United States using that frequency may broadcast between sundown and sunrise. *Also see* radio, types of stations.

Click-and-mortar   Traditional retail stores that conduct consumer business on the Internet (e.g., barnesandnoble.com). It is a play on words with traditional retail stores referred to as being constructed out of brick and mortar.

Click rate   The percentage of impressions that resulted in users clicking on an ad banner or other type of online advertisement.

Clicks   1. In the online advertising industry, clicks refer to the number of times a user clicks the mouse button on an ad banner or other type of online advertisement. 2. Describes the number of Web pages a person must go through (by pressing a mouse button) in order to reach a certain destination.

Clickstream   The path a user takes while navigating Web pages or cyberspace in general—that is, how the user goes from one website or Web page to others. Advertisers and online media providers have developed software that can track users' clickstreams. *Also see* bitstream.

Click-through (rate) (CTR)   The process of clicking on an advertisement on a Web page to access the advertiser's page (e.g., full advertisement, offer, promotion, website). The "rate" is a measure of users that have clicked through (or clicked on) one or more online ads, and therefore it is an indication of online ad readership.

Clients and Profits   A company offering software systems to advertising agencies, graphic design studios, marketing firms, and public relations firms for tracking production, media, and accounting. Website: clientsandprofits.com

Clip art   Ready-made printed or computerized graphic (illustrations, borders, backgrounds) that can be electronically copied and used in a document. Clip art can be found on various websites and is available for sale.

Closed captioning (CC)   The audio portion of a TV program "printed" on the TV screen, allowing viewers to read what is being said. This requires a device to be connected to the TV set.

Closed-circuit TV   Television programming transmitted by cable or other nonbroadcast means to specific receivers, such as only to a company's employees within an office building.

Closed-end diary   A diary used by research companies, filled out by survey respondents, that has prompting aids to help a respondent fill in specific information. For example, it might display a list of TV programs and ask respondents which programs are typically viewed. The respondents' answers are therefore akin to aided awareness as opposed to unaided or top-of-mind awareness (which do not include prompts).

Closed-end question   A question in a questionnaire used by research companies that has the possible answers printed on the questionnaire—a multiple-choice question. This is the opposite of an open-ended question.

Closing billboard (CBB)   A short (usually five-second) commercial at the end of a radio or TV program that (usually) identifies a sponsor of the program, such as "This program was brought to you by . . ." If this mention appears at the beginning of a program, it is called an opening billboard (OBB). There is no MBB.

Closing date   The deadline set by a publication for the receipt of material (keyline or mechanical) for an advertisement to appear in a forthcoming issue.

Cluster   1. A logical unit of file storage on a computer's hard disk. 2. A grouping of people who share the same or very similar demographic characteristics, lifestyle characteristics, or both without (necessarily) regard to their geographic location. Usually, clusters are unique (unduplicated) segments of the population: no person or household is designated as being in more than one cluster. *Also see* 1. ACORN, 2. ClusterPLUS, 3. PRIZM.

ClusterPLUS   A geodemographic clustering system that was purchased by Claritas and absorbed into PRIZM.

Clutter   1. Many different commercials (either airing sequentially, at different times within a radio or TV program, or both) that compete for the listener's or viewer's attention. 2. Many different print advertisements printed within a small area of space, on a page, or on sequential pages, but typically not adjacent to substantial editorial. **3.** Many out-of-home posters or billboards within a small geographic area. "Billboard alley" is a phrase used to describe a location, such as a stretch of space next to a major artery, where posters and billboards are constructed one right after the other.

CM   *See* cable modem.

CMA/CMSA   *See* consolidated metropolitan statistical area.

CMO   *See* C titles.

CMR   *See* **1.** TNS Media Intelligence/CMR, **2.** certified marketing representative.

CMRi   *See* Competitive (report).

CMTS   *See* cable modem termination system.

Coat out   *See* blank out.

Coaxial cable   The primary type of cabling used by the cable television industry, widely used for computer networks and often by telephone companies. The cabling consists of a copper wire surrounded by insulation, then a grounded shield of braided wire (copper mesh), and finally, outside insulation. The shield minimizes electrical and radio frequency interference. Although more expensive than standard telephone wire, it is much less susceptible to interference and can carry much more data. *Also see* fiber-optic cable.

COBOL   A computer programming language used primarily for business applications that run on large computers. It is short for *common business oriented language.*

Code Division Multiple Access (CDMA)   A digital wireless technology developed by Qualcomm that simultaneously uses multiple channels over the full bandwidth of a wideband channel (known as a spread spectrum technique). The technique scatters radio signals across a wide range of frequencies. It is used in some digital cellular, personal communications services, and wireless networks. CDMA-One is early CDMA technology. CDMA2000 provides voice and data capabilities. The *W* in WCDMA stands for *wideband*.

Coefficient of correlation   A statistic representing how closely two variables co-vary (correlate) or how a change in one variable affects a change in the other variable. It can vary from -1 (perfect negative correlation) through 0 (no correlation) to $+1$ (perfect positive correlation). For example, if the coefficient of correlation between level of academic education and personal income is, for example, 0.8, it would suggest that the higher one's education levels the higher one's income level.

Coincidental survey   A survey usually involving radio listening or TV viewing—but can involve other media forms or product/service usage—that occurs while the program is on the air. Survey telephone calls are made systematically throughout the program. For example, the interviewer might ask a respondent, "What TV program are you viewing right now?" The findings of these types of surveys are often used to compare to other survey methods (e.g., People Meters, diaries) to determine the validity of the latter.

ColdFusion Markup Language (CFML)   A proprietary language developed by Allaire. It is an extension of hypertext markup language (HTML). CFML tags link HTML pages to database servers. Files created with CFML have the file extension .cfm.

Collateral material   Any visual or auditory material produced and distributed to reinforce an advertising media campaign or to act as a substitute for media advertising. Collateral includes items such as point-of-purchase displays, trade show exhibits, booklets/brochures, and newsletters.

Column   An area of copy in a magazine or newspaper that runs vertically down the page with its width held constant throughout an entire publication.

Column inch   A unit of space used in newspaper ad units. It measures one column wide by one inch deep.

COM   The serial port on a PC. It is an abbreviation of the word *communications*.

Com (.com)   *See* domain name.

Combination rate   1. A discounted rate given to an advertiser that advertises in both morning and evening editions of a newspaper. 2. A discounted rate for an advertiser that uses more than one vehicle in a group of publications owned by one publishing company. Related to, but different from, bundled deals or multimedia buys.

Combined reach   The total reach of more than one media vehicle. *Also see* only-only-both.

Combo   1. In spot TV, the purchase of one or more spots (commercials) in two time periods or programs for a combined single price. The combination cannot be separated and purchased for individual rates. 2. In spot radio, the purchase of one or more spots on two stations, often an AM and an FM owned by the same company, for a single discounted price.

Comdex   Acronym for Computer Dealers Expo. An electronics (high-tech) hardware and software exposition at which new products are traditionally launched. The first Comdex was in 1978.

Commercial   A radio or TV advertising message. *Also called* a spot. Although traditionally incorrect, some refer to commercials as ads, the latter designating a print advertisement.

Commercial audience   The viewers or listeners who are actively engaged in a radio or TV commercial.

Commercial avoidance devices   *See* ReplayTV, TiVo, videocassette recorder.

Commercial break   *See* break position.

Commercial exposure potential   The number of possible recipients (viewers or listeners) of a commercial message.

Commercial fingerprinting   *See* pattern recognition.

Commercial impressions   *See* impressions.

Commercial integration cost   *See* integration cost.

Commercial length   The duration of a radio or TV commercial expressed in seconds—for example, 10s, 15s, 30s.

Commercial minutes   The number of 60-second time segments that radio and TV stations and networks set aside to air commercials. The number of commercial minutes typically varies by time of day—that is, by daypart.

Commercial pod   A grouping of commercials and (sometimes) non-program material in which (usually) more than one advertiser's commercials air. Also referred to as a "commercial interruption," "commercial break," or "now a word from our sponsor."

Commercial pool   A group of ready-to-air radio or TV commercials from which an advertiser can select a commercial to be broadcast. In most cases the advertiser supplies the stations with multiple commercials (executions), which stand at the ready to be trafficked by the station.

Commercial protection   *See* competitive separation.

Commercial time   *See* commercial minutes.

Commission   1. The payment made by an advertiser to the buying agent (e.g., a media agency) for services rendered (such as media planning and media buying). It is usually expressed as a percentage of gross media billings handled by the agent. 2. The portion of a gross media payment made to a media supplier by an advertiser, which is returned to the advertiser's buying agent. Technically, this commission is really a discount offered by a media vehicle to qualified media buying agents (e.g., a media agency) and often directly to the advertiser if the advertiser placed the advertising directly with the media vehicle.

Commissionable   Advertising rates proposed by media suppliers that contain a commission provision.

Common carrier   The term used to describe a telephone company, but which applies to any point-to-point communications relay service. It is a privately owned economic entity that is granted monopoly rights under various state and federal legislation to ensure adequate and nondiscriminating service at reasonable rates. AT&T is a common carrier. A broadcast station cannot be a common carrier.

Common gateway interface (CGI)   A standard way for a Web server to process a user's request to access and view a Web page. The most common CGI is when a user fills out a form on a Web page, sends it in to be processed by an application program, and receives back a confirmation that it was processed.

Communication channel planning   *See* channel planning.

Communications satellite   A device in geosynchronous orbit 22,300 miles above the equator, staying in the same position above the ground at all times. This allows satellite antennas that transmit and receive signals to be aimed at an orbiting satellite and left in a fixed position. For purposes of this dictionary, it is used for radio and TV transmissions. Satellite programmers broadcast, or uplink, signals to a satellite that they either own or from which they lease channel space. The signals are often scrambled, or encrypted, to prevent unauthorized reception before they are retransmitted to Earth. The uplinked signals are received by a transponder located on the satellite. The transponder is a device that receives the signals and transmits them back to Earth after converting them to a frequency that can be received by a ground-based antenna (a downlink). Typically there are 24 to 32 transponders on each satellite. Each satellite occupies a particular location in orbit, and operates at a particular frequency assigned by the Federal Communications Commission.

Community antenna relay service (CARS)   The microwave frequency band that the Federal Communications Commission has assigned to the cable TV industry to transport TV signals.

Community antenna television (CATV)   (Obsolete) Now simply called cable television.

Comp(limentary)   Something that is given free (complimentary), such as copies of magazines or newspapers commonly given by the publication to people who affect decisions to advertise in the publication. Comp copies are not counted in total "paid" circulation.

Compact disc (CD)   A small digital disk on which data has been recorded. A CD player uses a beam of laser light to read the data and convert it to digital sound of very high quality. Sony standardized it at 74 minutes of sound, the length needed to hold Beethoven's Ninth Symphony. Originally marketed specifically for sound, CDs now hold data of all sorts to be read by CD-ROM players.

Compact disc read-only memory (CD-ROM)   An optical storage technology that uses compact discs to store and play back data. CD-ROM technology was originally used for encyclopedias, dictionaries, and software libraries, but now it is often used in multimedia applications. A basic CD-ROM can hold about 600 megabytes or more, which is equivalent to the storage capacity of about 400 floppy disks. CD-ROMs have become a favorite medium for installing programs since they cost only slightly more to manufacture than floppy disks, and most major software applications come on at least five floppies.

Competitive (report)   The compilation of media spending, media usage, or media delivery by products or services competitive to the advertised product or service.

Competitive parity   A determination that an advertiser's media budget is (or should be) at the same level as one or more of its direct competitors.

Competitive separation   The agreed time or spatial distance between competitors' commercials or ads within a media vehicle—

for example, not having competitors' TV commercials back to back or within the same commercial pod.

Composition (audience) *See* audience composition.

Compression 1. The process of making computer data smaller so less disk space or file space is needed to represent the same information. The data can therefore be transmitted in less time. 2. With audio or video signals, such as with a TV commercial, the speeding up of the signal to reduce the amount of time it takes to view it. For example, if a produced 30-second commercial runs over 30 seconds, it can be compressed down to 30 seconds without affecting the audio/video effectiveness in the listener's ears or viewer's eyes. 3. With TV programming, speeding up the program to reduce the amount of time it takes to view it, thereby allowing for the insertion of more commercials within normal timing parameters.

Computer programming language The "vocabulary" used to instruct a computer to perform specific tasks. Among the nearly 200 different languages that can be used for these instructions, in addition to those that are commonly used for creating websites and pages, are C, COBOL, C++, Delphi, JavaScript, Pascal, Python, Rexx, Smalltalk, Unified Modeling Language (UML), Transaction Authority Markup Language (XAML), and Extensible Markup Language (XML).

ComScore A research company that measures online buying activity, customer behavior, and customer preferences. It was founded in 1999 and purchased Jupiter Communications' Media Metrix unit in 2002. Website: comscore.com

Concept test A test of consumer reaction to a description of a product or service rather than to the product or service itself.

Conference Board, The A nonprofit, nonpartisan organization that brings leaders together to find solutions to common problems and to objectively examine major issues that have an impact on business and society. It creates and disseminates knowledge about management and the marketplace to help businesses strengthen their performance and better serve society. Working as a global, independent membership organization in the public interest, The Conference Board conducts research, convenes conferences, makes forecasts, assesses trends, publishes information and analysis, and brings executives together to learn from one another. Website: conference-board.org

Confidence level   The likelihood that the sampling error in a survey result will fall within a specified range, usually expressed in terms of standard errors. For example, one standard error equals 68 percent likelihood, two standard errors equals 95 percent likelihood, and 3 standard errors equals 99 percent likelihood. So if a research study reports that a TV program received a 10 rating and the confidence level for this finding was at 1 standard error, and if the same exact research was conducted 100 times, then at least 68 of these studies would produce the same rating estimate. Likewise, if the exact research was repeated only once, the chances are 68 out of 100 that the finding would again be a 10 rating. *Also see* **1.** projection, **2.** sampling error, **3.** tolerance.

Confirmation   The written or verbal acceptance by a media seller of the purchased media schedule.

Consecutive week discount   A discount provided by a media vehicle for placing advertising activity on consecutive weeks.

Consolidated metropolitan statistical area (CMSA)   As defined by the Federal Office of Management and Budget, a CMSA is an area that meets the requirements to qualify as a metropolitan statistical area and also has a population of one million or more, if component parts of the area are recognized as primary metropolitan statistical areas. *Also see* metropolitan area.

Consumer Confidence Index   A report of consumers' assessment of U.S. economic conditions. It is based on a representative sample of 5,000 U.S. households. NFO WorldGroup, a member of The Interpublic Group of Companies, conducts the monthly survey for The

Conference Board. Questionnaires are mailed to a nationwide representative sample of 5,000 households, of which roughly 3,500 typically respond. Each month, a different panel of 5,000 households is surveyed. Data has been collected since 1967. The questions asked to compute the indexes have remained constant throughout the history of the series. The index is based on responses to five questions included in the survey: (1) respondents' appraisal of current business conditions, (2) respondents' expectations regarding business conditions six months hence, (3) respondents' appraisal of the current employment conditions, (4) respondents' expectations regarding employment conditions six months hence, and (5) respondents' expectations regarding their total family income six months hence. For each of the five questions, there are three response options: positive, negative, and neutral. The response proportions to each question are seasonally adjusted. For each of the five questions, the positive figure is divided by the sum of the positive and negative to yield a proportion called "relative" value. For each question, the average "relative" for the calendar year 1985 is then used as a benchmark to yield the index value for that question. The indices are then averaged together as follows: Consumer Confidence Index—average of all five indexes, Present Situation Index—average of indexes for questions one and three, and Expectations Index— average of indexes for questions two, four, and five.

Consumer magazine   A magazine targeted to consumers as opposed to, for example, a trade magazine that is directed to specific businesses. *Time* is a consumer magazine; *Advertising Age* is a trade magazine.

Consumer Magazine Audit Report   *See* Audit Bureau of Circulations.

Consumer price index (CPI)   Produced by the Bureau of Labor Statistics (BLS, a federal agency), the CPI is monthly data on changes in the prices paid by urban consumers for a representative basket of goods and services. The CPI reflects spending patterns for each of two population groups: all urban consumers (CPI-U) and urban wage earners and clerical workers (CPI-W). The CPI-U represents about 87 percent of the total U.S. population. It is based on the expenditures of almost all residents of urban or metropolitan areas, including professionals, the self-employed, the poor, the unemployed, and retired persons, as well as urban wage earners and clerical workers. The CPI-U is the statistic generally cited by the media in reporting the status of the CPI. Not included in the CPI are the spending patterns of persons living in rural nonmetropolitan areas, farm families, persons in the Armed Forces, and those in institutions such as prisons and mental hospitals. The CPI frequently is called a cost-of-living index, but it differs in important ways from a complete cost-of-living measure. Both the CPI and a cost-of-living index would reflect changes in the prices of goods and services, such as food and clothing, that are directly purchased in the marketplace, but a complete cost-of-living index would go beyond this to also take into account changes in other governmental or environmental factors that affect consumers' well-being. The CPI market basket is developed from detailed expenditure information provided by families and individuals on what they actually bought.

Consumer profiling   A formal summary or analysis of consumer data used to describe distinctive features or characteristics of consumers and often of consumers' purchasing habits. Data is captured in various ways, such as via online and offline transactions (including cookies and credit cards) and personal interviews (in person, over the phone, or via e-mail).

Consumer research   A type of advertising research that (depending on the size and scope of the specific study) is used to determine multiple phenomena, such as consumer buying habits, reaction to advertising, and consumer wants and needs. It can be conducted using various methodologies, such as focus groups, personal interviews, telephone interviews, or self-administered questionnaires.

Contemporary hit radio   A radio programming format of current rock-flavored music. It is also known as Top 40.

•

Contiguity   1. Two radio programs scheduled next to each other in time and sequence without any commercial interruptions. 2. A group of data fields that are within close proximity of each other and can be processed one after the other in sequence.

Contiguity rate   (Obsolete) 1. Discounted rates offered to advertisers who sponsor contiguous programs in broadcast media. 2. Discounted rates offered to advertisers who buy contiguous commercial time slots.

Continuity discount   A rate discount given to an advertiser who purchases a specific schedule within a series of a publication's issues. *Also called* frequency discount.

Contract   *See* advertising contract.

Controlled circulation   The circulation of a magazine that is sent free and addressed to specific individuals who elect to receive the publication.

Control market(s)   Geographic area(s), such as a metro area or TV market, against which test market results are compared. For example, the effect of an increased media spending plan tested in market X would be compared to market Y, where market Y was held constant without any increased spending.

Convergence   The coming together of multiple electronics and telecommunications industries with the resulting merging of consumer devices, such as the computer, telephone, and television. It is the opposite of divergence.

Convergent programming   Television programs that are tied to the Internet whereby viewers can interact with or participate in certain aspects of the program—for example, as a game show guest or by casting a vote in response to a question. *Also see* 1. enhanced TV, 2. Wink.

Conversion factor   A percentage applied to a number (e.g., a household rating) to obtain a different number (e.g., a women ages 18 to

34 rating). The reason for using conversion factors is to estimate audience delivery for demographics that are not reported in the original research. The factors are predicated on previous or related research that offers specifics or guidelines for estimating nonreported demographics—that is if a point of reference is required rather than just guessing.

Converter   A device that is attached to a TV set and cable system and allows the TV to receive the increased number of channels offered by cable systems.

COO   *See* C titles.

Cookie   A small piece of information about a computer user that is stored on the user's computer when the user clicks on something on a website. It is used to verify a registered user of a website without requiring the user to sign in every time he or she accesses that site. Technically, it is called an HTTP cookie.

Coop (.coop)   *See* domain name.

Co-op advertising   Advertising that is funded jointly by the manufacturer and the retailer; in other words, they cooperate with advertising expenditures.

Co-op announcements   Commercial time made available in network programs to the network's owned and operated or affiliated local stations for sale to national or local advertisers; that is, the networks are cooperating with the local stations.

Cooperation rate   The number of research study respondents who agree to participate in the study, as a percentage of all people originally contacted for participation. For example, if 1,000 are contacted and 200 agree to participate, the cooperation rate is 20 percent. The higher the cooperation rate, the more likely the respondents represent the original universe that was contacted.

COPPA   *See* Children's Online Privacy Protection Act of 1998.

COPPR   *See* Children's Online Privacy Protection Rule.

Copy split   Running different versions of a print advertisement in different portions of the same issue of a publication's total circulation, such as in different geographic areas or an A/B split.

CORE Media Systems, Inc.   Founded in 1992, CORE is a systems solutions provider to the advertising and media buying industries. It offers a line of software products focused on the business needs of these industries and customized solutions to meet specific situations. Website: core-systems.com

Corporate advertising   Advertising that promotes the image of a corporation versus a product. It is not uncommon for corporate advertising to be directed to investors. It is often called image advertising.

Corporation for Public Broadcasting (CPB)   A private, nonprofit corporation created by Congress in 1967 that promotes public telecommunications services (television, radio, and online) for the American people. It is the largest single source of funding for public television and radio programming. Most CPB-funded TV programs are distributed through the Public Broadcasting Service (PBS). *Also see* National Public Radio.

Correlation coefficient   *See* coefficient of correlation.

Correspondence (analysis)   Analytical and often graphically displayed research that shows the relationships between multiple variables, such as the relationship between product consumption levels and lifestyle behaviors. It generally answers questions like, "How does a particular lifestyle (or demographic) correspond (relate) to frequency of store visits?"

Cosponsorship   A sponsorship of a media vehicle (broadcast program, magazine ad) shared by more than two noncompeting advertisers.

Cost accounting   A managerial accounting activity designed to help managers identify, measure, and control operating costs (salaries, rent, utilities) relative to income (revenue). Most cost accounting systems assign operating costs to each product, service, or client, typically on the basis of the proportionate time employees spend working on a particular product, service, or client.

Cost efficiency   A reference to a media unit's or media schedule's cost relative to its audience delivery, usually expressed as cost per thousand.

Cost per click (CPC)   An agreed payment by an online advertiser to an online publisher each time a user clicks on the advertiser's ad.

Cost per inquiry (CPI)   *See* per inquiry.

Cost per point (CPP)   The cost to deliver the equivalent of one rating point (1 percent) of a specific audience segment with a specific media schedule or media vehicle. For example, a media schedule that costs $10,000 and delivers 100 target rating points (TRPs) has a CPP of $100. CPPs quite often are used for radio/TV planning and buying, but they can be used for any media form for which audience data is available. For radio and TV, CPPs are generally used by media planners for critical analysis of daypart mix or programming type alternatives. CPPs vary by daypart for both radio and TV. For example, prime-time TV typically has a higher CPP than daytime TV. Therefore, a media planner can determine how many TRPs can be purchased within a specified media budget by using one or another daypart mix. CPP data can be obtained based on previous buys in the medium (or dayparts), adjusted for predicted marketplace conditions in play for the planned advertising period, or through syndicated research sources such as SQAD. Once total TRP affordability is determined, the media planner can then calculate the reach/frequency generated by various daypart mixes and come to a conclusion about which mix is best (in terms of reach/frequency). A media buyer uses CPP in order to measure the cost-efficiency of one TV program versus another, or one station versus another. Unlike the predicted CPPs used by a media planner, the media buyer uses actual CPPs based on the actual costs and estimated audience delivery determined during a negotiation with the media seller. Curiously, but traditionally, spot TV buyers use CPP as an analytical tool, while buyers of national TV use cost per thousand (CPM). CPP is related to but different from CPM. CPP is based on rating points (percentages), while CPM is based on numbers of people (or homes). For either CPP or CPM, it is critical that the same demographic audience be used throughout the analysis.

Formula:

cost ÷ rating (or TRPs) = CPP

Example:

$1,000 ÷ 10 = $100

Converting a CPP to CPM:

Formula:

CPP × 100 ÷ market's population (expressed in thousands) = CPM

Example: assume market population = 2,000,000

$100 × 100 = $10,000 ÷ 2,000 = $5.00

Cost per thousand (CPM) The cost per 1,000 people (or homes) delivered by a medium or media schedule. The delivery can be net (e.g., average program audience) or gross (e.g., impressions). For example, a media vehicle that costs $10,000 and has an audience of 500,000 men ages 18 to 49 has a CPM of $20. Media planners use CPM analyses to determine the relative cost-efficiency of alternative media forms or specific uses of those forms. For example, within a defined media budget, an analysis might reveal that the CPM for TV is $10.00, for radio $5.00, and for magazines $7.00. This could point the planner in the direction of favoring radio, followed by magazines, and then TV in formulating a media plan. The lower the CPM, the more (gross) audience can be purchased within a given budget. The more audience that can be purchased, the greater the chance of reaching more people. CPM is related to but different from cost per point (CPP). CPP is based on rating points (percentages), while CPM is based on numbers of people (or homes). For either CPP or CPM, it is critical that the same demographic audience be used throughout the analysis.

> *Formula:*
>
> cost ÷ audience × 1,000 = CPM
>
> *Example:* assume media audience = 2,000,000
>
> $10,000 ÷ 2,000,000 × 1,000 = $5.00
>
> *Shortcut Formula:*
>
> cost ÷ audience expressed in thousands = CPM
>
> *Example:*
>
> $10,000 ÷ 2,000 = $5.00

Converting CPM to CPP:

> *Formula:*
>
> (CPM × market population expressed in thousands) ÷ 100 = CPP
>
> *Example:* assume market population = 2,000,000
>
> $5 × 2,000 ÷ 100 = $100

Cost plus   A compensation scenario whereby a company (e.g., a media agency) is paid for its services by its clients based on the actual costs incurred by the company, plus a margin for profit. Actual costs include proportionate salaries for employees who work on the account (based on hours worked on the account as a percentage of typical annual hours worked), pro-rated employee benefits, and overhead. *Also see* cost accounting.

Cost ranking report   A ranking of magazines (or other media forms) based on reach, composition, CPM, or a variety of other variables of a specific target group. For example, it might be said that magazine X is ranked number one because within a defined budget it reaches more men ages 18 to 24 than any other publication shown in the analysis.

Couch potato A person who spends much time sitting or lying down, usually watching television.

Council of American Survey Research Organizations (CASRO) The trade association of survey research businesses, representing nearly 200 companies and research operations in the United States, Canada, and Mexico. Website: casro.org

Country A radio programming format consisting of ballads, and contemporary and classic songs with a traditional, rural American influence.

County size *See* Nielsen county size groups.

Cover 1. The front cover, inside front cover, inside back cover, and back cover of a magazine. 2. The percentage or number of people exposed to an advertising schedule. The term is used in European countries. The U.S. equivalent is the term *reach*.

Coverage The percentage of a population group covered by a medium. Commonly used with print media to describe their average issue audience within defined demographic or purchasing groups. It is akin to a rating. *Also see* 1. broadcast coverage area, 2. coverage area.

Coverage area 1. The geographic area reached by a radio or TV station's signal—that is, the broadcast coverage area. 2. The geographic area covered by the publication's typical distribution (circulation) pattern.

Covering The illegal practice in which spots sold by a network or syndicator are preempted (covered or replaced) by local advertisements without the permission of the national advertiser.

Cover position Reference is to magazine ad placement. The second cover is the inside of the front cover, the third cover is the inside of the back cover, and the fourth cover is the outside back. Ads placed in these positions usually command a premium price versus inside-the-magazine positions.

Cover wrap   An additional cover stapled or glued to a magazine, most often used for circulation and other promotional messages. *Also see* outsert.

Cowcatcher   (Obsolete) A commercial at the beginning of, and forming a part of, a radio or TV program, with advertising for a product or service that is not mentioned again in the program.

CPB   *See* Corporation for Public Broadcasting.

CPC   *See* cost per click.

CPI   *See* 1. consumer price index, 2. per inquiry.

C++   A computer programming language, often used for graphic applications.

CPM   *See* cost per thousand.

CPO   *See* C titles.

CPP   *See* cost per point.

CPT   An acronym sometimes used for *cost per thousand.*

CPU   *See* central processing unit.

CR   *See* classic rock.

Cramming   A practice in which telephone customers are billed for enhanced features that they have not ordered, such as voice mail, caller-ID, and call-waiting.

Crash   An unexpected shutdown of a computer program or the entire computer system.

Crawler   *See* spider.

Credit check   The process of a media vendor evaluating an advertiser's or an advertiser's buying agent's financial credit standing to determine if the vendor will or will not require cash in advance for any media schedule purchased by or on behalf of the advertiser.

Credit memo   An alternative to a cash payment in which the media supplier issues a memorandum (or equivalent) that authorizes the advertiser to deduct that amount from the next payment to the supplier.

Critical mass   Having enough customers, sales, or market share for a marketer to be profitable.

CRM   *See* customer relationship marketing.

Cross-platform deal   An integrated communications package purchased by an advertiser using two or more of the media or nonmedia vehicles offered by a media conglomerate. Typically, the deal encompasses at least advertising and often promotional efforts. The usual strategy driving a cross-platform deal is to reach targeted consumers at various touch points (i.e., different media forms) to both drive awareness and convince the consumer to take action. It is not uncommon for the deal to also include elements for customer relationship marketing (CRM), following the customer from the initial purchase through affinity programs and repurchase cycles. *Also see* bundled (media) deals.

Crosstab   **1.** Cross-tabulating two or more distinct sets of data (usually found in syndicated media research reports) to yield one set of data. For example, combining media audience data for women ages 18 to 34 with household income and marital status to yield married women ages 18 to 34 in households with $50,000+ income. **2.** A product of Telmar that is an analysis system for identifying target market opportunities, product usage, and creating media delivery profiles. This application includes vehicle prototyping, means and medians, correspondence analysis, cluster analysis, QuadMapping, and customized reports.

CRT   *See* cathode ray tube.

C-store display   Point-of-purchase displays positioned at the entrance of convenience stores (e.g., 7-Eleven).

CTAM   *See* Cable and Telecommunications Association of Marketing.

CTIA   *See* Cellular Telecommunications Industry Association.

C titles   All of the upper management functional titles in a company, such as CEO (chief executive Officer), CFO (chief financial officer), CIO (chief information officer), CMO (chief marketing officer), COO (chief operating officer), CPO (chief privacy officer), and CTO (chief technology officer).

CTO   *See* C titles.

CTR   *See* click-through (rate).

Cume (cumulative) audience   The total unduplicated media audience accumulated over a particular period of time—such as the total audience of program X for its entire half-hour airing or the total audience of radio station Y during morning drive. People tune in and tune out of radio and TV programs as the programs are airing. To establish a cume audience, the number of people who view five or more minutes of a program are added together, making sure to not count any one person more than once. *See* 1. rating, 2. turnover rate.

Cume (cumulative) persons   An Arbitron term for the total number of different persons who tune in for at least five minutes to a radio station during the course of a daypart.

Cume (cumulative) rating   1. The reach of a radio or TV program (or station), as opposed to the average rating of that program, expressed as a percentage of the population universe. 2. An Arbitron term for the cume persons audience expressed as a percentage of all persons estimated to be in the specified demographic group.

Current issue   A publication's issue that is currently on sale at newsstands.

Customer relationship marketing (CRM)   Tracking customer behavior for the purpose of developing marketing and relationship-building processes that bond the consumer to the brand. It often involves one-to-one customer service and personal contact between the company and the customer. CRM is also referred to as customer relationship management and continuous retention marketing.

Cut-in The insertion of a commercial, at the local level, which replaces the commercial originally placed in a national broadcast program for national airing. It is generally used to test media, alternative commercial executions, or both. It requires that the same advertiser own both the cut-in and the national commercial. *Also see* covering.

Cybernetics Coined by Norbert Weiner in 1943, cybernetics is concerned with discovering what mechanisms control systems, and in particular, how systems regulate themselves. The systems can be computer science, biological and artificial control systems, social philosophy, and epistemology (the limits to how people know what they know).

Cyberspace Coined by William Gibson in his 1984 novel, *Neuromancer*, cyberspace is the electronic medium of computer networks in which online communication takes place. It primarily refers to the digital world constructed by computer networks, and in particular, the Internet.

Dailies Refers to newspapers that are published at least five days a week, generally Monday through Friday.

Daily effective circulation (DEC) The number of adults ages 18 and older who have the opportunity to be exposed to a specific out-of-home advertising display on an average day. The DEC is reported in the Traffic Audit Bureau's (TAB's) "Plant Operator Statement." The TAB requires an audit every three years. Official traffic counts are generally available from departments of transportation at city, county, or state agencies. Where these official counts are not available, the plant operator performs manual counts. Various adjustments are made to the raw traffic data to account for the number of people in a car, the number of hours the advertising unit is illuminated, and converting two-way traffic into a one-way count. For example, the national vehicle load factor currently used is 1.38 adults ages 18 and older per car. The use of the word *effective* does not necessarily have bearing on the communication value or impact of the advertising. *See* Traffic Audit Bureau.

Daily rate The cost of an advertisement that will appear in the daily (Monday through Friday or Monday through Saturday) edition of a newspaper.

Daniel Starch and Staff *See* Roper ASW.

DARPA   *See* Internet.

DAT   *See* digital audiotape.

Database   A collection of data (information) obtained from one or more sources and organized for easy retrieval, tabulation, and analysis of the data. The data can come from primary sources, such as from customers or from secondary sources (e.g., research studies).

Database marketing   Advertising to specific individuals or groups of individuals who share common traits (e.g., demographic, lifestyle, or buying behavior). Most database marketing is conducted via direct mail, with a growing trend to also use the Internet (e.g., via e-mail) to reach specific population segments.

Data compression   A technique that eliminates gaps, redundancies, and empty fields in data records in order to save computer storage space.

Data mining   Sorting or analyzing information from a database to isolate patterns or trends.

Data over cable service interface specifications (DOCSIS)   A standard interface for cable modems.

Datatech Software Corporation   A supplier of in-house business systems for advertising agencies, media buying services, and in-house media departments. Website: dtsoft.com

Daughterboard   A printed circuit computer logic board that plugs into another circuit (usually the motherboard) that offers additional computer functions (such as enabling 3-D graphics).

Daughter window   An advertisement on a website that is associated with a banner ad on the same site. Typically, the banner ad appears first, then the daughter window.

Day after recall   A research method used to measure how many people can recall an advertising message one day after exposure to an advertisement or commercial.

Daypart   *See* 1. radio dayparts, 2. TV dayparts.

Daypart distribution   *See* daypart mix.

Daypart mix   The distribution of audiences in each radio or TV daypart, typically expressed as percentages of target rating points (TRPs) in each daypart. For example, a TV daypart mix might be composed of 25 percent early news programming, 50 percent prime time, and 25 percent late news. A media planner analyzes various daypart mixes to determine which mix produces the greatest audience delivery. Evaluating daypart mixes requires keeping the budget constant: each mix must cost the same amount of money. To calculate how many TRPs can be purchased within a defined budget, multiply the cost per point (CPP) of each daypart in a particular daypart mix by the percentage of TRPs each daypart is to receive, add the products to obtain a weighted CPP, and then divide the budget by the weighted CPP.

Example (within a $1,000 budget):

	CPP	Mix	Weighted CPP	Mix	Weighted CPP
Day	$10.00	50 percent	$ 5.00	25 percent	$ 2.50
News	$30.00	50 percent	$15.00	75 percent	$22.50
Total		100 percent	$20.00	100 percent	$25.00
Affordable TRPs:			50		40

Daypart optimization   The combination of radio or TV dayparts that within a defined media budget offers the highest reach or effective reach of a predetermined demographic group. Although these calculations can be done manually, daypart optimization generally requires a computer program that analyzes a multitude of various combinations.

Daytime   *See* 1. radio dayparts, 2. TV dayparts.

Daytime station (daytimer)   A radio station that broadcasts only during the day (from sunrise to sunset).

DB   *See* 1. decibel, 2. delayed broadcast.

DBS   *See* direct broadcast satellite.

DBSA   *See* Satellite Broadcasting and Communications Association.

D channel   (ISDN data channel) A data connection between the telephone company's switching equipment and their customers' ISDN equipment.

D-commerce (digital commerce)   A part of e-commerce (electronic commerce) used by companies that sell content (news, data) and that can be delivered digitally to the user over the Web.

D counties   *See* Nielsen county size groups.

DDS   *See* Donovan Data Systems.

DeadQ   *See* Marketing Evaluations/TvQ.

Dealer tag   *See* tag.

DEC   *See* daily effective circulation.

Decibel (dB)   A unit of measurement used to express relative difference in power or intensity, usually between two acoustic or electric signals. The higher the decibel level, the louder the sound. As a logarithmic unit (based on 10), an increase of 10 dB means that the sound is 10 times as loud—for example, 70 dB is 10 times as loud as 60 dB. Ordinary speaking voice is at 10 dB, a chainsaw at 100 dB, and a rock music concert at 110 dB.

Decile   One-tenth of a group. A tertile is one-third, a quartile is one-fourth, and a quintile is one-fifth. A reptile is a cold-blooded, usually egg-laying, vertebrate.

Deck   A printed presentation or document. *Also see* double-decker.

Decryption   The process of decoding data that has been encrypted into a secret format. Decryption requires a secret key or password.

Dedicated line   A telephone line that provides a direct connection from a computer to the Internet.

Default   A user-controlled setting on a computer that causes the computer to automatically make something happen, such as connect to a particular device or software program. For example, a computer probably has a default setting for printing documents on a specific printer connected to the computer.

Defrag(mentation)   To optimize a computer's hard drive using a software program that combines and deletes bytes in order to make the computer run more smoothly and often faster. *Also see* fragmentation.

Degauss   To demagnetize something, such as removing the magnetic field that builds up within a computer display, or to erase information from a magnetic disk or other storage device.

Delayed broadcast (DB)   A network TV program that is recorded during its original broadcast so its recorded version can be broadcast at a later time or date by a local station. The usual purpose of doing this is to allow for programming to be delivered to viewers at the same local time in various markets, thereby overcoming time zone changes. For example, a program that is telecast out of New York City at 9:00 P.M. would ordinarily be delivered in central daylight time at 8:00 P.M., mountain time at 7:00 P.M., and Pacific time at 6:00 P.M. With a DB, markets in each time zone would receive that program at 9:00 P.M. local time.

Delphi   A computer programming language. It is similar to Visual Basic, which is based on BASIC programming language, but Delphi is based on Pascal.

Demographic editions   Special editions of magazines directed to specific demographic audiences—for example, an edition received by only upper-income subscribers—that contain targeted editorial and advertising.

Demographics   The characteristics of people and population segments, especially when used to identify consumer markets. Popular demographics used in media planning and buying typically include gender, age, household income, education levels, household size, and ethnicity. *Also see* **1.** demography, **2.** geodemographics, **3.** lifestyle.

Demography   The study of the characteristics of population groups in terms of size, distribution, and other vital statistics. *Also see* demographics.

Demoware   A software product that can be downloaded to give the user a demonstration of the product, but does not contain the entire product. It is meant to entice the user to buy the full product. *Also see* **1.** freeware, **2.** shareware.

Department of Transportation (DOT)   The federal, state, or city government agency that regulates, studies, and issues statistics on vehicular traffic flow. DOT studies are the basis of most daily effective circulation audits done by the Traffic Audit Bureau.

Description tag   A description of a Web page or website as written by the author of the page or site. The tag typically appears in search engine listings.

Descriptive extra line   An extra line of copy in a Yellow Pages listing, designed to give additional information in a larger-size type.

Designated market area (DMA)   Nielsen Media Research's definition of a TV market. It is a group of counties in which metro-area stations achieve the largest audience share of total people hours of viewing. DMA markets are nonoverlapping areas used for planning, buying, and evaluating TV audiences. Each of the 3,080 counties (or equivalents such as boroughs or parishes) in the United States is assigned to only one DMA. The assignment of a county into the DMA does not indicate that people in TV homes in that county view only the originating TV stations. Quite often people can also receive distant signals from stations located in adjacent or faraway DMAs. However, a county is designated into a specific DMA because the majority of the viewing done in that county is done on the originating TV stations. The viewing data and DMA designations are updated annually. *Also see* spill-in/spill-out.

DHTML   *See* dynamic hypertext markup language.

Diad   An in-depth interview involving the interviewer and the respondent. Also known as a one-on-one interview.

Dial around   Long-distance services that require consumers to dial a long-distance provider's access code (or "10-10" number) before dialing a long-distance number, to bypass or "dial around" the consumer's chosen long-distance carrier in order to get a better rate.

Diary   A self-administered questionnaire that is often used to collect radio and television audience data on a continuous basis. Respondents simply record their media usage patterns for one week or so, and a research company compiles the data into audience profiles for programs, stations, and networks. *Also see* Nielsen diary.

DID   *See* direct inward dialing.

Digest page   A print advertisement measuring 5 inches wide by 7 inches high. So called because it is the same size as a *Reader's Digest* magazine.

Digital   The use of the binary system in electronic transmissions, such as in a digital computer or with radio or TV programming, via cable or fiber-optic cable. Digital describes any system based on discontinuous data or events. For example, computers are digital machines, because at their most basic level they can distinguish between just two values, 0 and 1, or off and on. The opposite of digital is analog. Most analog events, however, can be simulated digitally. Although digital representations are approximations of analog events, they are useful because they are relatively easy to store and can be electronically manipulated.

Digital audiotape (DAT)   An audiocassette on which sound has been recorded using digital technology, to be replayed on an electronic device (DAT player) that reads and reproduces the original sound with a very high level of quality.

Digital compression The conversion of audio or video signals into a digital series, allowing for more data to be transmitted over a wire (coaxial, fiber-optic, or telephone) or to be written to a magnetic disk. The implementation of digital compression could allow cable TV homes to receive 400 to 500 channels.

Digital divide Loosely defined as the disparity between those who have access to Internet technology and those who don't. In July of 1999, the U.S. Commerce Department released a report called "Falling Through the Net: Defining the Digital Divide," which found that households with annual incomes of $75,000 or more were 20 times more likely than families in the lowest income bracket to have Internet access and 9 times more likely to have computers.

Digital radio An enhancement to regular radio that eliminates static and lets broadcasters transmit textual information, such as news updates, weather alerts, and information about songs, with the audio signal. Compared to AM/FM analog transmitters that can transmit only one station, digital transmitters can transmit up to six stations at once, and use less power than analog AM and FM signals. Sound waves can be processed as a series of digits. Each number gives the height of the sound wave at a particular instant. These numbers are then transformed into a digital signal consisting of 1s and 0s (binary code with 1 equaling electrical charge and 0 equaling no charge—essentially "on" and "off"). Each combination of 1s and 0s represents the height of the original sound wave. *Also see* digital video.

Digital receiver An electronic device that produces CD-quality sound without static. It uses a tiny computer that sorts through multipath echoes and reconstructs an interference-free signal. It can monitor signal strengths and use this information to switch automatically from a fading signal to a new, more powerful one. It can automatically find stations carrying programming of a specific type;

display song titles, artist and album names, and lyrics as well as traffic and weather information; allow for paging services and text services; receive pay radio services, such as pay-per-listen live concerts; and list stations sequentially by call letter or name to allow for easy tuning.

Digital service line   *See* T-carrier.

Digital set-top box   A device that converts digital encoded TV broadcasts so they can be viewed on an analog TV set.

Digital subscriber line (DSL)   A telecommunications line that provides a fast and constant connection to the Internet and does not require the user to dial in to an Internet service provider. The many types of DSL include asymmetric DSL (ADSL), high bit-rate DSL (HDSL), single-pair high bit-rate DSL (SHDSL), integrated services digital network DSL (IDSL), symmetrical DSL (SDSL), and very high bit-rate DSL (VDSL). *Also see* **1.** cable modem, **2.** integrated services digital network.

Digital TV (DTV)   A new technology for transmitting and receiving broadcast television signals. DTV provides clearer resolution and improved sound quality. *See* digital video.

Digital versatile disc   *See* digital video disc.

Digital video   An alternative way of storing or distributing video signals that is usually converted from an analog video source. Digital video signals are represented by "1s" and "0s," while an analog video signal is represented by a fluctuating voltage signal that is stored on magnetic tape. *Also see* digital radio.

Digital video disc (DVD)   A high-density compact disc for storing large amounts of data, especially high-resolution audio-visual material. *Also called* digital versatile disc.

Digital video interactive (DVI)   Transmission and reception of any kind of audio, visual, or electronic material, such as television and computer data.

Digital video recorder (DVR)   *See* personal video recorder.

Digital video server   A computer at a central location that receives commands from the TV viewer through a video-on-demand application. Once the request is received, the server sends back what the viewer requested.

Digital watermarking   Technology that places an inherent digital identity into all media content, allowing media owners or issuers to verify content, authenticate content, link media to related databases, manage and track digital assets, and prevent unauthorized copying. It also allows research companies to "track" radio and TV commercial airings. When these commercials air, the research companies' monitoring stations (computer robots) can capture pertinent information such as the date and time of the airing as well as the radio/TV station or network airing the commercial. Audio digital watermarking is used by AudioAudit and Verance; video digital watermarking is used by TNS Media Intelligence/CMR, Teletrax, and Nielsen SIGMA. *Also see* pattern recognition.

DINKS   Acronym for *dual income no kids*. A demographic household group composed of two adults, who each have outside income and do not have any children living at home.

Diorama   A backlit out-of-home display often located in airports, bus terminals, and sports arenas.

Direct broadcast satellite (DBS)   Reception of radio or TV signals directly from a satellite via a "personal" satellite dish that is owned or leased by an individual household. Dishes are of various sizes, with the smallest being approximately 18 inches in diameter. Cable TV operations are essentially satellite operations in that local cable systems receive their programming via satellite but then retransmit the signals to their subscribing households. This retransmission could degrade the audio and video signals to a greater or lesser degree on the way to a customer's home. Satellite TV, on the other hand, eliminates the intervening wiring and provides a direct link from the satellite to the customer's antenna (dish) in a 100 percent digital video and audio feed.

Direct Broadcast Satellite Association (DBSA)   *See* Satellite Broadcasting and Communications Association.

Direct cost (expense)   Those costs incurred by a company that are attributable to a specific client (customer), such as an advertising agency that incurs travel expenses on behalf of a specific client.

Direct inward dialing (DID)   Individual telephone numbers for each of a company's employees, whereby calls can be made directly to an employee without having to be routed through a live telephone operator/receptionist or computer answering machine. *Also see* private branch exchange.

Directional advertising   Advertising that directs people to the seller's physical location, such as an outdoor poster that says "Exit 21 for Paula's Pizza Kitchen."

Direct mail   A form of advertising that uses the U.S. mail to deliver advertising messages (e.g., letters, brochures).

Direct mail, attributes   All media forms have positive and negative attributes. The following are some of the attributes of advertising via direct mail: highly selective target audiences can be reached through the use of mailing lists (databases); advertiser has complete geographic control, down to the individual; advertiser has unlimited reach potential; advertiser can somewhat control the timing delivery of the advertising message (depending on mailing and delivery dates); advertiser has total control over the medium because it is the editorial environment; advertiser has unlimited creative flexibility; messages can be personalized; vehicle is audience controlled (nonintrusive) because recipient decides if the envelope will be opened; tangible permanency allows for repeat readership; coupons can be distributed; production costs can range from low (for simple letters) to very high (for brochures); mailing costs alone make it a high cost-per-reader medium; consumer responses can be tracked by geodemographic variables; and responses can be placed in a database for follow-up, repeat mailings, and customer relationship marketing efforts.

Direct marketing   Selling (advertising) directly to a consumer (or business), as opposed to general marketing, which sells (advertises) indirectly via mass and niche media forms. Direct marketing relies heavily on the use of databases and direct media, such as direct mail, the Internet, and telephone.

Direct Marketing Association (DMA)   The largest trade association for businesses interested in direct, database, and interactive global marketing, with about 4,700 member companies from the United States and 53 foreign nations on six continents. Founded in 1917, its members include catalog companies, direct mailers, teleservice firms, Internet marketers, and other at-distance marketers from every consumer and business-to-business segment, both commercial and nonprofit, as well as companies that provide supplies and services to marketers. Website: thedma.org

Direct response advertising   Any form of advertising that requests a consumer to respond directly to the advertiser—for example, by calling an 800 telephone number to place an order—as opposed to going to a retail store to buy a product. Often called DR or DR advertising, it includes, for example, DRTV (Direct Response TV) and direct mail.

Direct to consumer (DTC)   Advertising by a pharmaceutical company of ethical drugs (prescription medicine) directed to the consumer (end user) as opposed to trade advertising directed to physicians. Although a physician's prescription is needed to purchase the drug, the hope of the advertiser is that the consumer will either request the prescription from his or her physician or at least raise the subject with the physician, thereby creating an overall demand for the drug.

Disc jockey (DJ)   A radio personality who plays recorded music and acts as an announcer and (often) a commentator on the music. The term comes from *disc*, which was a phonograph record but now applies to any form of recording (e.g., a compact disc).

Disclosure   *See* full disclosure.

Disconnects   Subscribers who have terminated their subscription to, or who have been terminated from, cable TV service.

Discount   A reduction from the usual price of an advertising unit(s) granted to the advertiser in recognition of (usually) a quantity purchase of the medium.

Discrep   *See* discrepancy.

Discrepancy   The difference between the agreed price or specific placement of a radio or TV commercial and the invoiced price or placement (as shown on an affidavit of performance).

Discriminant analysis   A statistical method of predicting the future performance of, for example, an advertising effort based on an evaluation of past performance among discrete audience segments. So if an advertiser knows the response to past advertising efforts among a specific demographic group, the chances are that future advertising to the same group (even if they are different individuals) should produce the same or similar results.

Dish (antenna)   A parabolic or spherical-shaped antenna that is used for satellite communication, broadcast reception, space communication, radio, astronomy, and radar. *Also see* 1. direct broadcast satellite, 2. earth station.

Disk(ette)   A removable computer storage medium that is used in conjunction with a floppy disk drive. The term usually refers to the magnetic medium housed in a rigid plastic cartridge measuring 3.5 inches square. It can store up to 1.44 megabytes (Mb) of data. Some older computers provide drives for magnetic diskettes that are 5.25 inches square and capable of holding 1.2 Mb of data. These were sometimes called "floppy disks" or "floppies" because their housings are flexible. The term *floppy* is still used for the smaller, rigid disk.

Disk operating system (DOS)   This usually refers to any computer operating system but is most often a reference to MS-DOS (Microsoft disk operating system). It was originally developed by Microsoft for IBM-compatible personal computers.

Dispersion   The level of scattering commercials or ads across programs or print vehicles. To a great extent, the level of dispersion determines the level of reach that can be obtained with a media campaign. For example, a high dispersion schedule, indicating the use of many different TV programs (radio stations, magazines), will probably generate more reach than a low dispersion schedule that concentrates commercials in fewer programs. The lowest dispersion schedule is one that concentrates commercials in very few programs, such as scheduling three to five commercials per week in "strip" programming. The reason for the various reach accumulation levels has to do with "duplication" rates. A combination of many different programs has a greater probability of attracting more "unduplicated" viewers versus a combination of fewer programs where viewer duplication levels are higher. The highest level of duplication is found in repeated episodes of the same program, from week to week or in strip programs. High dispersion schedules often cost more than lower dispersion schedules because a media buyer is forced to select increasingly less cost-efficient programs in order to achieve dispersion goals. Therefore, within a given media budget, a high dispersion schedule will yield fewer affordable target rating points (TRPs) than a lower dispersion schedule. The moral of the story is that the reach advantage of a high dispersion schedule might be mitigated by cost factors that could lower total affordable TRPs (and therefore reach).

Display advertising   Newspaper advertising that typically uses various "creative" elements, such as large type, illustrations, photography, and color, and whose most distinguishing feature is that it does not resemble typical "classified" advertising.

Disposable income   The amount of an individual's income, after taxes have been paid, that is available for spending and saving.

Distant signal   A TV broadcast station's signal that is not considered "local" to the community (as defined by the Federal Communications Commission). Cable systems usually import distant signals via a satellite antenna, but the FCC limits the number of distant signals a cable system can offer its subscribers.

Distribution   1. A publication's total number of distributed copies, whether or not the copies are actually purchased by consumers. 2. The allocation of national media delivery into each local market (e.g., into DMAs). 3. The allocation of a medium's total audience into the various demographic groups. *Also see* frequency distribution.

Distribution hub   A location in a cable TV network that performs like a head end and receives some or all of its TV program material from a master head end.

Divergence   The replacement of the multicapable, all-in-one personal computer (PC) by small, single-purpose consumer electronic devices, such as a PDA (personal digital assistant). Divergence is the opposite of convergence.

DJ   *See* disc jockey.

DK   Abbreviation for "don't know," indicating that the respondent in a research study did not know the answer to a question.

DMA   *See* 1. designated market area, 2. Direct Marketing Association.

Docking station   An electronic device that typically sits on a desk, into which a laptop computer can be installed to connect to peripheral devices (such as a printer and a monitor).

DOCSIS   *See* data over cable service interface specifications.

Dollar volume   An advertiser's gross expenditures in a media vehicle that the medium uses to calculate cash discounts that the advertiser qualifies for, based on the medium's rate card.

Domain   A group of computers and devices on a network that are administered as a unit with common rules and procedures. Domains are assigned an Internet protocol (IP) address on the Internet.

Domain name   The part of a uniform resource locator (URL) that locates an organization or other entity on the Internet. For example, www.arfsite.org is composed of the host server (www) where the domain name is, and the name of the organization or organization Web address (arfsite). The suffix *.org* describes the type of organization—in this case, organization, public or noncommercial. The suffixes in use or that are being proposed for use are *.aero* (air-transport industry), *.arts* (arts and cultural entities), *.biz* (businesses), *.com* (commercial), *.coop* (cooperatives), *.edu* (educational), *.firm* (business), *.gov* (government), *.info* (information services), *.mil* (military), *.museum* (museums), *.name* (individuals), *.net* (network), *.org* (organization, public or noncommercial), *.pro* (professions), *.rec* (recreation and entertainment), *.store* (merchants), and *.web* (Web services). *Also see* Internet Corporation for Assigned Names and Numbers.

Donovan Data Systems (DDS)   A company offering software systems that are used by the advertising industry to manage the buying and selling of media advertising. DDS clients use the systems via their personal computers (PCs) or terminals, which are linked through a dedicated communications network to data processing centers. DDS products are used by media researchers, media buyers, planners and client accounting staff at ad agencies, buying organizations, and major advertisers. Website: donovandata.com

Donut   Slang for a radio or TV commercial that is produced with a blank time span (a hole) in it for the insertion of customized copy (creative) prior to airing. For example, a TV :30 or a radio :60 might contain a :05 to :15 hole in which local copy is inserted on a market-by-market basis. Unlike doughnuts, the hole is not sold separately. *Also called* a slug.

Doorway page   *See* splash page.

DOS   *See* disk operating system.

DOT   *See* Department of Transportation.

Dots per inch (DPI or Dpi)   The metrics used to measure print and screen resolution.

Double billing   An illegal practice wherein a vendor (e.g., an advertising agency or a medium) submits a false invoice—for example, showing the wrong costs or billing for commercials that did not air.

Double carding   Placing two advertisements for the same product in the same subway or commuter train car. The idea behind this placement is to extend reach, provide a higher level of frequency, or provide a combination of both reach and frequency.

Double-decker   An out-of-home media term for when advertising displays are stacked on top of each other, such as one poster unit on top of another. These types of units are usually placed in high traffic areas. *Also called* deck or stack.

Double spotting   Two commercials for the same advertiser airing within the same commercial pod without instructions from the media buyer (or the media buying agent's traffic department) to do so. If a network or station is instructed to air two commercials in the same pod, such as with bookend commercials, it would not technically be known as double spotting.

Double truck   The pages facing each other in the exact center of a newspaper section where the copy runs across the margin without interruption. This is different from a "spread." By definition, there can be only one double truck in any given section of a newspaper. Curiously, there is no single truck.

Doughnut   *See* donut.

Downcut   The loss of audio or visual, or both, at the end portion of a commercial, usually caused by a technical error at the point of transmission. *Also see* upcut.

Downlink/uplink   In satellite communications the downlink is the link (communications connection) from the satellite to Earth; an uplink is the link from Earth to the satellite.

Download   To transfer a file(s) to a computer from another source, such as from another computer or the Web. When a user loads a Web page into the browser, that user essentially is downloading the page from the server on which it is hosted.

Downstream   The flow of signals from the cable system control center through a distribution network to the customer.

DPI   *See* dots per inch.

DR   *See* direct response advertising.

Drill down   To investigate or evaluate something (e.g., data) down to very fine (granular) details.

Drive time   *See* radio dayparts.

Drop down menu   A list of commands or features that appear below the menu typically found at the top of the display screen of a computer program such as Microsoft Word. When a user clicks on one of the items on the menu (e.g., "File"), a list of options drops down (e.g., New, Open, Close), any of which can be clicked on to access that function.

Drop lines   Coaxial cable connecting the cable in the street to the subscriber's TV set.

DRTV   Direct response television. TV commercials that request the viewer to respond directly to the advertiser (or its agent) via a website, telephone number, e-mail, or mail. *Also see* direct response advertising.

DSL   *See* digital subscriber line.

DS1, DS2, DS3, DS4   *See* T-carrier.

DTC   *See* direct to consumer.

DTV   *See* digital TV.

Dual liability   *See* sequential liability.

Dub   As a noun, it is a copy of the original audio or video recording. As a verb, it is producing one or more copies of an audio or video recording or commercial. *Also called* dupe.

Dub house   A company that makes dubs.

Duopoly   An economic or political condition in which power is concentrated in two persons or groups, such as the ownership of media outlets in a given geographic market. The Federal Communications Commission (FCC) has various ownership rules, currently based on the number of media outlets in a market and the percentage of potential audience that each outlet has. Under fire from legislative and corporate critics, the FCC is continuously evaluating which rules should be changed and how. For example, one of the current rules is that ownership by one company is restricted to two FM band or two AM band radio stations in the same market, and further, that the combined audience of the two stations cannot exceed 25 percent of the market's population.

Dupe   *See* dub.

Duplication   Viewers, readers, or listeners who have been exposed two or more times to a vehicle or schedule within a particular time frame. For example, assume two magazines each have 100 readers, but 10 of the readers read both of the magazines. Therefore, 10 percent of magazine A readers are duplicated with magazine B readers. The combined duplication of magazines A and B is 5 percent (10 divided by 200 combined readers). Duplication rates between pairs of magazines (or pairs of TV programs or radio stations) are the foundation for producing formulas for estimating the total reach of a media schedule. *Also see* dispersion.

DVD *See* digital video disc.

DVI *See* digital video interactive.

DVR Digital video recorder. *See* personal video recorder.

Dynamic ad placement The process of inserting an advertisement into a Web page in response to the user's request—that is, the user clicked on something on the Web page to request the advertisement.

Dynamic content Content on a website or Web page that changes often whereby successive clicks on the site or page (for example, daily) will reveal revised or different content.

Dynamic hypertext markup language (DHTML) A markup language that describes how text and images are displayed on a Web page. It allows for an advertisement on a Web page to be created and deployed in a "layer" above the HTML content, thereby obscuring the content below it. Ads using DHTML are also known as layered ads or floating ads.

Dynamic Logic A research company specializing in measuring online advertising effectiveness. It serves online advertisers, ad agencies, and publishers with feedback regarding the branding effectiveness of their specific online advertising campaigns. Website: dynamiclogic.com

Dynamic rotation The delivery of ad banners on a rotating or random basis as opposed to static placement of an ad on the same page all the time. This offers the potential for each user to see a different message and for ads to be seen in more than one place on a website.

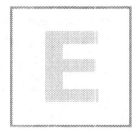

E When used as a prefix, it refers to *electronic*, as in e-mail.

Ear candy Sound effects (e.g., music) added to a website to make the site more appealing to users. *Also see* eye candy.

Early adopter A person who is among the first to use a new product or service.

Early fringe (EF) *See* TV dayparts.

Early morning (EM) *See* TV dayparts.

Early news (EN) *See* TV dayparts.

Earned rate A rate (usually discounted and for print media) earned by an advertiser based on the frequency of ads running or the volume of advertising placed over a specific time period.

Earth station A mechanical or electrical device used for transmitting or receiving messages. It consists of a disk antenna (dish) and receiving equipment directed toward a geosynchronous satellite.

Easy listening A radio programming format composed of light instrumental and vocal music largely from the 1940s through the 1970s. It is sometimes called "beautiful music."

EBI *See* effective buying income.

E-business   Electronic business. A company that earns all or part of its income (revenue) using the Internet.

E-commerce   Electronic commerce. Conducting business online via the Internet. *Also see* click-and-mortar.

Econometrics   The application of mathematical analysis principles to economic problems, specifically those pertaining to business and finance. Econometrics uses a specialized statistical technique for large masses of assembled data. Multifarious phenomena affect a company's sales, such as advertising, pricing, direct marketing, product news, the economic climate, weather, and competitive activity. Econometric analysis isolates the specific contribution each ingredient has on sales (or store traffic, etc.) and thereby determines the effectiveness of advertising and other marketing activities in terms of actual sales and return on investment (ROI). Assuming availability of a substantial amount of detailed data for each ingredient being analyzed, analyses can also be conducted to determine the ROI for aspects such as each TV daypart used in a campaign. *Also called* marketing mix modeling and ROI analysis.

EDI   *See* electronic data interchange

Edison Media Research   A company that conducts survey research and provides strategic information to radio stations, television stations, Internet companies, newspapers, cable networks, record labels, and other media organizations. Website: edisonresearch.com

E-distribution   Electronic distribution. *See* e-fulfillment.

Editorial   A written opinion transmitted via a newspaper, magazine, TV program, or other medium. An editorial is distinguished from typical "news." Most major metropolitan newspapers, for example, have an editorial page.

Editorial classification   Designating each piece of magazine or newspaper editorial into a category, such as news, fashion, food, and entertainment.

Editorial copy   All written material in a publication that is not advertising.

Edu (.edu)   *See* domain name.

Educational channel   A TV station that contains educational programming and might or might not contain advertising.

EF   Early fringe. *See* TV dayparts.

Effective buying income (EBI)   Equivalent to "disposable income" because it counts a person's net income (after taxes, etc.). EBI is used in the bulk measurement of market potential, indicating the ability to buy products and services. Developed by Market Statistics.

Effective circulation   *See* daily effective circulation.

Effective frequency   A level of exposure during a specified period of time to the media vehicle(s) in which an advertiser has a commercial or advertisement. There have been many research studies and points of view concerning what level of frequency is supposedly "effective." The most notable are Ogilvy and Mather's study (1965) concluding that all levels are effective, General Electric (1968) concluding 2 to 3 is effective, DuPont study (1968) stating 3, Colin McDonald (1971) stating 2, Herbert Krugman (1972) stating 2 to 3, Alvin Achenbaum (1977) stating 3 to 10, Mike Naples (1979) stating 3 or more, and John Philip Jones (1995) stating 1. The chosen level depends on the media planner's judgment (which may or may not be based on critical research). The period of time can be, for example, within one day, one week, four weeks, or more, again based on the planner's judgment. The effect (i.e., the effectiveness) can be creating awareness for the advertised product or service, retention of the message over time, a consumer's response to the message (such as buying the product), or any other criteria judged to be important to the success of the advertising. Designating an effective frequency level (such as 2 or more) automatically supposes that (1) less frequency is ineffective and (2) all exposures above this level are of equal importance. This may or may not be accurate. It can be argued (using 2+ as an example) that a frequency of 1 is less effective but not totally ineffective, and that 3 exposures are more effective than 2, and that 10 exposures are wasteful. The astute planner can therefore make other judgments and put values on each frequency level with, say, 2.0 being at 100 percent value, while lower and higher levels of frequency are at less than 100 percent value. If such values are assigned, the planner would multiply the reach at each frequency level by the value and add the products to obtain a weighted reach. Importantly effective frequency measures not the advertising itself, but only the media vehicle(s) in which the advertising appears. It is not quite a leap of faith, but it is assumed that if a person consumes a medium (e.g., viewing TV, listening to radio), that person has a good opportunity to also be exposed to the advertising in that medium. *Also see* **1.** effective reach, **2.** frequency (average), **3.** frequency distribution, **4.** recency, **5.** three hits.

Effective reach   A level of delivery (reach) during a specified time period that is deemed "effective." The level may or may not be tied to an effective frequency level. For example, a media planner might judge that at least a 50 reach is needed each week of the advertising campaign or a 50 reach at the 2+ frequency level. In the former, the level of frequency of exposure to the advertising is not stated and therefore not important; in the latter, the planner has judged that those people who are reached should be exposed to the advertising at least two times. As with effective frequency, "effective" can be judged in many ways, such as creating awareness, advertising retention, and consumer action. Effective reach measures vehicle exposure not advertising exposure. It is assumed that if a person is exposed to a media vehicle, that person has a good opportunity to also be exposed to the advertising in that medium. *Also see* **1.** frequency distribution, **2.** reach, **3.** recency, **4.** three hits.

Efficiency   Generally refers to the relative cost of delivering media audiences. Relativity deals with comparisons to other media forms or vehicles. *See* **1.** cost per point, **2.** cost per thousand.

E-fulfillment   Electronic fulfillment. Using the Internet to deliver digitized products to a user (subscriber or purchaser), such as books, music, and software. Also referred to as e-distribution.

8-sheet poster   An out-of-home poster panel usually measuring 5 feet by 11 feet. It is also known as a junior panel because it has the same proportions as, although smaller than, a 30-sheet poster.

E-journal   Electronic journal. A publication, such as a newsletter, that is published only electronically for access via the Internet.

Electronic data interchange (EDI)   The exchange of documents (e.g., media invoices, media buys) between different companies (e.g., a TV station and an advertising agency) using a computer network such as the Internet.

EM   Early morning. *See* TV dayparts.

E-mail (or Email)   Electronic mail. Mail that is electronically transmitted by a computer. E-mail sends messages instantaneously anywhere in the world, for less money than mailing a letter or phoning someone. There is no standard spelling for *e-mail*. Either E-mail (uppercase, hyphenated), e-mail (lowercase, hyphenated), or email (lowercase, not hyphenated) is equally accepted. The hyphenated version, however, does punctuate that it is "electronic," such as with e-commerce and e-tailing.

E-marketer   Electronic marketer. A research company that provides Internet and e-business statistics. Its reports combine original analysis with aggregated numbers from leading sources worldwide. The company was founded in 1996. Website: emarketer.com

Embellishment   Special effects attached to the face of an outdoor unit, such as letters, figures, mechanical devices, or lighting. *Also see* extension.

Emoticons   Typed characters that create a representation of an emotion. An example is the "smiley," which is an on-its-side representation of a smiling face as shown within the following brackets: [:-)].

EN   Early news. *See* TV dayparts.

Enamel proof   A camera-ready proof of an advertisement printed on coated glossy paper and sent to a publication for reproduction.

En banc   An informal meeting held by the Federal Communications Commission (FCC) to hear presentations on specific topics by diverse parties. The commissioners, or other officials, question presenters and use their comments in considering FCC rules and policies on the subject matter under consideration.

Encoda   A company that provides products and services including Internet applications, digital automation, and electronic business and media convergence solutions. Products are used by broadcasting, advertising, and new media industries, including television networks and stations, radio stations and networks, media buyers, and media sales representatives. Encoda was created in September 2000 when Columbine JDS Systems, Inc., merged with Enterprise Systems Group, Inc. Website: encodasystems.com

Encoding commercials   The digital encoding of radio or TV commercials in the audio track, which is detectable only by specialized electronic equipment. The technology is used to capture and report on which commercial execution aired (ISCI code or AD/ID) when and where. *See* **1.** AudioAudit, **2.** broadcast verification system, **3.** Nielsen Monitor-Plus, **4.** pattern recognition, **5.** SIGMA, **6.** Teletrax, **7.** Verance.

Encryption   **1.** The process of electronically translating an audio or TV signal into a secret code so that a decoder is needed to receive the original signal. **2.** Using a secret code to secure computer data. To read an encrypted file, you must have access to a password (secret key). Unencrypted data is called plain text; encrypted data is called cipher text.

End rate   The rate given to an advertiser after all discounts are applied.

Enhanced service provider   A business that offers to transmit voice and data messages and simultaneously adds value to the messages it transmits. Examples include telephone answering services, alarm/security companies, and transaction processing companies.

Enhanced TV (ETV)   Interactive television technology that allows marketers to send hypertext markup language (HTML) data and graphics through a small part of the regular analog broadcast signal. The viewer can click on the displayed data or graphic if the TV is equipped with a special set-top box device. *Also see* Wink.

E-publishing   Electronic publishing. Publishing some type of written, auditory, or visual material on the World Wide Web—that is, publishing without paper.

ESOMAR   European Society for Opinion and Marketing Research. Founded in 1948, ESOMAR has over 4,000 members in 100 countries, both users and providers of research. Members come from advertising and media agencies, universities, and business schools, as well as public institutions and government authorities. Its mission is to promote the use of opinion and marketing research in order to improve decision making in business and society worldwide. Website: esomar.org

Estimate billing   Invoicing an advertiser based on the predicted (estimated) cost of a media schedule before the final media invoice is received by the buying agent. The purpose of this practice is to obtain payment from the advertiser so media bills can be paid in a timely manner. Also called a prebill. *Also see* float.

Estimated rating   *See* rating.

E-tailing   Electronic retailing. Retail commerce conducted online. Often, the e-tailer does not have a brick-and-mortar location.

eTelmar   Created to provide Telmar's media planning software over the Internet using a Web browser. Website: etelmar.com

Ethernet   A type of networking technology for local area networks (LANs) that uses coaxial cable to carry radio frequency signals between computers. It operates at a rate of 10 megabits per second (Mbps).

Ethnic media   Media targeted to a specific ethnic group, such as African-Americans or Hispanics.

ETV   *See* Enhanced TV.

Evaliant Media Resources   Founded in 1998, Evaliant is an international provider of online advertising data. It was purchased by Taylor Nelson Sofres (TNS) and operates under CMRi, the Internet division of TNS Media Intelligence/CMR. Website: evaliant.net

Evening   *See* radio dayparts.

Event marketing   Marketing products or services by using or sponsoring events such as art exhibits, concerts, and sports.

Exabyte   Approximately one quintillion bytes (1,024 petabytes). In numerical sequence, bytes are counted as kilobyte, megabyte, gigabyte, terabyte, petabyte, exabyte.

Exclusive cume listeners   The number of different people who listen to a given radio station and no other radio station during a specific radio daypart, as reported by Arbitron.

Exclusive readers   Within a combination of magazines as specified in a media plan, these readers read one magazine but not any others in the schedule.

Exclusivity   The granting to one advertiser by a media vehicle to be the only advertiser within that advertiser's competitive category. Typically, exclusivity is granted for major sponsors using the media vehicle, who have purchased multiple commercials (or advertisements) in the vehicle. Exclusivity can be granted for the entire telecast of a TV program (or radio program, etc.), or for a specified segment of the program (e.g., during a given half-hour or specific feature).

Exposure   A person's physical contact (audio, visual, or both) with an advertising medium or message.

Extensible   Computer programming language, system, or protocol that can be modified by changing or adding features.

Extensible Hypertext Markup Language (XHTML)   A programming language developed by the World Wide Web Consortium that is a reframing and follow-on version of Hypertext Markup Language (HTML). The primary difference between XHTML and HTML is that the former can be extended (extensible) by anyone that uses it.

Extensible Markup Language (XML)   A version of SGML (Standard Generalized Markup Language) designed especially for Web documents. It allows designers to create their own customized tags, enabling the definition, transmission, validation, and interpretation of data between applications and between organizations. It was developed by the World Wide Web Consortium.

Extension   1. A constructed shape added onto, and typically outside the physical parameters of, an out-of-home bulletin to enhance the advertising. *Also see* embellishment. 2. The agreed delay beyond the normal closing date for delivery of advertising creative materials (mechanical or keyline) to the publication.

Extranet   The connection of two or more intranets. For example, company A will allow access to its intranet by company B, typically for certain kinds of information. An extranet can be established, for example, by a media agency to allow one of its clients to access data the agency created for the client.

Eye candy   Graphics or photography added to a website to make the site look more appealing to users. *Also see* ear candy.

E-zine   Electronic magazine. A magazine published in electronic form for viewing on the Internet, such as mediapost.com and medialifemagazine.com.

Facing　The direction an out-of-home poster or bulletin faces—for example, a south-facing poster can be seen by northbound traffic.

Facsimile (fax)　An electronic transmission from one location to another of a printed page or image using a fax machine.

Family　A radio programming format that is a mix of music, news, and talk designed for all age groups.

Family Friendly Programming Forum　An association of major advertisers that encourages the TV networks, studios, and the television production community to create and air more prime-time programs that are relevant and interesting to a broad audience and that the average parent would enjoy viewing together with a child. The forum offers the TV networks seed money to develop G-rated programs. If the networks decide to create pilots from the ideas, the forum then asks its corporate members to reimburse the fund.

FAQ　Frequently asked question. Often found on websites and sales promotional literature, FAQs are listed, along with answers, to questions that a company has found, or predicts it will find, to be the most popular queries about the company and its products or services.

Far forward right-hand page　A position request for an advertisement to be placed as near as possible to the beginning of a magazine issue on the right-hand page. It was once believed that advertisers had a better chance of having readers see their ads (i.e., ad readership scores would be higher) if placed in this position. Advertising readership studies conducted by Starch (now RoperASW) revealed virtually no difference in Starch scores between far forward, far back, or between right or left-hand pages.

Farm out   To give work out to people other than a company's employees. For example, an advertising agency might outsource media buying to another company. Also referred to as outsourcing.

Farm publication   A publication targeted to farmers and related occupations that focus on agricultural topics.

Farm Publication Audit Reports   *See* Audit Bureau of Circulations.

Farm Publisher's Statement   *See* Audit Bureau of Circulations.

Fax   *See* facsimile.

FCC   *See* Federal Communications Commission.

Feature   **1.** An ad within a retailer's circular. **2.** A product ad within a retailer's newspaper ad. **3.** Any radio or TV program that the network or local station deems to be "special."

Federal Communications Commission (FCC)   An independent U.S. government agency, directly responsible to Congress. The FCC was established by the Communications Act of 1934 and is charged with regulating interstate and international communications by radio, television, wire, satellite, and cable. The FCC's jurisdiction covers the 50 states, the District of Columbia, and U.S. possessions.

Federal Trade Commission (FTC)   A government agency, established in 1915, whose purpose is to enforce a variety of federal antitrust and consumer protection laws. The FTC seeks to ensure that the nation's markets function competitively, vigorously, efficiently, and free of undue restrictions. It also attempts to eliminate acts or practices that are unfair or deceptive.

Feeder lines   Coaxial cables that branch from the trunk lines past individual homes and to which drop lines are connected to provide cable TV in individual homes.

Femtosecond   *See* second.

Fiber-optic cable   Wiring with pure glass strands encased in it. This kind of cable wiring can transmit significantly more information (video, audio, or text) than conventional cable or phone lines. *Also see* coaxial cable.

Fiber optics   Thin glass fibers used for transmitting information. Light beams are transmitted along optical fibers. A fiber is about the thickness of a human hair. A light beam, such as that produced by a laser, can be modulated to carry information such as text files or audio/visual signals from a single source to a person's TV set.

FIFO   *See* first-in, first-out.

File extension   The letters following the "dot" in a file name that indicate the format or type of file. For example, in the file name "A-to-Z.doc," the extension *doc* indicates it is a Word document and can therefore be opened or viewed in Microsoft Word.

File transfer protocol (FTP)   A means of exchanging files between computers on the Internet.

Finger   A computer program that lets a user find out the name associated with an e-mail address—whether or not the person sought is online at the present moment—and possibly additional information, depending on what data is stored about that person on that computer.

Fingerprinting commercials   *See* pattern recognition.

Fire sale   *See* opportunistic buy.

Firewall   A security device for computer software that prevents unauthorized access into the computer's files.

Firm (.firm)   *See* domain name.

First cover   *See* inside front cover.

First-in, first-out (FIFO)   **1.** A method of inventory cost accounting where the first goods purchased are assumed to be the first sold, so the ending inventory consists of the most recently purchased goods. **2.** In computer programming, a processing approach where the oldest work request is handled first. *Also see* last-in, first-out.

First generation   The first version of a particular product, such as software.

First run   Programming that has not been previously broadcast.

First to market   Introducing a product or service into the marketplace before any competitors with the same or similar product.

Fiscal year (FY)   Any 12-month period, defined by the company, in which accounts are balanced. *Also see* calendar year.

Fixed position   **1.** A radio or TV commercial unit purchased with nonpreemption guarantees; that is, the media seller cannot remove a commercial without the advertiser's permission (except in extenuating circumstances, such as a news flash/bulletin). **2.** A position guaranteed to the advertiser within a specific section or adjacent to specific editorial in a magazine or newspaper.

Fixed rate   The price of a radio or TV commercial that guarantees the spot will air in an agreed specific time slot without preemption (except in extenuating circumstances, such as a news flash/bulletin).

Fixed wireless   Wireless devices that remain in fixed locations, such as an office or in one's home, as opposed to mobile or portable wireless devices. Fixed wireless devices typically obtain their electrical power from the location's utility mains, as opposed to mobile or portable devices that rely on a battery.

Flagging   A tear in the paper of an out-of-home poster, causing the advertisement to hang loose and "flag" in the wind.

Flagship   The most important one of a related group, such as a company's bestselling product or most prestigious store.

Flash   A rich media form of online advertising that allows movies and animation to move seamlessly across a Web page. It used to be known as FutureSplash.

Flash approach   An outdoor display with a very short approach, such as a panel that is viewable from no more than 100 feet by people in a car traveling at normal speed.

Flash paint   A schedule of out-of-home, permanent, painted bulletins in a market for a short period of time, such as for 2 to 4 months, versus the typical 12-month purchase for these units.

Flat rate   The nondiscountable rate charged by a magazine or newspaper for advertising. *Also called* a onetime rate.

Flexface   *See* flexform.

Flexform   A process used in outdoor advertising where the creative message is printed on vinyl (or similar material) and stretched across and around an outdoor board. Sometimes called flexface or flexible face.

Flexible face   *See* flexform.

Flexies   A multipage preprinted insert, usually printed on newspaper stock and distributed in newspapers as a freestanding insert.

Flight   A period of time during which advertising runs.

Flighting   Scheduling media advertising for a period of time (e.g., four weeks), followed by a hiatus, then (if so scheduled) another flight of advertising. *Also see* 1. adstock, 2. pulsing.

Float   The time between an advertiser's payment to its agent (e.g., a media agency) and the agent's payment to a supplier (e.g., a TV station). During this period the agent could invest all or part of the advertiser's payment in order to earn interest on the investment.

Floating ad   An advertisement on a Web page that is created and displayed in a "layer" above the hypertext markup language (HTML) content, thereby obscuring the content below it. The ad appears to float over the top of the page.

Floating island   A single print advertisement on a page, which is surrounded by editorial.

Floating point operations per second (FLOPS)   A measurement of the speed of microprocessors. It includes operations that involve fractional numbers, which take much longer to compute than integers. In larger computers, FLOPS are measured in megaflops (1 million floating point operations per second), gigaflops (1 billion), and teraflops (1 trillion).

Floppy (disk)   *See* disk(ette).

FLOPS   *See* floating point operations per second.

Flowchart   A typically graphic summary of recommended media that shows some details about their usage through an advertising period, such as an annual flowchart listing weekly target rating points (TRPs) by media form or annual budget by media form.

FM   *See* frequency modulation.

Focus group   A group of people brought together to discuss and comment on a specific subject, such as an advertising strategy, a new product, or an advertisement or commercial. The group typically consists of people who share the same demographic composition as the advertiser's target audience. The focus group session is structured and moderated by a trained professional. The number of people in the group is at the discretion of the moderator, but generally consists of 8 to 12 people.

Footprint   **1.** The geographic area in which a satellite transponder's signal can be received by an earth station dish. This coverage area is graphically similar to a footprint. **2.** A digital code ascribed to commercials or programs that allows computers to track over-the-air activity. **3.** The amount of space a particular unit of hardware or software occupies. For example, hardware with a small footprint suggests that its absolute size is small; software with a small footprint takes up less space in a computer. *Also see* **1.** geostationary earth orbit system, **2.** satellite.

Forced combination   Newspapers owned by the same publisher that sell advertising space only in the combined editions of the newspapers.

Foreign advertising   Ads placed in Yellow Page directories that are distributed in geographic areas distant from the core area in which the advertiser's business is physically located.

Format   *See* 1. radio programming formats, 2. standard page, 3. tabloid.

Forrester Research, Inc.   A research firm that analyzes the future of technology change and its impact on businesses, consumers, and society. Companies use the research as a source of insight and strategy to guide their business technology decisions. Founded in 1983. Website: forrester.com

FORTRAN   A computer programming language used primarily for applications that require extensive mathematical computations. Short for *formula translator.*

4As   *See* American Association of Advertising Agencies.

4C, 4CP, 4CPB   Four color, four-color page, four-color page bleed. *See* four-color page.

Four-color page   A magazine or newspaper advertisement that uses three colors plus black and white. Abbreviated as *4CP* or *P4C.* If it is a "bleed" ad, it is abbreviated as *4CPB* or *P4CB.*

Four-color process   The printing process that uses four ink colors (black, magenta, cyan, and yellow) to produce a printed image that matches the color of the original image.

Fourth cover   The back cover of a magazine. A magazine has four covers: front, inside front (also called second cover), inside back cover (IBC or third cover) and back cover (fourth cover).

Fractionals   *See* fractional unit.

Fractional unit   An advertising unit less than a page in size.

Fragmentation   1. The condition of a computer operating system's file system where files are divided into pieces and scattered throughout the system. As files are created or changed, the operating system needs to store parts of files in noncontiguous clusters. Fragmentation over time can slow a computer's operation. *Also see* 1. audience fragmentation, 2. defrag(mentation).

Frames   The simultaneous loading of two or more Web pages at the same time within the same screen.

Franchise   1. A business established or operated under an authorization to sell or distribute a company's goods or services in a particular area, such as McDonald's fast-food store franchise. 2. The legal authorization required under law from a state or local government for the establishment of a cable television service servicing a defined geographic area.

Franchise buy   An order for commercial time that provides the advertiser special options or rights, as with a sponsorship.

Franchise position   A position in a newspaper or magazine (usually sold at a premium price) for which an advertiser is granted a permanent franchise or right to its use as long as it is renewed periodically.

FreeDemographics.com   Provides free, unlimited access to U.S. Census data.

Free publication   A publication that can be obtained without cost to the reader, such as *Pennysaver*.

Freestanding insert (FSI)   A preprinted advertising message that is inserted into, but not bound into, print media (generally into newspapers). A more accurate term, but one that is not used, would be free-floating insert.

Freeware   Free software available on the Internet for downloading. *Also see* 1. demoware, 2. shareware.

Frequency (average)   The number of times the average person within a target audience has an opportunity to be exposed to an advertiser's messages within a specified time period. The "average person" is (1) a part of the group that was reached by the scheduled media—that is, people not reached by the scheduled media forms are not counted in the average, and (2) designated as average only to indicate the weighted midpoint of frequency. For example, if half the people had an exposure opportunity of 2.0 and half an exposure opportunity of 1.0, the average person would have a frequency of 1.5. Indeed, no person reached is exposed to 1.5 commercials. Some receive more than average frequency and some less. "Exposure" is for the media vehicle(s) in which the advertiser has placed commercials or ads, not specifically for the advertising contained in those vehicles. Advertising exposure therefore assumes that people consuming the purchased media forms have a good opportunity to be exposed to the advertising in those forms. The "time period" can be for any length of time deemed appropriate by the media planner, such as one week or four weeks. Frequency is typically reported in combination with "reach" and commonly calculated out to one decimal point, such as 1.0, 1.1, or 1.2. Although frequency levels can be shown with two decimal points (or more), it seems ludicrous to do so, given that the calculations are based on target rating points (which are estimates) and algorithms are used for reach estimates. *Also see* 1. band, 2. effective frequency, 3. effective reach, 4. frequency distribution, 5. opportunity to see.

Formula:

TRPs ÷ reach = frequency

Example:

100 ÷ 50 = 2.0

Frequency discount   A cost discount given to an advertiser, which is based on the number of ads scheduled within a specific period of time, such as six ads within one year. *Also see* 1. open rate, 2. volume discount.

Frequency distribution   The array of reach at each frequency level. During a media campaign, people are reached with different rates of exposure. For example, if a campaign encompassed the use of one ad in each of three magazines, it would be found that some people would read only one of the magazines, some read two, and some read all three. Therefore, different people have opportunities to be exposed to one, two, or three ads. Hypothetically, the campaign might have a total reach of 50 (percent). A frequency distribution (based on various formulas, which in turn were based on various tabulations of actual data) delineates the percentage of reach at each frequency level. In the preceding example, 30 percent of people received a frequency (exposure opportunity) of 1.0, 15 percent a frequency of 2.0, and 5 percent a frequency of 3.0. In other words, reach has been arrayed for each frequency level.

	Frequency Level	Reach	Target Rating Points (TRPs)
	1.0	30	30
	2.0	15	30
	3.0	5	15
Average frequency	1.5		
Total:		50	75

Also see 1. effective frequency, 2. effective reach, 3. frequency (average), 4. quintile distribution, 5. recency, 6. three hits.

Frequency modulation (FM)   A clear radio signal, without static or fading, that results from adjusting the transmitting wave's frequency to the originating sound. FM is conveyed to the radio wave by slightly changing the wave's frequency—similar to changing the color of light by passing it through various shades of tinted glass. Operating frequencies are expressed in megahertz (MHz); for example, a station broadcasting at 96.7 MHz has a frequency of 96,700,000 cycles per second. U.S. stations operate on frequencies that are 0.2 MHz (200 kilohertz [kHz]) apart from each other, such as 96.5, 96.7, 96.8. In Europe, stations operate on frequencies that are 100 kHz apart.

Frequency (periodicity)   Something occurring at intervals, such as the daily, weekly, or monthly issuance of a publication.

Fringe area   The outermost geographic reach of a radio or television station's signal.

Fringe time   *See* TV dayparts.

Front-end/back-end   A front-end computer application or program is one that a user interacts with directly; a back-end computer applications is one that supports the front-end service.

Frontispiece   The advertising position opposite the opening of the main editorial section in a magazine.

Frontload   A scheduling tactic where the bulk of the advertising weight (media delivery) is scheduled in the beginning days or weeks of an advertising campaign. The purpose of frontloading is to generate high levels of media delivery (reach, frequency, or both) with the belief that the advertising will break through the clutter of advertising, be seen (or heard), and be remembered for a longer period of time.

Front of book   A term used in magazine insertion orders specifying that the advertisement must run in the first 50 percent of a particular magazine issue's pages. *Also see* far forward right-hand page.

FSI   *See* freestanding insert.

FTC   *See* Federal Trade Commission.

FTP   *See* file transfer protocol.

FUBAR   An acronym for "fouled up beyond all recognition." Different words can be used for one or more of the letters, such as *repair* or *recovery* instead of *recognition.*

Full disclosure   The practice of a media buying agent to give the advertiser a copy of the medium's affidavit of performance and invoice to verify that the agent's media billing to the advertiser is accurate.

Full run   Refers to all editions of a newspaper that are distributed within one day, as opposed to, for example, zone editions.

Full service   A radio programming format that is community-oriented programming including news, community events, sports, and often farm reports.

Full service agency   An advertising agency that provides multiple services (usually in-house) to an advertiser, such as creative, market research, media planning and buying, and other resources. Many of the larger advertising agencies have spun off (unbundled) their media departments and formed "media agencies" to handle planning and buying.

Full showing   1. The purchase of many or all outdoor bulletins in a specific geographic area for a specific time period. A full showing indicates that 100 percent of the population in a community will have an opportunity to see the advertising at least once. This is different from a #100 showing. *Also see* showing. **2.** A transit advertising buy that places an advertisement on every bus, train car, or subway car.

Fusion   **1.** Combining respondent level data from separate research samples in order to link consumer consumption and media patterns as if they were reported by one source. Respondents from each database are matched up based on a list of shared demographic information, such as age, gender, or income. The greater the list of matched demographic variables, the greater the reliability in the overall findings. The primary media purpose of fusing databases is for estimating cross-media duplication to obtain multimedia reach of specific campaigns. *Also see* single source data. **2.** A radio programming format of soft instrumental music. Also known as New Age.

FY   *See* fiscal year.

G Abbreviation for *gamma*, Greek for *one million. Also see* **1.** gigabit, **2.** gigabyte, **3.** MPAA ratings.

GAA *See* gross average audience.

Gallup Organization A market and media research supplier that specializes in copy research, tracking, concept testing, media research, claims substantiation, spokesperson testing, and event sponsorship. Website: gallup.com

Gatefold A folded advertising page that when unfolded is bigger in dimension than the regular page.

Gateway A computer network point (node) that serves as an entryway to another computer network. A gateway node controls traffic within a network; a host node delivers data transmissions such as Web pages to a user.

Gazunta Media slang for the mathematical function of division, such as two gazunta four twice.

GB *See* gigabyte.

Gbps *See* gigabits per second.

GDP *See* gross domestic product.

Generation X, Y, Z   Nomenclature for people born within specified years where economic and technological phenomena had a demonstrable effect on cultural and behavioral characteristics. GenXers were born between 1965 and 1979, GenYers between 1980 and 1995, and GenZers from 1995 on. GenZers are also broadly referred to as the new generation and sometimes (although technically incorrect as of this writing) include tweens and teens. Baby boomers, born between 1946 and 1964 are the parents of GenXers. People born before 1946 are usually called old people, although many, including this author, would argue that definition.

Geodemographic mapping   Demographic data graphically displayed on a map. Typically, the demographic information is color coded (e.g., low income is yellow, average income is blue, and high income is red) and electronically printed on the map, showing where each demographic grouping is located within a particular piece of geography.

Geodemographics   The demographic description of people living in specific geographic areas. *Also see* **1.** ACORN, **2.** MicroVision, **3.** PRIZM.

GEOS   *See* geostationary earth orbit system.

Geostationary earth orbit system (GEOS)   A communication system that includes a satellite in geosynchronous equatorial orbit (GEO) located directly above the equator, exactly 22,300 miles out in space. It always stays directly over the same spot on Earth. A geosynchronous orbit can also be called a geostationary orbit.

Geosynchronous (satellite)   *See* geostationary earth orbit system.

Ghost site   A website that is no longer maintained but is still available for viewing. It is also called a gravesite.

GHz   *See* gigahertz.

GIF   *See* graphics interchange format.

Gig   Verbal shorthand for a gigabit or gigabyte.

Gigabit (G)   One billion bits of data transmission in a telecommunications system. The term is used to measure data communication speed.

Gigabits per second (Gbps)   A measure of the bandwidth of a telecommunications medium (the total information flow over a given time). Bandwidth is also measured in kilobits per second (kbps) or in megabits per second (Mbps), depending on the medium and transmission method.

Gigabyte (G or Gb)   Approximately one billion bytes (1,024 megabytes). In numerical sequence, bytes are counted as kilobyte, megabyte, gigabyte, terabyte, petabyte, exabyte.

Gigabits per second (Gbps)   A billion bits per second of data flow in a telecommunications medium.

Gigaflop   *See* floating point operations per second.

Gigahertz (GHz)   One billion cycles of electrical frequency per second. Kilohertz (KHz) is 1,000 cycles per second; megahertz (MHz) is 1,000,000 cycles per second. Named after Heinrich Rudolf Hertz, a German physicist who was the first to produce radio waves artificially.

Global positioning system (GPS)   A highly accurate geographic location system that communicates with orbiting satellites and precisely pinpoints structures in terms of exact latitude and longitude.

GNP   Gross national product. *See* gross domestic product.

Golden oldies   *See* oldies.

Googol   Typically, any enormous number. Technically, the number 10 raised to the hundredth power (1 followed by 100 zeros).

Googolplex   Just about the biggest number this side of infinity. It is the number 10 raised to the googol power, which is equivalent to the number one followed by a googol of zeros.

Gospel   A radio programming format consisting of evangelical music.

Gov (.gov)   *See* domain name.

GPS   *See* global positioning system.

Grade A and B contours   A Federal Communications Commission requirement of specific levels of transmission signal strength for certain areas on a TV station's coverage pattern.

Grade 1–6   A grade given to television picture quality: 1 = excellent, 2 = good, 3 = passable, 4 = marginal, 5 = inferior, 6 = unusable.

Grandfather clause   An allowable continuance based on circumstances existing prior to the adoption of some policy.

Grandfathered   1. An exception made for existing enterprises to operate as they have in the past despite new laws or regulations to the contrary. 2. Preferential treatment exhibited by a media seller to a long-standing advertiser of that medium—for example, lower rates, preferred positioning.

Granular   Describes highly detailed data or information.

Graphical user interface (GUI)   A software front end that provides an interface between the user and the applications on the user's computer, typically showing the applications with icons. It is what the user sees on the computer screen.

Graphics interchange format (GIF or gif)   One of the two most common types of images used on the World Wide Web, the other being JPEG (Joint Photographic Experts Group). The pictures and graphics seen on Web pages are usually in GIF, because these files are small and download quickly.

Gravesite   *See* ghost site.

Gravure   *See* rotogravure.

Greenfield Consulting Group   A qualitative research consultancy founded in 1983 that, among other things, conducts customized consumer surveys online. The company was purchased by WPP in 2002. Website: greenfield.com

Gross   The total number or amount exclusive of any deductions or discounts, as opposed to net.

Gross audience   A medium's total audience regardless of duplication. This is synonymous with gross impressions.

Gross average audience (GAA)   The combined audiences (average ratings) of a TV program's total airings. It is termed "gross" (not "net") because it includes duplicated viewers.

Gross billing   The amount of dollars claimed by a media agent (e.g., ad agency, media agency) as to how much money was planned, placed, or both by the agent on behalf of their advertiser clients in various media. Gross billing is based on the gross costs of the purchased media forms, without regard to any commissions or fees earned by the agent.

Gross circulation   The maximum amount of people who pass an outdoor display and have an opportunity to see it.

Gross cost   The total cost of a media vehicle or a media schedule, which includes the cost discount typically offered by a media supplier to the media buyer. Most media vehicles offer qualified buyers (e.g., ad agencies, media agencies) a 15 percent discount off the gross cost. This discount is commonly, but incorrectly, known as the agency commission. Because agency compensation structures have changed over the years, the "15 percent agency commission" has nearly become obsolete. Nonetheless, media sellers continue to discount their gross costs by 15 percent. Therefore, when a qualified buying agent (for example) purchases a commercial or ad for $100 (gross), the seller is expecting payment of $85 (net). The $15 difference is either kept in whole or in part by the agent as a commission or service fee, or returned in whole or in part to the advertiser client.

Gross domestic product (GDP)   The measure of country's output generated through production by labor and property, which are physically located within the confines of that country. In the United States, GDP is reported by U.S. Department of Commerce, Bureau of Economic Analysis. It includes the following: personal consumption, government expenditures, private investment, inventory growth, and trade balance. The government calibrates the relative prices of these goods, and their relative importance to the economy every year. There are two types of GDP: nominal and real. Nominal GDP is measured in current prices, without any adjustment for deflation or inflation in prices; real GDP includes the rate of change in prices of goods and services. Many news reports simply use *GDP* as a term to describe this announcement. The actual announcement focuses on the real GDP. In addition, newspapers will often refer to the rate of growth during the most recent quarter and will not always refer to the fact that it is reported at annual rates of change. This is contrasted to the reports of the consumer price index, which are reported at actual percentage changes in the index for a single month and not at annual rates. In December 1991, the Bureau of Economic Analysis began using the GDP rather than the gross national product (GNP) as the primary measure of U.S. production. This figure facilitates comparisons between the United States and other countries, since it is the standard used in international guidelines for economic accounting. The GNP is the total dollar value of all final goods and services produced for consumption in a society during a particular time period. Its rise or fall measures economic activity based on the labor and production output within a country. The figures used to assemble data include the manufacture of tangible goods such as cars, furniture, and bread, and the provision of services used in daily living such as education, health care, and auto repair.

Gross impressions   *See* impressions.

Gross national product (GNP)   *See* gross domestic product.

Gross rating points (GRPs)   The sum of all ratings delivered by a given list of media vehicles. For example, if one commercial is scheduled in each of two TV programs, each with a 10.0 rating, that will accumulate 20 GRPs. The reason for using the word *gross* is to indicate that there is (or probably is) duplication between the two ratings: some of the people who viewed program A might also have viewed program B. Therefore, the two programs combined do not "reach" 20 percent of people—they reach the "equivalent" of 20 percent of the people. The concept can be more easily seen in the purchase of a combination of programs whose combined ratings exceed 100. Because a rating is a percentage of a population universe, it is impossible to reach more than 100 percent of that universe. GRPs are synonymous with TRPs (target rating points). When the concept of GRP originally came into being, only household data was available. In time, companies like ACNielsen and Arbitron began to study people viewing TV programs, and eventually issued people ratings for TV programs. To distinguish between household and people ratings, advertisers began to differentiate between the two by using GRPs to designate households (HH) and TRPs to designate a specific target audience. Today, the terms are used interchangeably. Regardless of which term is used, a demographic must be stated (e.g., household GRPs or TRPs, women ages 18 to 34 GRPs or TRPs) so the analyst and the reader have a clear understanding of the dimension. GRPs are used to cost out media schedules (with cost-per-point data) and to calculate reach/frequency.

Formula:

reach × frequency = GRPs

Example:

50 × 2.0 = 100

Ground station   An Earth-based transmitting and receiving station for satellites.

Group discount   A lower advertising rate given to an advertiser who runs ads or commercials in a group of publications or radio/TV stations owned by the same company.

GRPs   *See* gross rating points.

Guerilla marketing   Marketing that is unconventional, nontraditional, not by-the-book, extremely flexible, and usually at a low cost. The term stems from a *guerilla*: a member of an irregular, usually indigenous, military or paramilitary unit, which operates in small bands in occupied territory to harass and undermine the enemy by using tactics such as surprise raids.

GUI   *See* graphical user interface.

Gutter   The space on the inside margin of a printed page within a magazine or newspaper.

Gutter bleed   To extend an illustration or copy to cover the inside margin (gutter) of a printed page.

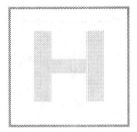

Hacker A very knowledgeable and clever computer programmer. The usual connotation (although not necessarily correct) is someone who illegally breaks into a computer system.

Half banner ad *See* interactive marketing unit.

Half-life *See* adstock.

Half-page spread An advertisement in a magazine or newspaper that spreads (runs) across two facing pages. The total ad space is equivalent in size (square inches) to a full-page ad.

Half showing A transit advertising buy that places an advertisement on every other bus, train car, and so on.

Hall's Magazine Reports A listing of editorial pages, by editorial category, for (currently) 113 consumer publications. Published by R. Russell Hall. Website: magazine.org

Halo effect The effect a product or service, or a product or service's advertising, has on another product or service offered by the same manufacturer or advertiser. The effect can be any number of things, such as advertising awareness, brand name recognition, quality perceptions, and so forth. For example, advertising for Campbell Soup's tomato soup could have a halo effect on other Campbell Soup products. The absolute quantitative effect can be measured via econometric analysis. Media planners sometimes use these findings, or their own intuition and guesstimates, to adjust media delivery levels for a second product based on the halo effect of the first product.

Ham radio   *See* amateur radio.

Handheld Device Markup Language (HDML)   A computer language that allows the text portion of Web pages to be accessed via a wireless device, such as mobile (cellular) phones and personal digital assistants.

Handhelds   *See* personal digital assistant.

Hard disk   The rigid storage medium located with a computer's hard drive.

Hard drive   The mechanism in a computer that stores all the electronic information needed to run the computer, as well as all of the software installed in the computer.

Hard interconnect   *See* interconnect.

Hardwired   Online ads set in a fixed position on a Web page and delivered each time that page is delivered. The opposite of dynamic rotation.

Harris Interactive   A worldwide market research and consulting firm. Harris Interactive is most widely known for The Harris Poll. Website: harrisinteractive.com

HDML   *See* Handheld Device Markup Language.

HD-ROM   *See* high density read-only memory.

HDSL   *See* digital subscriber line.

HDTV   *See* high definition TV.

Head of household   The person in a household who has primary decision-making responsibility for the household and lives in the dwelling.

Head end   The control center of a cable TV system, where incoming signals (such as TV programming from a communications satellite) are amplified, converted, and transmitted to subscribers of the system. A head end is also used to provide a cable operator's subscribers with Internet access via a cable modem termination system (CTMS), which sends and receives digital cable modem signals on a cable network. In 2002, there were 10,613 head ends in the United States.

Heavy metal   A radio programming format within the overall designation of "rock," but with harsher and usually louder sound than rock itself.

Heavy-up   A media scheduling device that increases advertising delivery (e.g., target rating points [TRPs]) above the average level used in the media plan, during a specific period of an extended advertising campaign. For example, instead of running a six-week campaign of 100 TRPs per week, 150 TRPs might be scheduled for each of the first two weeks and 75 weekly TRPs sustained for the remaining four weeks. The purpose of a heavy-up is to produce higher levels of reach, frequency, or both during the heavy-up (to introduce new creative, reinforce a promotion, etc.). *Also see* flighting.

Hertz (Hz)   A unit of measurement of electrical vibrations. One Hz is equal to one cycle per second. Named after Heinrich Rudolf Hertz, a German physicist who was the first to produce radio waves artificially.

HH GRPs   *See* gross rating points.

HHI   *See* household income.

Hiatus   A period of nonactivity between advertising flights.

Hi-fi   1. (Obsolete) A color advertisement preprinted on one side of a continuous roll of smooth coated paper so that the ad resembles a wallpaper pattern, which can be fed into a newspaper's press. This allowed the newspaper to print on the reverse side. 2. (Obsolete in usage, but not in concept) The electronic reproduction of sound, especially from broadcast or recorded sources, with minimal distortion. From the words *high fidelity*.

High band   1. The frequency band used in broadcast videotape recorders, providing a high-quality image through increased bandwidth. 2. TV channels 7 to 13. Low band is TV channels 2 to 6.

High bit-rate digital subscriber line (HDSL)   *See* digital subscriber line.

High definition TV (HDTV)   A television system that has twice the standard number of scanning lines per frame (1,125 lines of horizontal resolution as compared with the current U.S. NTSC standard of 525 lines). HDTV provides a higher quality, sharper video image.

High density read-only memory (HD-ROM)   As with compact disc read-only memory (CD-ROM), this is an optical storage technology that uses discs to store and play back data. Storage capacity, at about 160 gigabytes, is 300 times that of a CD-ROM.

High spot bulletin   An outdoor bulletin that delivers more potential audience exposure than an average bulletin in that community or city.

High spotting   A technique of placing radio commercials in specific hour segments rather than in broader daypart segments, such as placement in the 7:00 to 8:00 A.M. time slot rather than in morning drive time (6:00 to 10:00 A.M.). This technique, as opposed to spots being rotated throughout the daypart, could produce a higher average rating within the daypart.

Highway Beautification Act (HBA)   Congress passed the HBA in 1965 in an attempt to preserve the scenic beauty of America's highways. The act was designed to prohibit construction of new billboards on scenic and rural federal-aid highways, and to require the removal of illegal billboards (those erected without proper permits).

Signed by President Lyndon B. Johnson, the act is sometimes referred to as the Lady Bird Johnson Act.

Hit   The retrieval of any item, like a page or a graphic, from a Web server. When a user calls up a Web page and it has four graphics on it, this is counted as five hits (one for the page and four for the graphics). A related term is *page requests* (or *page views* or *page impressions*), which is the number of times a user requests a Web page from a server.

Hitchhike   A brief commercial mention immediately after the sponsor's final commercial in a broadcast program.

Hold   (Nearly obsolete) A type of order that is a nonbinding, verbal contract between the buyer (on behalf of the advertiser) and the media salesperson prior to making a binding order. Buys used to be negotiated by the media buyer and then placed on hold until the advertiser (client) had an opportunity to see and sanction the buy. Notwithstanding, a buy placed on hold was tantamount to a firm buy and cancellable only under unusual circumstances (e.g., when a media budget was cut at the last minute).

Holding power   The ability of a TV program or specific episode of that program to retain audience throughout the length of its telecast.

Holdover audience   The number of viewers of a TV program's audience who viewed programming on the same channel in the time slot immediately prior.

Home page   The first page or front page of a website, which serves as the starting point for navigating through the site.

Homes passed   The number of homes that have cable TV feeder lines in place close to them, although they might not necessarily have hooked up to receive cable TV. It is an indication of the potential number of subscribers to cable TV. *Also see* penetration.

Homes using TV (HUT)　The percentage of homes tuned into TV during a particular time of the day. HUT, like its related term *rating*, is a percentage and is usually expressed without a percentage sign. A 50 HUT at 9:00–9:15 P.M., for example, states that 50 percent of TV homes in a particular piece of geography (e.g., a DMA or the United States at large) are tuned into TV (any channel) during that quarter hour. HUT levels vary by time of day, day of the week, and month of the year. Generally, HUT levels are highest in prime time and in nonsummer months. HUT is often used as one of the steps in estimating a future program's rating. For example, because HUT levels do not change substantially from year to year for a specific time period, the total potential audience for any time period for any particular date can be estimated. From this, a share estimate can be applied and, using the formula that follows, a rating estimated. *Also see* 1. people using radio, 2. people using TV, 3. rating, 4. share.

　Formula:

　rating ÷ share = HUT

　Example:

　5.0 ÷ 10 (percent) = 50 (percent)

Horizontal cume　The cumulative audience rating for two or more programs in the same time period on different days.

Horizontal half page　A unit size in a magazine or newspaper positioned either on the lower or upper half of a page.

Horizontal publication　A trade magazine.

Horizontal rotation　The rotation of commercial messages on a radio or TV station during the same time period on different days of the week or month. *Also called* horizontal saturation.

Horizontal saturation　*See* horizontal rotation.

Host　A computer system that can be accessed by a user working on a computer that is away from the system. The term is used when two computer systems are connected by modems and telephone lines. The system containing the data is called the host, while the user's computer is generally known as a remote terminal. The term also refers to a computer that is connected to a TCP/IP network, including the Internet.

Hot adult contemporary   A radio programming format that is a blend of current and recent hits, but targeted to a younger demographic group.

Hot link   The text or graphic on a website that when clicked on, automatically takes the user to another Web page or a different area of the same page. A hot link is also called hyperlink, hypertext, or link.

House agency   *See* in-house agency

Household audience   The number of households in which at least one member viewed at least five minutes of a TV program. The household member can be anyone ages two years and older. *Also see* gross rating points.

Household income (HHI)   The annual income of a household derived from all members of the household, or average annual income of a group of households. HHI data is often used to describe one of the demographic characteristics of a media form or vehicle.

Households using television (HUT)   *See* homes using TV

Housewife time   (Obsolete) This referred to the daytime radio daypart (10:00 A.M. to 3:00 P.M.) that had proportionately more female than male listeners.

HTML   *See* hypertext markup language.

HTML banner   An ad banner that uses hypertext markup language so the user can click on various parts of the banner.

HTML e-mail   E-mail formatted with hypertext markup language, which allows graphics and text to appear in the body of the e-mail.

For HTML e-mail to appear on a computer screen, both the sender and receiver must have HTML e-mail capability.

HTML+   *See* hypertext markup language.

HTTP   *See* hypertext transfer protocol.

Hub   **1.** A secondary cable head end. Large cable systems are often served by multiple hub sites. **2.** The convergence point in data communications where data arrives from one or more directions and is sent out in one or more other directions.

HUT   *See* homes using TV.

Hypergraphic   A graphic image in a World Wide Web document coded to form a link to another file. If clicked on, it will take the user to the linked file.

Hyperlink   The text or graphic on a website that when clicked on, automatically takes the user to another Web page or a different area of the same page. A hyperlink is also called a hot link, hypertext, or link.

Hypermedia   The extension of hypertext that includes sound, graphics, and video, in addition to text. Hypermedia and hypertext are commonly interchangeable terms.

Hyperstitial   A Web-based advertisement that occurs before, after, or during a user's session with a website. It usually contains graphics, streaming media, or applets. They appear (pop up) on websites without user permission. A hyperstitial is a full-screen-sized ad, while an interstitial is smaller.

Hypertext   A computer system that allows a user to access additional data linked to a Web page by clicking on certain areas (links) on that Web page. *Also see* hypermedia.

Hypertext markup language (HTML)   The formatting code used to create Web pages and the protocol used to distribute Web pages. HTML uses tags to structure text into headings, paragraphs, and lists. HTML+ is a proposed superset of HTML designed to extend the capabilities of the language to incorporate better support for multimedia objects in documents. *Also see* **1.** dynamic hypertext markup language, **2.** standard generalized markup language, **3.** tag.

Hypertext transfer protocol (HTTP)   The prefix on all World Wide Web addresses.

IAB *See* **1.** Interactive Advertising Bureau; **2.** Internet Architecture Board.

IANA *See* Internet Corporation for Assigned Names and Numbers.

IAP *See* Internet access provider.

IBC *See* inside back cover.

ICANN *See* Internet Corporation for Assigned Names and Numbers.

ICOM The International Communications Agency Network, Inc., is an association of independent advertising and marketing communications agencies. Founded in 1950, the National Federation of Advertising Agencies became the International Federation of Advertising Agencies in 1980 and was renamed ICOM in 1998. Website: icomagencies.com

ID *See* identification.

Identification (ID) A short, usually 10-second long TV commercial (10 seconds visual with 8 seconds of audio).

IDSL *See* digital subscriber line.

IETF *See* Internet Engineering Task Force.

IFC   *See* inside front cover.

Illuminated panel   An out-of-home poster panel or bulletin that is lit at night.

IM   *See* instant messaging.

Imagery transfer   The recollection of the visual elements of a TV commercial after a consumer hears only the audio elements (typically from a radio commercial). A 1968 NBC study found that 72 percent of the respondents were able to play back the primary visual elements in TV commercials after hearing just the audio portions over the telephone. Radio listeners, upon hearing the audio part of a commercial, then complete the pattern of the whole commercial in their own minds. By association, the sound portion of the commercial will evoke a mental image of the sight portion. In 1993, Statistical Research, Inc., replicated the essence of the study and confirmed the imagery transfer phenomenon. This research led media planners to schedule a radio flight following a TV flight with the belief that the elements of the TV commercial would "carry through" during the radio flight. Although the effect is logical, it is operable only among those radio listeners who were exposed to the TV advertising.

Immediately preemptible (IP)   A TV spot purchased with the full understanding that a station can cancel it without prior notification to the buyer. These kinds of placements usually cost less than a nonpreemptible commercial.

Imported signal   A broadcast signal from outside the local area transmitted to subscribers by a cable TV system—for example, reception in Los Angeles of WGN/Chicago.

Impression   A single exposure of an audience member to an advertising unit.

Impressions   1. The gross sum of all media exposures (numbers of people or homes) without regard to duplication. Impressions are the same as gross rating points (GRPs) or target rating points

(TRPs), but are expressed in absolute audience numbers rather than as a percentage. 100 GRPs is the same as 100 percent of the population in a defined geographic universe. For example, if someone schedules 100 men ages 18 and older GRPs or TRPs in national TV, 100 million men impressions (the population of men in the United States) will be generated. Because impressions are "gross," they include duplicated audiences and are therefore not used for reach calculations. Impressions are, however, used to compare the total delivery (head count) of alternative media efforts and to calculate cost-efficiency. 2. For online advertising, it is the number of times an ad banner (or other type of ad) is downloaded by the user.

Formula:

GRPs (or TRPs) × the number of people in the population group = impressions

Example:

200 (percent) × 1,000,000 = 2,000,000

IMS   *See* Interactive Market Systems.

IMU   *See* interactive marketing unit.

Independent prime   (Obsolete) TV spots purchased on independent (nonnetwork affiliated) stations during prime time.

Independent station   A broadcast station that is not affiliated with a network. Also called indy.

Index   A form of percentage that relates numbers (variables) to a base, with the base always representing 100. An index shows a change in magnitude relative to the base. For example, a 110 index indicates a 10 percent positive change, while a 90 index indicates a 10 percent negative change. To obtain an index, divide a number by its base and remove the decimal point. For example, if 50 percent of TV program A's audience is composed of women ages 18 and older, versus 40 percent of the population, the index would be 120 (60 ÷ 50 = 1.25 = 125 index). If 40 percent of the audience is men ages 18 and older versus 50 percent of the population, the index would be 80 (40 ÷ 50 = 0.80 = 80 index). Indices are often used to demonstrate the concentrations, proportional relationships, or skews of media forms or media vehicles. The preceding example shows that program A skews to women (25 percent above the base population). Note that indices are void of decimal places and rounded to the nearest whole number. Using decimals defeats the purpose of easy visual scanning. *Also see* **1.** brand development index, **2.** category development index.

Formula:

variable percentage ÷ base percentage × 100 = index

Examples:

60 ÷ 50 = 1.20 × 100 = 120 index

50 ÷ 75 = .67 × 100 = 67 index

Indicia   A page within a publication that contains information such as the name, issue date, publication frequency, and subscription price.

Indirect costs   Costs that a company indirectly incurs in providing a product or service for sale—for example, rent, utilities, equipment maintenance—that is not attributable to a specific client but to all clients. *Also called* overhead. *Also see* cost accounting.

Indy   *See* independent station.

Inflation   An increase in the general price level of goods and services, such as the upward movement of advertising media costs.

In-flight publication   A magazine published for or by an airline that is distributed free of charge to passengers.

Info (.info)   *See* domain name.

Infomercial   A long-form (e.g., 30 minute) broadcast commercial that provides much more information than can be supplied in a typical 30- or 60-second commercial. Most infomercials contain a direct response mechanism, such as an 800 telephone number. Many of them air during typically low homes-using-TV (HUT) periods, such as Saturday and Sunday mornings and overnight when prices for airtime are typically low.

Information superhighway   Coined by then vice president Al Gore, it refers to the Internet. Now also referred to as the Infobahn (from the German *Autobahn*).

Information technology (IT)   A term that mostly applies to computers and computer software and that refers to all of the devices used for creating, exchanging, storing, or using information, as well as the design and practical application of the devices themselves.

Information Technology Industry Council (ITIC)   A trade association representing the top U.S. providers of information technology products and services. ITIC promotes policies that advance industry leadership in technology and innovation, open access to new and emerging markets, support e-commerce expansion, protect consumer choice, and enhance the global competitiveness of its member companies. Website: itic.org

Infrared (port)   The range of invisible radiation wavelengths that can be used to transmit data. A port enables devices to exchange data without using cables.

Inherited audience   The carryover audience from one program to the next on the same TV channel—that is, the viewers who do not switch channels when one program ends and another begins.

In-home readers   A magazine's reading audience that reads the publication in their own home, as opposed to reading it elsewhere (e.g., at a doctor's office, on an airplane). Various research studies have indicated that people reading in their own home spend more time with the magazine, read more pages, and therefore have a better chance of being exposed to the advertising in the magazine. *Also see* primary readers.

In-house agency   An advertising (or related) resource owned by the advertiser and often located in the advertiser's offices. Media sellers view in-house agencies as if they were independent ad agencies or media agencies: in-house agencies receive the same discounts off gross costs as those offered the independent agencies.

In-program   A TV commercial that appears within a TV program, as opposed to during the break between TV programs. Based on various research studies, media planners and buyers believe that the amount of viewing audience is greater, and that viewer attention to commercials is greater, for commercials that appear in-program versus during the break.

Insert   A magazine or newspaper advertisement printed separately from a publication, which is either bound into the publication or loosely inserted. *See* freestanding insert.

Insertable   A local cable TV system that accepts commercials to be inserted into the network cable TV programming that it retransmits to its subscribers. The insertion is by contractual agreement with the network.

Insertion   An ad placement in a print vehicle.

Insertion order (IO)   The written document sent to a magazine or newspaper that confirms the placement of a purchased advertisement in the publication. It typically contains detailed information such as the insertion date, size of the ad, and cost.

Inside back cover (IBC)   An advertising position within a magazine. A magazine has four covers: front, inside front (also called second cover), IBC (third cover), and back (fourth cover).

Inside front cover (IFC)   The first inside page position within a magazine. A magazine has four covers: front, IFC (also called second cover), inside back (third cover), and back (fourth cover).

Instant messaging (IM)   A communications service that enables a private real-time e-mail conversation with another individual.

Institutional advertising   *See* corporate advertising.

Instructional Television Fixed Service (ITFS) A microwave broadcast technology created and licensed by the Federal Communications Commission for use by educational institutions to distribute instructional television programs to schools.

In-tab sample The number of completed respondent interviews or diaries used by research companies to create audience estimates. In-tab indicates those interviews that will be tabulated for the research report.

Integrated marketing Marketing a product or service with coordinated (integrated), multiple media and nonmedia forms of communication, such as mass media, public relations, and in-store displays, with each reinforcing essentially the same marketing or advertising strategy or message.

Integrated service digital network digital subscriber line (IDSL) *See* digital subscriber line.

Integrated services digital network (ISDN) A fiber-optic or copper wire that carries digital information in a communications network. It is commonly referred to as an ISDN line. It allows for the simultaneous transmission of computer data, voice, and fax on a single line quickly (i.e., at up to 128 kilobits per second). *Also see* 1. cable modem, 2. digital subscriber line.

Integration cost The cost charged by a broadcast network to physically integrate an advertiser's commercial announcement into a program. Tantamount to a service charge, advertisers pay this fee on top of any cost for the placement of any commercial in any program.

Interactive Advertising Bureau (IAB) Founded in 1996, the IAB is an industry association involved in interactive advertising. Its activities include evaluating and recommending guidelines and best practices, fielding research to document the effectiveness of interactive media, and educating the advertising industry about the use of interactive advertising and marketing. Membership includes companies that are actively engaged in the sale of interactive advertising and marketing. Website: iab.net

Interactive cable TV   A two-way communications system that allows the viewer to receive and respond (interact) to what is being telecast via an electronic device, such as a remote control.

Interactive marketing   Using computer technology and devices (e.g., websites, CDs) to collect information from, and directly communicate with, prospective customers and current users of a product or service.

Interactive marketing unit (IMU)   A term used by the Interactive Advertising Bureau (IAB) to describe the types of advertisements found on websites and search engines. The IAB has published the following voluntary guidelines for IMU sizes: medium rectangle—300 by 250 pixels, square pop-up—250 by 250 pixels, vertical rectangle—240 by 400 pixels, large rectangle—336 by 280 pixels, rectangle—180 by 150 pixels, full banner—468 by 60 pixels, half banner—234 by 60 pixels, micro bar—88 by 31 pixels, button 1—120 by 90 pixels, button 2—120 by 60 pixels, vertical banner—120 by 240 pixels, square button—125 by 125 pixels, wide skyscraper—160 by 600 pixels, and skyscraper—120 by 600 pixels.

Interactive Market Systems (IMS)   A company that integrates data and systems for information analysis and media planning requirements. IMS was founded in 1969 and is owned by VNU. IMS and MediaPlan merged in 2002. Website: imsusa.com

Interactive media   Media forms (e.g., TV, personal computers, and wireless devices) that allow the consumer to electronically interact with the video/audio/text being transmitted to the consumer.

Interactive television (ITV)   Combining interactive technology with television. In theory, it will enable two-way communication between a TV viewer and an online service provider. *Also see* **1.** interactive video data service, **2.** Wink.

Interactive video data service (IVDS)   A communication system, operating over a short distance, that allows nearly instantaneous two-way responses by using a handheld device at a fixed location. Viewer participation in game shows, distance learning, and e-mail on computer networks are examples. This TV system uses radio signals to transmit data to and from a subscriber's home. The service uses a set-top box that provides a graphic overlay of messages over ordinary broadcast or cable programming, and allows the viewer to respond using a remote control. The user's response could be, for example, immediately ordering an advertised product or playing along with a quiz show. An IVDS band is a minute portion of the radio spectrum (218–219 megahertz) set aside by the Federal Communications Commission for carrying signals for interactive video data service. *Also see* Wink.

Intercept interview   A research study conducted in person with respondents who are approached or intercepted outside of their homes on a random basis. *Also see* mall intercept.

Interconnect   Two or more cable systems within close proximity to each other and typically located within the same DMA, which agree to sell commercial time in combination with each other. The media costs are usually less than the combined cost of buying time on each system individually. An interconnect also accepts just one copy of the commercial(s) to be aired instead of having the advertiser supply copies to each purchased system. The interconnected systems are linked together to air commercials simultaneously (if possible). However, not all local systems in an interconnect have commercial availabilities in all of the network cable programming being purchased by the advertiser. A "hard" or "true" interconnect is linked by cable or microwave. A "soft" interconnect is a group of systems with an agreement to insert commercials into programs or time periods, but they are not electronically interconnected. *Also see* insertable.

Interface   A computer program that interacts between a user and an application. Computer technology offers three types of interface: (1) user interface (keyboard, mouse, and menus on a computer system), (2) software interface (the language for communicating between applications), and (3) hardware interface (wires, plugs).

Interim Publisher's Statement   A magazine's or newspaper's circulation claim issued to, but not audited by, the Audit Bureau of Circulations. The statement covers the first half of the publisher's statement's period—that is, a 3-month period ending (for magazines) March 31 and September 30, and (for newspapers) December 31 and June 30. The statement is issued at the publisher's option between the normal biannual ABC reporting periods.

International Circulation Managers Association   *See* Newspaper Association of America.

International Standard Commercial Identification (ISCI)   The unique codes by which all radio and TV commercials are identified. The code is composed of four letters and a series of numbers. The first two letters are uniform for each advertiser or agency; the two letters and a number sequence that follow serve to differentiate various commercial executions. Advertisers use ISCI codes to instruct stations on which commercials to air where and when. In 2002, it was proposed that ISCI be replaced by advertising digital identification (Ad-IDs). ISCI is pronounced "I-sky."

International Telecommunication Union (ITU)   A civil organization established to promote standardized telecommunications on a worldwide basis. Website: itu.int

Intermercial ads   *See* interstitial.

Internet   A series of interconnected computers located throughout the world that facilitates data communication. It connects millions of computers that can communicate with any other computer as long as all are connected to the Internet. Information uses a variety of protocols to travel over the Internet. The World Wide Web is one of the ways that information can be shared over the Internet (using hypertext transfer protocol [HTTP]). The first recorded description of what is today the Internet was a series of memos written by J. C. R. Licklider of MIT in August 1962 discussing his "Galactic Network" concept. He envisioned a globally interconnected set of computers through which everyone could quickly access data and programs from any site. Licklider was the first head of the computer research program at DARPA (Defense Advance Research Projects Agency, now called ARPA), a department within the U.S. Defense Department. Today's Internet was originally designed so that a communication signal could withstand a nuclear war and serve military institutions worldwide. The Internet is also used for e-mail (using simple mail transfer protocol—SMTP), Usenet news groups, instant messaging, and file transfer protocol. Internet spelled with a lowercase *i* usually refers to a group of local area networks.

Internet access provider   A company that provides individuals or organizations access to the Internet. *Also see* Internet service provider.

Internet ad types   The most popular advertising units are banner, button, daughter window, Flash, floating, interstitial (transitional), intermercial, pop-under, pop-up, and skyscraper. *Also see* interactive marketing unit.

Internet Alliance (IA)   An organization of Internet policy professionals representing the Internet online industry at the state, federal, and international levels. Website: internetalliance.com

Internet Architecture Board (IAB)   A technical advisory group of the Internet Society. Among its responsibilities are architectural oversight (providing oversight of the architecture for Internet protocols and procedures) and standards process oversight (providing oversight of the process used to create Internet standards). It acts as a liaison between the Internet Society (ISOC) and other standards bodies.

Internet Assigned Numbers Authority (IANA)   *See* Internet Corporation for Assigned Names and Numbers.

Internet, attributes   All media forms have positive and negative attributes. The following are some of the attributes of advertising on the Internet: target audiences can be reached by virtue of the appeal and selectivity of sites, relatively high levels of reach can be obtained through the purchase of advertising on multiple sites, timing of the delivery of the advertising message can be controlled by the minute, advertising addresses the consumer while consumer is shopping online (for information, products, services), consumer instantly interacts with or responds to the advertiser, consumer response can be tracked for follow-up and customer relationship marketing efforts, unlimited copy length is available, advertising copy can be changed almost immediately, and advertising production costs can vary from low (for simple banner ads) to very high (for rich media alternatives).

Internet broadcasting   *See* low power radio.

Internet Corporation for Assigned Names and Numbers (ICANN) A private, nonprofit organization that is responsible for managing Internet protocol addresses and domain names. These services were previously performed by the Internet Assigned Numbers Authority (IANA).

Internet domain   *See* domain name.

Internet Engineering Task Force (IETF)   A loosely self-organized group of people who contribute to the engineering and evolution of Internet technologies. It is the principal body engaged in the development of new Internet standard specifications. The IETF is unusual in that it is not a corporation and has no board of directors, no members, and no dues.

Internet protocol   A communications scheme that enables information to be routed from one network to another.

Internet radio   *See* streaming media.

Internet service provider (ISP)   A company that provides access to the Internet, and usually also website building and design and website hosting. Before a user can connect to the Internet, the user must first establish an account with an ISP. The service provides a software package, username, password, and an access phone number.

Internet Society (ISOC) A professional membership society with more than 150 organization members and 11,000 individual members in over 182 countries. It provides leadership in addressing issues that confront the future of the Internet, and is the organization home for the groups responsible for Internet infrastructure standards, including the Internet Engineering Task Force (IETF) and the Internet Architecture Board (IAB).

Internet telephony *See* voice over Internet protocol.

Interpolate Filling in unknown values in a sequence by examining known values. For example, in the known sequence 3, 6, X, 12, Y, one can interpolate that $X = 9$ and $Y = 15$.

InterSell A software system from Telmar-Harris with the ability to quickly find and demonstrate the competitive advantage that a medium can add to a client's or potential client's advertising plan.

Interstitial Literally, in between. Any Web-based advertisement that occurs before, during, or after a user's session with a website. It usually contains graphics, streaming media, or applets. They appear (pop up) on websites without user permission. They are also known as transitional ads, intermercial ads, splash pages, and Flash pages. *Also see* hyperstitial.

Intranet A private network inside a company or organization that uses the same kinds of software found on the public Internet, but is only for internal use.

Invoice A bill issued by one who has provided products or services to a customer, such as a medium's invoice to an advertiser.

IO *See* insertion order.

IP *See* **1.** immediately preemptible, **2.** Internet protocol.

IP (Internet protocol) address   A number that uniquely identifies a computer on the Internet to other host computers.

ISCI   *See* International Standard Commercial Identification.

ISDN   *See* integrated services digital network.

Island position   In electronic or print media, a commercial or advertisement that is surrounded by editorial or programming, but no other advertising.

ISOC   *See* Internet Society.

Isolated 30   A 30-second TV commercial that is surrounded by programming.

ISP   *See* Internet service provider.

Issue date   The date a magazine begins its distribution to readers, which usually precedes the cover date.

Issue life   The length of time it takes a magazine to be read by the maximum number of people who will read the magazine. It is commonly accepted that a weekly publication takes approximately 4 weeks to accumulate its total reading audience; a monthly takes approximately 12 weeks. *Also see* readers per copy.

IT   *See* information technology.

ITFS   *See* Instructional Televisions Fixed Service.

ITI   *See* Information Technology Industry Council.

ITU   *See* International Telecommunication Union.

ITV   *See* interactive television.

IVDS   *See* interactive video data service.

Jack Myers Report A publication (and research report) focusing on leading economic forecasts for the media industry. The daily *Jack Myers Report* newsletter features insights and observations on the media and advertising economy, industry trends, media technology, television programming, and online media developments. Jack Myers provides consulting services for corporate senior management on revenue building and the impact of new technologies on traditional businesses. Website: jackmyers.com

Java A computer programming language that is specifically designed for writing programs and can be safely downloaded to a computer through the Internet and immediately run without fear of viruses or other harm to the computer or its files.

JavaScript A computer programming language that shares many of the features of Java, but was developed for Web authors to design interactive sites.

Jazz A radio programming format consisting of instrumentals and vocals.

Jointly and severally liable *See* sequential liability.

Joint Photographic Experts Group (JPEG) One of the two most common types of images used on the World Wide Web, the other being GIF (graphics interchange format).

JPEG   *See* Joint Photographic Experts Group.

Jump page   **1.** An advertising page on a website that appears temporarily in order to capture the user's attention for a promotion or to gather user information in a survey. **2.** In website maintenance, a page that is posted temporarily to redirect the user to a new unique resource locator (URL). **3.** In website design, a website page that provides a "jumping off" point for users who need to locate information on the Web quickly and efficiently.

Junior page   An advertisement in print media that is smaller than a full page and is surrounded only by editorial matter. It might look something like a *Reader's Digest* full-page ad floated in the middle of a *Time* magazine page.

Junior panel   A scaled-down version of a 30-sheet poster (usually 5 feet by 11 feet). *Also called* 8-sheet poster.

Junior spread   Two facing junior page advertisements in a magazine or newspaper.

Junk mail   Any form of promotional mail that the recipient believes is misdirected or not useful.

Jupiter Communications   *See* Jupiter Media Metrix.

Jupiter Media Metrix   A research company that measures the end-to-end impact of the Internet and new technologies on commerce and marketing. It was founded in September 2000 as a result of the merger of Jupiter Communications and Media Metrix. Jupiter Communications, established in 1986, was the first research firm to cover the most essential dynamics of the Internet economy. Media Metrix pioneered Internet and digital media measurement in 1996. In 2002, the Media Metrix division of Jupiter was sold to comScore, with eventual plans to merge Media Metrix with comScore's Media Solutions. Website: jmm.com

K   Abbreviation of *kilo*, the Greek word for *one thousand*. The financial and communications industries use *K* to represent 1,000, and the computer industry uses *K* to represent either 210 or 1,024. Nonetheless, media professionals prefer Latin to Greek and use *M* to represent 1,000. *See*, for example, kilobyte and cost per thousand.

Ka-band   A range of microwave frequencies operating between 17.7 and 31.0 gigahertz and reserved for satellite communication. *Also see* **1.** C-band, **2.** Ku-band.

Kantar Media Group (KMR)   An integrated research, information, and software group, specializing in media and survey research solutions and media analysis software systems. KMR is owned by WPP.

Kb   *See* kilobyte

Kbps   *See* kilobits per second.

Kelsey Group, The (TKG)   Founded in 1986, The Kelsey Group provides research, advice, and events regarding communications, local media, and electronic commerce. The company's focus is on how new technologies, together with business, economic, and social trends, affect local businesses and people within larger enterprises. Website: kelseygroup.com

Keyline   *See* mechanical.

KHz   *See* kilohertz.

Kickback   An illegal, secret payment made in return for awarding a contract, such as placing advertising with a media vendor.

Kids ProductQ   *See* Marketing Evaluations/TvQ.

Kilo   Greek for *one thousand*.

Kilobit   One thousand bits.

Kilobits per second (Kbps)   A measure of the bandwidth of a telecommunications medium (the total information flow over a given time). Bandwidth is also measured in megabits per second (Mbps) or in gigabits per second (Gbps), depending on the medium and transmission method.

Kilobyte (KB)   Approximately one thousand bytes, but technically 1,024 bytes. In numerical sequence, bytes are counted as kilobyte, megabyte, gigabyte, terabyte, petabyte, exabyte.

Kilohertz (kHz)   One thousand cycles of electromagnetic currency per second. The term is used for radio wave transmissions as well as the clock speed of computer microprocessors. Megahertz (MHz) is one million cycles per second (100 kHz); gigahertz (GHz) is one billion cycles per second. Named after Heinrich Rudolf Hertz, a German physicist who was the first to produce radio waves artificially.

Kiosk   A freestanding, backlit display of different sizes, having three or four sides on which advertisements are shown. Usually found in places such as airports, train stations, and malls.

KMR   *See* Kantar Media Group.

KN/Statistical Research   A research company specializing in media audience measurement for the Internet, radio, television, and Yellow Pages. *KN* stands for Knowledge Networks. The company was originally named Statistical Research, Inc. (SRI). Website: statistical research.com

Ku-band   A range of microwave frequencies operating between 10.9 and 12.75 gigahertz. Ku-band is primarily used for satellite communications, particularly for transmission from a remote location back to a TV network or station for broadcasting. *Also see* 1. C-band, 2. Ka-band.

Lady Bird Johnson Act   *See* Highway Beautification Act.

Lady of the house (LOH)   (Obsolete) A term used in Nielsen TV reports that referred to the female head of the household.

LAN   *See* local area network.

Landline   Traditional wired phone service.

Land mobile service   A public or private radio service providing two-way communication, paging, and radio signaling on land.

Laredo Group, The   Founded in 1996, The Laredo Group provides research, training, and consulting dedicated to Internet advertising and revenue generation. Website: laredogroup.com

Last-in, first-out (LIFO)   1. A method of inventory cost accounting whereby the last goods purchased are assumed to be the first goods sold, so that the ending inventory consists of the first goods purchased. 2. In computer programming, a processing approach whereby the most recent work request is handled next and the oldest request does not get handled until it is the only remaining request. *Also see* first-in, first-out.

Late fringe (LF)   *See* TV dayparts.

Late news (LN)   *See* TV dayparts.

Law of supply and demand   First, in the legal sense it is not a law, but an economic reality. The law of demand holds that if supply (e.g., the number of TV commercials available for sale) is held constant, an increase in demand (e.g., for the commercial time) leads to an increased market price (e.g., the media cost), while a decrease in demand leads to a decreased market price.

Layered ad   An advertisement on a Web page, constructed using dynamic hypertext markup language (DHTML). The layered advertisement is created and deployed in a "layer" above the HTML content, thereby obscuring the content below it. Also known as a floating ad.

LCD   *See* liquid crystal display.

Lead   A person or household that wishes to receive more information about a company or its products or services. A qualified lead is a person or household that meets the marketer's criteria for a prospective buyer—for example, the person or household has a certain amount of income or is a certain age.

Lead generation   A marketing or advertising process or technique that attempts to accumulate leads.

Lead time   Usually refers to the amount of time between the start of negotiating a radio or TV buy to the day that the first commercial will air (the on-air date). It can also refer to any media purchase, or for that matter, any task.

Lead-in/lead-out   A program that precedes (lead in) or follows (lead out) another. TV media buyers analyze TV program rating trends and estimate future rating performance, based in part on the strength or weakness of lead-in and lead-out programs. For example, a program with a strong lead-in (i.e., the lead-in program has a high rating) stands a better chance of also receiving a relatively high rating, because many viewers of the lead-in will automatically carry over into the next program. This concept was especially true before remote controls—that is, when viewers had to manually switch channels on the TV set. Now that nearly all TV households have a remote control, and channel switching (and surfing) is as easy as the touch of a button, the lead-in dynamic is less powerful.

Leased access   A public access cable system channel for which programmers pay a fee for use and are thereby permitted to sell commercial time in their programming.

Leased channel   A cable TV channel leased to a third party for that party's use by the local cable system operator.

Least squares   *See* regression analysis.

Letterpress   Printing from type with a raised surface as opposed to printing from plates with relief printing. *Also see* 1. lithography, 2. offset, 3. rotogravure.

Level playing field   An environment in which all companies in a given market must follow the same rules and are given an equal ability to compete. For example, in giving magazines a request for proposal, all should receive the same request without any favoritism shown to any of the magazines prior to the submissions.

LF   Late fringe. *See* TV dayparts.

Lifestyle   Pertains to the nondemographic characteristics of people when describing their behavior, such as recreational habits. Also commonly called psychographics.

LIFO   *See* last-in, first-out.

Lightbulb   *See* pulsing.

Line   *See* agate line.

Lineage   The number of agate lines of newspaper space accounted for by one advertisement or a series of advertisements. The term is used on newspaper rate cards to show cost discount levels once a certain number of total lines (for all advertisements combined) are purchased by an advertiser.

Line network (Obsolete) The term was in use when a TV network transmitted signals from one station to the next through telephone lines. It is now simply called a TV network, with transmission typically accomplished via a satellite.

Liner A 10- to 20-second prerecorded or live on-air radio mention of an advertised product or service, usually tied to a promotion. It is similar to a TV ID.

Lineup *See* station lineup.

Link Text or images on a Web page that a user can click on in to connect to another document. Links are most commonly thought of as the technology that connects two Web pages or websites. Links are also called hot links, hyperlinks, and hypertext.

Liquid crystal display (LCD) The screen used on flat panel monitors, cell phones, digital watches, and other devices. It uses liquid crystals to display information. *Also see* **1.** cathode ray tube, **2.** plasma screen.

LISP A computer programming language typically used for artificial intelligence applications. It is an acronym for *list processor*.

List broker A person or organization that administers direct-mail advertising lists, often selling them to clients.

Lithography A printing process using a flat surface of (usually) zinc or aluminum in which the image or text to be printed is treated to retain ink while the remainder of the surface is not. *See* **1.** letterpress, **2.** offset, **3.** rotogravure.

Little America (or Little U.S.) A method for simulating in test market(s) the media weight generated by a national plan in the average market. This method is used to test the viability of one or more national media plans before it is implemented nationally or rolled out across the United States. The methodology treats the test market(s) as if it were the United States at large (i.e., a little U.S.). National media in the national media plan are translated (simulated) into the test market(s) using their local equivalents. For example, spot TV is used to simulate national TV using the same dayparts; local or regional editions of magazines are used to simulate national editions, and where local or regional editions are not available, either similar magazines or newspaper supplements are used. Local media in the national plan are first "averaged" and then translated into the test market(s). Averaging local media requires "weighting." For example, if the national plan calls for 100 target rating points (TRPs) in TV markets representing 50 percent of U.S. households, then the average U.S. market is receiving 50 TRPs [(100 × 50 percent) + (0 × 50 percent) = 50]. As with any in-market test, it is very important to select test markets that are representative of the United States at large. It is also wise to select more than one test market in the event that any one market suffers the consequences of dramatic economic or environmental change during the test. *Also see* **1.** as it falls, **2.** rollout, **3.** weighted average.

Live feed   Transmitting a live radio or TV program or segment as it is happening, as opposed to videotaping it for a later transmission.

Live tag   A short message (usually about 5 seconds) transmitted live by an announcer at the end of, but within, a radio or TV commercial.

LMA   *See* local marketing agreement.

LMDS   *See* local multipoint distribution service.

LN   Late night. *See* TV dayparts.

LNA   Leading National Advertisers. *See* TNS Media Intelligence/ CMR.

Load factor   The average number of persons riding in each vehicle, which is used by outdoor media companies to estimate audience counts. Based on government research, the national average load factor is 1.38 adults ages 18 and older per vehicle.

Local area network (LAN)   A computer network that spans a small area, like a room, a building, or a set of buildings. Workstations and personal computers in an office are commonly connected to each other with a LAN. LANs can be connected using cabling, telephone lines, or radio waves. *Also see* wide area network.

Local cable TV   Broadcast and cable-originated TV programming delivered within the geographic area covered by a cable system. There are over 10,000 local cable systems (head ends) in the United States, with about three out of four TV homes subscribing to cable TV. *Also see* **1.** homes passed, **2.** interconnect.

Local channel station   A radio or TV station licensed by the Federal Communications Commission to broadcast within a limited geographic area.

Local cut-ins   *See* cut-in.

Local marketing agreement (LMA)   The agreement of two or more separately owned radio stations in the same market to have one entity (e.g., a sales representative) sell commercial time on the stations as a combination buy.

Local media   Advertising media whose audiences are primarily within a relatively small geographic area, such as a metro area or TV market, as opposed to regional or national media forms that cover much greater geographic areas. Examples of local media are local cable TV, local consumer magazines, daily newspapers, various out-of-home media, spot radio, and spot TV.

Local multipoint distribution service (LMDS)   A broadband radio service that enables a two-way transmission of voice, high-speed data, and video.

Local newspapers   *See* local media.

Local origination programming   TV programming produced by or under the control of a local cable system.

Local program   TV programming produced by or under the control of a local TV station.

Local rate   Advertising rates that are offered by the local media to local advertisers and are typically less than the rates offered to national advertisers.

Locally edited supplement   A Sunday magazine newspaper supplement owned and edited by the newspaper distributing it, such as the *New York Times Magazine. Also see* newspaper distributed magazines.

Log   A listing created and kept by radio/TV stations and networks showing which commercials should air, or did air, at what times. *Also see* International Standard Commercial Identification.

LOH   (Obsolete) *See* lady of the house.

Loss leader   A product or service sold at substantial discount, and sometimes at a loss, in order to attract customers to a store.

Low band   TV channels 2 to 6. High band is TV channels 7 to 13.

Low power radio   Very local, small-scale broadcasting, such as (1) broadcasting over the air with AM, FM, or shortwave signals; (2) transmission via power lines (e.g., on a college campus), also known as carrier-current; (3) hooking an FM receiver up to the cable TV service; (4) transmitting via coaxial cable that is buried near the surface of the ground or running through walls; and (5) placing an audio file on a website, also known as Internet broadcasting.

Low power TV (LPTV)   The same as broadcast TV, but limited in geographic coverage by its low power (signal strength). These stations operate on existing VHF (very high frequency) and UHF (ultra high frequency) bands and can originate programming (either pay TV, advertiser supported, or noncommercial) or retransmit the signal of a consenting station.

Loyalty program   A marketing program designed to retain current customers (as well as attract new customers) of a product or service by rewarding regular customers with incentives or other benefits, such as frequent flyer programs.

LPTV   *See* low power TV.

LTC   Last telecast. The final (last) telecast of a program, advertising flight, or commercial schedule.

M 1. Roman numeral for 1,000. Media professionals prefer Latin to Greek (and therefore use *M* instead of *K—K* for *kilo*, meaning *one thousand*), while the financial and computer industries prefer Greek to Latin (and therefore use *K* instead of *M*). *See*, for example, kilobyte and cost per thousand.

MAA *See* Mobile Marketing Association.

Maestro TV Planning A daypart reach and frequency system for network, local market, and cable television. The budget and daypart allocation feature allows automatic calculation of schedules. A software product of Telmar.

Magazine format A TV programming term borrowed from the magazine industry, in which a TV program is organized into different features, each with its own story, similar to the way a magazine is organized (e.g., *60 Minutes*).

Magazine page exposure (MPX) Used by Mediamark Research, Inc. as a measure of how frequently readers look at an average page (editorial or advertising) in a magazine. The concept is based on earlier independent research of ad page exposure.

Magazine Publishers of America (MPA) An industry association for consumer magazines. Established in 1919, the MPA represents more than 240 U.S.-based publishing companies with more than 1,400 titles. Website: magazine.org

Magazine supplement   *See* newspaper distributed magazine.

Magazines, attributes   All media forms have positive and negative attributes. The following are some of the attributes of advertising in consumer magazines: specific target audiences can be reached via the selection of specific editorial formats; they can be purchased on a national, regional, or local market basis (either because of an individual magazine's geographic distribution pattern or through geographic editions of national magazines); issue dates vary from one publication to another; single copy sales happen on various days; actual readership, by either primary or secondary audiences, happens over time; high-resolution color reproduction is available; long copy advertisements are available; it is a reader-controlled (relatively nonintrusive) medium—the reader essentially decides whether to turn the page and be exposed to the advertising; the magazine's tangible permanency offers the opportunity for repeat readership of the same advertisements (magazine page exposure); magazines can be used to distribute coupons and reader response cards; and it takes time for magazines to build their total reading audience—approximately 4 weeks for a weekly and 12 weeks for a monthly.

Mainframe   A very large computer capable of supporting thousands of computer users simultaneously.

Makegood   **1.** In radio or TV, a commercial position is offered by a station or network to make up for a scheduled commercial that did not or will not air. Reasons why a scheduled commercial did not or will not air include station trafficking error, preemption by another advertiser (that typically is willing to pay a higher price), movement of the purchased program from one time slot to another, or pre-emption of the purchased program (in whole or in part) due to, for example, a news bulletin. **2.** The free repeat of a print advertisement to compensate for the publication's error in the original insertion, or if the publication's issue in which the advertiser's ad ran missed the publication's rate base.

Mall intercept   A research study conducted in person with respondents who are approached or intercepted in shopping malls.

MAN   *See* metropolitan area network.

Management information systems (MIS)   A company's computer systems (or a division or department) that provide information about the business and its operations.

Manager of information services (MIS)   A person who manages a company's management information services.

Manas   *See* MediaPlan.

M & A   *See* mergers & acquisitions.

Marcom   An abbreviation for marketing communications.

Margin   **1.** The difference between the cost and the selling price of a commodity. **2.** The difference between a company's operating costs and its income from the sales of its products or services. This is typically expressed as a percentage of income. For example, if a company has $850,000 in operating costs (e.g., salaries, rent) and an income (revenue) of $1 million, it has a margin of $150,000, or 15 percent. It is also called gross profit (i.e., profit before taxes).

***Marketer's Guide to Media* (MGM)**   Data covering media audiences and media costs for most major media forms. Published semiannually by *Adweek*.

Marketing Evaluations/TvQ   A research company that produces Q Scores—information about the familiarity, appeal, and commitment people have to various TV programs, performers, and products. Q Score services use The People Panel, a cooperating consumer panel of over 50,000 member households for data collection, diary studies, product tests, telephone surveys, attitude and usage tracking, and for screening concepts and ideas. Scores are reported for TV broadcast and syndication programs (TvQ), cable TV programs (CableQ), performers and characters (PerformerQ), cartoon characters (CartoonQ), products—company, product, and brand (ProductQ), kids' products (Kids ProductQ), sports—program and personalities (SportsQ), and past performers (DeadQ). Website: qscores.com

Marketing mix modeling   The application of the principles of mathematical analysis to economic phenomena, specifically those pertaining to business and finance. Multifarious phenomena affect a company's sales, such as advertising, pricing, direct marketing, product news, the economic climate, weather, and competitive activity. Marketing mix modeling uses a specialized statistical technique for analyzing all of this assembled data. The technique isolates the specific contribution each ingredient has on sales (or store traffic, etc.) and thereby determines the effectiveness of advertising and other marketing activities in terms of actual sales and return on investment (ROI). Assuming availability of a substantial amount of detailed data for each ingredient being analyzed, analyses can also be conducted to determine the ROI for, as an example, each TV daypart used in a campaign. *Also called* econometrics and ROI analysis.

Marketing Research Association (MRA)   Founded in 1954, MRA provides its members with a variety of opportunities for advancing and expanding their marketing research and related business skills. MRA acts as an advocate with appropriate government entities, other associations, and the public. Website: mra-net.org

Marketing Science Institute (MSI)   Established in 1961, MSI is a nonprofit institute serving as a bridge between business and academia. Its mission is to initiate, support, and disseminate leading-edge studies by academic scholars, which address research issues specified by member companies. MSI functions as a working sponsorship and brings together executives with leading researchers from approximately one hundred universities worldwide. Website: msi.org

MarketMate Radio   A local market radio planning tool that generates detailed, market-sensitive reach and frequency analyses without requiring any station-specific data. A product of Interactive Market Systems.

MarketMate TV   A local market television planning system that generates market-sensitive reach and frequency results for all TV markets by accessing individual market population and viewing data. A product of Interactive Market Systems.

Markup   1. *See* tag. 2. The amount of money (or percentage) added to a basic cost and charged to the customer along with the basic cost. For example, a 17.65 percent markup on the net production cost for a TV commercial yields a 15 percent commission on the gross cost (e.g., $85 × 1.1765 = $100; $100 − $85 = $15 commission).

Mass magazine   A general-interest magazine with mass appeal.

Mass media   All advertising media that have general (mass) appeal.

Master antenna television (MATV)   A TV antenna that serves multiple dwelling complexes, such as hotels and apartment houses.

Master contract   A written agreement between an advertiser and a media vehicle covering all products to be advertised. It is also known as a blanket contract.

Master head end   A head end that collects TV program material from various sources and distributes it to distribution hubs in the same geographic area.

Masthead   1. The title of a newspaper displayed at the top of the front page. 2. The section of a magazine or newspaper that details information such as the title and address of the publication, publisher, and staff.

Material closing date   The last date a publication is willing to accept creative material (e.g., a mechanical) for insertion of advertising in a specific issue.

Materials   The creative material (e.g., a mechanical) needed by a publication to print an advertisement.

Maximizer Run   A report generated by Arbitron that shows custom demographic, geographic, or daypart audience delivery data not commonly reported in the typical ratings report. Previously called "AID Run."

Mb   *See* megabyte.

M-banking   Conducting banking transactions using a mobile phone (cell phone).

Mbone   Short for multicast backbone. It is an extension to the Internet to support multicasting: two-way transmission of data (e.g., audio and visual) between multiple sites. Unlike transmission control protocol/Internet protocol (TCP/IP), which divides messages into packets and sends each packet independently, Mbone allows a packet to have multiple destinations and it is not divided until the last possible moment.

Mbps   *See* megabits per second.

M-commerce   Coined by Jack Meyers, it includes transactions over mobile devices, advertising, and downloads that involve payment.

MDS   *See* multipoint distribution system.

Mean   Commonly called the "average," the mean is the sum of all numbers on a list divided by the number of items on the list. For example, in a list comprised of the numbers 1, 1, 3, 7, 8, the mean is 4 ($20 \div 5 = 4$). The median for this list is 3 and the mode is 1.

Mechanical   A camera-ready pasteup of artwork that includes type, photography, and artwork or line art, all on one piece of art board. Also known as a keyline.

Media   Plural for *medium*. The communication vehicles that may or may not contain advertising, such as the Internet, radio, magazines, mail, newspapers, out-of-home media, television, and Yellow Pages.

Media agency   An organization that specializes in media research, media planning, and media buying, and does not offer any services for the creation of advertising messages. In the late 1990s, the advertising industry saw a change in nomenclature away from buying service to "media agency." This happened for two reasons: (1) most buying services also offered media planning, ergo the name was not appropriate; and (2) most of the largest advertising agencies spun off their media departments into stand-alone, quasi-independent media planning and buying services, ergo the redesignation to "media" agency from "ad" agency. *Also see* **1.** advertising agency, **2.** boutique advertising agency.

MediaAnalysisPlus (MAP)   Founded in 2001, MAP is an independent consultancy that concentrates on media accountability. It offers media auditing, econometric analysis, media training, strategic media consultation, as well as media agency searches. Website: mediaanalysisplus.com

Media audit   Similar to, but more granular than, a post-analysis of a media schedule in which actual audience delivery and actual cost are compared to the original media plan or media buy to determine how the media buy faired vis-à-vis goals. A media audit is typically conducted by an independent third party (i.e., not the advertiser or the advertiser's media buying agent).

Media Audit, The   Founded in 1971, The Media Audit is a multimedia, qualitative audience survey that covers over 450 target items for each rated medium's audience. These items include socioeconomic characteristics, lifestyles, business decision makers, product purchasing plans, retail shopping habits, travel history, supermarket shopping, stores shopped, products purchased, fast-food restaurants eaten in, soft drink consumption, brands purchased, health insurance coverage, leisure activities, banks used, credit cards used, and other selected consumer characteristics important to local media and advertisers. The Media Audit is a product of International Demographics, Inc. It is fully owned and operated by its founders and current employees. Website: themediaaudit.com

Media Framework   With Snapshots' market profiles as its flagship service, Media Framework was established in 1999. It focuses on providing the advertising and marketing industries with analyses of each local market to assist them in the process of making informed decisions. Website: mediaframework.com

Media imperatives   An analytical system developed by Simmons to evaluate the extent to which one medium complements another in their combined ability to target audiences. The analysis indicates, for example, which media form is imperative for a particular audience, based on the audience's consumption levels of that medium.

Media kit   A brochure or equivalent issued by a medium that contains promotional and sales material, such as descriptions of the medium, specific advertising offers, and media rates.

Mediamark Research, Inc. (MRI)   A research company that offers comprehensive demographics, lifestyle, product usage, and exposure to all forms of advertising media collected from a single sample. Mediamark conducts more than 26,000 personal interviews with consumers (ages 18 and older) throughout the continental United States to produce syndicated reports and data for electronic access. Each year, the sample is completely redrawn, with 13,000 new respondents entering the survey every six months. Fieldwork is done in two waves per year, each lasting six months (April to September and October to March), so each report represents two waves of interviewing. Because reports come out twice each year (spring and fall), each report overlaps the previous with six months of interviewing fieldwork. The Doublebase report rolls up 24 months of interviewing (not the most recently released four reports) and therefore represents the most recent two spring reports. Two different methods are used to question the respondent. First, a personal face-to-face interview is used to collect demographics and data related to media exposure (including magazines, newspapers, radio, television, cable, and outdoor). Then at the end of the interview, the fieldworker leaves behind a self-completing questionnaire booklet covering personal and household usage of some 500 product categories and services and 6,000 brands. MRI is owned by NOP World, a United Business Media company. Website: mediamark.com

Media Metrix   *See* Jupiter Media Metrix.

Media mix   The use of two or more different media forms in one advertising plan, usually scheduled either simultaneously or in close timing to each other. There are many reasons for mixing media forms: (1) to reach people not reached with the first medium, (2) to provide additional repeat exposure in a secondary medium after optimum (or near optimum) reach is obtained in the first medium, (3) to use the intrinsic values of a medium to extend the creative effectiveness of the advertising campaign—for example, music on radio or the delivery of coupons in print media, and (4) to reach people at different times of the day based on typical media consumption habits—for example, radio reaches more people than TV in the morning while the opposite is true at night. It must be kept in mind that when combining two different media forms, not all people will be exposed to both forms. Some will be exposed to only medium A, some to only medium B, and some to both. *Also see* **1.** imagery transfer, **2.** only-only-both, **3.** random combination.

Median   A mathematical form of "average" representing the midpoint in a sequence of numbers sorted by magnitude. Essentially, half of the numbers on the list are above the median and half are below the median. For example, in a list comprised of the numbers 1, 1, 3, 7, 8, the median is 3. The mean for this list is 4, and the mode is 1.

MediaPlan   A company that provides media and marketing software. MediaPlan was founded in 1985 and introduced Manas, the world's first media flowchart software. MediaPlan is a division of Spectra Marketing, owned by VNU. Interactive Market Systems and MediaPlan merged in 2002. Website: mediaplan.com

Media Rating Council (MRC)   An organization whose charter is to maintain industry confidence and credibility in audience research. MRC members consist of blue-chip advertising and media companies. MRC came into being as the Broadcast Rating Council (BRC) in 1964 as a result of a congressional investigation into claims of ratings irregularities and falsification of data findings. Fear of government regulation of the ratings industry caused the broadcasters of the day to form the BRC. The BRC then evolved into the Electronic Media Rating Council and more recently, into the MRC. MRC accreditation of research methodologies indicates that the data produced is within known degrees of reliability. This is not to say, however, that methodologies not accredited by the MRC are invalid.

Medium　The singular form of *media*, such as the radio medium and the magazine medium.

Meg　Verbal shorthand for a megabit or megabyte.

Megabit (Mb)　One million binary pulses. It is commonly used to measure the amount of data transferred in one second between two telecommunication points. Some define megabit as 1,048,576 bits, and use *megabit* and *megabyte* (MB) interchangeably. Megabit applies to communication speed, while megabyte applies to computer storage capacity.

Megabits per second (Mbps)　A measure of the bandwidth of a telecommunications medium (the total information flow over a given time). Bandwidth is also measured in kilobits per second (kbps) or in gigabits per second (Gbps), depending on the medium and transmission method.

Megabyte　Commonly considered 1 million bytes, but technically 1,048,576 bytes (1,024 kilobytes). Megabyte applies to computer storage capacity, while megabit applies to communication speed.

Megaflop　*See* floating point operations per second.

Megahertz (MHz)　One million cycles of electromagnetic currency per second. The term is used for radio wave transmissions as well as the clock speed of computer microprocessors. Kilohertz (kHz) is 1,000 cycles per second; gigahertz (GHz) is 1 billion cycles per second. It is named after Heinrich Rudolf Hertz, a German physicist who was the first to produce radio waves artificially.

Mendelsohn Affluent Survey   A research product of Mendelsohn Media Research that reports readership of more than 90 publications among the richest segment of the adult population. It also reports broadcast media exposure, demography, expenditures, investments, alcohol consumption, travel, and automobile ownership in the affluent market. Website: mmrsurveys.com

Mendelsohn Affluent Travel Survey   *See* Mendelsohn Affluent Survey.

Mendelsohn Media Research   Founded in 1975, Mendelsohn Media Research offers a broad range of custom and syndicated advertising and media research services. Syndicated measurements include the Mendelsohn Affluent Survey and the Mendelsohn Affluent Travel Survey. The company also specializes in custom mail surveys, including subscriber studies, editorial surveys, and print media evaluations. Website: mmrsurveys.com

Merchandising   Any form of hard goods or services that complement advertising and are provided free or at a nominal charge by the media purchased for advertising. Some media buyers think of merchandising as added value received in consideration of placing advertising with the media.

Mergers & acquisitions (M & A)   A term commonly used to refer to one or more companies that have either merged or acquired one or more other companies. A merger is the union of two or more commercial interests or corporations. The identity of the merged companies might or might not lose their individual identity. An acquisition is one company taking over controlling interest in another company.

Metabrowser   An online application that can jump across websites, gather information, and organize it on one page.

Meta refresh   HTML (hypertext markup language) coding on a website that redirects a visitor to a new page. Meta refresh tags are used by websites that have changed addresses but want visitors to be able to access the new address by going through the old one. The user typically receives a message that reads, for example, "This site has moved to a new location. Please wait a moment and you will automatically be brought to the new location."

Meta tag   An HTML (hypertext markup language) tag that provides information about a Web page but does not affect how the page is displayed. The meta tag provides information such as who created the page, and keywords that represent the page's content. The tag(s) is used by search engines to find the website or page.

Meter   *See* set-tuning meter.

Metered markets   Local markets (DMAs) where Nielsen Media Research uses set-tuning meters (which are different from People Meters) to report household ratings. The local metered-market ratings from 53 markets (as of 2001) are usually available in the morning following the previous day's TV usage. For this reason, they are usually called "metered-market overnights" or "preliminary" estimates. When reporting all markets, the household ratings are weighted by size of market, with each rating point representing nearly 70 million households. Nationally, each rating point represents just over 102 million households (as of 2002).

Metro area   *See* metropolitan statistical area (MSA).

Metropolitan area   Defined by the Federal Office of Management and Budget, a metropolitan area generally is a core area containing a large population nucleus, together with adjacent communities that have a high degree of economic and social integration with that core. Included among metropolitan areas are metropolitan statistical areas (MSAs), consolidated metropolitan statistical areas (CMSAs), and primary metropolitan statistical areas (PMSAs). In addition, New England city and town areas (NECTAs) are an alternative set of areas defined for the six New England states. As contained in the 1990 U.S. Census, there are 362 metropolitan areas in the United States, 268 MSAs, 21 CMSAs, and 73 PMSAs.

Metropolitan area network (MAN)   A computer network designed for a metropolitan area, city, or town. It is typically larger than a local area network (LAN), but smaller than a wide area network (WAN).

Metropolitan statistical area (MSA)   Often referred to simply as "metro area," an MSA is a geographic area defined by the Federal Office of Management and Budget. An MSA consists of one or more counties that contain a city of 50,000 or more inhabitants, or contain a Census Bureau–defined urbanized area and have a total population of at least 100,000 (75,000 in New England). Counties containing the principal concentration of population—the largest city and surrounding densely settled area—are components of the MSA. The MSA also includes contiguous or additional counties when the economic and social relationships between the central and additional counties meet specific criteria. Radio stations and newspapers commonly use an MSA in stating their respective media audience delivery within a specified market. TV media audiences, on the other hand, are typically shown within a TV market (designated market area). *Also see* total survey area.

MHz   *See* megahertz.

Microprocessor   *See* central processing unit.

Microsecond   *See* second.

Microsoft disk operating system (MS-DOS)   The operating system for IBM personal computers and IBM-compatible computers. It was developed by Microsoft for IBM.

MicroVision   A segmentation and consumer targeting system that classifies every U.S. household into one of 50 unique market segments. Classifications are based on the demographic, lifestyle, socioeconomic, buying, media consumption, and behavior characteristics of households within every ZIP+4 geography. A product of Claritas. Website: claritas.com

Microwave   That part of the radio spectrum above 500 megahertz (short wavelength) used for point-to-point communications where line-of-sight communications is not possible or necessary.

Middle of the road (MOR)   A radio programming format that is becoming obsolete. The format combines news, information, and popular music.

Middleware   Software that connects two otherwise separate applications, such as flight schedules and seat assignments.

Milline rate   (Obsolete) The cost of one million agate lines (without discount) divided by the circulation of a newspaper. It has since been replaced by cost per point and cost per thousand.

Millions of instructions per second (MIPS)   (Obsolete) A measure of a computer's speed and power. It measures the number of machine instructions that a computer can execute in one second.

Millisecond   *See* second.

Millward Brown IntelliQuest   The technology research center of the Millward Brown Group. It provides marketing research services that enable clients to understand and improve the strategic position of their brands, products, media, or channels. It offers custom research solutions, market and brand tracking, media research, along with business-to-business online marketplace tracking. Website: intelliquest.com

Millward Brown International   A global research firm specializing in advertising tracking and awareness studies. Millward Brown is a member of The Kantar Group, the research and consultancy arm of WPP Group. Website: millwardbrown.com

MIME   *See* multipurpose Internet mail extensions.

Minimum depth   The minimum amount of advertising space in a newspaper that an advertiser is required to run. Generally, the minimum depth of an ad is one inch for every column it is wide.

Minute-by-minute profile   An audience flow analysis used to study audience gains and losses during specific minutes of a TV program.

Minute-by-minute ratings   TV household ratings for each minute of broadcasting that determine how many homes are viewing a particular station (or program) during the average 60 seconds of each minute. Nielsen Media Research can estimate these ratings in sample homes with a set-top box (metered markets) that records when a TV set is on, and to what station it is tuned, 24 hours a day, 7 days a week, 365 days a year. Minute-by-minute ratings are at the heart of TV optimizer software, because they help gauge the "real" audience duplication of two or more TV programs.

MIP   *See* mobile Internet provider.

MIPS   *See* millions of instructions per second.

MIS   *See* 1. management information systems, 2. manager of information services.

MMA   *See* Mobile Marketing Association.

MMDS   *See* multipoint microwave distribution service.

MMS   *See* multimedia messaging service.

Mnemonic   1. In commercials or advertisements, it is something that aids the viewer's/listener's memory, such as a rhyme, graphic, or tangible object. Often referred to as a mnemonic device. 2. In computer programming, it is a word or string of characters that is easier to remember than what it stands for, and therefore similar to an acronym.

Mobile billboard   A flatbed truck equipped with one or more poster panel units. The truck can either be parked at specified venues or driven around designated localities. *Also see* 1. Porta-panel, 2. rolling billboard.

Mobile Internet provider (MIP)   An Internet service provider (ISP) dedicated to providing wireless service.

Mobile Marketing Association (MMA)   An association representing the interests of mobile (wireless) marketing and advertising vendors. MMA's goal is to foster the mobile marketing industry and protect the interests of consumers. Formed through the merger of the Wireless Marketing Association and the Wireless Advertising Association. Website: mmaglobal.org

Mode   The number that occurs most frequently in a list of numbers. For example, in a list comprised of the numbers 1, 1, 3, 7, 8, the mode is 1. The mean for this list is 4, and the median is 3.

Modem   A device or program that enables a computer to transmit data. Computer information is stored digitally, whereas information transmitted over telephone lines is transmitted in analog form. A modem converts between these two forms. Modem is an acronym for modulator-demodulator.

Modern rock   A radio programming format that bridges the contemporary hit radio and alternative rock formats.

Mom and pop (store)   A description of a comparatively small, privately owned retail store that is not part of a larger chain.

Monitor-Plus   *See* Nielsen Monitor-Plus.

Moore's law   In 1965, Gordon Moore, cofounder of Intel, realized a trend: each new microchip contained roughly twice as much capacity as its predecessor, and each chip was released within 18 to 24 months of the previous chip. He reasoned that if this trend continued, computing power would rise exponentially over relatively brief periods of time. Loosely applied, "technology" doubles every couple of years.

MOR   *See* radio programming formats.

Morning drive (AM drive)   *See* radio dayparts.

Morph (morphing)   Transforming one image into another with a cinematic effect, by using a computer, such as morphing a man into a wolf.

Motherboard   The main circuit board of a computer that contains the central processing unit and other components. *Also see* daughterboard.

Moving average   The mean average of a series of numbers that is updated periodically to yield the latest data in order to track trends. For example, if a TV program's rating in four consecutive weeks is 10, 6, 5, 15, then the straight average of the four weeks is 9 and the moving average (cumulatively by week) is 10, 8 [(10 + 6) ÷ 2], 7 [(10 + 6 + 5) ÷ 3], and 9 [(10 + 6 + 5 + 15) ÷ 4].

Moving Picture Experts Group (MPEG)   A type of audio/video file found on the Internet. The term also refers to the family of digital video compression standards and file formats developed by the group. MPEG-1 is a standard for CD-ROM video and audio. MPEG-2 is a standard for full-screen, broadcast-quality video. MPEG-4 is a standard for video telephony.

Moving Picture Experts Group, Audio Layer 3 (MP3)   A popular music download format. MP3 produces CD-quality music in a compressed file that can be transferred quickly and played on any multimedia computer with MP3 player software. The technology creates sound files a tenth the size of standard CD music files with very little loss of sound quality. As a result, huge numbers of Internet users have taken to trading MP3 files back and forth, or posting them on download sites, often in violation of industry-owned copyrights.

MPA   *See* Magazine Publishers of America.

MPAA ratings   A rating system established and implemented by the Motion Picture Association of America for movies. The ratings are G (general audience, all ages admitted), PG (parental guidance suggested, some material may not be suitable for children), PG-13 (parents strongly cautioned, some material may not be suitable for children under 13 years of age), R (restricted, a person under 17 requires accompanying parent or adult guardian), and NC-17 (no one under 17 admitted).

M-payments   Making payments (e.g., using a credit card) via a mobile phone (cell phone).

MPEG   *See* Moving Picture Experts Group.

MP3   *See* Moving Picture Experts Group, Audio Layer 3.

MPX   *See* magazine page exposure.

MRA   *See* Marketing Research Association

MRC   *See* Media Rating Council.

MRI   *See* Mediamark Research, Inc.

MSA   *See* metropolitan statistical area.

MS-DOS   *See* Microsoft disk operating system.

MSI   *See* Marketing Science Institute.

MSO   *See* multisystem operator.

M-Street   An online publication concentrating on the radio industry. Website: mstreet.net

M-trade   Conducting stock transactions using a mobile phone (cell phone).

Multicast   **1.** A message sent out by a host to multiple devices on a network. **2.** A type of audio and video broadcasting over the Internet that requires at least 128 Kbps modem speed hardware and special software. *Also see* Mbone.

Multichannel multipoint distribution service (MMDS)   Technology used for wireless broadband access to the Internet. Also known as multipoint microwave distribution service.

Multichannel video distribution and data service   A television technology that is digital, wireless, and local. It offers high-speed Internet access. It is akin to digital cable but has no cables. The Federal Communications Commission approved the technology in April 2002.

Multimedia   An advertising campaign that uses more than one medium. *Also see* media mix.

Multimedia messaging service (MMS)   An enhancement of short messaging service that allows more complex transmissions, such as incorporating audio and video with traditional text messages.

Multiplexing   To combine multiple signals (analog or digital) for transmission over a single line or medium, such as transmitting several feeds of the same cable TV network with the same programming at different times of the day.

Multipoint distribution system (MDS)   A Federal Communications Commission–authorized common carrier service for short distances (under 25 miles) that has line-of-sight transmission of a single channel of TV programming to selected locations.

Multipoint microwave distribution service (MMDS)   Technology used for wireless broadband access to the Internet. Also known as Multichannel Multipoint Distribution Service.

Multipurpose Internet mail extensions (MIME)   A specification for formatting messages so they can be sent over the Internet. MIME defines how an e-mail message is sent in code and then decoded by the recipient computer. In addition to e-mail applications, many Web browsers support various MIME types, which allows the browser to display files that are not in hypertext markup language (HTML). S/MIME supports encrypted messages.

Multiset household   A household with more than one TV set.

Multisystem operator (MSO)   A company that owns or operates more than one local cable system, such as Adelphia, AOL/Time

Warner, AT&T Broadband, Cablevision, Charter, Comcast, and Cox.

Multitasking   Consuming more than one advertising medium at any particular moment, such as reading a newspaper while listening to the radio.

Murphy's Law   In 1947, an Air Force engineer by the name of Edward A. Murphy observed: "If there are two or more ways to do something, and one of those ways can result in a catastrophe, then someone will do it." The common and often used variation of what he said is: "If anything can go wrong, it will."

Museum (.museum)   *See* domain name.

Must-carry (retransmission or rule)   A 1992 Federal Communications Commission Cable Act requiring a cable system to carry signals of both commercial and noncommercial television broadcast stations that are "local" to the area served by the cable system.

Mystery shopper   A person sent by a research company into a business location to act in the role of a customer in order to evaluate the business or employee performance.

Na or n/a   Abbreviation for *not applicable, no answer, not available, not affiliated,* and possibly other *nos* and *nots.*

NAA   *See* Newspaper Association of America.

NAB   *See* **1.** National Association of Broadcasters, **2.** Newspaper Advertising Bureau.

NAB code   (Obsolete) A National Association of Broadcasters code that was followed by nearly all broadcasters and dealt with programming and advertising standards, such as how many commercial minutes and program interruptions per hour a TV station or network should have. The code was disbanded in 1982.

NABSS   *See* Nielsen Agency, Broadcaster and Syndication Service.

NAC   *See* radio programming formats.

NAD   *See National Audience Demographics.*

NAICS   *See* North American Industry Classification System.

Name (.name)   *See* domain name.

Nanosecond   *See* second.

NARC   *See* National Advertising Review Council.

Narrowband   A connection over a computer network that supports a relatively low bit rate. It can carry audio frequencies but not visual transmission. It typically operates at a speed of 64 kilobits per second (kbps) or less, as compared to broadband, which operates at rates of 1.544 megabits per second (Mbps) or higher, and wideband, which operates at speeds ranging from 64 kbps to 1.544 Mbps. *Also see* baseband.

Narrowcasting   A term used to describe special-interest programming that is designed for small, select audiences.

National Advertising Review Council (NARC)   An advertising industry self-regulatory body. NARC's mission is to foster truth and accuracy in national advertising through voluntary self-regulation. NARC was formed in 1971 when the Association of National Advertisers, the American Association of Advertising Agencies, and the American Advertising Federation formed an alliance with the Council of Better Business Bureaus to create an independent self-regulatory body. Website: narcpartners.org

National Association of Broadcasters (NAB)   A full-service trade association that promotes and protects the interests of radio and television broadcasters in Washington, D.C., and around the world. NAB is the broadcaster's voice before Congress, federal agencies, and the courts. Website: nab.org

National Audience Demographics **(NAD)**   A Nielsen Media Research report published five times per year that provides national audience demographic data by program and time period.

National Cable and Telecommunications Association (NCTA) Formerly the National Cable Television Association, NCTA is the principal trade association of the cable television industry in the United States. Founded in 1952, its primary mission is to provide its members with a single, unified voice on issues affecting the cable and telecommunications industry. It represents cable operators serving more than 90 percent of the nation's cable television households and more than 200 cable program networks, as well as equipment suppliers and providers of other services to the cable industry. Website: ncta.com

National Cable Television Association   *See* National Cable and Telecommunications Association.

National Center for Supercomputing Applications (NCSA)   A research center that helps define the future's high-performance computing infrastructure for scientists and for society. NCSA creates the hardware, software, and tools that will make up the grid. This grid will assemble the country's most advanced technologies into a single system that will advance science beyond what is possible today. NCSA opened its doors in January 1986 as one of the five original centers in the National Science Foundation's Supercomputer Centers Program and a unit of the University of Illinois at Urbana-Champaign. The center has earned and maintains an international reputation in high-performance computing and networking and in developing innovative software applications. In 1992, the center introduced NCSA Mosaic, the first readily available graphical Web browser. Website: ncsa.uiuc.edu

National Mail Order Association (NMOA)   An association that provides business resources for companies involved in direct marketing. Website: nmoa.org

National media   Advertising media vehicles whose audiences are nationwide, such as network TV, network radio, and full-run editions of national magazines. *Also see* local media.

National projection   To estimate U.S.-wide activity based on data representing less than the entire United States. For example, if an advertising effort in markets representing 10 percent of U.S. population costs $1,000, the national cost of that effort would be $10,000. This projection would be adjusted up or down based on the idiosyncrasies of the media used—for example, using network TV in lieu of spot TV in all U.S. markets might cost less for the same media delivery.

National Public Radio (NPR) Founded by the Corporation for Public Broadcasting (CPB) in 1970, NPR is a private, nonprofit organization that provides leadership in national news gathering and production. It is a nationwide interconnection of 680 noncommercial stations that also broadcasts worldwide and via the Internet. *Also see* Public Broadcasting Service.

National rate of spending The level of spending in a market or group of markets projected to show how much it would cost to buy the same schedule in all U.S. markets. This is only a rough indication of the national cost, because it assumes (incorrectly) that the media costs in the selected markets are proportionately the same as the remaining U.S. markets. Costs by medium across markets vary substantially.

Formula:

market's spending ÷ market's percent of U.S. population = national rate of spending

Example:

$100,000 ÷ 10 percent = $1,000,000

National Television Standards Committee (NTSC) An organization that defines the television video signal format used in the United States. The European equivalent is Phase Alternation Line (PAL).

NCSA *See* National Center for Supercomputing Applications.

NC-17 *See* MPAA ratings.

NCTA *See* National Cable and Telecommunications Association.

NDA *See* nondisclosure agreement.

Near video on demand (NVOD) The capability of receiving movies or other programming fare via cable TV or direct broadcast satellite (DBS) near the time a consumer wishes to view a program, such as within 15 minutes of the desired time. *Also see* video on demand.

NECTA   *See* New England cities and towns area.

Negotiate   To arrange or settle by discussion and mutual agreement. Negotiations happen between a media buyer and a media seller. They typically involve discussions about placement of commercials in specific programs or dayparts (or, e.g., placement of advertisements in sections of magazines), the cost of the placements, and tangential elements such as added value, cancellation rights, competitive separation, and makegood understandings.

Net   **1.** A media audience that is not duplicated with any other media audiences for all of the media and vehicles used in a media schedule. **2.** Equivalent to reach. **3.** The amount of payment due to a media supplier for carrying advertising. **4.** Sometimes used as an abbreviation for *Internet. Also see* gross.

Net (.net)   *See* domain name.

Net circulation   *See* circulation.

NETCOSTS   (Obsolete) A media research report published by Ephron, Papazian & Ephron, Inc., that listed industry-average costs paid for national TV advertising. It was sold to SQAD in 2001.

Net coverage   *See* coverage.

Net domestic product   The gross domestic product minus depreciation on a country's capital goods.

Net income   The income for a product, service, or company that is derived after costs are subtracted from revenue.

Net paid circulation   The circulation of a magazine or newspaper that is accounted for by copies purchased as single copies, such as at a newsstand, or through subscription.

Net radio   *See* webcasting.

Net rating point   *See* rating.

NetRatings   *See* Nielsen/NetRatings.

NetScore   An online traffic measurement service designed to provide indicators of online business performance for both e-commerce and content sites. Website: netscoreonline.com

Netspot   Software that accesses Nielsen Media Research data to show how network television programs deliver audiences in local markets. Using Nielsen Network Program by DMA (designated market area) data, combined with a user's predetermined delivery goal for each market, a user can see how a planned TV schedule over-delivers or underdelivers media audiences (ratings converted to impressions) relative to the goal in each market. A software product of Telmar.

NetValue   A worldwide market research company founded in 1998 that concentrates on Internet usage. Its system of measurement is based on panels strictly representative of the Internet user population, and analyzes all Internet use, over and beyond the simple measurement of website audiences. Website: netvalue.com

Network   **1.** A broadcast TV, cable TV, or radio entity that provides programming and sells commercial time in programs that air nationally or regionally via affiliated or licensed local stations, such as ABC television network. **2.** Any connection of two or more computers that enables them to communicate. Networks may include transmission devices, servers, cables, routers, and satellites.

Network affiliate   *See* affiliate.

Network feed   Transmission of network programming, typically via satellite, to stations that are affiliated with the network. The feed may be aired live or taped for a later broadcast.

New adult contemporary   A radio programming format of soft, light vocals and instrumental music with a jazzy sound.

New age   A radio programming format of soft instrumental music. Also known as fusion.

Newbie   A person who is new to the Internet, but the term can be applied to any media form or occupation.

New England cities and towns area (NECTA)   As defined by the Federal Office of Management and Budget, an NECTA is a county-based alternative to the city- and town-based metropolitan statistical area and consolidated metropolitan statistical area. The county composition of an NECTA reflects the geographic extent of the corresponding MSA(s) or SMSA(s). NECTAs are not defined for individual primary metropolitan statistical areas. *Also see* metropolitan area.

New Millennium   A buying system that provides advertising agencies with the ability to perform pre-buy analyses, track negotiations and scheduling of ad time, evaluate overall performance in terms of delivery and cost, and perform reconciliation and subsequent accounting functions. A product of Nielsen Media Research.

Newspaper Advertising Bureau   *See* Newspaper Association of America.

Newspaper Advertising Co-op Network   *See* Newspaper Association of America.

Newspaper Association of America (NAA)   A nonprofit organization representing the newspaper industry. NAA members account for nearly 90 percent of the daily circulation in the United States and a wide range of nondaily U.S. newspapers. The association focuses on six key strategic priorities that collectively affect the newspaper industry: (1) marketing, (2) public policy, (3) diversity, (4) industry development, (5) newspaper operations, and (6) readership. NAA was founded in 1992 by the merger of seven associations serving the newspaper industry: American Newspaper Publishers Association (founded in 1887), Newspaper Advertising Bureau, Association of Newspaper Classified Advertising Managers, International Circulation Managers Association, International Newspapers Advertising and Marketing Executives, Newspaper Advertising Co-op Network, and the Newspaper Research Council. Website: naa.org

Newspaper Audit Report   *See* Audit Bureau of Circulations.

Newspaper designated market   The geographic area in which the publisher believes the newspaper has its greatest strength. The term is used for reporting circulation to the Audit Bureau of Circulations. *Also called* primary market area.

Newspaper distributed magazine   A magazine format publication usually distributed in the Sunday edition of local newspapers and carried as a supplement to the newspaper. *Also called* supp or supplement. The *New York Times Magazine* is an example of a locally published supplement, and *Parade* is an example of a syndicated supplement.

Newspaper distributed magazines, attributes   All media forms have positive and negative attributes. The following are some attributes of advertising in newspaper distributed magazines: they are essentially a mass medium directed to adults with little if any demographic targeting capability; they can be purchased nationally or locally in just about any market; a goodly portion of the adult population can be reached; timing delivery of the advertising message can be controlled by week (e.g., Sunday); because over 90 percent of readership happens on the issue date, advertising can be delivered almost immediately; long copy advertisements are available; the medium is reader-controlled (relatively nonintrusive)—that is, the reader essentially decides whether to turn the page and be exposed to the advertising; because of their tangible permanency, they offer the opportunity for repeat readership of the same advertisements; they can be used to distribute coupons; and ad production costs are relatively low.

Newspaper Publisher's Statement   *See* Audit Bureau of Circulations.

Newspaper Research Council   *See* Newspaper Association of America.

Newspapers, attributes   All media forms have positive and negative attributes. The following are some attributes of advertising in newspapers: specific target audiences can be reached by placing advertisements in specific sections of the newspaper; they can be purchased nationally or locally in just about every market; through the purchase of zoned editions, advertisements can appear in specific ZIP codes; a goodly portion of the adult population can be reached through the purchase of major metro dailies and Sunday newspapers; high reach levels are obtainable only through the purchase of nearly all the newspapers distributed within a specific geographic area; timing delivery of the advertising message can be controlled by day of the week; because over 90 percent of readership happens on the issue date, advertising can be delivered almost immediately; formatting by section allows for placement of advertisements in a compatible editorial environment; long copy advertisements are available; newspapers are a reader-controlled (relatively nonintrusive) medium—that is, the reader essentially decides whether to turn the page and be exposed to the advertising; because of newspapers' tangible permanency, they offer the opportunity for repeat readership of the same advertisements; they can be used to distribute coupons; and ad production costs are relatively low.

Newsstand circulation   Copies of a magazine or newspaper that are sold and purchased at outlets (such as newsstands) selling single copies, as opposed to copies sold through subscriptions.

News/talk (sports)   A radio programming format with information programming primarily featuring call-in participants and personality hosts. May or may not also include sports.

NFO WorldGroup   A company that provides research-based marketing information and counsel on market evaluation, product development, brand management, customer satisfaction, pricing, distribution, and advertising effectiveness. Key market sectors include packaged goods and foods, health care, financial services, high-tech and telecommunications, travel and leisure, automotive, and business-to-business. Website: nfor.com

NHI   *See* Nielsen Homevideo Index.

NHSI *See* Nielsen Hispanic Television Services.

NHTI *See* Nielsen Hispanic Television Services.

Niche A special area of demand, such as among a specific demographic group, for a product or service, as opposed to mass appeal. Niche often precedes various nouns, such as in *niche marketing*, *niche markets*, and *niche media*.

Nielsen Agency, Broadcaster and Syndication Service (NABSS) A service that provides continuous audience estimates for all national broadcast network television programs and national syndicated programs. NABSS combines the marketing staffs of Nielsen Television Index (NTI), which was established in 1950, and Nielsen Syndication Service (NSS), which was established in 1985.

Nielsen Broadcast Data Systems (BDS) A Nielsen Media Research resource that provides off-the-air music tracking for the entertainment industry. Employing a digital pattern recognition technology, Nielsen BDS captures song detections on more than 1,200 radio stations in more than 130 markets in the United States and Canada.

Nielsen county size groups Designation of all U.S. counties into one of four categories as defined by Nielsen Media Research, based on 1990 U.S. Census household counts. They are commonly referred to as A, B, C, and D counties. "A" counties are those within the 21 largest metropolitan statistical areas; "B," those with more than 85,000 households that are not in "A"; "C," those with 20,000 to 84,999 households; and "D," all remaining counties. The intent is that A counties account for 40 percent of total U.S. households, B counties account for 30 percent, and C and D counties each account for 15 percent. Media practitioners use this data to determine the delivery skews of national TV programs. For example, a program that has proportionately higher ratings in A counties is said to skew to urban areas; a program with relatively higher ratings in C or D counties is said to skew to rural and farm areas.

Nielsen diary   The device used by Nielsen Media Research to collect TV viewing information from sample homes in every television market in the United States. Each year Nielsen processes approximately 1.6 million paper diaries from households across the country for the "sweeps" ratings periods. The paper-viewing diaries are mailed out to randomly selected households in all 210 local TV markets in the United States. Each person in the household in the diary sample is asked to write down what programs and channels he or she views over the course of that one week. *Also see* 1. audimeter, 2. People Meter, 3. sweeps.

Nielsen Hispanic Television Services (NHTI and NHSI)   Started in November 1992, Hispanic Services provides comprehensive measurement for Hispanic television viewing and Spanish-language television in the United States. Nielsen Hispanic Television Index (NHTI) is the first electronic metered service to report Hispanic audience measurement on a national basis. NHTI uses the people meter—the same measurement tool used to report total U.S. audience behavior—with a separate sample of more than 800 Hispanic households. Nielsen Hispanic Station Index (NHSI) reports on local TV, providing viewing information in 16 television markets with significant Hispanic populations. Like its national counterpart, the NHSI service began in 1992. A product of Nielsen Media Research.

Nielsen Homevideo Index (NHI)   NHI was established in 1980 and provides a measurement of cable, pay cable, VCRs, DVD players, satellite dishes, and other new television technologies. The data are collected through the use of people meters, set-tuning meters, and paper diaries. Included in the NHI service is measurement of interactive television systems. A product of Nielsen Media Research.

Nielsen Media Research   The company is synonymous with television ratings and audience estimates. The ratings provide an estimate of audience size and composition for television programmers and commercial advertisers. Nielsen's television audience research information is used to buy and sell television time, to help programmers make program decisions, and to help broadcasters decide which programs should be placed on which days and times. The company also provides information about competitive advertising expenditures and audience reach for print, radio, and television, as well as information about computer usage and the Internet. Nielsen Media Research shares a common heritage with the ACNielsen Company. The companies split up in 1996 as part of a strategic restructuring. Before that, both companies had been part of the A.C. Nielsen Company, which was founded in 1923 by a 26-year-old engineer, Arthur C. Nielsen, Sr. Nielsen Media Research and ACNielsen are now owned by VNU. Website: nielsenmedia.com

Nielsen Monitor-Plus In 1986, Nielsen Media Research introduced an automated recognition system called Monitor-Plus to collect commercial data. Monitor-Plus uses Ad*Sentry, a technology known as "computerized pattern recognition" that permits Nielsen Media Research to monitor commercial activity on broadcast networks, cable networks, syndication, and local television stations in most of the major markets. The system is passive and requires no manual insertion of artificial codes. Nielsen Monitor-Plus links television ratings and cost data (from SQAD and other sources) to commercial occurrence data and tracks share-of-spending and share-of-voice. Nielsen Monitor-Plus enables marketers and their agencies to track advertising activity across 15 categories of media, including television, radio, and print. Ad*Views is software that allows the user to work with Monitor-Plus information directly from their desktop or laptop computers. Website: nielsenmedia.com

Nielsen/NetRatings Research that provides Internet audience information and analysis that is required for strategic decision making in the Internet economy. It is owned by Nielsen Media Research and ACNielsen. The basis for audience measurement data and analysis is click-by-click Internet user behavior measured through a comprehensive, real-time meter installed on computers throughout the world. NetRatings acquired the assets of AdRelevance in 2002. Website: netratings.com

Nielsen Sports Marketing Service (NSMS)   Established in 1995, this marketing unit focuses on the special information needs of sports teams, leagues, and marketers, as well as stations, networks, unwired networks, and production companies. A product of Nielsen Media Research.

Nielsen Station Index (NSI)   Established in 1954, NSI provides local market television audience measurement. This service provides continuous metered-market overnight measurement in 53 markets and diary measurement in all 210 designated market areas in the United States. A product of Nielsen Media Research.

Nielsen Syndication Service (NSS)   *See* Nielsen Agency, Broadcaster and Syndication Service.

Nielsen Television Index (NTI)   *See* Nielsen Agency, Broadcaster and Syndication Service.

:90   A 90-second TV commercial.

NMOA   *See* National Mail Order Association.

No-charge spots   A radio or TV commercial given to an advertiser at no cost, usually as part of a paid advertising schedule.

Node   A connection point or processing center in a computer network for either redistribution of data (a gateway node) to another node or to an end point (host node) for data transmission. A node can be a computer or some other device, such as a printer.

Nominal gross domestic product   *See* gross domestic product.

Nondisclosure   The practice of masking detailed costs shown on a media supplier invoice, before it is sent by a media buying agent to the advertiser.

Nondisclosure agreement (NDA)   A signed agreement between two parties that stipulates that information given to the second party by the first party cannot be divulged to any third party during a specified period of time. Such an agreement comes into play when an advertiser gives confidential data to its advertising agency.

Nonduplication rule   *See* cable nonduplication rule.

North American Industry Classification System (NAICS)   The numerical coding system developed by the Bureau of Budget used in the classification of business establishments according to the principal end product manufactured or service performed at that location. The NAICS was developed jointly by the United States, Canada, and Mexico to provide new comparability in statistics about business activity across North America. The NAICS code for advertising and related services is 5418. The NAICS has replaced the Standard Industrial Classification Code (SIC).

Nostalgia/big band   *See* radio programming formats.

Noted   The percentage of a magazine's readers who claimed to have seen a particular advertisement in the magazine. *See* Starch readership scores.

NPD (National Product Data)   Founded in 1953, NPD provides comprehensive marketing intelligence collected and delivered online for a wide range of vertical markets. NPD tracks both purchasing behavior and attitudes among the same consumers to inform subscribers about what is happening in their industries and why. NPD also measures both retail product movement and e-commerce for a complete view of items in each market tracked. In 1981, NPD invented the handheld scanner for consumer sales tracking for packaged goods, and subsequently licensed the technology to ACNielsen. Website: npd.com

NPR   *See* National Public Radio.

NSI   *See* Nielsen Station Index.

NSMS   *See* Nielsen Sports Marketing Service.

NTI   Nielsen Television Index. *See* Nielsen Agency, Broadcaster and Syndication Service.

NTSC   *See* National Television Standards Committee.

Number portability   A term used to describe the capability of individuals, businesses, and organizations to retain their existing telephone number(s) and the same quality of service when switching to a new local service provider.

NVOD   *See* near video on demand.

O & O   *See* owned and operated.

OAAA   *See* Outdoor Advertising Association of America.

OBB   *See* opening billboard.

Objectives, media   These are the stated goals of a media plan. Some refer to them as strategies. Despite nomenclature, objectives are the road map that illustrates where a company is and where it wants to be—what it wants to accomplish with advertising media. Objectives typically address the questions of *who* (target audiences), *when* (timing of delivery), *where* (geography), and *how much* (media delivery parameters), as well as any other important media delivery goals. Defining a precise target audience is extremely important. Focusing on the people you want to reach with advertising will minimize wasted delivery to unimportant population segments, and thereby increase cost-effectiveness and result in increased reach/frequency to the most important segment. Timing has to do with the period of time a company will advertise, expressed both in terms of start and end dates for the campaign, as well as any adjustments within that overall period. Adjustments might include, for example, the need for increased media delivery during certain important days or weeks. Geographic objectives detail which markets will receive advertising support and the method used to determine how budgets or media delivery will be allocated to each market. Delivery parameters deal primarily with reach/frequency: how many of the target audience does the company want to reach and how often. Media objectives are an extension of the marketing and advertising objectives, and they must therefore fully reflect the goals stated in the marketing plan. All objectives must be media-actionable. For example, it is not actionable to state "increase awareness" without stating how many people need to be reached and how often. Media objectives must be written before a media plan is devised. If a plan does not or cannot completely fulfill an objective, the planner should state the reason—rather than changing the objectives after the plan is written. *Also see* tactics, media.

OEM   *See* original equipment manufacturer.

Off card   A negotiated advertising rate not expressly stated in a published rate card.

Offline   **1.** Computer operations conducted when not connected to the Internet—for example, reviewing e-mail files. **2.** Non-Internet (interactive) media forms, such as radio, TV, and print. **3.** (Jargon) Private discussions outside of open meetings.

Offline browser   A browser that lets a user download a website, or parts of it, very quickly so the user can review it offline.

Off-network   TV programming that has originally aired on network TV and is sold for airing in the syndication market.

Offset   A printing process that puts the surface of paper in contact with another surface (such as a rubber cylinder) that has been freshly inked with the image or text to be printed. *Also see* **1.** letterpress, **2.** lithography, **3.** rotogravure.

Oldies   A radio programming format of vocal or instrumental music from the 1940s to the 1980s. Also referred to as golden oldies.

Omnibus study (or survey)   A research study that examines a number of unrelated topics or issues.

On air   The first date that a scheduled radio or TV advertising campaign is physically broadcast (cablecast).

One color (1C)   The addition of one basic color to a black-and-white print advertisement.

One-on-one interview   An in-depth interview involving the interviewer and the respondent. Also known as a diad.

1+ Reach   *See* Reach (1+).

One sheet   An out-of-home poster usually measuring 2 feet by 4 feet and physically produced on one sheet of paper. These can be found on walls next to convenience stores and various other locations.

One-time-only (OTO)   A commercial or program that airs only once.

Onetime rate   *See* open rate.

:120   A two-minute radio or TV commercial.

One-way system   The ability to receive TV programming through a broadband network, but no ability to interact (respond) as would be possible with a two-way system.

Online auction   An auction for the sale and purchase of items conducted via a website, such as eBay.

Online Privacy Alliance (OPA)   A cross-industry coalition of more than 80 global companies and associations committed to promoting the privacy of individuals online. Its sole purpose is to define privacy policy for the new electronic media in addition to fostering an online environment that respects the consumer's privacy. Website: privacyalliance.org

Online Publishers Association (OPA)   A trade association, OPA represents a particular segment of online publishers. Website: online-publishers.org

Online service provider (OSP)   A company, such as AOL, that provides customer-only content to its subscribers. Most OSPs offer Internet access like an Internet service provider (ISP), but maintain a private network that is only accessible to its subscribers.

Online services   A software service offered to consumers with a personal computer (PC) and interface capabilities, which links customers to information, programs, and entertainment via computer networks available worldwide.

Online survey   Market or opinion research conducted via the Internet, either through a website or via e-mail.

Only-only-both   A description of the reach of two or more different media forms or media vehicles used in an advertising campaign. Whenever two media are combined, some of the target audience receives only one medium and some receive both media. One of the purposes of using two or more media forms is to extend reach; ergo the additional reach must be against those who are not exposed to the first medium. Only-only-both is a display of audience reach for those receiving only medium A, only medium B, and both A and B.

To calculate only-only-both, one first needs the reach of the two media forms in question. This can be obtained via various computer software programs or by using the random combination technique.

Formula:

Reach of A+B combined − the reach of B = the reach of only A (i.e., this audience was not exposed to medium B)

Reach A+B combined − the reach of A = the reach of only B (i.e., this audience was not exposed to medium A)

Reach of A+B combined − [the reach of only A + the reach of only B] = the reach of those exposed to both A and B.

Example:

Reach of A = 60 (percent)

Reach of B = 50 (percent)

Reach of A+B combined (using random combination) = 80 (percent)

80 − 50 = 30 (30 percent exposed to only A)

80 − 60 = 20 (20 percent exposed to only B)

80 − [30 + 20] = 30 (30 percent exposed to both A and B)

Also see media mix.

On-sale date   The date of a magazine issue indicating when it is physically available for sale. This date almost always precedes the cover date.

OOH   *See* out-of-home media.

OPA   *See* 1. Online Privacy Alliance, 2. Online Publishers Association.

Op-ed   *See* opposite editorial.

Open-end co-op   *See* unlimited co-op.

Open-end diary   A diary, which a survey respondent fills out for a research company, that does not have prompting aids to help the respondent fill in specific information. For example, an open-end diary might ask what TV programs the respondent typically views, rather than prompting the respondent by listing TV programs. The respondent's answers are therefore akin to top-of-mind awareness or unaided awareness as opposed to total awareness (which includes prompts) and aided recall. *Also see* closed-end diary.

Open-ended question   A question in a research questionnaire that has no set of responses listed on the questionnaire. This is the opposite of a closed-end question.

Opening billboard (OBB)   A short (usually five-second) commercial at the beginning of a radio or TV program, which (usually) identifies a sponsor of the program, such as "This program is brought to you by . . ." If this mention appears at the end of a program, it is called a closing billboard (CBB). There is no MBB.

Open rate   The maximum rate shown on a publication's rate card that is charged for a particular size advertisement that will appear in the magazine or newspaper (usually) only once within a 12-month period. This rate creates a base against which various cost discounts are calculated for placing additional ad space in the publication. *Also see* 1. frequency discount, 2. volume discount.

Operating system (OS)   The primary program running on a computer, such as MS-DOS, OS/2, Macintosh, and Windows. Every computer must have an OS to run other programs. The OS is the foundation software of a computer system, responsible for controlling and launching the installed applications and computer peripherals (e.g., a printer).

Operator service provider (OSP)   A common carrier that provides services from public phones, including pay phones and those in hotels and motels.

Opportunistic buy   A purchase of one or more media vehicles, generally made immediately prior to airdate (or closing date), which usually costs less than if purchased well in advance. The reason for the lower cost is that media airtime and space are perishable. If they are not sold to advertisers, the media companies do not receive any revenue. Therefore, media companies would rather have less income for a particular commercial or advertisement than no income. Although the media costs are usually lower, there is no guarantee that any media time or space will be available at the last minute, which makes opportunistic buying a dicey proposition. An opportunistic buy is also sometimes referred to as a "fire sale."

Opportunity to hear (OTH)   *See* opportunity to see.

Opportunity to see (OTS)   While media practitioners in the United States use the term *frequency*, those in other countries favor OTS—perhaps because it is a more accurate description of the dynamic reality of media exposure. Frequency implies (albeit incorrectly) that once a number is shown in a media plan (e.g., a 3.0 frequency), then the target audience is exposed to the advertising in the media being used for a particular advertising campaign. Indeed, frequency indicates the probable consumption level of the media forms, not necessarily the advertising in those forms. Frequency of exposure to media vehicles is no more than a one-way street: the media are delivered to the target audience, and the audience therefore has an opportunity to be exposed to the media. The fact that a TV program is delivered to a person does not guarantee that the person will in fact be exposed to the advertising in that medium. Therefore, "opportunity to see" becomes a more accurate assessment of media dynamics. The same concept is used for radio with opportunity to hear (OTH).

Opposite editorial (op-ed)   An advertising position or editorial feature that is physically positioned opposite a newspaper's editorial page.

Optical fiber   A very thin thread of pure glass able to carry one thousand times the amount of information possible with copper wire. The end of an optical fiber is thinner than a human hair and smaller than the period at the end of this sentence. By contrast, the end of copper wire is thicker than a human hair.

OptiMax   A national television reach and frequency and optimization system that uses a weekly database. This software program allows the planner, buyer, and seller to optimize on budget, reach, or effective reach. A product of Interactive Market Systems.

Optimization   1. The process used to make a media plan or media buy as cost-efficient as possible by generating as much media audience (e.g., reach or impressions) per dollar invested. 2. A print software program that creates a best schedule that can be brought into reach and frequency programs. The user specifies the target, the list of magazines or newspapers, and the goals such as budget, reach, and frequency. Optimization then produces the most cost-efficient schedule, taking into account must-buys, minimums and maximums, and volume discounts. A product of Interactive Market Systems.

Optimizer   Although an optimizer has usually referred to TV media, it can apply to just about any media form. It is a computer reach and frequency analysis that generates an "optimal" schedule given a specific set of parameters, such as budget level and reach goal. It calculates the reach of various combinations of TV programs, or dayparts, in order to find the highest reach within a given budget. It uses respondent level data—that is, specific people within the research sample (such as the Nielsen sample). It is based on the Nielsen recorded audience for the middle minute of a quarter hour of viewing. Minute-by-minute viewing is required for a pure optimization, but these ratings are only available for household viewing (not people viewing), and only through customized Nielsen Media Research reports. In addition to hard data (e.g., number of viewers), optimizers can include program weights (e.g., the user's perception of a program's value).

Media planners think of optimizers as buying tools, while media buyers view them as planning tools. When an optimization is "run," it is unknown whether specific TV programs have commercial availability. Therefore, the product of an optimization may or may not be executable; that is, there might not be any commercial time available for sale in the TV programs "recommended" by the optimizer. Furthermore, because TV commercial costs are negotiable, it is unknown how much a TV program will actually cost until a buy is negotiated. Therefore, cost input by program is an estimate that leads to an estimate of optimized reach. In reality, optimization is a looping process. It starts with (1) a media planner doing a computer analysis based on a desired target and the buyer's estimated costs; (2) the results are given to a buyer for implementation; (3) due to a continuously dynamic marketplace, the buyer invariably finds that either the specified programs are not available or costs are different than the original input; and so (4) the buyer seeks a new direction, and the planner conducts further analysis.

If optimizers are useful (in either the planning or buying stage), they are only useful for national TV. National TV has continuous viewing research, as opposed to spot TV, which is not monitored as frequently. The largest TV markets (designated market areas), for example, are studied only seven times per year. With infrequent reporting, it is impossible to determine viewing patterns for nonreported days. Lack of research is exacerbated in smaller markets, which are studied only two to four times per year. The smaller a program's rating, the fewer the number of people in Nielsen's sample who viewed that program. The smaller the sample size, the more unstable the findings. Therefore, typical packages of high, average, and lower rated programs automatically contain a degree of sampling instability. Optimizers were first created in Europe and gained favor in the United States during the late 1990s.

Opt-in e-mail   Promotional e-mails requested by the individual receiving them. Opt-in e-mails are targeted to specific people; often, they are personalized based on a person's want of specific information, products, or services. For example, if a user frequents amazon.com, that user can opt-in to automatically receive an e-mail when certain kinds of books are published. Opt-in e-mail is also referred to as permission e-mail. *Also see* spam.

Orbit   A schedule of TV commercials that airs between programs or at the half-hour break of one-hour or longer programs. For example, a prime-time orbit can consist of Monday, 8:30 P.M.; Tuesday, 9:00 P.M.; and so on. An orbit has three distinct attributes: (1) by running as adjacencies, commercial costs are usually lower than media buys that schedule commercials in-program; (2) rotation through various days and time periods results in more reach than a less-dispersed schedule; and (3) an orbit is not as targeted to specific audiences as a program-specific schedule. *Also see* **1.** rotation, **2.** run of station.

Org (.org)   *See* domain name.

Original equipment manufacturer (OEM)   A company that purchases computer components from manufacturers, often adds other hardware or software, and then sells the final product under a specific brand name.

OS   *See* operating system.

OSP   *See* **1.** online service provider, **2.** operator service provider.

OTH   Opportunity to hear. *See* opportunity to see.

OTO   *See* one-time-only.

OTS   *See* opportunity to see.

Outdoor Advertising Association of America (OAAA)   A trade association representing the outdoor advertising industry. Founded in 1891, the OAAA is dedicated to promoting, protecting, and advancing outdoor advertising interests in the United States. With nearly 1,100 member companies, the OAAA represents more than 90 percent of industry revenues. Website: oaaa.org

Outdoor synergy   A software product that calculates multimarket and multimedia analysis for outdoor bulletins, posters, shelters, and eight-sheets. Media variable results are quickly calculated and displayed graphically on a flowchart or in customized reports. Synergy works with Traffic Audit Bureau (TAB) data, which can be customized for either a specific outdoor plant operator or provided with an industry average database for nationwide analysis. A software product of Telmar.

Outdoor Visibility Rating System (OVRS)   A system of grading a poster panel's "visibility" and assigning it a relative rating. It is based on factors such as the maximum distance from which it can be seen and any obstructions that can affect viewing. OVRS ratings are calculated by plant operators.

Outdoor, attributes   All media forms have positive and negative attributes. The following are some of the attributes of advertising on outdoor posters and bulletins: outdoor advertising is essentially a mass medium directed to the population at large; very high levels of reach can be obtained through the purchase of multiple units; timing delivery of the advertising message can only be controlled (essentially) by month; advertising can be purchased one unit at a time in a specific geographic area, thereby making it the second most local medium (direct mail is the most localized of all media forms); because nearly all advertising appears for at least one month, outdoor offers high levels of frequency; it offers significant creative flexibility (through the use of various extensions and embellishments); because of a relatively short exposure duration (while travelers pass by a unit), copy must be relatively short; and it is considered the lowest cost-per-thousand (impressions) medium.

Out-of-home media (OOH)   Any advertising media forms that can be seen or heard outside of one's home. This includes, but is not limited to, outdoor bulletins and posters, advertising on or in trains or buses (transit advertising), in-store media, airport advertising, bus shelters, bike racks, and skywriting.

Out-of-home readers   Those people reading a magazine outside their own homes. If a person reads a magazine in a neighbor's home, that person is still an out-of-home reader. Likewise, and logically, a person reading a magazine at an airport, in a doctor's office, or at a hair salon is an out-of-home reader. Various research studies have shown that an out-of-home reader typically spends less time reading a magazine than an in-home reader. Less time reading is an indication that there is likely less exposure to the average page (editorial and advertising). With likely less exposure, media planners often discount those readers when evaluating magazine media audiences, such as in a ranker.

Outsert   A page or card enclosed with a magazine in a polybag and used for circulation promotion purposes. *Also see* cover wrap.

Outside back cover   *See* back cover.

Outsource   Work done for a company by people other than its employees. For example, an advertising agency might outsource media buying to another company. Colloquially referred to as farming out (a project or task).

Overhead   Costs that a company incurs in providing a product or service for sale, such as rent, utilities, and equipment maintenance, which are not attributable to a specific client but to all clients. *Also called* indirect costs. *Also see* cost accounting.

Overnight   *See* radio dayparts

Overnights   A Nielsen Media Research report that provides daily household ratings for selected metered markets.

Override   The continuation of an outdoor advertising program beyond a contracted period. It is usually provided by the outdoor company at no additional cost to an advertiser.

OVRS   *See* Outdoor Visibility Rating System.

Owned and operated (O & O)   Radio and television stations that are owned and operated by radio or TV networks. *Also see* affiliate.

PA *See* 1. prime access, 2. TV dayparts.

Pacific Rim Countries in the Far East that border the Pacific Ocean.

Packet A bundle of data or a piece of a message transmitted over a computer network.

Page four-color bleed (P4CB) A full-page advertising unit that is printed in four colors and "bleeds"; that is, it extends the illustration or copy to the edge of a page so there is no white border. Two facing full-page advertisements where one or both of the pages bleed is known as a spread four-color bleed (S4CB).

Page impressions *See* page requests.

Page requests The number of times a user requests a Web page from a server. *Also called* page views or page impressions. This is one of the methods, sometimes preferred, for tallying traffic estimates for a page. A related term is *hits*, which counts the number of times that all the elements on a page are accessed (text and graphics).

Page views *See* page requests.

Paging system A one-way mobile radio service where a user carries a small, lightweight miniature radio receiver capable of responding to coded signals. These devices, called pagers, emit an audible signal, vibrate, or do both when activated by an incoming message.

Paid circulation A classification of subscriptions or purchases of single copies of a magazine or newspaper, based on payments in accordance with standards set by the Audit Bureau of Circulations.

Paint out *See* blank out.

Painted bulletin (paint) *See* bulletin.

Painted wall A form of outdoor advertising where the advertisement is painted (usually) on the side of a large building.

PAL 1. *See* Phase Alternation Line. 2. A national media allocation system, which takes into account market-by-market differences in media delivery for network, syndicated, and cable television, as well as magazines. PAL evaluates performance, by market, of a national media schedule in terms of gross impressions or gross rating points and budget. A product of Interactive Market Systems.

P&L *See* profit and loss.

Panel 1. A poster panel in outdoor or transit advertising. 2. A preselected group of people used more than once over a period of time and from whom information is collected (e.g., product purchases and opinions).

Panel research Research findings from a panel.

Paper buy A radio or TV schedule that delineates all details (e.g., station program, time, cost, audience delivery) but which has yet to be booked with the station(s). The purposes of a paper buy are to evaluate the buy vis-à-vis buying guidelines and specifications, and to present a possible buy to an advertiser prior to its booking with the stations or networks.

Paradigm The assumptions, concepts, values, and practices that are shared by a group of people, a community, or the population at large.

Paradigm shift   When a majority of people accept a partial or total change (shift) of an assumption, concept, value, or practice. For example, banking online, versus in person or by mail, required a paradigm shift.

Parallel port   A "plug" used to connect an external device, such as a printer, to a personal computer. A parallel port uses a 25-pin connector. *Also see* **1.** port, **2.** serial port, **3.** universal serial bus.

Participation   (Obsolete) A commercial that appears in-program, as opposed to between programs during a break.

Pascal   A computer programming language that forces programmers to design programs methodically and carefully, and is therefore a popular teaching language.

Passalong (secondary) readers   Readers who did not purchase the magazine, do not live in the same household as the person who purchased it, but obtained it secondhand, such as from a primary reader, a reception room, or a friend. "Secondary" is somewhat of a misnomer since many passalong readers are not even the second person to read a particular copy of a magazine.

Pattern recognition   A software technology used by research companies (e.g., Nielsen Monitor-Plus and TNS Media Intelligence/CMR) to monitor television commercial airings. A computer is "shown and taught" to remember specific commercials. When these commercials air, the research companies' monitoring stations (computer robots) can capture pertinent information, such as the date and time of the airing as well as the TV station or network airing the commercial. Also referred to as fingerprint technology. *Also see* digital watermarking.

Pay cable   Programs or services provided to basic cable subscribers for an additional fee—for example, HBO. *Also called* premium cable.

Pay per click (PPC)   A payment model used for online advertising in which the advertiser pays the publisher based on the number of click-throughs that are generated.

Pay per lead (PPL)   A payment model used for online advertising in which the advertiser pays the publisher based on the number of qualified leads that were generated for the advertiser. *Also see* per inquiry.

Pay per view (PPV)   A telecast, usually of a special event, for which cable TV subscribers pay a onetime fee to view.

PBS   *See* Public Broadcasting Service.

PBX   *See* private branch exchange.

PC   *See* personal computer.

PCS   *See* personal communications service.

PDA   *See* personal digital assistant.

PDF   *See* Portable Document Format.

Pending client approval   (Obsolete) A negotiated radio or TV schedule that is placed with a station(s) or network and is ostensibly booked, but first requires the advertiser's final approval. The negotiated schedule is therefore held intact by the station until approval is granted. A similar term is *on hold*.

Penetration   The percentage of people (or homes) within a defined demographic universe who are physically able to be exposed to a medium. Cable TV, for example, has a national penetration level of approximately 75 percent, because three out of four homes are able to receive cable TV. Newspapers ostensibly have a 100 percent penetration level, because every person in a market is able to purchase a copy of the newspaper. *Also see* coverage.

People hours of viewing   Used by research companies, such as Nielsen Media Research, to calculate the share of viewing of TV stations in a given geographic area (e.g., designated market area). For example, if a person views station A and station B, each for five hours, that person represents ten people hours of viewing. In a real-world situation, a market with one million people could tally approximately fifty million people hours of viewing during an average week.

People Meter   An electronic metering system placed by Nielsen Media Research in randomly selected households. The meter records when the TV set is on, what channel or station is being tuned, and who is viewing. A fixed box is placed on or near the television set, and each member of the household is assigned a personal viewing button. Often, a remote clicker is also personalized for each household member. Survey respondents are required to click on their button when viewing and click off when they stop viewing. These personal buttons allow Nielsen Media Research to determine who is watching which program and when. The People Meter is used to produce household and persons audience estimates for broadcast and cable networks and nationally distributed barter-syndicated programs.

People using radio (PUR)   The percentage of all people within a defined demographic group listening to radio at a particular time— for example, 7:00–7:15 A.M., or during morning drive. *Also see* 1. rating, 2. share.

Formula:

rating ÷ share = PUR

Example:

5 ÷ 10 (percent) = 50

People using TV (PUT)   The percentage of people within a defined demographic group viewing TV at a particular time—for example, during 6:00–6:15 P.M., or prime time. Identical to PVT: people viewing TV. *Also see* 1. homes using TV, 2. rating, 3. share.

Formula:

rating ÷ share = PUT

Example:

5 ÷ 10 (percent) = 50

People viewing TV   *See* people using TV.

Perfect binding   A process that uses glue rather than staples or stitching to bind the pages of a periodical or book. The resulting flat edge is at a 90-degree angle to the front and back covers.

PerformerQ   *See* Marketing Evaluations/TvQ.

Per inquiry (PI)   The number of inquiries received as a result of a direct-response advertising campaign, divided by the media cost of the commercial (or schedule of commercials). An inquiry could be, for example, a telephone call to an 800 number to order a product. PI rates (or costs) are used to evaluate the relative performance (and effectiveness) of specific commercials, radio or TV programs, and time periods. Although PI rates are losing favor as a method of buying airtime, the direct response buyer would negotiate them with the media seller wherein the medium would receive payment based on the number of inquiries received as a result of advertising on that medium (i.e., the advertising cost per inquiry, or the cost charged by the media supplier for each inquiry received). *Also see* pay per lead.

PERL   A computer programming language typically used for processing text. It is an acronym for *Practical Extraction and Report Language.*

Permanent (bulletin or display)   An outdoor bulletin that permanently remains at a specified location throughout the term of a contract and usually for long periods. *Also see* rotary.

Permission e-mail   *See* opt-in e-mail.

Personal communications service (PCS)   Any of several types of wireless, voice, or data communications systems, typically incorporating digital technology. PCS is a Federal Communications Commission classification, for which licenses are most often used to provide services similar to advanced cellular, mobile, or paging services. However, PCS can also be used to provide not only wireless communications services to homes, office buildings, and other fixed locations, but also those that allow people to place and receive communications while away from their homes or offices.

Personal computer (PC)   Although technically an IBM product, it commonly refers to any IBM-compatible computer made by dozens of manufacturers. A Macintosh computer is not a PC.

Personal digital assistant (PDA)   A handheld portable computer (e.g., the Palm Pilot) that contains various software and features, such as an address book, calendar, and memo pad. State-of-the-art PDAs also offer wireless access to the Internet.

Personal video recorder (PVR)   A consumer device that uses a hard disk drive to record TV programs. It is the digital successor to videocassette recorders; it stores programs digitally on a high-capacity computer hard drive instead of on removable tapes. *Also see* 1. ReplayTV, 2. TiVo.

Petabyte   Approximately one quadrillion bytes (1,024 terabytes). In numerical sequence, bytes are counted as kilobyte, megabyte, gigabyte, terabyte, petabyte, exabyte.

P4C, P4CB   *See* page four-color bleed.

PG   *See* MPAA ratings.

PG-13   *See* MPAA ratings.

Phase Alternation Line (PAL)   The video signal format used in Europe. The U.S. equivalent is National Television Standards Committee (NTSC).

PI   *See* per inquiry.

PIB   *See* Publishers Information Bureau.

Pica   A unit of measurement in print media. There are six picas to an inch. *Also see* agate line.

Pickup rate   Discounted advertising rates earned when ads are repeated within a short period of time (usually between 3 and 10 days) in the same newspaper—such as an ad running on Sunday and repeated on Wednesday.

Picosecond *See* second.

Piggyback (Obsolete) Airing two completely separate commercials for two different products from the same advertiser combined within a single announcement—for example, a :30/:30. These sixty-second commercial lengths used to be the norm in TV. Stations and networks would not sell advertising units of less than 60 seconds. By combining two :30 commercials, advertisers were able to buy TV media at half price (for half the time) for each of two brands. Over time, the :30 unit became the norm.

PIN 1. An acronym for Personal Identification Number as used, for example, at automatic teller machines. 2. The devices in dot-matrix printers that press ink on paper to create an image (text, etc.) The more pins a printer has, the higher the quality of the image it is capable of producing. 3. A male end of a computer connection device.

Pink Sheets *See* Audit Bureau of Circulations.

Pirate station *See* low power radio.

Pixel A single-colored dot. The smallest element of an image or picture on a TV or CRT (cathode ray tube) screen.

Place-based media Advertising at a physical location, such as on bike racks at a retail store.

Plant The factory that produces and physically places outdoor media.

Plant capacity The total number of poster panels or bulletins physically available in an outdoor plant.

Plant operator The owner of an outdoor advertising company.

Plant Operator Statement Published by the Traffic Audit Bureau (TAB) for out-of-home media, the statement provides documentation that TAB has verified the circulation numbers of the outdoor plants based on field audits conducted by TAB. It is published after a field audit is completed. It is presently available for bulletins, 30-sheet posters, 8-sheet posters, and transit shelters.

Plasma screen   A computer video display in which each pixel on the screen is illuminated by a tiny bit of plasma or charged gas. Plasma screens are thinner than a cathode ray tube and brighter than a liquid crystal display.

PMA   *See* primary market area.

PM drive   *See* radio dayparts.

PMSA   *See* primary metropolitan statistical area.

Pocketpiece   The common term for the Nielsen Television Index report that is published weekly and provides audience data for network TV programs.

Pod   *See* commercial pod.

Pod position   The specific position a commercial has within a pod, such as first position or second position.

Point-of-purchase display (POP)   An advertising display at the place where consumers purchase goods or services, such as a counter card at a retail outlet. *Also called* point-of-sale (POS).

Polybag   A polyethylene or plastic bag in which a home-delivered copy of a newspaper is inserted, or the bag wrapped around a magazine. Ads can be printed on the bag or inserted into the bag along with the newspaper or magazine. Product samples can also be inserted into the bag used for newspapers.

Pool   *See* spot-buying pool.

POP   *See* point-of-purchase display.

Pop-up ad   An online ad, such as an interstitial, that pops up on a website without the user requesting it. *Also see* **1.** pop-under ad, **2.** interactive marketing unit.

Pop-up coupon   A coupon, typically perforated and of heavier stock than the pages of the publication, that is bound into a publication. The reference to pop-up is because it pops up as the reader turns the pages in a magazine. *Also called* a bind-in card or tip-in card.

Pop-under ad   An online ad that appears in a separate window beneath an open window and pops up only when the window is closed, moved, resized, or minimized. *Also see* **1.** pop-up ad, **2.** interactive marketing unit.

Port   **1.** The place where information goes into a computer, out of a computer, or both. Personal computers have internal ports for connecting disk drives, display screens, and keyboards, and external ports for connecting peripheral devices, such as modems and printers. **2.** On the Internet, *port* often refers to a number that is shown in a universal resource locator (URL), following a colon right after the domain name. *Also see* **1.** parallel port, **2.** serial port, **3.** universal serial bus.

Portable Document Format (PDF)   The file format of documents viewed and created by the Adobe Acrobat Reader, Acrobat Capture, Adobe Distiller, Adobe Exchange, and the Adobe Acrobat Amber Plug-in for Netscape Navigator.

Portable People Meter (PPM)   A pager-sized device that is carried by consumers and automatically detects inaudible codes that TV and radio broadcasters, as well as cable networks (and some websites), embed in the audio portion of their programming using encoders provided by Arbitron. At the end of each day, the survey participants place the PPM into a base station that sends the collected codes (e.g., the radio listening information) to Arbitron for tabulation. By collecting multimedia usage from a single source (a person), PPM allows for cross-media duplication analysis and therefore integrated media planning. First tested in Manchester, England, the PPM has undergone U.S. in-market testing in 2000–2002.

Portal   A website that serves as a starting point for going to other destinations or activities on the Web, such as e-mail, shopping, games, and weather.

Porta-panel   A mobile poster panel that is wheeled to a given location such as a supermarket parking lot. *Also see* **1.** mobile billboard, **2.** rolling billboard.

POS   Point-of-sale. *See* Point-of-purchase display.

Position request   A request made by an advertiser or its buying agent for the ad to be positioned in a specific location within a magazine or newspaper, such as adjacent to food editorial or not facing another advertisement.

Post analysis   An analysis and evaluation of a media schedule after it runs. It is generally based on physical evidence of its running, such as a broadcast station affidavit of performance or magazine tear sheets. It typically reports the schedule's audience delivery in effect at the time the schedule ran. For example, if a TV schedule aired in January, the January Nielsen Station Index would be used for the post-analysis; if a magazine advertisement ran in January, the magazine's January circulation, as reported in the Publisher's Statement, would be used. *Also see* media audit.

Post-buy analysis   *See* post-analysis.

Poster panel   An outdoor advertising structure on which a preprinted advertisement is displayed, as distinguished from a bulletin. Also referred to as an 8-sheet poster or 30-sheet poster, depending on its size. An 8-sheet poster is equivalent in size to eight 1-sheet posters; a 30-sheet poster is equivalent in size to thirty 1-sheet posters. A common 30-sheet poster size is 10 feet, 5 inches by 22 feet, 8 inches.

Post-expiration copies   *See* arrears.

Posting Placing or painting an advertisement on any kind of outdoor or transit advertising unit.

Posting date The date when a poster program is scheduled to commence.

PostScript **1.** A computer programming language for printing documents on laser printers, as well as images on other types of electronic devices. **2.** If shown as two words (*post script*), it is a message at the end of a letter following the writer's signature, abbreviated as *P.S.* A second postscript on the same letter is abbreviated as *P.P.S.*, from the Latin *post postscriptum* (additional postscript).

Post-turn An outdoor unit with a slanted face that allows three different copy messages to revolve intermittently. Sometimes referred to as a Trivision.

POV Acronym for point of view (opinion).

PPC *See* pay per click.

PPL *See* pay per lead.

PPM *See* Portable People Meter.

PPV *See* pay per view.

Prebill *See* estimate billing.

Preempt *See* preemption.

Preemptible rate (Obsolete) A generally lower cost paid for a broadcast commercial unit, which gives the broadcaster the right to preempt the spot and sell it to another advertiser at a higher price. Because the vast majority of commercial placements are now preemptible, the term is no longer necessary. *Also see* immediately preemptible.

Preemption Replacing a regularly scheduled radio/TV program or commercial with another program or commercial. For example, a TV network might preempt a regularly scheduled program for a special news bulletin, or a TV station might preempt a commercial for an advertiser with another from a different advertiser because the latter was willing to pay a higher cost.

Preferred position   The placement of an advertisement in a specific location within a magazine or newspaper at the buyer's request. These placements sometimes command a premium price.

Premiere panel   A standardized display format measuring 12 feet, 3 inches by 24 feet, 6 inches in overall size. Premiere panel units offer the impact of a bulletin by using a single-sheet vinyl face stretched over a standard 30-sheet poster panel.

Premiere square   A standardized display format measuring 25 feet, 5 inches by 24 feet, 6 inches in overall size. The premiere square uses a single-sheet vinyl face stretched over two stacked 30-sheet poster panels. In some markets, this same technique can be applied to stacked 8-sheet poster panels measuring 12 feet, 6 inches by 12 feet, 1 inch in overall size.

Premium cable   Programs, services, or both provided to basic cable TV subscribers for an additional fee—such as HBO. *Also called* pay cable.

Pre-post   A practice conducted by radio and TV buyers in which a mock post-analysis is conducted for a hypothetical media schedule before it goes on air. This exercise gives the buyer an approximation of the total target rating point (TRP) delivery of the schedule had it aired in the past. It incorporates share estimates from the latest Nielsen Station Index (or Arbitron rating book) and homes using TV (or people using TV, people using radio) estimates from the same period as the planned program but one year earlier.

Preprint   A reprint of a magazine or newspaper advertisement produced before the ad appears in the publication. Preprints are often used to promote future advertising to the trade.

Preprinted insert   An advertisement printed by the advertiser and given to the publication in appropriate quantities (i.e., according to the circulation of the publication in which it will run) for insertion and distribution in a forthcoming issue.

Price elasticity   The degree to which customers respond to a product's price changes in terms of their purchase behavior. A product has price elasticity if a small change in price is accompanied by a large change in demand—the product is then elastic (or responsive to price changes). A product is inelastic if a large change in price is accompanied by a small change in demand.

Primary audience   *See* primary readers.

Primary market area (PMA)   A geographic area defined by a newspaper in which the publisher believes the newspaper has its greatest strength. *Also called* newspaper designated market.

Primary metropolitan statistical area (PMSA)   As defined by the Federal Office of Management and Budget, a PMSA consists of a large urbanized county or a cluster of counties (cities and towns in New England) that demonstrate strong internal economic and social links, as well as close ties with the central core of the larger area. Upon the recognition of PMSAs, the entire area they belong to becomes a consolidated metropolitan statistical area. *Also see* 1. metropolitan area, 2. metropolitan statistical area.

Primary readers   Magazine readers who purchased the magazine at newsstand or via subscription, as well as the members of the purchasers' households who claim to have read or looked into the magazine. *Also see* in-home readers.

Primary research   Creative, market, or media research conducted by an advertiser, or by a research company or person specifically for the advertiser. *Also see* syndicated research.

Prime access (PA)   A TV daypart immediately preceding a TV station's designation of prime time and in which local stations were originally charged by the Federal Communications Commission to broadcast programs in the interest of the local community. Prime access now contains various local or syndicated programs. Generally, prime access is the half hour from 7:30 P.M. to 8:00 P.M. eastern standard time. *Also see* TV dayparts.

Prime access rule   A Federal Communications Commission rule that prohibits all network-affiliated TV stations in the top 50 U.S. markets from carrying more than three hours of network programming between 7:00 P.M. and 11:00 P.M. eastern standard time. This led to the creation of the prime access daypart. *Also see* TV dayparts.

Prime number   A positive whole number divisible without a remainder by only itself or one, such as 5, 7, 11.

Prime time (prime)   A general reference to the time period in broadcast media that attracts the most viewers or listeners. *Also see* 1. radio dayparts, 2. TV dayparts.

Print media   Any printed publication, whether or not it carries advertising. This includes magazines, newspapers, newsletters, and pamphlets.

Private branch exchange (PBX)   A telephone exchange (system) within an enterprise that uses, but does not provide, telephone services. A PBX is owned by the enterprise, not a telephone company. It allows, for example, for calls between the enterprise's employees on local lines, while also allowing all users to share a certain number of external lines.

PRIZM   Created in the early 1970s, PRIZM was the first of the lifestyle segmentation systems. Like many of the segmentation systems, it operates on the simple principle of "birds of a feather flock together." In other words, people of similar demographic and lifestyle characteristics tend to live near each other. PRIZM applies this principle by assigning every neighborhood in the United States to one or another of 62 clusters. Each cluster is unique: no household is assigned to more than one cluster. Each cluster describes the predominant demographics and lifestyles of the people living in that neighborhood. A product of Claritas. Website: claritas.com

Pro (.pro)   *See* domain name.

Product protection   The separation of commercials or advertisements between competitive brands.

ProductQ   *See* Marketing Evaluations/TvQ.

Profile   The demographic or lifestyle characteristics of a medium's audience. For example, if magazine X readers tended to be concentrated within the young adult demographic group, it would have a young adult profile.

Profit and loss (P&L)   Also known as an income statement, a P&L shows business revenue and expenses for a specific period of time. The difference between the total revenue and the total expense is gross income (before taxes). A key element of this statement, and what distinguishes it from a balance sheet, is that the amounts shown on the statement represent transactions over a period of time, while the items represented on the balance sheet show information as of a specific date (or point in time).

Progressive adult radio   *See* adult alternative.

Projection   An estimate of the characteristics or magnitude of a total population universe based on a sampling of the population. For example, Arbitron projects the total audience of a market's radio stations based on the listening habits of a sampling of the population. *Also see* **1.** confidence level, **2.** sampling error, **3.** tolerance.

Prolog   A computer programming language based on formal logic and often used for artificial intelligence applications. Short for *Programming Logic*.

Promotion   Activities, materials, devices, and techniques used to supplement the advertising and marketing efforts and help coordinate those efforts with the overall selling effort.

Proof   A sheet of printed material (e.g., an advertisement) made to be checked and corrected. *Also see* slick.

Prorate   To distribute or divide proportionately. For example, if a media plan allocates the budget evenly to each of six months, then the budget has been prorated over those six months.

Protocol   The language or procedures used between computers to transfer information, such as the established method of exchanging data over the Internet.

Prototype   An estimate of a media vehicle's audience (often of a magazine) based on the audience delivery of a similar magazine(s). A prototype is used when a magazine has not yet been measured for audience delivery by a research company, or when an unmeasured publication's estimate of audience duplication is needed in order to estimate reach/frequency for a media schedule that includes the unmeasured publication.

PSA   *See* public service announcement.

Psychographics   The use of demographics to study and measure attitudes, values, lifestyles, and opinions for marketing or advertising purposes. It is a contraction of *psychological* and *demographics*. It is often used as an alternative term for *lifestyle*.

Public access   A channel that is reserved for a community and contains programming for and by that community without stipulations on content. Open to the public on a first-come, first-serve basis by the station.

Public Broadcasting Service (PBS)   A membership organization (not a network) charged with providing programming to its 349 member stations. PBS commissions, acquires, and distributes more than 2,000 hours of programming every year with funding from the Corporation for Public Broadcasting (CPB), the member stations, corporations, foundations, strategic partnerships, and viewers. It was founded by the CPB in 1969. *Also see* National Public Radio.

Publicity   Published or word-of-mouth information that attracts attention to a company, event, person, product, or service. *Also see* public relations.

Public relations   Planned efforts to establish, support, and maintain a company's, person's, product's, or service's image with the public. These services are provided by public relations agencies, public relations agents or consultants, and the company's in-house public relations personnel.

Public service announcement (advertisement) (PSA)   A commercial or advertisement that promotes programs, activities, or services regarded as servicing community interests. PSAs are typically run by the media free of charge. *See* Advertising Council, The.

Public television   A TV station that promotes programs, activities, and services in the public interest. It used to be synonymous with noncommercial TV programming, but has evolved to include stations that accept commercials, albeit on a limited basis and generally within stricter content guidelines than found with commercial stations.

Publishers Information Bureau (PIB)   A membership organization that tracks the amount and type of advertising carried by consumer magazines. With a membership representing roughly 85 percent of consumer magazine advertising volume in the United States, PIB is recognized as the primary source for consumer magazine advertising data. The Magazine Publishers Association administers PIB and contracts with an outside firm to measure, compile, and publish the data for its reports. Website: magazine.org/PIB

Publisher's Statement (to the ABC)   A notarized document made by the publisher stating the magazine's or newspaper's total circulation (and related data). *See* Audit Bureau of Circulations.

Pub set   That part of a magazine or newspaper advertisement that is set in type by the publication. For example, the mechanical for an advertisement announcing a mortgage rate, sans the mortgage rate, would be sent to a newspaper. Just prior to printing the ad, the newspaper would be instructed what the rate is and set that rate within the ad.

Pulsing   A media scheduling technique that has advertising running for short bursts with short hiatuses between each burst. The length of the burst or hiatus could be a day, several days, or a week. Longer periods move the tactic within the framework of "flighting." It is often called a "lightbulb" technique, because it is similar to a turning a lightbulb on and off. The concept behind pulsing is that people's memories don't immediately fade after exposure to advertising, so an advertiser can sustain a short hiatus without significantly jeopardizing advertising awareness. Therefore, a pulsing technique can ostensibly extend the length of media campaign (assuming that the hiatuses are essentially part of the campaign). *Also see* **1.** adstock, **2.** recency.

PUR   *See* people using radio.

Purchase cycle   The typical period of time between purchases of a specific type of product or service. For example, the purchase cycle of a car might be three to five years while milk is three to five days.

PUT   *See* people using TV.

PVR   *See* personal video recorder.

PVT   *See* people using TV.

Python   *See* computer programming language.

QRCA *See* Qualitative Research Consultants Association.

Q Scores *See* Marketing Evaluations/TvQ.

Qualified respondent A person who meets certain criteria for a particular study and therefore qualifies to be included in the study. Respondents may be qualified by characteristics such as age, income, and brand used.

Qualitative research Research that is based on the quality or type of a group and applied to advertising audience research in order to determine the quality of audience responses to advertising. *Also see* quantitative research.

Qualitative Research Consultants Association (QRCA) A non-profit organization with the primary goal of enhancing the quality and standards in the qualitative research industry. Website: qrca.org

Quantitative research Research that is based on the measurement of quantity (amount), such as the actual numbers of audience members, and applied to advertising audience research in order to accurately measure market situations. *Also see* qualitative research.

Quantity discount *See* volume discount.

Quarter hour cume The reach of a radio/TV program or station during a particular 15-minute segment. Unlike an average rating, which reports the media audience during the average minute of a 15-minute segment, the cume reports all listeners or viewers who spent at least five minutes with the medium during the 15-minute segment.

Quarter showing   A transit advertising buy that places an advertisement on every fourth bus, train car, and so forth—that is, in 25 percent of the available places.

Quartile   One-fourth (25 percent) of a group. A tertile is one-third, a quintile is one-fifth, and a decile is one-tenth.

Quintile   One-fifth (20 percent) of a group. A tertile is one-third, a quartile is one-fourth, and a decile is one-tenth.

Quintile distribution   A display of frequency (or related data) among audiences grouped into equal fifths of reach. All media forms attract people at different levels of exposure, ranging from heavy consumers of the medium to lightly exposed users or nonusers of the medium. The same phenomenon usually occurs with product consumption—ranging from those who buy and use more of a product than the average person to those who do not use the product. To calculate a quintile distribution, a complete frequency distribution that shows the reach at each frequency level is necessary first. Using this distribution, the following can be determined: (1) what one-fifth of the total reach is, and (2) on average, how much frequency is delivered to each quintile, starting with the least amount of frequency on the distribution down to the most amount of frequency. Using the following frequency distribution, one-fifth of the total reach is 10 ($50 \div 5 = 10$), the top 10 percent has a frequency level of 1.0, and the next 10 percent of reach has an average frequency of 1.5—composed of 5 percent who receive a frequency level of 1.0 (i.e., 5 gross rating points [GRPs]) plus 5 percent who receive a frequency level of 2.0 (i.e., 10 GRPs). The 5 GRPs and 10 GRPs are added together and divided by the 10 reach to yield the average frequency of 1.5. The same arithmetic sequence is used for each succeeding quintile.

Frequency	Reach	Reach as Part of Each Quintile				
		Lightest	Next	Next	Next	Heaviest
1.0	15	10	5	-	-	-
2.0	8	-	5	3	-	-
3.0	7	-	-	7	-	-
4.0	6	-	-	-	6	-
5.0	4	-	-	-	4	-
6.0	3	-	-	-	-	3
7.0	3	-	-	-	-	3
8.0	2	-	-	-	-	2
9.0	1	-	-	-	-	1
10.0	1	-	-	-	-	1
Total Reach	50	10	10	10	10	10
GRPs	170	10	15	27	44	74
Frequency	3.4	1.0	1.5	2.7	4.4	7.4

Quintile distributions were used mostly to determine the average frequency of exposure to the heaviest media-consuming group (the top 20 percent) in order to decide whether or not a secondary medium should be added to the first medium planned, or if a second commercial execution (e.g., a new commercial) should be aired. The belief (based on available research at the time) was that if the top 20 percent received an average frequency of exposure of 25 or more, it was time to add a second medium, i.e., the commercial effectiveness wore out and a second commercial execution was needed. The concept has lost favor with media planners and advertisers, and was replaced with an assessment of media delivery based on effective reach or optimized reach.

R *See* MPAA ratings.

RAB *See* Radio Advertising Bureau.

RADAR Acronym for *radio all dimension audience research*: national radio audience data. Listening data is collected throughout the year using both diaries and telephone interviewing techniques. Arbitron purchased RADAR from Strategy Research, Inc., in 2001.

Radio Advertising Bureau (RAB) An industry organization that represents commercial radio stations and promotes their use by advertisers. Website: rabmarketing.com

Radio, attributes All media forms have positive and negative attributes. The following are some attributes of advertising on radio: specific target audiences can be reached via the selection of specific programming formats; radio can be purchased either nationally (via broadcast networks) or locally (out of nearly 300 separate radio markets); radio has high reach potential (if many stations in a market are purchased); radio offers immediacy of audience delivery; timing of the delivery of commercials to listeners can be controlled by time of day and day of the week; commercials can be placed in complementary environments based on programming formats; various standard commercial lengths can be purchased (the most common are :30 and :60); commercials can elicit visual elements, either through the listeners' own imaginations or through "imagery transfer"; radio is an advertiser-controlled (intrusive) medium—that is, it is delivered to consumers without their request; commercial production costs are typically less than TV; and radio does not necessarily offer the high attention value of other media forms.

Radio dayparts   Standard time periods used to both plan and buy media. The dayparts are (using eastern standard time) morning drive (or AM drive), 6:00–10:00 A.M.; daytime, 10:00 A.M.–4:00 P.M.; afternoon drive (or PM drive): 4:00–7:00 P.M.; evening, 7:00 P.M.–midnight; and overnight, midnight–6:00 A.M. Morning and afternoon drives are also often called prime time.

Radio Market Reports (Arbitron)   *See* Arbitron.

Radio programming formats   A programming genre that refers to the overall content that a radio station broadcasts. Some stations broadcast multiple genres on a set schedule. Over the years, formats have evolved and new ones have been introduced. Many radio formats are designed to reach a specifically defined segment or niche of the listening population, based on such demographic criteria as age, ethnicity, and cultural background. Among the most popular formats are active rock, adult alternative, adult contemporary, album-oriented rock, alternative, American country, black/rhythm and blues, blues, classical, classic country, classic hits, country, classic rock, easy listening, family, full service, fusion, gospel, heavy metal, hot adult contemporary, jazz, middle of the road, modern rock, new age, news/talk, nostalgia/big band, oldies, religious, rhythm and beach, rhythm and blues, soft contemporary, and variety.

Radio station classifications   *See* radio, types of stations.

Radio, types of stations   Classifications that are determined by the Federal Communications Commission and categorize radio stations by frequency and power restrictions. The following classifications apply to AM (amplitude modulation) stations. Class I (clear channel stations) serve the largest possible area. They operate 24 hours a day at 50,000 watts. Class I-A is the dominant station broadcasting on its assigned frequency throughout North America—for example, WBBM Chicago. Class I-B is one of two dominant stations on the continent broadcasting on its frequency—for example, KNX Los Angeles and CBA Moncton, New Brunswick, Canada, are both at 1070 MHz. Class II stations operate on the same group frequencies as Class I, have smaller signal areas, and are required to reduce power at night to not interfere with Class I stations; for example, KRBE Houston (10,000 watts) operates at 1070 MHz. Class III/Class IV are regional and local stations serving narrow geographic areas and operating on 250–5,000 watts. The following classifications apply to FM (frequency modulation) stations. Classes B and C have the largest coverage areas. Class B is usually limited to a maximum power of 50,000 watts and has antennas up to 500 feet above the ground with a typical coverage of a 75-mile radius from the transmitting tower. Class C operates with power up to 100,000 watts and antenna height of up to 2,000 feet with a typical coverage of a 90-mile radius from the transmitting tower. Class A stations serve specified local areas and have lower power and antenna height.

RAM   *See* random access memory.

R&B   *See* rhythm and blues.

R&D   Research and development. The division or department within a company that is responsible for creating new products or services.

Random access memory (RAM)   The hardware inside a computer that retains memory on a short-term basis. This information is stored temporarily while the user is working on it. Increasing the amount of RAM increases the speed at which a computer works, because more of a program may be loaded into the working space at one time, and thus less time is spent accessing parts of the program from the hard drive.

Random combination   A mathematical formula for obtaining the total audience reach for two media forms used in an advertising campaign. Various research studies have shown how reach builds within a medium. From these studies, various formulas have been devised to estimate reach based on specific levels of media usage. No widely published definitive research, however, shows how two or more media forms used in the same advertising campaign build reach. An industry-accepted practice is to combine the reach of each media form by using one or another of the following random combination formulas. Both result in the same answer. Both assume that as more reach is added, the rate of duplication between the two forms increases.

Formula A:

100 percent − [(100 percent − reach of medium A) × (100 percent − reach of medium B)] = combined reach

Example:

Assuming reach of medium A is 50 (percent) and reach of medium B is 40 (percent)

1 − [(1 − 0.5) × (1 − 0.4)]

1 − (0.5 × 0.6)

1 − 0.3 = 0.7 = 70 combined reach

Formula B:

(reach of A + reach of B) − (reach of A × reach of B) = combined reach

Example:

Assuming reach of medium A is 50 (percent) and reach of medium B is 40 (percent)

(0.5 + 0.4) − (0.5 × 0.4)

0.9 − 0.2 = 0.7 = 70 combined reach

A planner can adjust the formula based on macro judgments of duplication levels. For example, if the planner believes that medium A and medium B have extremely little duplication, then the combined reach can be increased, for example, by 10 percent. Using the preceding 70 reach, that level can therefore be increased to 77. Conversely, if the planner believes the duplication between the two media forms is very high, the 70 reach can be adjusted downward. The same formulas can be used for three or more media forms. The process is to randomly combine two of the media forms and use the combined reach as if it was the reach of medium A, and then combine that with the reach of medium C.

Random digit dialing   A process used in consumer research or telemarketing where a selection of telephone numbers are picked by chance, often by a computer. This allows listed, unlisted, and new numbers equal chances of being called.

Random duplication   Using a mathematical formula, as opposed to actual research data, to determine the audience duplication of two or more media forms or media vehicles. *Also see* random combination.

Random sampling   Giving all people within a specified demographic or lifestyle universe equal chances of being selected as respondents in a research study.

Ranker   A report showing media ranked in a particular order, such as magazines ranked according to cost per thousand, or radio stations ranked according to average quarter rating.

Rate   1. The cost of an advertisement. 2. The magnitude of change from a base, such as the rate of cost increases.

Rate base   A magazine's circulation, upon which advertising space rates are based. The rate base is usually slightly less than what is shown on a publication's audited circulation (or sworn circulation statement). The rate base might or might not be guaranteed by the publisher. If it is guaranteed, and the audited circulation for the period in question is less than the guarantee, the publisher may proportionately reduce the advertising rate charged to the advertiser and give the advertiser a rebate or a makegood.

Rate card   A pamphlet, brochure, single sheet of paper, or text on a website that states the costs for advertising on or in an advertising vehicle, as well as other pertinent information relating to the media vehicle, such as circulation and mechanical requirements for advertising.

Rate differential   The difference between national and local newspaper advertising rates. Nearly all newspapers offer a lower rate to local advertisers than to national advertisers.

Rate holder   (Obsolete) A unit of space or time, usually small, that is used to maintain or establish a contractual agreement over a period of time.

Rate protection   The period in which an advertiser's rate is protected from any increases.

Rating   The percentage of a given population group consuming a medium at a particular moment. It is generally used for broadcast media, but it can be used for any medium. For example, to say that a TV program had a 10 rating of adults ages 18 to 49 is to say that 10 percent of the adult population, ages 18 to 49, viewed the average minute of the program. Ratings not only apply to specific demographic groups, but also to specific geographic areas. For example, a rating can apply to one market, such as a designated market area or metro area; to a region, such as the Northeast; or to the United States at large. The accumulation of ratings results in gross rating points (GRPs), which in turn lead to calculations of reach and frequency. For example, if ten 10-rated programs are purchased, the result is the purchase of 100 GRPs, which hypothetically can result in a 50 reach with a 2.0 frequency. *Also see* **1.** gross rating points, **2.** homes using TV, **3.** people using radio, **4.** people using TV, **5.** share.

Formula:

HUT × share (or PUT × share, and so forth) = rating

Example:

50 (percent) × 10 (percent) = 5

Rating services   Syndicated media research suppliers that report audience levels for the different media.

Ratio   The relationship between two quantities expressed as a fraction, an actual relationship, or a percentage. For example, if a product's advertising budget is $100 and the product's sales are $1,000, the ratio of advertising to sales can be shown as 1/10, 1:10, or 10 percent.

Reach   The number of different individuals (or homes) exposed to commercials or ads in a media schedule. It is a "net" number that eliminates all duplication; that is, reach counts an individual or home only once regardless of how much frequency is delivered to that person or home. For example, if two magazines each have a total audience of 1 million readers, but 500,000 of the combined 2 million readers are the same people, the reach of the two magazines combined is 1,500,000 (2,000,000 − 500,000 duplicated). Reach is usually expressed as a percentage of a specific population group. For example, if the preceding example talked about teens ages 12 to 17 and there were 10,000,000 teens in the United States, then the reach of the two magazines would be 15 percent (1,500,000 ÷ 10,000,000 population base). For radio and TV, reach is typically shown by week or cumulatively for a four-week period or longer. For out-of-home media, reach is typically shown for a one-month period. Internet media can produce the equivalent of reach numbers for a given day, week, or longer period. Newspaper and magazine reach is generally shown for the issue life of the publication. Newspapers are assumed to have a one-day issue life, ergo newspaper reach is for a given day. Weekly magazines tend to a have a 4-week issue life, and monthly magazines a 10- to 12-week issue life. Therefore, reach for magazines is assumed to accumulate over a 4- to 12-week period depending on the magazines used. *Also see* **1.** effective reach, **2.** frequency, **3.** gross rating points, **4.** only-only-both, **5.** random combination, **6.** reach curve, **7.** recency.

Formula:

TRPs or GRPs ÷ frequency = reach

Example:

100 ÷ 2.0 = 50

Reach curve   A diagram showing reach accumulation as additional target rating points (TRPs) are added to a media schedule. The curve is generally depicted within a graph where the horizontal axis shows progressively higher TRP levels and the vertical axis depicts progressively higher reach levels. Reach accumulation is rarely, if ever, a straight line. As more and more TRPs are added to a media schedule, the odds are that there is more and more audience duplication. Each additional rating point, therefore, has an increasingly diminished chance of adding new audiences. Frequency, however, is depicted with a straight line. If the reach/frequency of alternative TV schedules were plotted on graph paper, and the respective dots connected, the reach line would curve (showing diminishing returns as TRPs are increased) and the frequency line would be straight.

Reach (1+)   The amount of media audience reach among people who are exposed to at least one advertising message. It is synonymous with "reach," because no one can be reached with less than one exposure to advertising.

Reach (3+)   *See* effective reach.

Reader response   A measurement of advertising readership based on information requests, letters received, and orders placed as a result of advertisements.

Readership   1. The percent of a publication's audience who recall reading a particular advertisement in that publication. 2. The total number of individuals in a selected group (e.g., adults, males, females ages 18 to 34) who claim to be readers of a magazine or newspaper. Different research companies use different methodologies to determine readership, such as self-administered questionnaires, personal interviews, or telephone interviews. *Also see* 1. passalong readers, 2. primary readers, 3. readers per copy.

Reader service card   An insert in a magazine that readers use to request additional information about a product featured in an advertisement within the magazine.

Readers per copy (RPC)   The average number of readers who read or looked into an average issue of a magazine or newspaper, divided by the publication's circulation. The readers can be primary or pass-along, regardless of where the publication was read.

Formula:

average issue audience ÷ circulation = RPC

Example:

5,000,000 ÷ 1,000,000 = 5

Reading days   The average number of days the average reader spends reading an average issue of a publication.

Reading time   The average length of time spent reading an average issue of a publication.

Read most   The percentage of a magazine's readers who read more than half of the copy of an advertisement in a magazine. *See* Starch readership scores.

Read-only memory (ROM)   The prerecorded instructions on a computer. Once data has been written onto a ROM chip, it cannot be removed and can only be read. Most personal computers contain a small amount of ROM that stores programs, such as the program that boots the computer.

Read some   The percentage of a magazine's readers who read any part of an ad in a magazine. *See* Starch readership scores.

Real gross domestic product   *See* gross domestic product.

Reality programming (shows)   TV programs using real-life situations with people who are not professional actors—that is, "real" people, such as "Survivor" and "Fear Factor."

Real time   Technology that allows a user to access something instantaneously. Literally, real time is this very moment that you are reading this definition—not a second before or after. There is no such thing as fake time.

Rebate   Money back from a media seller to an advertiser for non-delivery of the agreed purchase with the medium. Usually, a rebate is for a portion of media the schedule that was not delivered as negotiated.

Reboot   The process of restarting a computer after it jams, freezes, or supposedly crashes.

Rec (.rec)   *See* domain name.

Recall   *See* **1.** aided recall, **2.** unaided recall.

Recency   The advertising scheduling tactic of providing reach, without regard to frequency, for as many weeks as possible in order to deliver ad messages immediately prior to purchase decisions. Recency states that "the most recent exposure in a series of exposures does most of the work"—for example, convincing a person to visit a store or take advantage of a sale. By way of example, if a person runs out of bread, he or she will be more receptive to a commercial about a specific brand of bread and therefore can be more motivated to buy that brand as soon as possible. Recency theory suggests that advertising be as continuous as possible (because it is not known when someone will run out of bread). However, recency scheduling must be balanced with communication needs. If a sale goes on for only one week, scheduling advertising too far in advance is counterproductive and scheduling advertising after the sale ends is foolish. The recency theory is predicated on the research of John Philip Jones, as published in his 1995 book *When Ads Work—New Proof That Advertising Triggers Sales*, and supported in many articles written by Erwin Ephron.

Recent reading   A technique used by researchers to determine the average issue audience of print media. The technique requires a respondent to sort cards (or the equivalent) that have been labeled with a magazine's or newspaper's logo into two piles: "read the last issue" or "did not read the last issue." *Also see* through-the-book.

Reciprocal   A number related to another in such a way that when multiplied together their product is 1. For example, the reciprocal of 85 is 1.1765. To obtain a reciprocal, divide 1 by the number in question—for example, $1 \div 0.85 = 1.1765$.

Rectangle ad   An online ad size. A rich media rectangle uses rich media technologies such a HTML (hypertext markup language), Flash, and Java. *Also see* interactive marketing unit.

Redemption   The return of something distributed by an advertiser back to the advertiser or its agent—for example, the redemption of price-off coupons distributed in a newspaper, redeemed at a supermarket, and then returned to the advertiser.

Redemption rate   The number of coupons redeemed divided by the number of coupons distributed. For example, if 1 million price-off coupons were distributed via a magazine, and 20,000 were redeemed (e.g., at a supermarket), the redemption rate would be 2 percent.

Regional edition   An edition of a national magazine that is distributed in a particular geographic location—for example, the northeast edition. Regional editions are typically constructed to accommodate advertisers wishing to advertise in specific geographic areas. Sometimes the regional edition also carries regionalized editorial matter.

Regional magazine   A magazine editorially designed for, and typically distributed primarily in, a particular geographic region, such as *Sunset* for the western region and *Southern Living* for the southern region.

Regional network television   The purchase of only one or more geographic regions, but not 100 percent of the full network lineup of stations. Regional buys were popular when the broadcast networks had unsold national inventory (commercial time) and were willing to sell the inventory on a regional basis. However, this method of buying required that 100 percent of all geographic areas be sold to one or more advertisers for any particular commercial slot.

Regional sports network   A network of stations that are located in a limited geographic area and have agreed to televise a commercialized sporting event(s).

Regression analysis   A statistical technique for investigating and modeling the relationship between variables in order to predict future values. It is used extensively in econometrics, for establishing audience reach curves, and for a host of other analytical needs. There are many types of regression analysis: exponential, logistic, nonlinear, multivariate, polynomial, and—most commonly used in advertising and marketing—linear. Essentially, a linear analysis fits a straight or curved line that best connects the observations in data points. The line is mathematically constructed to minimize the collective distances between the data points and the line. The distance is technically known as a residual, and the "best fit" is one where the sum of the squared residual values is minimized. This is known as the "least squares" regression fit.

Regular panel   Any outdoor poster that is not illuminated.

Religious   *See* radio programming formats.

Reminder advertising   Typically a low level of media delivery scheduled only to remind a target audience of the advertiser (or the advertiser's previous creative message).

Remnant space   The advertising space for a specific geographic portion of the publication's circulation that was left over (not purchased) by an advertiser. Rather than filling this hole with editorial, a publisher sells the space to an advertiser, generally at a discount (versus a straight prorated cost of a full-run buy). Typically, remnant space availabilities are not known or sold until the magazine has closed its books on national and regional edition purchases.

Remote   The broadcast of a radio or TV program from a location other than the normal studio location. It is usually conducted as a promotional device on behalf of an advertiser, such as from a retail store to promote its grand opening.

Repaint   The physical repainting of the advertiser's creative message on an out-of-home bulletin as contracted for during the original purchase of the bulletin.

Repeat   1. Any rebroadcast of a TV program that has previously aired. All off-network programs sold in syndication are repeats. *Also called* a rerun. 2. The running of an advertisement more than one time. *Also see* pickup rate.

Repeater station   *See* boosters.

Rep firm   A media sales company that represents stations or publications in various markets for national advertising sales. Typically, the stations and publications do not have sales offices in the markets where the rep firm sells.

ReplayTV   A personal video recorder that allows the user to pause viewing, have the device automatically record what is being telecast, and then replay what was recorded while TV viewing was paused. As with a videocassette recorder (VCR), the user can fast-forward past unwanted video. It is a successor to VCRs, storing programs digitally on a high capacity computer hard drive instead of removable tapes.

Representative sample   A group of people that proportionately represent the total population universe from which they were selected.

Reprint   A reproduction of a print ad produced after the ad has run in a publication.

Repurpose   To convert something for reuse in a different format or environment. TV networks, for example, air original programming on their broadcast network and then again on their owned cable network.

Request for information (RFI)   A request given by an advertiser to an agency (e.g., advertising, direct response, media, promotion, public relations) to answer specific questions to help the advertiser decide if the agency is a suitable candidate to be hired by the advertiser.

Request for proposal (RFP) **1.** A request given by media buyers to media sellers for a specific proposal to advertise within their medium. Typically, the buyer will give the seller various parameters and objectives, such as timing, creative units that are planned, and the need for promotions or added value. **2.** A request given by an advertiser to an agency (e.g., advertising, direct response, media, promotion, public relations) for a specific proposal to hire that agency. This form of RFP usually contains a list of questions that need to be answered by the agency (e.g., size of company, client list). Technically, this form of RFP is more a request for information.

Rerun *See* repeat.

Residual A fee paid to the talent for reruns of programs or commercials in which the talent appeared or was heard.

Resolution **1.** For a printer, a measurement of dots per inch (DPI), describing the sharpness of an image. **2.** For a computer monitor or television set, the number of pixels and lines on the screen. **3.** For sound boards, the number of bits used to encode sounds.

Respondent A person who participates in a market or media research study. All respondents combined together equal a "sample."

Respondent level data Data that is obtained from the research supplier and cites the actual responses from the respondents (the sample) before the findings are projected to a larger population universe.

Retail rate A newspaper advertising rate offered to local retailers. Retail rates are often less than the rates offered to national advertisers. *Also see* rate differential.

Retail trading zone (RTZ) Defined by the Audit Bureau of Circulations, RTZ refers to an urban area outside of the city zone that accounts for a high proportion of a market's retail sales and is also included within a newspaper's circulation.

Retention (level)   The percentage of people who remember specific advertising (e.g., a TV commercial) or a specific brand even after visual or audio exposure to that advertising or brand has ceased. *Also see* adstock.

Return on investment (ROI)   The incremental sales return on the advertising expenditures invested in media. ROI can also apply to other returns, such as increases in advertising awareness, and to nonmedia investments. *Also see* econometrics.

Revenue   The monetary amount of annual sales for a product, service, or company.

Rexx   A computer programming language. Short for *restructured extended executor language.*

RFI   *See* request for information.

RFP   *See* request for proposal.

Rhythm and beach   A radio programming format similar to rhythm and blues, but with a definitive beat and aimed at the adult contemporary audience.

Rhythm and blues   A radio programming format consisting of soul music with a mellow beat and rich vocals.

Rich media   Online media that accommodate advertising using animation, sound, video, interactivity, or any combination of these elements.

Rich media banner   *See* interactive marketing unit.

Rich media rectangle ad   *See* rectangle ad.

Rich media skyscraper ad   *See* skyscraper ad.

Rich text format (RTF or rtf)   A file extension for a simple text-based document.

Riding the boards   A physical inspection of the poster panels or bulletins that comprise a showing. The "riding" refers to driving around from location to location. If you are surfing the Net while riding the boards, you can have an auto accident.

Right of first refusal   An agreement (sometimes contractual) between an advertiser and a media vehicle that offers the advertiser one last notification that the specific advertising unit or schedule being considered will be purchased by another advertiser should the first advertiser refuse to buy it.

RMR   Radio Market Reports. *See* Arbitron.

Roadblock   A tactic used in radio or TV that calls for scheduling commercials across many or all stations or networks at the same time in order to expose the advertising ostensibly to all the listeners or viewers consuming that medium at that time. The tactic is meant to block the listener or viewer from avoiding the commercial regardless of which station is tuned. Invariably, roadblocking results in a premium cost, because stations or networks are purchased regardless of their competitive cost-efficiency. Roadblocking was a popular tactic when there were relatively few TV stations. In today's environment, an advertiser would have to purchase dozens of stations or networks to have an effective roadblock.

Roaming   The ability to get access for telephone calling, personal digital assistant cellular connections, and access to the Internet when away from home at a price considerably less than the regular long-distance charges. For example, if someone lives in Chicago and typically connects to the Internet from Chicago, but travels to New York, that person can call a designated provider in New York and pay for a local phone connection (and perhaps a small service charge).

Robust   Something that is marked by richness or is powerfully built or sturdy. The term applies to many areas of advertising and media, such as "robust data" (based on methodologically sound research), "robust computer" (a personal computer that will not easily break down), and "robust software" (capable of performing many functions.

ROI   *See* return on investment.

Rolling billboard   A form of outdoor advertising consisting of a truck that can electronically produce digital messages on its exterior or that carries a printed billboard on its exterior. *Also see* 1. mobile billboard, 2. porta-panel.

Rollout   A marketing procedure where product or service availability, and advertising, is progressively expanded into more geographic areas over time. It generally follows test-marketing the product or service, and is typically used for new product introductions.

ROM   *See* read-only memory.

ROM BIOS   *See* basic input-output system.

Rome Report   A media research report showing advertising expenditure data for trade publications.

ROP   *See* run of press.

Roper ASW   A unit of NOP Worldwide that specializes in advertising and marketing research. The Roper Company merged with Audits and Surveys Worldwide (ASW) to form RoperASW. Among its products is Starch readership scores. Website: roperasw.com

ROS   *See* 1. run of site, 2. run of station.

Rotary (bulletin or display)   An out-of-home bulletin that is moved to different locations in a market at fixed timing intervals, usually every 60 or 90 days. *Also see* permanent (bulletin or display).

Rotation   1. The scheduling of radio or TV commercials at different times each day within the time periods purchased. The reasons for rotating commercials in this manner are twofold: (1) it usually produces a higher reach level for the campaign than would repeating airings in the same time slots each day, and (2) by allowing the stations flexibility in scheduling, rotation typically results in a lower cost. **2.** Moving an out-of-home bulletin to a different location at stated intervals (e.g., every month), which is commonly called a rotary bulletin. *Also see* **1.** run of station, **2.** orbit.

Rotator   A radio or TV commercial in a rotation.

rotogravure   A printing process that uses an engraved or etched image or text on a cylindrical printing surface (usually copper) whereby the ink is held within the etched crevices. Paper is run through a rotary press that prints both sides of the paper at the same time. *Also see* **1.** letterpress, **2.** lithography, **3.** offset.

Router   A device used to connect one recognized computer network to another, such as with a local area network. A router connects a local network to an Internet service provider (ISP) for Internet access. Routers receive packets of data, filter them, and forward them to a final destination using the best route.

RPC   *See* readers per copy.

RTF   *See* rich text format.

RTZ   *See* retail trading zone.

Run of paper   *See* run of press.

Run of press (ROP)   A media buyer's request to run an advertisement anywhere in the publication without regard to the newspaper section or position on the page. ROP is also commonly used to describe any form of newspaper advertising.

Run of site (ROS)   An online advertising media purchase to run ads on any page of a website.

Run of station (ROS)   A tactic used in radio and in TV media wherein commercials are scheduled throughout the day and night at the discretion of the station or network, as opposed to the media buyer negotiating for specific time periods or programs. Typically, an ROS schedule costs less than a time-period or program-specific schedule. *Also see* **1.** orbit, **2.** rotation.

Runs   The number of times a program can be telecast over a specific period of time, according to the arrangement made between a program producer or syndicator and a TV network or local station.

Saddle stitched   The binding process whereby a publication is held together by staples through the middle of the fold—for example, *Time* magazine. *Also see* perfect binding.

SAG   *See* Screen Actors Guild.

Same-store sales   Sales for retail chain stores that have been in existence for the two periods being compared. Using sales for the same stores to make sales comparisons between one year or month and another allows the chain to determine natural sales growth versus sales resulting from new stores.

Sample   The statistical selection of some respondents to express or exhibit the opinions or actions of the population universe that they represent. Sample selection is critical to the validity of the findings in a research study. For example, if a sample is composed of only women, the findings from the research cannot be projected to an adult (men and women) population. *Also see* biased sample.

Sampling error   The possible deviation in the reported finding of media audience research based on a sample, from what might be the actual finding had a complete census been done. It is often reported as "+/−" the reported number. *Also see* 1. confidence level, 2. tolerance.

Sandwich board   A form of out-of-home advertising worn by individuals. It consists of two signs hung from the shoulders of an individual, thereby "sandwiching" the person between the signs. If the ad message is unbelievable, it could be called a baloney sandwich board.

Satellite   (Geosynchronous) A device that is located 22,300 miles over the equator and is in a geostationary orbit over Earth. It receives transmissions from separate points on Earth and retransmits them for capture by earth stations (also known as downlinks), which in turn enable local cable systems (and the equivalent) to deliver the signals to subscribing households.

Satellite Broadcasting and Communications Association (SBCA)   The national trade organization representing all segments of the satellite consumer services industry. The association is committed to expanding the use of satellite technology for the delivery of video, data, voice, interactive, and broadband services. It is composed of direct broadcast satellite, C-band, broadband, and other satellite service providers, as well as programmers, equipment manufacturers, distributors, retailers, encryption vendors, and national and regional distribution companies. The SBCA was founded in 1986 through the merger of the Society for Private and Commercial Earth Stations (SPACE) and the Direct Broadcast Satellite Association (DBSA). Website: sbca.com

Satellite Home Viewer Improvement Act (SHVIA)   A 1999 Federal Communications Commission Act modifying the Satellite Home Viewer Act of 1988, SHVIA permits satellite companies to provide local broadcast TV signals to all subscribers who reside in the local TV station's market. SHVIA also permits satellite companies to provide "distant" network broadcast stations to eligible satellite subscribers.

Satellite Internet connection   An electronic connection whereby upstream and downstream data are sent from the provider to the user via a satellite. The user must be equipped with a satellite dish antenna and a transceiver.

Satellite (-fed) master antenna TV system (SMATV)   A master antenna TV system that picks up both broadcast and satellite transmissions and retransmits the signals (TV programs and commercials) to subscribers connected to the system. SMATV is generally found in apartment buildings.

Satellite radio   The digital transmission of radio signals from Earth to a satellite and back to Earth for reception on digital radios equipped to receive these signals. Satellite radio signals are static-free and can be received without interruption, even when radio is moved great distances (such as a car radio); the "broadcast" coverage area is virtually U.S.-wide.

Satellite station   A broadcast station that rebroadcasts the transmission of another station (generally operating in a nearby market) to an area that cannot otherwise be serviced by that station.

Saturation   Scheduling many commercials or advertisements within a short time period to create maximum impact for an advertiser's message. Sometimes also called a "blitz."

SAU   *See* standard advertising unit.

SBCA   *See* Satellite Broadcasting and Communications Association.

SBW   Spread black/white. *See* spread.

Scanner   1. A retail store's checkout-counter machine that electronically reads prices from the Universal Product Code imprinted on each item. These codes are fed into a central computer that allows for the tracking of inventory, distribution, buying patterns, and the effect of advertising. Determining the effect of advertising, however, requires additional marketing input, such as the specifics of the media effort leading up to and during the sales period being studied. Such advertising effectiveness studies are usually called econometric analyses. 2. A radio receiver that moves across a wide range of radio frequencies and allows audiences to listen to any of the frequencies. **3.** An electronic device used in the home or office that digitally copies printed images and transmits the images to a computer file.

Scanner wand   An electronic device provided by a market research company to be used by individuals in their home to scan the Universal Product Codes of products (such as packaged goods) that the individuals recently purchased. The collected data is then transmitted by phone lines from the individual's home to the research company, and sometimes married to media consumption data (such as TV-viewing habits of the individuals). *Also see* single source data.

Scarborough   A research company, founded in 1975, that conducts syndicated surveys of consumers in 75 local markets. Scarborough tracks more than 1,200 products, services, and retail shopping categories, and reports consumer retail shopping behavior, product consumption, media usage, and lifestyle and demographic characteristics. The company uses a combination of telephone interviews, self-administered questionnaires, and television diaries to collect its information. Scarborough is a joint venture of Arbitron, Inc. and VNU Marketing Information. Website: scarborough.com

Scatter   **1.** The purchasing of network TV time that is not purchased during an "upfront" media buy. The "scatter market" refers to the pricing of the available commercial inventory that was not sold in the "upfront market." **2.** Purchasing commercial time in many different programs in radio or TV media—that is, scattering commercials.

Scope of work (SOW)   A document that details the specific work to be done by a supplier for a company or individual. Among other things, it includes precisely what the delivered product or service should be (i.e., the deliverables), when the project will be completed (timing), and the fees to be paid for delivery of the product or service.

Screen Actors Guild (SAG)   A labor union affiliated with the AFL-CIO through the Associated Actors and Artistes of America. SAG represents its members through negotiation and enforcement of collective bargaining agreements that establish equitable levels of compensation, benefits, and working conditions for performers.

Script   A type of computer program written in computer programming language.

S curve   A curve on a graph that resembles the letter *S*. The curve is used, for example, in modeling the future adoption of a new product or service. For example, when the percentage of people who will purchase a new product is plotted along the *y* (vertical) axis, and time (e.g., days, weeks, months) along the *x* (horizontal) axis, it will often be found that at the lower ranges of *x* that there is very little response—the line climbs slowly over time and then begins to climb sharply until it peaks and levels off (or conceivably diminishes). *Also see* bell curve.

SDSL   *See* symmetrical digital subscriber line.

Seamless media   Coined by MIT Media Lab professors, it includes any media content that is transmitted digitally to a handheld, mobile, or portable device. Seamless media are distinguished from, for example, handheld TVs or radios. The federal government has mandated that all TV stations and networks in the United States become totally digital and completely cease analog transmission by January 2006, but most people are not holding their breath.

Search engine   A computer program that searches for specific keywords—input by the user—that are found in documents on the World Wide Web and Usenet newsgroups. The program produces a list of documents (sites) with brief descriptions that the user can click on to access a document.

Search engine optimization (SEO)   A process for increasing a website's chances to rank high on a list of search results. Because Internet users do not typically click through all pages of a search result, the higher a website ranks in the results of a search, the greater the chances a user will visit that site.

Seasonality   A display of data or a statement concerning the variations by season of a product's or service's sales or usage, or a medium's audience delivery. For example, lemonade sales skew to the summer when people tend to buy cold drinks, and television viewing levels are highest during the winter when people spend more time in their homes.

Second   1. The position after first. 2. A unit of time representing 1/60 of a minute. Technically, it is the time that elapses during 9,192,631,770 cycles of the radiation produced by the transition between two levels of the cesium 133 atom—but a different dictionary will explain what that means. A millisecond is 1 thousandth of a second; a microsecond, 1 millionth of a second; a nanosecond, 1 billionth of a second; a picosecond, 1 trillionth of a second; a femtosecond, 1 quadrillionth of a second; and an attosecond, 1 quintillionth of a second.

Secondary readers   *See* passalong readers.

Second cover   *See* inside front cover.

Second-generation tape   A videotaped copy of a videotaped copy of an original or master recording.

Secure Sockets Layer (SSL)   A protocol developed by Netscape for transmitting private documents over the Internet, such as credit card numbers.

Seen-associated   Now called "associated." The percentage of a magazine's readers who saw the advertiser's name in the ad. *See* Starch scores.

Selective binding   Binding together of specific sections (editorial, advertising, or both) of a magazine where the final product (the publication) is customized for specific target audiences. For example, a magazine might bind-in an extra section devoted to gardening and direct those copies to people who have a higher-than-average propensity for gardening.

Self-administered questionnaire   A research questionnaire in which the desired information is recorded by the respondent with or without the aid of an interviewer.

Seller's market   A media marketplace environment in which demand for advertising time or space is relatively high and media sellers are able to negotiate for higher media costs. It is the opposite of a buyer's market.

Sell-in   The process of the manufacturer selling goods to the retailer.

Sell-through   The process of the retailer selling goods to the consumer.

SEO   *See* search engine optimization.

Sequential liability   Designating the advertiser or the advertiser's media buying agent (but not both simultaneously) as having the responsibility for payment to the media of purchased advertising. In February 1991, the American Association of Advertising Agencies adopted the following statement as their position on agency liability for payments to media: "The agency shall be solely liable for payment of all media invoices if the agency has been paid for those invoices by the advertiser. Prior to payment to the agency, the advertiser shall be solely liable." This sentence became known as the "sequential liability policy": the advertiser has the liability until it pays the agency, and then the agency has the liability. The media considered the sequential liability policy as a self-serving declaration and went on record as rejecting it. The media have not changed their practices, and they continue to pursue agencies and clients if they were not paid. The media take the position that agencies and clients should be jointly and severally liable (i.e., dual liability). Many agencies have incorporated the sequential liability policy in their media orders. Unfortunately, most media orders are not countersigned. In fact, most media orders are given by e-mail or fax. Source: *Hall Dickler Kent Goldstein & Wood, LLP*—"Adlaw."

Serial port   A "plug" used to connect an external device, such as a mouse or a modem, to a personal computer. It can also be used to connect a printer, but most printers are connected to a parallel port. *Also see* **1**. port, **2**. universal serial bus.

Server   **1**. A host computer on a network that holds information (e.g., websites) and responds to requests for information from it (e.g., links to another Web page). **2**. The software that makes the act of serving information possible.

Service provider   A telecommunications provider that owns circuit switching equipment.

Setback   The distance between the out-of-home advertising structure and the line of travel. For example, if the distance between a bulletin and the highway is 20 feet, the bulletin has a 20-foot setback.

Set showing   An outdoor poster showing that has preselected locations and may not be sold to another advertiser during the term of the contract.

Sets in use (SIU)   (Obsolete) The term was replaced by *homes using TV*. Sets in use referred to the number of TV sets in use (turned on) at a given time, which was almost synonymous with the number of TV households viewing TV at a given time (because just about all households had only one TV set). Times have changed, and terms have changed.

Set-tuning meter   An electronic metering system used by Nielsen Media Research to provide set-tuning information on a daily basis. The information is collected from a sample of homes in 40 markets (separate from the People Meter), and overnight household ratings are reported on a daily basis for these local areas. This meter is placed onto the back of each television set in the home and monitors the tuning status of each TV set in the household.

Seven Sisters   The unofficial but industry-accepted name given to a group of magazines whose editorial focus was women: *Better*

Homes and Gardens, Family Circle, Good Housekeeping, Ladies' Home Journal, McCall's, Redbook, and *Woman's Day.* Note: *McCall's* changed its name to *Rosie* and has since ceased publication.

S4C, S4CB Spread four-color, spread four-color bleed. *See* spread.

SGML *See* standard generalized markup language.

Share (of audience) The percentage of homes using TV (HUT), or people using TV (PUT), or people using radio (PUR) tuned to a particular program or station at a particular time. Media buyers estimate future program shares in order to predict future program rating performance (see formula). Because of time differences, share is a more reliable estimating tool than merely looking at past rating performance of the same program or similar programs. For example, a program that had aired during a specific time and day (e.g., Monday from 8:00 to 8:30 P.M.) but is moved to a new time slot and day will probably not achieve the same rating that it had before. The reason is that different days of the weeks often have different usage levels (i.e., HUT, PUT). A different usage level directly affects the rating potential of any program. For example, if the HUT level for Monday from 8:00 to 8:30 P.M. is usually 50, and the program moves to a time slot where the typical HUT level is 45, chances are the program will garner a lower rating simply because not as much potential audience is available. A program's share is affected by many factors, such as the competitive programs airing at the same time, the genre, the cast, the writers, and the directors.

Formula:

Rating ÷ HUT = share

Example:

10 (percent) ÷ 50 (percent) = 20

Share of market The percentage of total category volume (e.g., dollars, units) accounted for by a brand. It is important that the category the advertiser competes in is accurately defined and relative to the advertiser's marketing objectives. The size of category volume will have a direct bearing on a brand's share of market and obviously on the strategies used to market the brand. For example, if the brand is apple juice, it must be decided whether it competes within the fruit drink category, soft-drink category, or beverage category (each of these being sequentially larger and therefore resulting in a sequentially smaller share of market for the brand).

Share of mind   A reference to the level of aided or unaided awareness of a particular brand within its total marketing category. It is not technically a specific "share" but more of a reference to a particular brand's relative standing in the category. For example, a new or unknown brand might have a low share of mind compared to a highly advertised well-known brand. Media planners sometimes incorrectly use the term to indicate a brand's share of spending or share of voice.

Share of spending   The percentage of total category media spending accounted for by a brand. Although media expenditure data is often analyzed to establish share data, the expenditure data for competitive brands is based on estimates primarily from syndicated research sources (e.g., TNS Media Intelligence/CMR and Nielsen Monitor-Plus). The resulting share-of-spending data, therefore, should not be used as a definitive and accurate statement, but more as a guideline. *Also see* **1.** share of voice, **2.** share of market.

Share of voice   A particular brand's advertising impressions or target rating points (TRPs) delivered to a specific target audience as a percentage of all the impressions or TRPs delivered to that target by all brands in the same product category. Although technically incorrect, some use share of voice to indicate share of spending. Because various marketers use different media forms, or schedule different uses of the same media forms, or pay different rates for the same media forms, media dollars do not always directly equate to the same level of impressions or TRPs. Conceivably, an advertiser that secures media at competitively low prices could have a relatively low share of spending, but a relatively high share of voice.

Shareware   Software offered free on a trial basis and available for downloading on the Internet. *Also see* **1.** demoware, **2.** freeware.

SHDSL   Single-pair high bit-rate DSL. *See* digital subscriber line.

Sheets   A way of designating poster panel size based on the number of pieces of paper originally needed to cover a poster panel area; for example, it used to take 30 sheets to cover the average panel (now called a 30-sheet poster).

Shelf life   **1.** The length of time a physical unit of a product remains on a supermarket shelf before the seller removes it due to its deteriorating qualities. **2.** A term loosely used to express the length of time a media vehicle stays, or can stay, in existence and continues to be advertiser supported.

Shelf talker   A small advertising message that is affixed to a shelf in a retail store and extends from the shelf.

Shelter magazine   A publication with an editorial focus on the home (e.g., decorating, home improvement, gardening, food, maintenance).

Shopper   A free newspaper that is distributed in local retail centers (usually grocery stores, convenience stores, etc.) and contains sales announcements and coupons.

Short messaging service (SMS)   A service for sending short text messages to cell phones, mobile and handheld devices, personal digital assistants, or pagers. Also known as text messaging. *Also see* multimedia messaging service.

Short rate   The dollar penalty an advertiser pays for not fulfilling print-media space requirements that were contracted for at the beginning of a given period, usually one year. The penalty is the difference in rate between the contracted rate and the actual earned rate per, for example, the medium's published rate card. Sometimes an advertiser comes up short on fulfilling its original purchase and therefore pays the rate it ordinarily would have paid had the original purchase been at the level of the final purchase.

Showing   1. Daily gross rating points (GRPs) generated by out-of-home media. For example, a #50 showing indicates that all of the posters or bulletins contained in the schedule will produce the equivalent of 50 GRPs each day the advertising is displayed. Likewise, a #100 showing is 100 daily GRPs, and a #25 showing is 25 daily GRPs. The showing size does not specifically relate to the number of units purchased. A #50 showing could be composed of various numbers of units, all depending on the daily effective circulation of each of the units purchased. 2. The number of posters displayed in transit media.

SHVIA   *See* Satellite Home Viewer Improvement Act.

SIC   *See* North American Industry Classification System.

SIGMA   A verification service provided by Nielsen Media Research that electronically detects airplays of videos distributed to television stations, broadcast networks, and cable networks.

Signature   The name given to a printed sheet of a magazine after it comes off the press and has been folded into 4, 8, 16, 32 pages and so forth. Two or more signatures are then bound together to create the entire publication. Coupons are often bound-in at signature breaks.

Sign off   The time of day a station stops broadcasting.

Sign on   The time of day a station begins to broadcast.

Simmons Market Research Bureau (SMRB)   A multimedia research company specializing in marketing and media information. It is generally referred to as simply Simmons. Their National Consumer Survey (NCS) encompasses over 8,000 brands, 400 product categories, all mass media venues, and lifestyle descriptors. Multimedia research includes information on adults, teens, kids, Hispanics, consumer online users, and computer professionals.

Approximately 30,000 adults, ages 18 and older, participate with each receiving one personal self-administered questionnaire and an additional household questionnaire that is completed by a designated member of the home. The personal questionnaire contains questions pertaining to media consumption, demographics, information on product or service usage, lifestyle and psychographic information, and shopping behavior. The household questionnaire contains questions pertaining to household products and services. Simmons is owned by Symmetrical Resources, Inc. Website: smrb.com

Simple mail transfer protocol (SMTP)   The standard Internet protocol for transferring electronic mail messages.

Simulcast   To broadcast simultaneously on AM and FM radio or by radio and television.

Single copy sales   Copies of a magazine that are sold at newsstands and similar places as opposed to by subscription.

Single-pair high bit-rate digital subscriber line (SHDSL)   *See* digital subscriber line.

Single source data   The reporting of data based on the product or service purchase patterns and media consumption habits from a single source. For example, the syndicated research produced by Mediamark Research, Inc., Scarborough, Simmons, and The Media Audit all contain product and media data based on their respondent samples. *Also see* fusion.

Sitcom   Abbreviation for a situation comedy TV program.

Site map   A visual model of the pages on a website that show the user a diagram of the entire site's contents. It is similar to a table of contents.

SIU   (Obsolete) *See* sets in use.

:60   A one-minute commercial.

Skew   A statistical deviation from symmetry that demonstrates a bias in the reported data for a particular segment of the data. For example, a magazine that has proportionately more younger readers than older readers (compared to the total population composition) is said to skew to a younger audience.

SKU   *See* stock-keeping unit.

Skyscraper ad   A tall, thin online advertisement. A rich media skyscraper uses rich media technologies such as HTML (hypertext markup language), Flash, and Java. *Also see* interactive marketing unit.

Skywriting   A form of out-of-home advertising in which a brief message is written in the sky by an airplane using a chemical substance to emit small puffs of smoke that form the letters of the message. Skywriting advertising is typically sold only on Earth's side of the sky.

Slamming   The term used to describe what occurs when a customer's long-distance service is switched from one long-distance company to another without the customer's permission. Such unauthorized switching violates Federal Communications Commission rules.

SLC   *See* subscriber line charge.

Slick   A camera-ready proof of an advertisement printed on glossy paper and sent to a publication for reproduction.

Slotting allowance   1. A fee charged by retailers to manufacturers for premium product placement in a store (e.g., shelf space), category exclusivity, or other special treatment. 2. On the Internet, the same concept as for retail stores but applicable to a domain's special treatment in search engines.

Slug   *See* donut.

Small office/home office (SOHO)   A term used for small businesses, whether or not they are headquartered in someone's home.

Smalltalk   A computer programming language.

SMATV   *See* satellite (-fed) master antenna TV system.

S/MIMe   *See* multipurpose Internet mail extensions.

SMRB   *See* Simmons Market Research Bureau.

SMS   *See* short messaging service.

SMSA   *See* standard metropolitan statistical area.

SMTP   *See* simple mail transfer protocol.

Snapshots   A comprehensive collection of media and market profiles that are used for advertising and marketing. Website: snapshotsinteractive.com

Snipe   Extra information that is usually printed on paper and glued on top of existing advertising copy on an out-of-home poster or bulletin and that updates the message on the snipe. For example, a snipe stating "now open" might be placed on top of copy that states "coming soon."

SNTA   *See* Syndicated Network Television Association.

Society for Private and Commercial Earth Stations (SPACE)   *See* Satellite Broadcasting and Communications Association.

Soft contemporary   A radio programming format of light, easy, relaxing, and usually current music, which often includes material from the 1970s and 1980s.

Soft interconnect   *See* interconnect.

SOHO   *See* small office/home office.

Sound order   A Yellow Pages Directory advertising order sent to a publisher.

SOW   *See* scope of work.

SPACe   *See* Society for Private and Commercial Earth Stations.

Space discount   A discount earned off the open rate (i.e., the one-time rate) for placing a specified amount of space in print media.

Spam   E-mails, often promotional in nature, that are sent out by an advertiser to large lists of recipients without regard to whether or not any of the recipients want the information—that is, without the recipient's consent. Spam is also known as unsolicited commercial e-mail (UCE) or simply junk e-mail. If people requested the e-mail (i.e., the promotion), it would be an opt-in e-mail.

Spanish Television Reach Evaluator for Targeting Campaigns to Hispanics (STRETCH)   A computer program published by Telemundo that allows analysis of TV reach/frequency among Hispanics and Spanish-dominant Hispanics by demographic cell.

SPARC   It stood for Spot Advertising Radio Costs, a media research resource reporting on the industry average cost-per-point for spot radio buys by market, daypart, demographic group, and calendar quarter. The research company SQAD now produces the same data but simply calls it Spot Radio Costs.

Specs (specifications)   *See* buying specifications.

Spectacular   An outdoor bulletin that is usually larger than 14 feet by 48 feet (the size of a standard bulletin) and is positioned at prime locations in a market. A spectacular often has embellishments.

Spectra Marketing   A research company that provides manufacturers, retailers, and brokers in the consumer goods industries with consumer segmentation, data integration, and retail intelligence. Spectra delivers analytical services through software, proprietary retail data, and consulting. Market Metrics was founded in 1985 and Spectra in 1988. The two companies merged in 1995. Spectra is a division of VNU. Website: spectramarketing.com

Spectrum   The range of electromagnetic radio frequencies used in the transmission of sound, data, and television.

Spider   A computer program that automatically finds Web pages. Spiders are used to feed pages to search engines. A spider finds and displays links to other Web pages. Spiders are also known as crawlers, wanderers, and Webcrawlers.

Spill-in/spill-out   Spill-in is the viewing of television broadcast emanating from a designated market area different from the market in which the signal is received (and viewed). For example, people in San Diego viewing Los Angeles stations are viewing spill-in programming. Spill-out is the opposite of spill-in: viewing taking place outside the originating TV market—for example, Los Angeles stations delivering audiences into San Diego. The extent of spill-in/spill-out is reported by Nielsen Media Research once yearly for each TV market. Media planners use the data to adjust planned target rating point (TRP) levels in various TV markets in recognition of essentially receiving free TRPs in a given market from other markets. For example, if the original goal is to deliver 100 TRPs in Los Angeles and San Diego, and Los Angeles is delivering the equivalent of 15 TRPs into San Diego, the media planner may opt to reduce the San Diego TRPs to 85 in order to deliver a total of 100 TRPs into the market. If this adjustment is made, it is necessary to have the same copy (creative execution) airing in both markets. Another use of the data is to determine the extent of delivery into markets where no advertising is desired, such as during an in-market test of a new product or alternative TV commercial.

Spillover   The extent to which a secondary target audience is exposed to the advertising meant for a primary target audience. For example, if an advertiser is targeting young men in a radio campaign, the odds are that older men, women, and teens will also be exposed to that advertising, albeit at lower levels (assuming that the media buy was properly made to the primary target audience).

Spin-off   A TV program derived from situations or characters from other programs. For example, "Law and Order SVU" is a spin-off of "Law and Order."

Splash page   The first page or front page that is seen on some websites and is the introduction to the website. It is not the home page. It usually contains a fancy animated (Flash) presentation. The website's main content is behind (after) this page. It is also referred to as a doorway page.

Split counties   A portion of a county that is composed of one or more ZIP codes and has been separately identified for purposes of ordering and controlling a consumer sample in, for example, ratings research reports. This results from a county receiving substantial TV or radio coverage from two distinctly separate markets. Audience figures for each portion are assigned to the appropriate radio or TV market.

Split run   A scheduling technique whereby two different advertisements are run in the circulation of a publication with no one reader receiving both advertisements. This can be accomplished via a geographic split, demographic split (if the publication offers demographic editions), subscription/newsstand sales split, or every-other-copy split (known as an A/B split).

Split :30   Two commercials, usually :15, either for the same product or service, or for related products or services, that air during a 30-second period on a station or network.

Sponsor   An advertiser who buys the exclusive right to the available commercial time within a given segment of a program or the entire program.

SportsQ   *See* Marketing Evaluations/TvQ.

Spot   1. The purchase of radio or TV commercial time on a market-by-market basis as opposed to a network (national) purchase. 2. A common reference, and essentially slang, for a radio or TV commercial. Hypothetically, a media buyer could buy 10 spots in spot and see spots run.

Spot-buying pool   (Obsolete) A group of spot radio or TV buyers at a media agency who do not have any specific client or market assignment, but make buys for any client in any market, as needed. The common practice of today is for a buyer to be assigned one or more markets and buy activity for all of the agency's clients in those markets, or for a buyer to be assigned one or more clients and buy all markets for those clients.

Spot color   The utilization of color in only certain areas of an advertisement.

Spot radio   The purchase of advertising time (commercials) on local radio stations, as opposed to on network (national) radio.

Spotted map   A map showing all the outdoor unit locations available, recommended, or purchased in a particular market.

Spot television   The purchase of advertising time (commercials) on local TV stations, as opposed to on network (national) TV. *Also see* designated market area

Spot times   The specific times commercials air.

Spread   **1.** The difference in price between what advertising in a medium "should have" cost and the price obtained by the advertiser's media buying agent. The difference is usually labeled "savings": the buyer secures advertising time or space for a lower cost than planned. Media buying companies sometimes work "on the spread" in order to earn a fee for their services—by keeping the difference. The question always remains as to how much the media purchase should have cost. **2.** An advertising unit designed to occupy two facing pages as a single unit of space. Common abbreviations are S4C (spread four-color), S4CB (spread four-color bleed), SBW (spread black/white). *Also see* **1.** center spread, **2.** double truck.

Spreadsheet   A multicolumn sheet of paper used for performing numerical work, such as found in MS Excel.

SQAD   SQAD originally stood for Spot Quotations and Data, but is now an acronym for Service Quality Analytics Data. SQAD features national and local media products for cost forecasting. National data includes network TV, cable, syndication, and Internet costs. Local data is reported for spot TV, spot Hispanic TV, spot radio, plus the summarized major media data of the *Media Market Guide*. It is recognized as the industry standard cost per point (CPP) guide for 30-second spots. Reported costs are average gross 30-second CPPs. They are determined from advertising agency data. Website: sqad.com

Square button   *See* button ad.

Square pop-up   *See* pop-up ad.

SRC   *See* Strategy Research Corporation.

SRDS   *See* Standard Rate and Data Service.

SSL   *See* Secure Sockets Layer.

Stack   *See* double-decker.

Staggercast   The time between the beginning of a program on one cable TV channel and the beginning of the same program on one or more other cable TV channels. For example, if a movie starts at 9:00 P.M. on channel 100, at 9:15 P.M. on channel 101, and at 9:30 P.M. on channel 102, it is staggercast 15 minutes. *Also see* near video on demand.

Standard advertising unit (SAU)   Established newspaper ad sizes given in specific column by inch measurements (in standard size newspapers, 6 columns by 21 inches; in tabloid size newspapers, 5 columns by 14 inches). The SAU is intended to make ad unit sizes comparable among separate newspapers despite different page layouts. *Also see* agate line.

Standard broadcast calendar   *See* broadcast calendar.

Standard error   *See* sampling error.

Standard generalized markup language (SGML)   An international standard for the publication and delivery of electronic information.

SGML is widely used to manage large documents that are subject to frequent revisions and need to be printed in different formats.

Standard Industrial Classification Code (SIC)   *See* North American Industry Classification System.

Standard metropolitan statistical area (SMSA)   *See* metropolitan statistical area.

Standard page   A full-page newspaper advertisement that conforms to the standard advertising unit nomenclature.

Standard Rate and Data Service (SRDS)   A provider of media rates and data of traditional media: direct marketing, magazine, newspaper, online, out of home, radio, and TV. It is owned by VNU. Website: srds.com

Standard size   *See* standard advertising unit.

Starch INRA Hooper   *See* RoperASW.

Starch readership scores   Print media advertising readership data produced by RoperASW through personal interviews of readers. Using a through-the-book recognition method, RoperASW does one-on-one interviews of 100 to 200 people for each publication studied. Four readership scores are reported: (1) Noted—the percentage who saw any part of the advertisement, (2) Associated—the percentage who saw the advertiser's name in the ad, (3) Read Some—the percentage who read any of the ad, and (4) Read Most—the percentage who read more than half of the copy. They are called Starch scores because the research was originally conceived and conducted by the Daniel Starch and Staff company. Daniel Starch and Staff eventually became Starch INRA Hooper, which was then purchased by Roper and eventually merged with Audits and Surveys Worldwide (ASW). RoperASW is owned by NOP Worldwide, which in turn is owned by United Business Media. Website: roperasw.com

STARS   1. Simmons Teenage Research Study, a media research study reporting on media and product/service consumption patterns among teenagers. *See* Simmons Market Research Bureau. **2.** Station Tracking and Ratings—a service offered by M-Street. Website: mstreet.com

Station avails   *See* availability.

Station count   The number of stations transmitting a program.

Station format   The type of programming carried by a radio station, such as adult contemporary music, news, and talk.

Station identification   A short, usually 10-second long TV commercial (10 seconds visual and 8 seconds audio). Typically abbreviated as ID.

Station lineup   The listing of stations carrying a regional or national radio/TV program.

Station total area   The geographic area in which a broadcast station's signal is received. With television, the area is usually greater than the geographic boundaries of a designated market area. With radio, the area is usually greater than a metro area.

Statistical error   *See* sampling error.

Statistical Research, Inc.   *See* KN/Statistical Research.

Steganography   Embedding hidden messages within audio and graphical material. It is intended for use on digital songs, movies, and e-books to monitor intellectual property. Steganography replaces bits of useless or unused data in a computer (such as graphics, sound, or text) with bits of different, invisible information. It literally means "covered writing." *Also see* watermarking.

Stereo (radio)   Reproducing sound in a way that captures the qualities of the original sound. It can be transmitted on an AM or FM band. The human ear can hear four characteristics of sound: (1) frequency—the rate at which air vibrates, (2) amplitude—the pressure of each vibration (loudness), (3) harmonic constitution—how much of the sound is its main frequency and how much is exact multiples (harmonics) of its main frequency, and (4) direction—the direction from which the sound is emanating. A microphone translates sound into an electrical signal. At least two microphones are used in stereophonic sound. Each captures a slightly different sound. Separate loudspeakers play back the signal from the original microphones. With only one speaker, a listener will hear only one "channel" (mono) regardless of how it was recorded. Commercials recorded in stereo can be heard in stereo.

Stickiness   The ability of a website (or page) to hold a user on that site or page, or have that user return to that site or page.

Stitching   A magazine binding method using saddle stitching or staples.

Stock-keeping unit (SKU)   A coding used by retailers to identify an item carried in inventory or stock. The term is often pronounced as "skew." If a particular SKU in a store has disproportionately high sales versus all other SKUs, one could say that sales skew to that SKU.

Store (.store)   *See* domain name.

Store-distributed magazine   Publications that are (for the most part) not sold through subscription but whose circulation depends on sales in retail stores.

Storyfinder   A research software tool that assists in learning more about a target group of consumers by looking at all the products and services used by that group. Storyfinder also provides a lifestyle analysis of a target market, including that target group's activities. A product of Interactive Market Systems.

STRATA Marketing, Inc.   A company that provides software applications for TV, radio, and print planning and buying. Website: stratag.com

Strategy, media   *See* objectives, media.

Strategy Research Corporation (SRC)   A marketing research firm serving the U.S. Hispanic market, Latin America, and the Caribbean. Owned by Markets Facts, Inc., which in turn is owned by Synovate. Website: synovate.com

Streaming media   Software that enables people to listen to radio or view television on the Internet but in real time and without downloading. In radio (which is also called Internet radio), this includes any audio that is broadcast (music, etc.) as well as photography, graphics, text, etc. In TV, this includes movie trailers, full-length movies, and live sports events. One distinct advantage of accessing radio or TV via the Internet is that there are no geographic limits to the broadcast signal.

Street furniture   Out-of-home advertising displays within close proximity to pedestrians for eye-level viewing or at a curbside to impact vehicular traffic. Street furniture displays include, but are not limited to, transit shelters, newsstands/news racks, kiosks, shopping mall panels, convenience store panels, and in-store signage.

STRETCH   *See* Spanish Television Reach Evaluator for Targeting Campaigns to Hispanics.

Stripping   Scheduling TV commercials in a strip program over multiple days within a given week. *Also see* strip programming.

Strip programming   The scheduling of a TV program's episodes at the same time on consecutive days. Strip programming is typically found in daytime, fringe, and prime access dayparts with programs airing Monday to Friday. Commercials airing in these programs over multiple days within a given week is commonly known as stripping. A related term for scheduling commercials in this fashion is *across the board.*

STV   *See* subscription television.

Subject to nonrenewal (SNR)   Commercial time that is available if the current advertiser does not renew its contract.

Subscriber   A home or person who pays for receiving an advertising medium or media vehicle, such as a subscription to cable TV or a magazine.

Subscriber line charge (SLC)   A monthly fee that telephone subscribers pay to compensate the local telephone company for part of the cost of installation and maintenance of the telephone wire, poles, and other facilities that link the home to the telephone network. These wires, poles, and other facilities are referred to as the "local loop." The SLC is one component of access charges.

Subscriber study   A research study that measures the demographics and (sometimes) the product or service consumption levels of a publication's audience. A subscriber study is typically commissioned by the publisher and conducted by an independent research company. A subscriber study is conducted if the publication is not studied within a syndicated research report (such as Mediamark Research, Inc., or Simmons), or it is a relatively new publication and syndicated research is not yet available.

Subscription television (STV)   An over-the-air premium program service that usually contains uncut first-run movies, transmitted in a scrambled signal that is decoded by the subscriber's set top device.

Sunday supplement   *See* newspaper distributed magazine.

Superstation   An independent TV station whose signal is transmitted throughout the United States via satellite. The term was coined by TV station WTBS, and is now used for other stations that meet the criteria.

Supplemental directory   A Yellow Pages directory that may be used outside a client's "home" directory coverage area.

Supply and demand   *See* law of supply and demand.

Supp/supplement   *See* newspaper distributed magazine.

Surfing (the Net)   Browsing Web pages by clicking on links that look interesting. It is like optically floating in a sea of links and catching (clicking on) a particular wave (e.g., ad banner).

Suspense   The illegal practice of a media agent keeping the monies paid by an advertiser for purchased media schedules that were incorrectly billed by the medium at a lower rate. The practice requires that the agent use estimate billing. The reason for the term is that buying agents cannot predict how much money, if any, will be accrued until well after invoices and client billing are reconciled.

Sustaining (period)   The period(s) of an advertising campaign that receives relatively low levels of media delivery in order to maintain (keep alive) an advertising presence in the consumer's mind. Sustaining periods follow a frontloaded or heavy-up period.

SWAG   Jargon for "systematic wild-ass guessing."

Sweeps   The period when Nielsen Media Research collects demographic viewing data from sample homes in every one of the 210 designated market areas in the United States. The term has been around since the beginning of TV measurement. These measurement periods are called sweeps because Nielsen mails out diaries to certain households around the country, and then collects and processes the diaries in a specific order. The diaries from the northeast regions are processed first, and then the diaries are swept up around the country, from the South, to the Midwest, and finally ending with the West. The standard sweep months include February, May, July, and November of each year. In some of the larger markets, the diaries are used to provide viewer information for up to three additional months (January, March, and October).

Switch pitch   (Obsolete) A radio or TV station presentation to an advertiser, advertising agency, or media agency that is meant to convince the advertiser to purchase that station for an advertising schedule by switching dollar investments off another station.

Sworn circulation   The nonaudited but printed statement by a publisher of a magazine's or newspaper's circulation.

Symmetrical digital subscriber line (SDSL)   *See* digital subscriber line.

Symmetrical Resources, Inc.   Founded in 1992, Symmetrical is the parent company of several media and marketing information companies. Under its corporate umbrella are four business units: Advanced Analytic Solutions (A2S), Simmons Market Research Bureau (SMRB), Simmons Custom Research, and Global TGI. Symmetrical Holdings is owned by its employees, the Arbitron Company, and the Kantar Media Group. Website: symmetrical.com

Syndex   Abbreviation for syndicated exclusivity rules. *See* cable nonduplication rule.

Syndicated Network Television Association (SNTA)   A trade group that promotes advertising in syndicated programming. Website: snta.com

Syndicated program   A radio or television program or series that is sold by syndicators to stations on a market-by-market basis without affiliated network involvement. Some syndicated programs are originally produced for syndication, such as "Wheel of Fortune." Some programs are off network programs, such as "Seinfeld." *Also see* barter syndication.

Syndicated research   Creative, market, or media research that is conducted by a research company and is sold to as many companies that will buy it (e.g., advertisers, advertising agencies). It is the opposite of proprietary research, which is exclusively owned by one company. Numerable examples are shown in this dictionary, such as Arbitron, Mediamark Research, Inc., Nielsen Media Research, and Simmons.

Syndication   1. A broadcast program carried on selected stations that may or may not air at the same time in all markets, such as the

"Oprah Winfrey Show." **2.** An independently written column or feature carried by many newspapers, such as "Dear Abby."

Synergy The interaction of two or more forces, such as two or more media forms, whereby the combined effect is greater than the sum of their individual effects. For example, if an advertiser purchases medium A, which reaches 50 percent of a target audience, and medium B, which reaches 40 percent of the same target audience, the two media combined, based on random combination, will reach 70 percent of the target audience.

Synovate A global amalgamation of all of the Aegis Group's marketing research companies, which include Market Facts and its subsidiaries (USA and Canada), Asia Market Intelligence (Asia), Pegram Walters and Sample Surveys Research Group (UK), INNER, MEMRB, Demoscopie and Market&More (Europe, the Middle East, and Africa), and Research Fact (Japan).

System operator A company, person, or other entity that operates a local cable system.

TAB   *See* Traffic Audit Bureau.

Table tents   *See* tent card.

Tabloid   1. A newspaper with a page size that is approximately half the size of a standard size newspaper. 2. A type of television program that is similar in concept and content to newspapers and that features unusual events, news, and speculative editorial.

TACA   *See* Transportation Advertising Council of America.

Tactics, media   The specific use of media to accomplish a media plan's objectives (strategies). For example, if the objective is to advertise nationally and also provide increased advertising pressure in selected markets, the tactic might be to use a combination of network, cable, and syndication TV as well as spot TV. *Also see* objectives, media.

Tag   1. The dealer identification aired at the end of a commercial. *Also see* live tag. 2. The sequence of characters or other symbols inserted in a text or word processing file to indicate how the file should look when it is printed or displayed, or to describe the document's logical structure. A tag is also called markup.

Tagged image file format (TIF or tif)   A graphic file format used for storing bit-mapped images on a personal computer.

Talk show   A type of TV program that contains—you guessed it—mostly talk.

TAP   *See* total audience plan.

TAPI   *See* Telephony Application Program Interface.

Tapscan   A computer program that incorporates Arbitron radio ratings data and allows alternative displays of the audience data.

Target audience   A group of consumers that an advertiser has deemed to be most important in terms of buying the advertiser's product or service, or whom the advertiser wishes to influence, as in the case of advocacy advertising. Target audiences can be defined by multiple demographics (e.g., gender, age, income, education), lifestyles (e.g., participates in sports, entertains at home), specific behaviors, attitudes, and so on. However, because media research data is typically limited in terms of reporting on demographics, lifestyles, and other such categories, it is important that any target audience descriptions be media-actionable. For example, it might be helpful for a copywriter to know that a target audience member is a young male who is bold and individualistic. But this type of social behavior is not reported in any standard syndicated media research study, thereby making it impossible to discern which media venues are best at reaching this target. A media-actionable objective might describe this target audience as men aged 18 to 24 who participate in sports such as road biking, swimming, in-line skating, or weightlifting. These demographic and participation traits are adequately reported in various research reports. The term is often interchanged with *target market,* but target market better identifies the geographic area(s) of interest. *Also see* buying target.

Target rating points (TRPs)   *See* gross rating points.

T-carrier (telecommunications carrier)   A leased telephone line connection capable of carrying voice and data. There are several digitally multiplexed T-carrier systems. T-carrier systems were originally designed to transmit digitized voice signals. Current applications also include digital data transmission. If an F precedes the T, a fiber-optic cable system is indicated at the same rates. T-1 (also known as DS1—digital signal first level) has a speed of 1.544 megabits per second (Mbps); T-1 (DS2), 6.312 Mbps; T-3 (DS3), 44.736 Mbps; T-4 (DS4), 274.176 Mbps; and T-5, 400.352 Mbps. T-1 is the fastest speed commonly used to connect networks to the Internet. T-3 is used mainly by Internet service providers to connect to the Internet.

TCP/IP   *See* transmission control protocol/Internet protocol.

TDD   *See* text telephony.

Tear sheet   The physical advertisement, which ran in a publication, that is torn out of the publication and given to the advertiser as proof of the ad running.

Teaser ad/commercial   An advertising message that has only bits of information about a product or service and may or may not contain the product name. It is meant to create interest in the product or service by nature of its nondisclosure, as well as word-of-mouth advertising. Two examples follow: the initial advertising for the remake of the movie *Godzilla*, in which only references to Godzilla's size were advertised; and the initial advertising for mlife without reference to what it really was.

Technology doubles . . .   *See* Moore's law.

Teens (teenagers)   From a marketing, advertising, and media research perspective, teens are typically considered people ages 12 to 17. Technically, a 12-year-old is not a teenager, and 18- and 19-year-olds are. But those ages 18 and older are considered adults, except, of course, in many bars. *Also see* tweens.

Telco   Short for telecommunications company, such as a telephone company.

Telecast   Transmission of a broadcast or cablecast TV signal.

Telecommunications Device for the Deaf (TDD) *See* text telephony.

Telecommunications Relay Service A free service that enables persons with TTYs (text telephony), individuals who use sign language, and people who have speech disabilities to use telephone services by having a third party transmit and translate the call.

Telecommuting Working outside a traditional office or workplace, and usually at home (such as in a SOHO [small office/home office]), but communicating with the traditional office or workplace via various telecommunication devices, such as e-mail, fax, and phone.

Teleconference A meeting of two or more people in separate locations using the telephone (and often a speaker phone).

TeleCume A national television reach/frequency and optimization system that allows access to the full details of the Nielsen Persons Cume Study. TeleCume relies on respondent level data to create custom demographics and daypart definitions. A product of Interactive Market Systems.

Telemarketing Marketing products or services by using the telephone to contact potential buyers.

Telematics The science of combining telecommunications with computers, such as is found in dial-up service to the Internet, wireless access to the Web, and wireless communication with global positioning systems used in automobiles.

Telephone coincidental survey A survey that is conducted over the telephone while the respondent is engaged in a specific activity, such as viewing a TV program. The live interview is coincident with the respondent's activity.

Telephony Application Program Interface (TAPI) A standard program interface that allows a user to talk over a telephone or videophone to other users.

Telescope   A national television planning system that generates reach/frequency results for network, cable, spot, and syndicated dayparts. A product of Interactive Market Systems.

Teletext   A broadcast service that transmits information to a TV set using unused scanning lines between frames of TV pictures.

Teletrax   A service of Medialink Worldwide, Inc., which employs a patented digital technology that monitors client programming whenever it is broadcast on television via satellite, cable, and terrestrially. Using Teletrax, owners of video content (news, sports programming, motion pictures, or advertising) embed an invisible digital watermark into their material whenever it is created, edited, distributed, broadcast, or duplicated. A network decoder then captures all incidents of the embedded video being broadcast and generates tracking reports for the content owners. Teletrax was launched in Europe in 2001 and as of this writing is establishing itself in the United States. Website: teletrax.tv

Television Bureau of Advertising (TVB)   A nonprofit trade association of America's broadcast television industry. TVB provides a diverse variety of tools and resources to support its members and help advertisers make the best use of local television. Website: tvb.org

Television household   A household that has at least one TV set. Ninety-nine percent of U.S. households have at least one TV set.

Television time periods   *See* TV dayparts.

Television, attributes   All media forms have positive and negative attributes. The following are some of the attributes of advertising on TV: specific target audiences can be reached via the selection of specific programming; TV can be purchased either nationally (via broadcast networks, national syndicated programs, or cable networks) or locally (essentially in each of 210 separate TV markets); regional sports can be purchased via cable TV; high levels of reach can be obtained quickly because just about everybody views TV;

timing of the delivery of commercials to viewers can be controlled by time of day and day of the week (videocassette recording and delayed replay are exceptions); commercials can be placed in complementary environments based on programming formats; various standard commercial lengths can be purchased (most common are :10, :15, :30, and :60); this media form is considered to have high impact (communication effectiveness) because commercials contain visual, audio, and movement elements; TV advertising is an advertiser-controlled (intrusive) medium—it is delivered to consumers without their request; quality commercials have high production costs; obtaining high levels of reach or continuity of advertising over time involves high absolute costs; and as with all mass media, there will probably be media delivery to audiences not within the target audience (spillover).

Telmar   A supplier of media planning software and support services. Subscribers can access syndicated data and manipulate the data to create media plans or make media buys. Telmar Radio Planning provides delivery analysis, including reach/frequency for multiple demographics and rank, and optimizes stations using multiple criteria. Telmar's Spot TV Buyer uses Nielsen NSI data to produce a spot market buy complete from analysis to insertion orders. The company was established in 1968. Website: telmar.com

10Base-T   An Ethernet local area network (LAN) cabling composed of a twisted pair of wires.

:10   A 10-second television commercial.

Tent card   An imprinted and folded advertising display that can stand free on a tabletop and be read on either side. Usually used at restaurants.

Terabyte   Approximately one trillion bytes (1,024 gigabytes). In numerical sequence, bytes are counted as kilobyte, megabyte, gigabyte, terabyte, petabyte, and exabyte.

Teraflop   A measure of computing speed equal to one trillion floating point operations per second.

Terahertz (THz)   One trillion hertz.

Tertile   One-third of a group. A quartile is one-fourth, a quintile is one-fifth, and a decile is one-tenth. A reptile is a cold-blooded, usually egg-laying vertebrate.

Tertile distribution   A display of frequency (or related data) among audiences grouped into equal thirds of reach. *See* quintile distribution.

Test market   A market (or markets) chosen for the purpose of conducting a test prior to implementation into a larger region or nationally.

Test market media translations   Purchasing media in one or more geographic markets (e.g., a designated market area) to test a media effort that is planned to run in a much larger geographic area (e.g., the United States at large). The need for a "translation" is that all the specific uses of the media forms that will eventually be used are not necessarily available in a test market. *See* **1.** as it falls, **2.** little America, **3.** rollout, **4.** weighted average.

Text messaging   A service for sending short text messages to cell phones, mobile/handheld devices, personal digital assistants, or pagers. Also known as short messaging service (SMS).

Text telephony (TTY)   Also known as TDD (Telecommunications Device for the Deaf), it is a machine that can be hooked up to a telephone and provide people who are hearing impaired with a way to use the telephone. They have a keyboard and a small screen like that on a computer, which allows them to type messages to others over the telephone.

T-5   *See* T-carrier.

TFN   'Til further notice. *See* 'til forbid.

T-4 *See* T-carrier.

Third cover The inside of the back cover of a magazine. A magazine has four covers: front, inside front (also called second cover), inside back cover (IBC or third cover), and back cover (fourth cover).

:30 A half-minute commercial.

30-Sheet *See* poster panel.

3/C *See* three color.

Three color (3/C) The use of two colors plus black and white in a print advertisement.

3G The third generation of mobile communications technology sanctioned by the International Communication Union. Analog cellular was the first generation, and digital PCS (personal communication service) was the second. 3G operates with up to 384 kbps bandwidth.

Three hits (3+) A term used to indicate the level of reach obtained among audiences exposed to three or more advertising messages within a given period of time (typically within a four-week period). The theory is that a consumer exposed to an advertising message three times (within a defined period) is "effectively" reached. The three-exposure level was a concept presented by Dr. Herbert Krugman in 1980, who theorized that three exposures to a TV commercial might be the basic number needed for effective communication. He entitled the exposure levels sequentially as "What is it?", "What of it?", and "The true reminder." Mistakenly, many believe that the third exposure happens within a four-week period and among media audiences that receive a 3.0 or higher frequency level. The third exposure, however, can happen months later when the person is ready to buy the product in question and therefore pays more attention to the commercial. Further, the third exposure ("the true reminder") is not necessarily the third. It could be the fourth, fifth, or tenth, and usually occurs when the person is "ready to buy"—that is, has a need for information or a want to purchase. The "three hits" theory is now commonly referred to as "Reach at 3+" *Also see* 1. effective reach, 2. recency.

3+ Reach   *See* Reach (3+).

Through-the-book   A research technique used to determine the average issue audience of print media wherein the interviewer has the respondent go through a magazine page by page (usually through a stripped-down version of the magazine that does not contain advertising) to determine if the respondent is actually a reader of that magazine. The technique is time-consuming and expensive, and many researchers now opt to use the "recent reading" technique to determine readership.

Tie-in advertisement   A print advertisement that relates to other advertising, such as an advertisement that promotes a specific product and is paid for by a grocery store versus the manufacturer.

Tier   Single or multiple channels offered over and above basic cable service and generally at an additional cost, such as HBO.

TIF or tif   *See* tagged image file format.

'Til forbid   Instructions by an advertiser to run a purchased schedule or advertisement(s) until notified to stop—that is, until forbidden to run any more. Also known as TFN ('til further notice).

Time banks   The purchase by a company (e.g., a media agency) of radio or TV commercial time on a station before any advertiser commitment is made, with the buying agent hoping to re-sell the time to paying advertisers, usually at a markup. This is unlike typical broadcast buying conducted by a buying agent directly for an advertiser. The supposed advantages for an advertiser buying commercials in this fashion rather than by usual buying practices are cost savings, or opportunities to obtain commercial positions in programs that are not available for sale in the open marketplace, or both. The possible disadvantages are that the buying agent's fee or commission is typically not divulged to the advertiser, and the advertiser will not necessarily know if the purchased inventory is necessarily at the lowest possible price.

Time buyer   The person who buys advertising time (commercials, spots) on radio and television.

Time period rating   The estimated rating for a station or network within a specific time period (e.g., 9:00–10:00 P.M.), which is averaged over a period of time without regard to programming changes during that period.

Time shifting   Generally refers to consuming programming, advertising, or both at a different time than the original time the programming or advertising was run. A videocassette recorder (VCR), for example, allows for recording programming and playing it at a later time. *Also see* **1.** ReplayTV, **2.** TiVo, **3.** video on demand.

Time spent listening (TSL)   An estimate of the number of quarter hours (or actual hours) the average person spends listening to radio during a specified time period.

Timings   The log times a commercial will air, or has aired, on a particular station.

Tip-in card (coupon)   An insert card (e.g., a reader response card) in a magazine that is bound into a magazine or glued onto an advertisement. *Also called* a bind-in card. *Also see* blow-in card.

TiVo   A personal video recorder that allows the user to pause viewing, have the device automatically record what is being telecast, and then replay what was recorded while TV viewing was paused. As with a videocassette recorder (VCR), the user can fast-forward past unwanted video. It is a successor to a VCR, storing programs digitally on a high-capacity computer hard drive instead of removable tapes.

TNS Media Intelligence/CMR   Commonly referred to as CMR (Competitive Media Reporting), it is a company that provides marketing communication and advertising expenditure information to advertising agencies, advertisers, broadcasters, and publishers. CMR was formed in 1992 with the following businesses folded into the CMR umbrella brand: Broadcast Advertisers Reports (BAR), Leading National Advertisers (LNA), Radio Expenditure Reports (RER), and Radio TV Reports. In June 2000, London-based Taylor Nelson Sofres (TNS), a provider of marketing information, acquired CMR. CMRi is the interactive division of TNS Media Intelligence/CMR. Website: cmr.com

Tolerance   A percentage allowance for possible variation from a reported statistic. For example, if a research company reports a finding that 10,000 people use a particular product, and the research company states that the finding is accurate within a ±10 percent tolerance, the actual finding in a complete census would therefore be 9,000 to 11,000. *Also see* **1.** confidence level, **2.** projection, **3.** sampling error.

Tombstone ad   Jargon for an advertisement for a professional individual (e.g., doctor, lawyer, banker) or company that meets specific legal requirements and regulations imposed on the industry represented in the advertising.

T-1   *See* T-carrier.

Top-down   Analyzing a subject or creating a media plan by starting from the highest level and working toward the bottom. For example, a national top-down media plan is created by first planning national media forms, and then adding local market media (if needed and affordable). *Also see* **1.** bottom-up, **2.** Netspot.

Top 40   *See* **1.** classic hits, **2.** contemporary hit radio.

Top-of-mind awareness (or recall)   A measure of a person's first mention to questions about an advertisement, commercial, company, product, or service. *Also see* **1.** aided recall, **2.** awareness, **3.** unaided recall.

Total audience plan (TAP)   A schedule of radio commercials airing in multiple time periods that is meant to accumulate high levels of audience reach on a station.

Total net paid   The number of copies of a publication, as reported by the Audit Bureau of Circulations, that were actually purchased (as opposed to given away free of charge). It includes subscription, newsstand, and other single copy sales.

Total paid   *See* total net paid.

Total survey area (TSA)   The geographic area in which Arbitron reports radio listening audiences—the area where radio signals from originating stations can be received. The area encompasses the metro survey area and may include additional counties located outside the metro that meet certain listening level criteria.

Trade advertising   Advertising targeted at wholesalers, retailers, and professionals to stimulate them to purchase products for resale to their customers or endorse products among their clientele.

Trade magazine   A professional magazine targeted at a specific industry or occupation, such as advertisers, architects, and engineers.

Trademark unit   An advertisement placed in alphabetical sequence in the Yellow Pages, the prominent feature of which is a brand name (product or service identification) coupled with a product logo or logotype, accompanied with copy text.

Traffic Audit Bureau (TAB)   An industry trade organization that authenticates the circulation data of out-of-home media. In specific instances, TAB also certifies advertising placement. TAB currently audits the circulation of 30-sheet posters, bulletins, 8-sheet posters, and shelter advertising displays. An audit methodology has also been completed for truck advertising. TAB also conducts advertising placement verifications for ski area displays. The plant operator is required to gather the raw traffic counts (before a TAB audit is conducted) for its locations. These come from either of two sources: official government data (mechanical) or, where the official counts do not exist or are greater than three years old, hand counts. Factors developed by TAB are used to accurately convert the official or manual vehicular counts (pedestrians can also be counted) into daily effective circulation (DEC). Website: tabonline.com

Traffic instructions   Printed instructions given to a medium on how creative materials (e.g., a commercial, print ad) should be inserted into the medium, such as which commercial should air in which TV program.

Traffic programming   Radio or TV programming centering on automotive traffic phenomena.

Traffic time   A reference to the radio dayparts of morning drive and afternoon drive. *Also see* radio dayparts.

Transaction Authority Markup Language (XAML)   A computer programming language that is used to coordinate and process online business transactions.

Transducer   A device for converting one form of energy into another, such as converting alternating current (AC) and direct current (DC) into sound.

Transit advertising   A form of out-of-home advertising that appears on transportation vehicles such as buses, taxis, subways, commuter trains, rapid transit, and ferries.

Transitional ads   An online advertisement that is displayed between Web pages when a user navigates between pages. *Also see* **1.** interstitial, **2.** interactive marketing unit.

Transit media, attributes   All media forms have positive and negative attributes. The following are some of the attributes of advertising with transit media (e.g., buses, trains, passenger terminals): it is essentially a mass medium directed to the population at large; very high levels of reach can be obtained through the purchase of multiple units; timing delivery of the advertising message can be controlled only by month; it can be purchased in specific neighborhoods; because nearly all advertising appears for at least one month, transit offers high levels of frequency; transit advertising offers creative flexibility (e.g., multiple executions within the same bus, painted trains); because of a relatively short exposure duration with some units (e.g., outside bus advertising), copy must be relatively short; and it is considered one of the lowest cost-per-thousand (impressions) media.

Transit poster (bus)   Posters attached to the exterior of buses. Common displays are king panels measuring 30 inches by 144 inches in overall size with a bleed copy area of 29 inches by 144 inches, queen panels measuring 30 inches by 88 inches in overall size with a bleed copy area of 29 inches by 88 inches, and side-tail panels measuring 21 inches by 70 inches in overall size with the same bleed copy area.

Transit poster (commuter rail)   Posters displayed in commuter rail stations and on trains.

Transit shelter   A curbside structure (street furniture) located at regular stopping points along urban bus routes. Backlit posters are affixed to transit shelter structures using a standardized display format measuring 69 inches by 48 inches in overall size with a bleed copy area of 67 inches by 46 inches.

Transmission control protocol/Internet protocol (TCP/IP)   A suite of communication protocols used to connect hosts on the Internet.

Transmit for Windows   Software that provides a full planning and post-evaluation system for television using continuous people meter data. A product of Telmar.

Transponder   Transmitter responder. A wireless communications device that picks up and automatically (usually instantaneously) responds to a signal. Transponders are used in communications satellites, as well as in many other places, where signals are received from an uplink and sent back to a downlink. They are similar in practice to a repeater station (boosters).

Transportation Advertising Council of America (TACA)   A marketing council within the Outdoor Advertising Association of America. TACA promotes the advancement of transportation advertising.

Triad   An in-depth interview involving two respondents and one interviewer.

Triopoly   Ownership by one company of three or more radio stations in the same market, with one of the stations being on the opposite band. *Also called* Trombo.

Triple A   *See* adult alternative.

Trivision   An outdoor unit with a slanted face that allows three different copy messages to revolve at intermittent intervals. Sometimes referred to as a post-turn.

Trombo   *See* triopoly.

TRPs   Target rating points. *See* gross rating points.

TRS   *See* Telecommunications Relay Service.

True interconnect   *See* interconnect.

Trunk lines   Coaxial cable distributing signals from a head end to feeder lines in a cable TV system.

TSA   *See* total survey area.

TSL   *See* time spent listening.

T-3   A leased telephone line connection capable of carrying data at 44,736,000 bits-per-second.

T-2   *See* T-carrier.

TTY   *See* text telephony.

Turnkey   A product or service that is supplied, installed, or purchased in a condition ready for immediate use—for example, a media-driven promotion in which the advertiser simply agrees to participate without having to create or coordinate the promotion. The term relates to the ease of use, as if the advertiser (or buyer) simply has to turn a key to take advantage of the product or service.

Turnover rate The extent to which a media vehicle changes audience within a specified time frame. In broadcast, it is often measured within a daypart.

Formula:

cumulative audience percent ÷ average quarter-hour rating = turnover

Example:

10 (percent) ÷ 0.5 = 20

TVB *See* Television Bureau of Advertising.

TV dayparts Time segments (or program types) into which all TV programming is designated for the convenience of reporting media research, media planning, and the selling and buying of TV time. Although designations vary based on venue (i.e., network TV, syndication TV, spot TV), the day of the week (e.g., Monday to Friday versus Saturday or Sunday), or geographic market (e.g., by time zone), the typical dayparts are (for eastern time): early morning (5:00 A.M.–10:00 A.M.), daytime (10:00 A.M.–4:00 P.M.), early fringe (4:00 P.M.–7:30 P.M.), early news (anytime it airs within the early fringe time period), prime access (7:30 P.M.–8:00 P.M.), prime (8:00 P.M.–11:00 P.M.), late news (11:00 P.M.–11:30 or 11:35 P.M.), late fringe (11:30 or 11:35 P.M.–2:00 A.M.), and overnight (2:00 A.M.–5:00 A.M.). *Also see* daypart mix.

TV-14 *See* TV Parental Guidelines.

TV-G *See* TV Parental Guidelines.

TV Guardian An electronic device that automatically detects and filters profanity and other offensive phrases in TV programs and movies played on a VCR. When any of the 100 offensive words or phrases in its databank is detected, it mutes the sound for the sentence and displays a replacement text on the screen. *Also see* **1.** TV Parental Guidelines, **2.** V-chip, **3.** Weemote.

TV-MA   *See* TV Parental Guidelines.

TV Market   *See* Direct Marketing Association.

TV Parental Guidelines   A rating system established in 1997 by the National Association of Broadcasters, the National Cable Television Association, and the Motion Picture Association of America. These ratings are displayed on the television screen for the first 15 seconds of rated programming and, in conjunction with the V-Chip, permit parents to block programming with a certain rating from coming into their home. Rating programs is voluntary on the part of broadcasters and cablecasters. It applies to all programming except news, sports, and unedited Motion Picture Association of America rated movies on premium cable channels. The ratings for programs designed solely for children are TV-Y (appropriate for all children), TV-Y7 (appropriate for children age seven and above), TV-Y7-FV (appropriate for children age seven and above, but contains fantasy violence that may be more intense or more combative than other programs). The ratings for programs designed for the entire audience are TV-G (general, suitable for all ages), TV-PG (parental guidance suggested, contains material parents may find unsuitable for younger children), TV-14 (unsuitable for children under 14 years of age), and TV-MA (mature audience only, unsuitable for children under 17 years of age).

TV-PG   *See* TV Parental Guidelines.

TV program types   The classification of TV programs into various genres, such as action/adventure, situation comedy, and drama.

TvQ Scores   A quantitative measure of people's familiarity with and commitment to viewing broadcast TV programs. *See* Marketing Evaluations/TvQ.

TV-Y, TV-Y7, TV-Y7-FV   *See* TV Parental Guidelines.

Tweens   People who are approximately 8 to 12 years old. They are between young children and teenagers. *Also see* teens.

24/7/365   Shorthand for 24 hours a day, 7 days a week, 365 days a year. Reference is to a store or resource (e.g., the Internet) that is open or available all of the time (including February 29th).

Twisted pair   A pair of wires twisted around each other to minimize interference from other circuits. Paired cable is made up of thousands of twisted pairs.

Two color (2C)   The use of one color in addition to black and white in a printed advertisement.

Two-way capability   The capability of a cable television system to receive and transmit signals from various terminals to any other point in a cable television system. Also known as interactive capability.

UCE Unsolicited commercial e-mail. *See* spam.

UHF *See* ultra high frequency.

Ultra high frequency (UHF) Channels 14 to 83 on a TV set. Technically, it is the frequency band (range of sound and wavelength frequencies) added to the VHF band for television transmission. VHF (very high frequency) is channels 2 to 13.

Umbrella plan A media plan, usually using national media forms, under which tailored local market efforts are implemented.

UML *See* Unified Modeling Language.

UMTS *See* Universal Mobile Telecommunications System.

Unaided recall (awareness) The percentage or number of consumers surveyed who are able to recall a product's or service's name (or a specific advertisement, commercial, or company) after being requested to cite any and all product names within an advertised category. The respondents are not given any prompts or lists to jog their memory. *Also see* **1.** aided recall, **2.** top-of-mind awareness.

Underdelivery Usually refers to a media schedule or media unit that actually produced less audience delivery than originally estimated by the buyer, the seller, or both.

Unduplicated audience *See* cume audience.

Unified Modeling Language (UML) A general-purpose computer programming language used for creating complex software.

Uniform Product Code (UPC) *See* Universal Product Code.

Uniform resource locator (URL) The unique address of a file that is accessible on the Internet. Typically, the address is in two to three parts. For example, the URL "http://www.arfsite.org/webpages/ primarypages/arfinfo" describes the type of access method being used (http—hypertext transfer protocol), and the location of the server that hosts the website (www.arfsite.org) for the Advertising Research Foundation. The third part indicates the exact location of a particular page (webpages/primarypages/arfinfo). All websites have URLs. *Also called* unique resource locator. *Also see* domain name.

Unit A single thing, such as an advertising unit: one radio or TV commercial, one magazine ad, one outdoor bulletin.

Unit rate (or cost) The cost of an advertising unit (radio or TV commercial, print advertisement).

Universal Mobile Telecommunications System (UMTS) Wireless technology that transmits text, digitized voice, video, and multimedia at speeds up to 2 megabits per second.

Universal Product Code (UPC) A bar code system that provides a unique code for each product sold at retail. The UPC can be scanned by laser, and transmitted to a computer to obtain the price and for monitoring sales and inventory. UPC is also referred to as Uniform Product Code.

Universal serial bus (USB) A physical receptacle (plug) on a computer into which up to 127 different low-speed peripheral devices (e.g., keyboard, mouse) can be connected. USB is beginning to replace parallel ports and serial ports. It has a maximum transfer speed of 12 megabits per second (Mbps).

Universe   The total number of individuals, items, or data from which a statistical sample is taken. For example, the U.S. household universe is just over 100 million.

Unlimited co-op   A cooperative in which payments are not limited to a co-op fund. Advertising qualifies without limit, provided it conforms to the terms of the supplier's co-op plan. *Also called* open-end co-op.

Unpaid circulation (copies)   The circulation of a magazine that is either distributed entirely free to recipients or is distributed at a price inadequate to qualify as "paid" as defined by the Audit Bureau of Circulations.

Unsolicited commercial e-mail (UCE)   *See* spam.

Unwired networks   A combination of selected local stations not connected by wire or satellite on which an advertiser can purchase commercial time usually at a discount compared to purchasing each station individually. Created by national sales representatives, an unwired network is technically not a network because each participating station broadcasts commercials independently. Media buys are quite similar to spot radio or spot TV buys in that they can be tailored by market and by station/format. They are not completely flexible, as the sales representative firm might not represent a desired station/format in all markets needed by the advertiser.

UPC   *See* Universal Product Code.

Upcut   The loss of audio, visual, or both on the beginning portion of a commercial. *Also see* downcut.

Upfront   A method for purchasing many commercials, negotiated well in advance of airdates, that encompasses multiple programs airing during a protracted period, such as for a one-year schedule. Upfront used to apply to only network broadcast TV programs. Purchases were made in the spring for commercial airings commencing mid-September (the beginning of the "new season") through the following 12 months. Upfront buys typically require that at least two calendar quarters (which may or may not be contiguous) be purchased. Upfront buys now also apply to cable TV, spot TV, and, in some instances, to print media. Purchasing in this fashion usually allows advertisers to select specific desired programs at a typically lower price versus purchasing commercial time after the upfront marketplace negotiations are completed (in a "scatter" market). An upfront advertiser usually negotiates with the networks for quarterly cancellation rights (a quarterly option to cancel a part or all of the commercial inventory purchased), audience delivery guarantees, and various other scheduling and flexibility options. *Also see* **1.** opportunistic buy, **2.** scatter.

Upgrade　To increase the value of a (typically) TV commercial by moving it to a different program or daypart, often without an increase in cost.

Uplink/downlink　In satellite communications, an uplink is the link (communications connection) from Earth to the satellite; the downlink is the link from the satellite to Earth.

Upload　To copy a file from a computer to a server or host system. It is the reverse process of download. If a user uploads and downloads continuously for a long period of time, that person can experience overload.

Upscale　A term used to describe the high-income segment of the population.

Urban adult contemporary　A radio-programming format that is a mix of urban and adult contemporary formats.

URL　*See* uniform resource locator.

USB　*See* universal serial bus.

Usenet　A worldwide bulletin board system accessible through the Internet and online service providers.

User friendly　Typically applied to computers or software, it is something that is easy to learn and use.

VAC *See* Verified Audit of Circulation.

VALS Established in 1978, VALS is one of the first major consumer segmentation systems based on values and lifestyle characteristics. VALS defines eight segments of adult consumers who have different attitudes and exhibit distinctive behavior and decision-making patterns: actualizers, fulfilleds, achievers, experiencers, believers, strivers, makers, and strugglers. Website: sric-bi.com

Value added *See* added value.

Variable Something that is likely to change. A variable has no fixed quantitative value. It is the opposite of a constant (something that does not change, unless you buy into Murphy: "The only thing constant is change."). For example, in the Pythagorean theorem, a, b, and c are all variables.

Variety A radio programming format that offers a broad selection of programming appealing to different audiences at different times of the day.

V-chip An electronic chip that works in conjunction with a television, VCR, or cable box. Users select a rating level appropriate for their children. V-chip reads the transmitted ratings code for all programming and automatically denies access to programming that exceeds the preset ratings limitations. *Also see* **1.** TV Guardian, **2.** TV Parental Guidelines, **3.** Weemote.

VCR *See* videocassette recorder.

VDSL Very high bit-rate digital subscriber line. *See* digital subscriber line.

Vehicle A specific medium, such as *Time* magazine and the Super Bowl TV program.

VEIL Video encoded invisible light. *See* broadcast verification system.

Venn diagram A field within which circular areas represent groups of items sharing common properties. The diagram is made up of two or more overlapping circles. It is often used in mathematics to show relationships between sets and to describe attributes and characteristics of items, such as things, people, places, events, and ideas. For example, assume there are two magazines, one has 100 readers, the other has 50 readers, and 10 of the readers read both of the magazines (i.e., 10 of the 100 and 10 of the 50 are the same people). This can be represented in a Venn diagram by showing two circles. One of the circles represents 100 readers; the other, which is half as large, represents the 50 readers. The circles overlap slightly to represent the 10 "common" readers. Specifically, the area covered by the overlap is 10 percent of the size of the larger circle and 20 percent of the size of the smaller circle. If a third magazine is added to the diagram, the same spatial exhibit is created using the third magazine's readers and duplication counts with the first two magazines. The diagram is named for John Venn (1834–1923).

Verance A company that monitors and verifies radio/TV airplay of advertising, music, and programming content wherever and whenever it airs. The company digitally encodes each commercial that it monitors and receives the encoded signals at various electronic monitors throughout the United States. Website: verance.com

Verified Audit of Circulation (VAC) Founded in 1951, VAC provides independent circulation audit and research services for paid and free community newspapers, shopping guides, alternative news weeklies, ethnic, niche and special interest publications, business, parenting and senior periodicals, trade and consumer magazines, and Yellow Pages directories. Website: verifiedaudit.com

Veronis Suhler Stevenson An independent merchant bank dedicated to the media, communications, and information industries. Since its formation in 1981, the firm has acted as a financial adviser across the full spectrum of media industry segments, including broadcasting; cable and entertainment; newspaper publishing; consumer magazines; business information services; consumer, professional and educational books; business-to-business communications; specialty media and marketing services; and the Internet. veronissuhler.com

Vertical button *See* button ad.

Vertical discount A discount applied to an advertiser's rate when several radio or TV time slots within a specific time period are purchased.

Vertical half page A magazine or newspaper advertising unit that divides the page in half vertically rather than horizontally.

Vertical publication A publication written for a specific profession, industry, or trade, as opposed to a mass audience.

Vertical rotation The scheduling of commercials across many time periods throughout the course of a day, week, or month with the intention of reaching as many different people as possible.

Vertical third page An advertising space unit that is equal to one-third of a page and runs vertically (profile) as opposed to horizontally (landscape).

Very high frequency (VHF) TV channels 2 to 13. Technically, it is the frequency band (range of sound and wavelength frequencies) for television transmission. UHF (ultra high frequency) is channels 14 to 83.

Very high-speed digital subscriber line (VDSL)   *See* digital subscriber line.

Videocassette recorder (VCR)   An electronic device for recording and playing back on a videocassette the images and sounds that originally appeared on television or that were electronically copied from another videocassette.

Videoconferencing   Conducting a conference (meeting) between two or more people at different locations by using computers to transmit audio and video.

Video description   An audio narration that is for television viewers who are blind or visually disabled and consists of verbal descriptions of key visual elements in a television program, such as settings and actions not reflected in dialogue. Narrations are inserted into the program's natural pauses and are typically provided through the secondary audio programming channel.

Videodisc   Video and sound recorded digitally via laser and viewed or listened to through a videodisc player.

Video encoded invisible light (VEIL)   *See* broadcast verification system.

Video on demand (VOD)   The capability of receiving movies or other programming fare via cable TV or direct broadcast satellite at exactly the time a consumer wishes to view the program. *Also see* near video on demand.

Videotape   An electromagnetic tape that electronically records sounds and pictures simultaneously and can be played back on videocassette recorder.

Videotext   A two-way interactive system that allows people to receive and manipulate text and graphic information on their TV set through a special device attached to the set.

Viewers per 1,000 viewing households (VPVHs)   The number of people within a specific population group tuned to a TV program in each 1,000 viewing households, as defined by Nielsen Media Research.

Viewers per set (VPS)   The number of people in a demographic group viewing a particular program, divided by the number of households reached by that same program.

Vignette   1. A small drawing or illustration that appears in the body text of an advertisement. 2. A short duration radio or TV program focusing on a specific subject. 3. A technique used in commercial production where several situations that emphasize the qualities of a product are shown in rapid sequence.

Viral marketing   A marketing tactic or advertising strategy that propagates like a virus. The techniques facilitate and encourage people to pass along an advertising message. *Also see* word-of-mouth advertising.

Virtual reality   A computer-generated "environment" that is presented to the user in a way that it appears real.

Virtual Reality Modeling Language (VRML)   A computer language (specification) used on the World Wide Web that presents three-dimensional images and sometimes allows user interaction.

Virus   A computer program that uses various techniques for duplicating itself and traveling between computers. They can vary from being harmless nuisances to causing serious problems, such as destroying files or disabling a computer.

Visual Basic   A computer programming language that is widely used for in-house application program development and for prototyping.

VMS   Via its VoiceTrak report, VMS is a research company that provides media expenditures based on voluntary surveys of media sources: local TV stations, cable systems and interconnects, radio stations, newspapers, out-of-home operators, and magazines. Website: vmsinfo.com

VOD   *See* video on demand.

Voice-over   The part of a TV commercial that is spoken by an announcer who is heard but not seen on the screen.

Voice over Internet protocol (VOIP)   Technology that allows voice communication by telephone using Internet protocol (IP) instead of voice recognition. *Also called* Internet telephony. For users who have free, or fixed-price Internet access, VOIP software essentially provides free telephone calls anywhere in the world.

Voice recognition   Technology that lets people operate a computer by using voice commands instead of typing.

VoiceTrak   *See* VMS.

VOIP   *See* voice over Internet protocol.

Volume discount   The price discount offered to advertisers who purchase a certain amount of volume from the medium, such as advertising pages. *Also see* 1. frequency discount, 2. open rate.

Volumetrics   The aggregate usage or spending by a particular demographic audience for specific products or services. For example, instead of data that reports the percentage of a demographic who use a product, or the percent of a demographic group who are above-average users of a product, volumetrics reports what percentage of total product usage is accounted for by a demographic group.

VPS   *See* viewers per set.

VPVHs   *See* viewers per 1,000 viewing households.

VRML   *See* Virtual Reality Modeling Language.

WAA Wireless Advertising Association. *See* Mobile Marketing Association.

Wallscape Murals painted or attached directly onto the exterior surface of a building.

WAN *See* wide area network.

WAP *See* Wireless Application Protocol.

WAP phones (Wireless Application Protocol phones) Mobile (cellular) phones that use WAP technology to access the Internet. The screen on a WAP phone can be used to deliver advertising.

Waste circulation A publication's circulation consumed by population groups or distributed in geographic areas that are not part of the target audience or geography.

Watermarking Embedding information into multimedia data (e.g., a radio or TV commercial) that is imperceptible and irremovable. The main application is the protection of intellectual property rights. For example, watermarking allows for embedding a copyright label into the image, which can identify the copyright holder. *Also see* **1.** digital watermarking, **2.** encoding commercials, **3.** steganography.

WCDMA   Wireless Code Division Multiple Access. *See* Code Division Multiple Access.

Wearout   A level of frequency, or a point in time, when an advertising message loses its ability to effectively communicate. The level varies by the product or service being advertised, the amount and intensity of directly competitive advertising, the medium used to convey the messages, and a host of other variables. Various research studies have indicated that TV commercials for "average" packaged goods tend to wear out after the target audience is exposed to the commercial 12 to 15 times (over indeterminate periods of time).

Web   1. *See* World Wide Web. 2. (Obsolete) A term that referred to broadcast TV networks.

Web (.web)   *See* domain name.

Webcasting   Broadcasting information using the Internet—in particular, the World Wide Web. Net radio, for example, uses streaming audio to deliver radio programming over the Internet. *Also see* multicast.

Webcrawler   Also known as a spider, this computer program automatically finds and displays Web pages, as well as finds and displays links to other Web pages.

Webinar   Coined by Beyond Technology Corp., this online marketing seminar is convened on the Internet in real time. Website: seebeyond.com

Web page   A document on the World Wide Web. Every Web page is identified by a uniform resource locator (URL).

Web programming language   A computer language used to create websites and pages. The most widely used Web programming languages are ADA, BASIC, C++, FORTRAN, HTML (hypertext markup language), Java, Lisp, PERL, PostScript, Prolog, and Visual Basic. *Also see* computer programming language.

Web server   A computer that delivers Web pages to users. For example, if http://www.arfsite.org/webpages/primarypages/arfinfo is entered in a browser, a message will be sent to the domain name (arfsite), the server will find the page named "webpages/primarypages/arfinfo," and it will appear on the screen.

Website   A location on the World Wide Web. All websites have at least one page and may contain additional documents and files. Every website is owned and managed by an individual, company, or organization. Once on a site (i.e., it appears on the computer screen), a user can make purchases, do searches, send messages, and conduct other interactive activities. There is no standard for its spelling. *Web site* (as two words with *Web* using a capital letter) or *website* (as one word without a capital letter) are equally acceptable. Whichever is chosen, it is best to consistently use one spelling to avoid confusing the reader with two different spellings. Also common is the reference to a website as a "homepage."

WebTV   A device for accessing the Internet from a TV with the use of a computer. All that is needed is a television, a phone line, and a WebTV Internet terminal.

Weemote   A television remote control device designed for young children, ages three to eight. While offering simple controls for a child to operate, it also features the parental control for selecting only those channels a parent wants his or her child to view.

Weighted average   Generally refers to the arithmetic average obtained by adding the products of numbers valued (weighted) by a predetermined percentage. For example, if 100 TRPs are scheduled in market A (10 percent of population) and 200 TRPs are scheduled in market B (5 percent of population), a weighted average of 133 TRPs are scheduled in the two markets combined: (100 × 10 percent) + (200 × 5 percent) divided by 15 percent.

Weighting   Assigning a quantitative value to each of several media vehicles to assist in comparisons. For example, if medium A is perceived as having a value of 100 percent and medium B a value of 50 percent, then the audience delivery of each of these media is multiplied by their respective values to yield a "weighted" audience against which cost-efficiency, reach, and other quantitative aspects can be judged. In this example, if medium A has a target audience delivery of 1,000 and a cost per advertising unit of $20, and medium B has a target audience delivery of 4,000 and a cost per advertising unit of $30, the audiences of each can be weighed by the values and the products divided into the costs to yield a weighted cost per thousand:

medium A = $20 ÷ (1,000 × 100 percent) = $20 CPM

medium B = $30 ÷ (4,000 × 50 percent) = $15 CPM

White paper An authoritative and usually educational report on a particular issue.

Wide area network (WAN) A computer network spanning very large geographic areas, such as cities, states, the nation, or the planet. It typically consists of two or more local area networks.

Wideband A medium-capacity communication system capable of carrying a wide range of frequencies. Wideband speeds range from 64 kilobits per second (kbps) to 1.544 megabits per second (Mbps), as compared to broadband, which operates at rates of 1.544 Mbps or higher, and narrowband, which typically operates at 64 kbps or less. *Also see* baseband.

Wi-Fi *See* wireless fidelity.

Wink A free interactive television service, offered by cable and direct broadcast satellite service providers. Wink delivers the interactivity synchronized to television programming and advertising. So while a person is watching a television program or commercial, interactive enhancements are available that the viewer can choose to see while watching that show or ad. The viewer can, for example, order products or request information, play trivia games, and access further information such as news, sports, or weather. Viewers access this enhancement by clicking on the "i" icon that appears on the upper left corner of the television screen. *Also see* interactive video data service.

Wired networks   Broadcast networks that are connected via satellite, telephone lines, or both.

Wireless Advertising Association (WAA)   *See* Mobile Marketing Association.

Wireless Application Protocol (WAP)   The global protocol that allows users to access information via handheld wireless devices (e.g., cell phones, pagers).

Wireless bitmap (WBMP)   A file format for use with wireless (mobile) computing devices, such as cell phones, pagers, personal digital assistants (PDAs), and palm-size personal computers. WBMP is part of the Wireless Application Protocol.

Wireless cable   A cable operator's transmission of programming to subscribing homes, over the airwaves via microwave frequencies.

Wireless fidelity (wi-fi)   Short-range radio signals to connect wireless-ready computers to high-speed access points that, in turn, connect to a mobile (cellular) phone network.

Wireless Markup Language (WML)   An Extensible Markup Language (XML) that is part of the Wireless Application Protocol (WAP) and is used to create and transfer Internet data to wireless narrowband handheld devices. WML is supported by almost every mobile phone browser around the world.

WMA   *See* Mobile Marketing Association.

WML   *See* Wireless Markup Language.

Women's service magazine   A magazine targeted at women with editorial featuring cooking, child-rearing, and other home-related subjects. *Also see* Seven Sisters.

Word-of-mouth advertising   Ostensibly free advertising that relies on people telling other people about a product or service.

Workhorse Software Company   A company specializing in developing media planning and media plan management software tools, such as MEDIATOOLS. Website: workhorsesoftware.com

World Wide Web   Commonly called the Web. A global hypertext system that uses the Internet as its transport mechanism. Created in 1989 at CERN, a research institute in Switzerland, the Web relies upon the hypertext transport protocol (HTTP), an Internet standard that specifies how an application can locate and acquire resources stored on another computer connected to the Internet. The Web is an information-sharing model that is built on top of the Internet. The Web uses HTTP to transmit data and browsers to access Web documents (called Web pages). The first Web page was shown on the Web on December 12, 1991.

World Wide Web Consortium (W3C)   A consortium of companies involved with the World Wide Web and the Internet to develop standards for its use.

W3   Short for *World Wide Web*.

W3C   *See* World Wide Web Consortium.

XAML *See* Transaction Authority Markup Language.

XHTML *See* Extensible Hypertext Markup Language.

XML *See* Extensible Markup Language.

Yankelovich A market research firm that produces, among other things, the *Yankelovich Monitor* report, which tracks American values, lifestyles, and buying motivations. Harris Interactive acquired the custom research division of Yankelovich in 2001. The custom research division conducts the majority of its research using the telephone. Website: yankelovich.com

Year to date (YTD) A period of time starting January 1 of the current year and ending on a specific date in the same year. Reporting YTD data, such as sales or media spending, requires the reporter to state the ending date—for example, YTD June 30.

Yellow Pages advertising Advertising within a telephone Yellow Pages directory.

Yellow Pages Integrated Media Association (YPIMA) YPIMA was established in 1988 with the merger of AAYPP and NYPSA. It was then called Yellow Pages Publishers Association (YPPA) and changed its name to YPIMA in 2002. YPIMA is currently comprised of publisher members and nonmember publishers who collectively produce more than 95 percent of all Yellow Pages directories and account for 98 percent of advertising revenues generated in North America. Website: yppa.com

Yellow Pages, attributes All media forms have positive and negative attributes. The following are some of the attributes of advertising in Yellow Pages: it is essentially a mass medium directed to the population at large with little if any demographic targeting capability, it can be purchased within comparatively small geographic areas, relatively high levels of potential reach can be obtained because every household with a telephone receives a free directory, timing delivery of the advertising message can only be controlled by year, advertising addresses the consumer while in the act of shopping for specific products or services, and production costs are relatively low.

YPIMA *See* Yellow Pages Integrated Media Association.

YPPA Yellow Pages Publishers Association. *See* Yellow Pages Integrated Media Association.

YTD *See* year to date.

Y2K Shorthand for the year 2000. It became popular prior to 2000 when the majority of the world's literate population thought that all computer systems would fail when the clock struck 01-01-00, whether or not you used your mouse. People thought that computers' internal clocks would read the new date as if it were the year 1900 instead of 2000, which in turn would cause massive shutdowns and miscommunications in computer systems, especially accounting and database systems. Just prior to Y2K, corporations and consumers spent enormous amounts of time and money to make every hardware, software, and embedded system component "Y2K compliant." As it turned out, the investment was not warranted. Nothing broke down. The world went on.

Zero base (budgeting, planning)   A method where any actions taken in the current or prior year are not taken into consideration when establishing a budget (or a plan) for the next year. Each item therefore starts from zero. This essentially forces all actions to be justified or rejustified before a budget (or plan) is implemented. It also forces a discipline whereby past actions are not necessarily repeated for the sake of expedience.

Zero cells   Disagreement between the Nielsen Media Research set-top meter and diary data—that is, when the meter indicates viewing but the diary data shows no record of viewing.

Zipping   Fast-forwarding through commercials or TV programs while playing back a videocassette recording.

Zone (zoned) editions   A way to buy a newspaper's circulation in only specific geographic areas. Newspapers divide their circulation into geographic zones (usually by ZIP codes) and sell advertising to be distributed only within the specific zone.

Media Formulas

Audience composition

audience of a demographic cell ÷ total audience = composition

Example: 500,000 ÷ 2,000,000 = 25 percent

Average   (*See* mean, median, mode, or weighted average)

Brand development index (BDI)

[(market A brand sales as a percentage of total universe sales) ÷ (market A population as a percentage of total universe population)] × 100 = BDI

Examples:

(10 percent ÷ 20 percent) × 100 = 50 (decimal and percentage sign deleted)

(10 percent ÷ 5 percent) × 100 = 200

Category development index (CDI)

[(market A category sales as a percentage of total universe sales) ÷ (market A population as a percentage of total universe population)] × 100 = CDI

Examples:

(10 percent ÷ 20 percent) × 100 = 50 (decimal and percentage sign deleted)

(10 percent ÷ 5 percent) × 100 = 200

Cost per point (CPP)

cost ÷ rating (or TRPs) = CPP

Example: $1,000 ÷ 10 = $100

Converting CPP to CPM (cost per thousand)

(CPP × 100) ÷ market's population (expressed in thousands) = CPM

Example: assume market population is 2,000,000

($100 × 100) ÷ 2,000 = $5.00

Cost per point   weighted for a daypart mix

(CPP × percent of TRPs in the daypart) + (CPP × percent of TRPs in the daypart)

Example:

	CPP	Mix	Weighted CPP
Day	$10.00	25%	$2.50
News	$30.00	75%	$22.50
Total		100%	$25.00

Cost per thousand (CPM)

(cost ÷ audience) × 1,000 = CPM

Example: assume media audience = 200,000

($1,000 ÷ 200,000) × 1,000 = $5.00

Shortcut: cost ÷ audience expressed in thousands = CPM

$1,000 ÷ 200 = $5.00

Converting CPM to CPP

(CPM × market population expressed in thousands) ÷ 100 = CPP

Example: assume market population is 200,000

($5 × 2,000) ÷ 100 = $100

Coverage

demographic audience ÷ demographic universe = coverage

Example: 1,000 ÷ 10,000 = 10 percent

Frequency of audience delivery

TRPs ÷ reach = frequency

Example: 100 ÷ 50 = 2.0

Gross cost to net cost

gross cost × (100 percent − commission percent) = net

Example: $100 × (100 [percent] −15 [percent]) = 85 [percent] = net

Gross rating points

reach × frequency = GRPs

Example: 50 × 2.0 = 100

Homes using TV (HUT)

rating ÷ share = HUT

Example: 5.0 ÷ 10 (percent) = 50 (percent)

Impressions

GRPs (or TRPs) × the number of people in the population group = impressions

Example: 200 (percent) × 1,000,000 = 2,000,000

Increase/decrease percentage

(the higher number − the lower number) ÷ the lower number = percent increase

Example: (10 − 8) ÷ 8 = 25 percent increase

(the higher number − the lower number) ÷ the higher number = percent decrease

Example: (10 − 8) ÷ 10 = 20 percent decrease

Index

(variable percentage ÷ base percentage) × 100 = index

Examples:

(60 percent ÷ 50 percent) × 100 = 120 index (i.e., 20 percent above the base)

(50 percent ÷ 75 percent) × 100 = 67 index (i.e., 33 percent below the base)

Mean, median, mode

Assume these set of numbers: 5, 5, 15, 25, 50

sum of all numbers ÷ the number of sets of numbers = mean

Example: (5 + 5 + 15 + 25 + 50) ÷ 5 = 20

middle number in a series of numbers arrayed in numerical order =
median

> *Example:* 15

the number that appears most frequently = mode

> *Example:* 5

National rate of spending

> market(s) spending ÷ market's percent of U.S. population =
> national rate of spending
>
> *Example:* $100,000 ÷ 10 percent = $1,000,000

Net cost to gross cost

> net cost ÷ net percent cost = gross cost
>
> *Example:* $100 ÷ 0.85 (percent) = $117.65

Only-only-both

To calculate only-only-both one first needs the reach of the two media
forms in question. This can be obtained via various computer software programs, or by using the random combination technique.

> *Formula:*
>
> Reach of A + B combined − the reach of B = the reach of
> *only A* (i.e., this audience was not exposed to medium B).
>
> Reach of A + B combined − the reach of A = the reach of
> *only B* (i.e., this audience was not exposed to medium A).
>
> Reach of A + B combined − the sum of the reach of *only A* +
> the reach of *only B* = the reach of those exposed to *both A
> and B.*

Example:

Reach of A = 60 (percent)

Reach of B = 50 (percent)

Reach of A + B combined (using random combination) = 80 (percent)

80 − 50 = 30 (30 percent exposed to *only* A)

80 − 60 = 20 (20 percent exposed to *only* B)

80 − [30 + 20] = 30 (30 percent exposed to *both* A *and* B)

People using radio (PUR)

rating ÷ share = PUR

Example: 5 ÷ 10 (percent) = 50

People Using TV (PUT)

rating ÷ share = PUT

Example: 5 ÷ 10 (percent) = 50

Quintile distribution

1. Array reach for each frequency level (lowest to highest frequency).
2. Assign one-fifth of total reach to each quintile.
3. Accumulate up to one-fifth of the reach from the frequency distribution within each quintile.
4. If reach within a quintile is less than the total reach at a particular frequency level, place the remainder into the next quintile.

Reach As Part of Each Quintile

Frequency	Reach	Lightest	Next	Next	Next	Heaviest
1.0	15	10	5	-	-	-
2.0	8	-	5	3	-	-
3.0	7	-	-	7	-	-
4.0	6	-	-	-	6	-
5.0	4	-	-	-	4	-
6.0	3	-	-	-	-	3
7.0	3	-	-	-	-	3
8.0	2	-	-	-	-	2
9.0	1	-	-	-	-	1
10.0	1	-	-	-	-	1
Total Reach	50	10	10	10	10	10
GRPs	170	10	15	27	44	74
Frequency	3.4	1.0	1.5	2.7	4.4	7.4

Random combination

Formula A:

100 percent − [(100 percent − reach of medium A) × (100 percent − reach of medium B)] = combined reach

Example: assuming reach of medium A is 50 (percent) and reach of medium B is 40 (percent)

$1 - [(1 - 0.5) \times (1 - 0.4)]$

$1 - (0.5 \times 0.6)$

$1 - 0.3 = 0.7 = 70$ combined reach

Formula B:

(reach of A + reach of B) − (reach of A × reach of B) = combined reach

Example: assuming reach of medium A is 50 (percent) and reach of medium B is 40 (percent)

$(0.5 + 0.4) - (0.5 \times 0.4)$

$0.9 - 0.2 = 0.7 = 70$ combined reach

Rating

HUT $\times$ share (or PUT $\times$ share, and so forth) = rating

Example: 50 (percent) $\times$ 10 (percent) = 5

Reach

TRPs (or GRPs) $\div$ frequency = reach

Example: 100 $\div$ 2.0 = 50

Readers per copy (RPC)

total audience $\div$ circulation = RPC

Example: 2,000,000 $\div$ 500,000 = 4

Share of audience

Rating $\div$ HUT = share

Example: 10 (percent) $\div$ 50 (percent) = 20 (percent)

Target (gross) rating points (TRPs or GRPs)

reach $\times$ frequency = GRPs

Example: 50 $\times$ 2.0 = 100

Tertile distribution

1. Array reach for each frequency level (lowest to highest frequency).
2. Assign one-third of total reach to each quintile.

3. Accumulate up to one-third of the reach from the frequency distribution within each quintile.
4. If reach within a quintile is less than the total reach at a particular frequency level, place the remainder into the next quintile

		Reach As Part of Each Quintile		
Frequency	Reach	Lightest	Next	Heaviest
1.0	16	16	-	-
2.0	9	4	5	-
3.0	8	-	8	-
4.0	7	-	7	-
5.0	6	-	-	6
6.0	5	-	-	5
7.0	4	-	-	4
8.0	3	-	-	3
9.0	2	-	-	2
Total	60	20	20	20
GRPs	216	24	62	130
Frequency	3.6	1.2	3.1	6.5

Turnover rate

cumulative audience percent ÷ average quarter hour rating = turnover

Example: 10 (percent) ÷ 0.5 = 20

Weighted average

[(market A TRPs × A percent population) + (market B TRPs × market B percent population)] ÷ (market A percent population + market B percent population) = weighted average

Example: [(100 × .10) + (200 × .05)] ÷ (.10 + .05] = 133